HARBOR LIGHTS

HARBOR LIGHTS

Gudmundina Haflidason

To order additional copies of this book, contact:
Xlibris Corporation
1-888-795-4274
www.Xlibris.com
Orders@Xlibris.com
48868

I want to thank my niece Constance Svanwheit for urging me to write this book. Otherwise this story would never have been told.

Location: Isafold in the year 1875
Isafold is now called Iceland.

CHAPTER ONE

In the middle of the Atlantic ocean nestles an enchanted Island which was named Isafold, and later changed to Iceland. It's beauty and mystic cannot be compared with any Island or country in the world.

It's Scandinavian people, fair haired and blue-eyed are equally enchanting. They are reserved and display a cold exterior. Yet, below the surface they are probably more honest and kinder than the average human being.

The people here in Iceland live only in about one-fifth of the country because of the glaciers. Reykjavik Harbor is a breathtaking sight as flags fly from the masts of the ships; blue for the heavens, red for the fire and white for the ice.

In the distance rugged mountain ranges can be seen where hundreds of white sheep are grazing. At the first sign of autumn sheep are driven down from the mountains and rounded into an old stone fold.

The Icelandic coastline is mystifying with the harsh but enchanting fjords. (rivers) Mount Hekla is the most active volcano Yet, the other volcanos unleashed and filled with fury have destroyed homes and caused much suffering and famine in past years.

Mountain sides are steep. At the base of some of them many one room homes have been constructed of sod and stone, with built-in beds around the wall called badsofa. (beds)

In the summertime it stays light all night. The country's seclusion and peace is broken by only the summer birds on the rocky shore. Iceland is located near the Artic Circle. Millions of seagulls are seen over head as strong winged seabirds and eiderducks with gray spots sit on the rocky shore paying no attention to the puffins nestling near by. Often black sand is seen arising displaying a beautiful expanse. For several days the Icelandic sea appeared to be in abnormal elevation. The huge waves were dark and angry looking, throwing a gloomy velocity of light over the small Hamlet of Elefu Vatn (Eleven Waters) in Grindavik. Soon lofty waves about twelve foot high moved with more than average scope, leaping fury in the direction of the Hamlet.

In Grindavik on February twenty-four, eighteen hundred and seventy-five, a beautiful red-haired baby girl was born to Hallbera and her husband, Olafur Sigurdsson Freyoteinsson. The baby was Hallbera's ninth child at the age of thirty-two. Only four children of the nine had survived; Sigurun who was twelve, Loftur age seven and Johanna who was born nine months after Porunn. Three sons and another daughter, Pordis, age one had drowned in the sea some years before.

The small house in Elefu Vatn was quiet and happy as the siblings watched peacefully over another baby girl sleeping on their mother's breast. Coming to Hallbera's bedside with a smile on his face Olafur kissed her on the check. "Our little girl has hair about the color of yours, elskan." (love)

Hallbera smiled. "Porunn's is redder than mine. My hair is more blonde."

Olafur picked up her hand from the bed. "Is that what you are going to name our baby?"

"Yes, Olafur if you agree," she replied half-asleep. Olafur kissed her on the forehead. "I see your almost asleep elskan. Come on children let your mother rest."

He then called out over his shoulder to Hallbera. "I'll arrange for the christening, Elskan." When Hallbera did not reply he was cognizant that his wife was lessening in strength.

Three months passed. The May sunshine glistened brightly over the hamlet. To day was Sunday and as every Sunday morning the church bells would chime at seven A.M. Far and wide from every direction, the small assemblage of villagers hurried toward the small Lutheran church. There were only five pews. Heavenly vibrating music resounded from the loft where a few men and women sang in choir robes with an organ. "O Gud veÐ pokkum peir fere notin og fere morgunn ljosiÐ . . . . (O God we thank you for the night and for the morning light." Yes this was a special Sunday. A new life was being christened after the morning church services.

The minister stood at the alter dressed in a red and gold trimmed satin robe. Draped over his back was a cross of telluride which is the only naturally occurring gold compound. In Hallbera's arms lay the honor child attired in a long, white lace christening dress reaching the floor. The sun sparkled through the small church window, casting a light over the infants red hair.

The minister's voice was low but clear: "AÐ hljotir pu frelsi Gud's barna . . . ." he uttered, sprinkling a scant amount of water on the infants head from a stone font holding the water from the Holy Sacrament of Holy Baptism. The minister then announced the baby's name . . . "Þórunn Òlafsdóttir."

In Iceland children do not take their father's last name. They are given the father's first name, adding dottir. (daughter) If the child is a male, son is added to father's first name.

Married women do not take the husband's name. Their own blood name they keep from birth to death. This way Icelanders do not lose their identity.

Evening took over the day. A soft, long expanse of shadows spread over the happy household of Olafur and Hallbera's modest home. Little three months old Þórunn lay in her cradle beside the kitchen table where the rest of the family were eating supper. Olafur glanced over at the happy faces as Hallbera perceived her husband was about to reveal the secret they had kept away from their children for awhile. "Family, I am about to announce some very important news to you." Clearing his throat all eyes rested on Olafur's serious features. "Your mother and I have decided to leave Grindavik and move to Sondum i MaDalland." (town)

"Nothing doing, Pabbi, (Papa) Grindavik is our home," cried out Loftur.

"I know, Loftur. But we will get another home. and I hear there are some new homes being constructed near the base of the mountain in Sondum i MaDallund. This house is pretty old, Loftur and quite expensive."

"And I have heard these new homes are attractive, but very small," replied Loftur, rising from the table and pacing the kitchen floor.

"Yes small, but the one room is very large. Plenty of space for badsofas (beds) to be built around the walls." Olafur's features turned grim and worried. "Iceland is going through some hard and difficult times, son. And they will get worse. And to live in Sondum i Madalland would be less expensive."

Sigurun rose from the table and kissed her father then re-filled her parents cups with fresh hot coffee. "But, Pabbi. isn't the ocean being so close to the village a threat to the town peoples' lives?"

"Yes, of course, Elskan. But Iceland is an Island There's water . . . . water everywhere. And don't forget the sea, the volcanos, the fjords. That's the kind of a land we are living in."

Hallbera rose from her chair. "And that's why we have lost five children to the sea." she injected bitterly, pushing the cradle into the bedroom.

Sigurun sat down again at the table. "What ever you and mamma have to do Pabbi, Loftur and I will help you. Of course Loftur and I will have to change schools. But that's alright. Baby Porunn isn't ready for school. She has about nine years yet," smiled Sigurun.

"Porunn of course will have to learn to read and write before the schools will accept her," stated Loftur grinning. "And Porunn will have to be able to swim," he added more cheerfully.

"Is it compulsory to be able to swim?" asked Sigurun.

"Yes. It's the law of the land," stated Olafur.

"And children have to be nine years old before they are allowed to enter school. At least that is the law in Iceland," interjected Hallbera returning from the bedroom.

Settled in their new home in Sondum all went well. With Sigurun's help Hallbera found time to utilize her past higher education. Hallbera had been given permission to use the new library which was built for clergy and statesmen. No private citizen was allowed on the premises. Hallbera's intellect cut the way for her for being one of Iceland's most intelligent citizen.

Thus the years passed. Sigurun was now fifteen years old and through with school. Loftur was age ten, Porrun three and now there was a new member in the family, a little girl named Johanna already two years old.

This morning Sondum was wet and dreary as pouring down rain continued drenching the small village.

When Olafur came home from the printing shop, his clothes were dripping wet. "Pabbi! Get those clothes off. you'll get pneumonia" called out Sigurun throwing down her dishtowel and pulling off his jacket.

"Don't worry about me, Elskan. "I'm a Viking, so I can take it."

"Well, I've noticed lately that this here Viking has been coughing lately."

Porunn came running with a towel and wiped the water from her father's face and head when he dropped down in a chair at the kitchen table and closed his eyes. He opened them again then glanced around the room. "Where is your mother, Sigurun? Not out in this weather I hope."

"Mamma is at the library, Pabbi. She will be home soon. I have super almost ready."

"I wish she wouldn't go there all the time. I miss her," complained Porunn. "Mamma should not leave us alone every day."

"You have your big sister, Sigurun," replied Olafur, in a tired tone of voice.

It was midnight. All the members of the household were tucked in their beds. Morning dawned. It had been a rough week. Olafur was very ill, coughing and unable to get much rest. However, last night Olafur slept quietly and the family also had a chance to acquire some much needed sleep.

The morning sun came out radiantly bright. The brilliant assemblage spread the small house with light. Olafur opened his pale blue eyes to find his family eating breakfast in much better spirits.

Loftur rose from his chair and moved to his father's bedside. "How are you feeling, Pabbi? I believe you slept pretty well last night."

"Much better Loftur. I hope I didn't keep you all up these last couple of nights."

"Last night was a much better night for you . . . . for all of us", stated Loftur.

"Come back here, Loftur and finish your oatmeal." cried out Hallbera.

Without a reply, Loftur patted his father's hand. "I'll be right back with some porridge for you and a nice cup of hot coffee."

Olafur smiled. "You've always been a good son, Loftur, thank you."

When Loftur came back with the oatmeal and coffee, Olafur was asleep. "Wake up Pabbi! Time for breakfast." When his father did not respond Loftur hurried back to the table. "Mamma, pabbi won't wake up!"

Rising from the table, and going to Olafur's bedside Hallbera saw that Olafur was dead. Pneumonia had taken his life. and the disease was running rabidly throughout the country. With no medications, few doctors cold houses little could be done to combat this serious disease.

The rain continued over the land. Hallbera, Loftur, Sigurun and the two small girls, Porunn and Johanna stood somberly before Olafur's casket, home-made by Loftur. The funeral Service held in the Lutheran Church was brief as the few villagers came to pay their respects. Beautiful church bells began to chime, then the ceremony of burying the dead was over.

Moving toward the rear entrance, the procession of mourners moved out of the church to the unkempt graveyard in the backyard.

The pallbearers walked slowly out of the wide back door to the fresh dug grave and placed the coffin down on the ground. The minister then mumbled a few words over the casket as it was lowered into the earth. Picking up some wet soil in the palm of his hand, he sprinkled some dirt over the plot. "Ashes to ashes, dust to dust." He then opened his hymnal And led the assemblage in song.

Closing his hymnal book he glanced at the mourners with deep reflection. Then in a monotone timber: "Our friend, Olafur Sigurdsson Freysteinsson, has now left this troubled world. The major problem of man is that of human existence with the emotions of anguish common to all man and the moral demand upon them. His temporal life on earth is now over." The minister paused and focused his eyes on the momentous group with a meditative expression, as if he were thinking this over. He then made a sign of the cross along the course of the mourners' heads. As they were lowering the casket into the ground the minister blessed the plot and muttered: "May Olafur Sigurdsson Freysteinsson rest in peace. AMEN!"

Overbearing with grief the family left and the assemblage of mourners moved closer to the burial plat and watched the casket being lowered deep into the wet ground. Loftur hurried away from the scene and headed for home. Remembering that he had his mother's umbrella he stopped and waited on top of the graveyard hill for his family. Loftur then espied his mother and sisters walking across the muddy, wet grass. With tears and rain obscuring his vision, he ran down the elevation and placed the umbrella over his mother's head, supporting her with his arm. Sigurun held Johanna's and Porunn's hands. She observed that the two small innocent girls did not realize what was going on or how permanent an affair it was, as they skipped laughing over the puddles on their way home to Sondum i Medallandi.

Porunn placed her arms around Sigurun's neck. "Why didn't Pabbi come home with us? she asked as she ate supper.

"I'll tell you tomorrow." With everyone in bed, Loftur handed Sigurun a cup of coffee, then pulled out a chair at the table and sat down. "How do you think Mamma is taking it, Sigurun?"

"I can't tell, Loftur. As you know, Mamma does not wear her heart on her sleeve like most people.

"Mamma seems extra tight inside," said Loftur.

"Well, everyone has their own way of grieving. It cannot be forced by another," stated Sigurun. "So all we can do is to help her with the work and make it as easy for her as we can." Glancing over the edge of her coffee cup at Loftur, she grimaced. "And now Mamma is seven months pregnant and Pabbi is gone. And only two more months 'til the baby is born. Pabbi was hoping the child would be a boy," smiled Sigurun.

"I know. Life sure can be cruel sometimes," replied Loftur with facial distortion.

"At least Mamma has us," stated Sigurun, tears dropping from her eyes, I'm fifteen now and you are eleven with the intellect of an adult." Standing up from the table Sigurun wiped the tears from her pretty blue eyes.

Time went by. Loftur and Sigurun helped their mother to get through the hard times. Sigurun's thoughtfulness and weighty presence was reflected every day in the love and support she gave her mother and family.

All went well. The family continued on as before and life took on a happier meaning.

Hallbera, the beautiful thirty-seven year old widow vaulted off her badsofa (bed) and glanced out of the small window over-looking the Icelandic sea. "I have never seen the ocean so restless and so black."

Sigurun occupying the bed next to her mothers stretched her arms sleepily and emitted a sigh. "Go back to bed, Mamma."

Ignoring Sigurun, Hallbera sat down on the bed and began to dress.

"Mamma, aren't you going back to bed? It's only five A.M.," persisted Sigurun pressing for a reply.

Porunn and Johanna raised their heads. "You woke me up, Sigurun," cried Porunn.

"And you woke me too," mumbled Johanna in her baby accent rubbing her eyes.

"You children go back to sleep," called out Hallbera. "I have to go to Hraungerd i Alftauert this morning to buy some fish for our supper tonight."

"But why so early, Mamma?" asked Sigurun.

"Because the fishermen's' boats come in about seven A.M. and as you know it is a long way, even though one does take the shore path." She rose with a twisting of her face and walked to the cubicle window overlooking the sea. The huge waves looked dark and angry, throwing a gloomy velocity of light over the small houses nestling against the cliffs then moving closer to the shore with volume, and being near prospect the waves leaped with fury in the direction of the village. Returning to her bed Hallbera sat down on the edge and continued dressing hurriedly. Sigurun observing her mothers labored breathing, sprang out of bed and slipped into a cotton smock over her nightdress. "Mamma, I'm going for you. And I'm going to Vigur. it would be a lot shorter and there will be many fishermen coming in with a lot of nice fish. The fish there is much better than in Hraungerd i Alftaueri."

"Yes, and a much higher price also," replied Hallbera breathlessly, slipping over her head her native Icelandic dress; a black long skirt, white silk blouse with a large silk bow on the front of the blouse and a short black satin bolero. Kneeling at her bed Hallbera pulled out a drawer where she kept her native skull cap with a long black tassel and placed it on the side of her head. Sitting down on her bed, Hallbera put on her lambskin shoes. "For instance, I need a pair of new shoes. I really cannot wear these much longer. But at least we can make our own shoes. Sheepskin is still very inexpensive." Rising from her bed Hallbera moved across the floor to Porunn and Johanna. When their mother approached their bed Porunn grasped her mother's arm. "Do you have to go, Mamma?"

"Yes, I'll be back soon with some delicious fish. Now, you and Johanna must mind your big sister while I'm gone."

All at once, Loftur jumped out of bed, and on bent knees pulled out his chest from under his bed. He opened the lid and took out a white freshly washed and ironed shirt from the chest.

"Loftur!" cried out Hallbera. "What are you doing! Put that shirt back. I ironed that shirt for church Sunday. She pulled it out of his hand and he pulled it back and held it behind his back.

"I'm going with you, Mamma. And I'm going to wear my best shirt so I will look real good because you look so pretty, Mamma." Hallbera's face softened.

Sigurun snatched the shirt out of his hands examining the wrinkles with disgust. "Look what you've done, Loftur after all Mamma's hard work." She gave her mother a quick glance. "You may as well let the little baby go so he can wear his nice white shirt." Throwing the shirt on Loftur's bed Sigurun looked over at him with wry features, "Hurry up, Mamma is waiting for you."

"If you are going with me, Loftur you'll have to hurry. And don't complain all the way that you're tired," stated Hallbera, picking up her gold belt off her bed and placing it around her waist. "Come on Loftur," she called out, and they headed for Hraungerd i Alftaueri on foot.

Sigurun standing in the doorway of the small structure watched her mother and only brother climb over the cliffs and head for the road. "Mamma!" shouted Sigurun over the loud noise of the tide whipping toward the shoreline. "Take the strand, Mamma it's a lot shorter than the road."

"Oh, I intend to, Sigurun," shouted Hallbera over her shoulder.

"You're walking too fast. Don't forget that you're pregnant."

"Don't worry about me, Sigurun I'll be fine. A brisk walk will do me good."

"What did you say, Mamma? I can't hear you. The roaring of the sea is getting louder," shouted Sigurun as her mother and Loftur continued on their way with deafened ears from the sea's sound of a bull's roar.

To expedite their time Hallbera began to walk faster. Lofter followed her closely, by advanced alternating steps. "Mamma, your walking too fast. I'm tired and we haven't even reached Hraungerd i Alftaueri yet."

Hallbera continued her velocity of speed with the bitter wind blowing her long, reddish blonde hair across her face, obscuring her vision. "Loftur quit lagging behind. Come up here and walk with me," shouted Hallbera. "You wanted to come, so come on!"

"You walk too fast," replied Loftur sluggardly. "How much farther?"

"We are almost there, son," she answered, slipping a straw basket off her arm and handing it to him. "Here, Loftur, you take it for awhile. My arm is tired."

"Why did you drag that thing along in the first place?"

"It's for the fish."

CHAPTER TWO

When they arrived at the wharf, numerous fishing vessels were bringing in nets of fresh fish. With a full basket of cod, Hallbera and Loftur headed back home. As they hurried along the shore the tide was coming in with unbelievable fury toward the land adjacent to the ragging sea. Cries of frightened sea birds could be heard attracting Hallbera's concerned attention. Loftur reached for his mother's hand. "Mamma, I'm scared."

"Nothing to be afraid of, Son. Nature is just showing us whose boss."

Moving spiritedly along, hand in hand they stepped over hundreds of dead birds lying on the path. Suddenly clouds of small diameter reached from the sky to the earth. Hallbera removed the basket from Loftur's arm. "I'll carry the fish the rest of the way home. And I believe we'd better take the road the rest of the way. The waves are getting too big and too close."

"But Mamma, the road is much farther."

"A little . . . But much safer."

"Hold my hand tight, Mamma, We're never going to make it home."

"We'll be alright as soon as we get on the road."

As they were about to leave the shore path Hallbera experienced a physical sensation of her son's hand slipping from her grasp . . . . and Loftur was gone! Oh God, a tidal wave!" she uttered to herself.

Gaining miracle strength she threw the basket of fish on the ground and ran headlong into the uncontrollable ocean. The opprobrious waves pulled her out to sea. Tossing, choking and coughing out water, she struggled desperately for her life and to find and save her son. Being an excellent swimmer she continued making a violent effort to stay alive. She was becoming weaker now that her lungs kept filling up with water. instead of air, thus depriving her of oxygen therefore poisoning her body, giving her two to five minutes to live. Then all at once Hallbera noted a white mass of something in the water.

Snatching wildly at the object she recognized Loftur's white shirt! "Thank you, God, Thank you God! It's got to be! It's got to be!" she uttered in a whisper too weak to emit a sound. Hallbera began pulling Loftur's unconscious body out of the water to the shore road, dropping down at short intervals to catch her breath. Having no time to spare, she dragged Loftur by his clothes to the shoreline, then unable to go another step, fell down again and collapsed on the rocky beach.

As Hallbera lay in a stupor, she was living through past events and emotions—a recall of a drowning incident. Recall—In her mind Hallbera was now a five year old little girl. Coming out on the veranda Hallbera called out to her mother who was picking wild berries. "Mamma, you said we're going to have a picnic by the Narrow Fjord (river) today."

"So we are, Hallbera. Go into the house and bring out my bonnet on the table and we'll go."

With a bright blue silk taffeta bonnet in her hand Hallbera handed her mother her hat. Gazing proudly at her daughter, Hallbera's mother straightened the child's collar. "My, Hallbera you look so pretty in your new pink dress. It sets off your long, reddish blonde hair and your pale gray eyes." Laughing, Hallbera whirled around to show of her long pretty sash. "Tie up my sash, please, then we can go Mamma."

Walking toward the Narrow Fjord, they moved to the edge of the river. "Don't go any closer to the water, Hallbera. The fjords are very deep in spots." About to step back, she noted a wild violet growing in the water between the stones at the river's bank.

"Oh, Mamma. Look at the beautiful flower. Purple just like my new sweater."

"We'll see a lot more violets on our way home. There will be enough for you to have a nice bouquet for your room."

"No, I want this one," retorted Hallbera with temper. Bending down on the bank. And stretching for the flower she fell into the river.

Throwing off her coat, her mother jumped into the water. Hallbera was not in view. Suddenly she saw the violet move and bubbles floated by the flower. Hallbera's mother swam into the moving water and lifted Hallbera out of the river and lay her down on the bank. And with immediacy her mother bent her leg and stooped forward so as to rest her weight of the body on a knee. Being a physician Hallbera's mother was knowledgeable to First aide treatment of manual form to restore consciousness.

After applying artificial resuscitation, the child was brought back to reality. Hallbera opened her soft blue gray eyes. "Mamma, I'm all wet and you are too. Where is my violet?"

"Nevermind," replied Hallbera's mother. We're going home. No picnic today. You could have drowned if you had been in the water any longer," retorted her mother. "and all because you didn't mind. It doesn't pay to be too independent, Hallbera."

Loftur and Hallbera lay on the beach in a stupor. Hallbera stirred and struggled to come out of her childhood past. Her bluish gray eyes caught Loftur's still body lying beside her. "Oh, God, give me strength to save my son!" she whispered, crawling on her hands and knees to her son's still body. Then all at once she was remembering her mother's manual form of treatment on her when she was a child. Developing her senses, she envisioned the incident and proceeded administering artificial resuscitation. With labored breathing, and no results, Hallbera fell back down on the rocky strand.

Being of a forceful and determined nature, Hallbera pulled herself up again and continued trying to revive her son. All at once Loftur began coughing. "Oh, dear God, you are sending me a message to not give up!" She continued again. but too exhausted and ill, she fell back onto the pebbles and wept.

Getting control of herself, Hallbera bent her ears to the noise of the sea. Everything appeared dark and quietus which caused cessation of action. And in this state of stillness, she slipped into a comatose slumber.

Loftur raised up coughing and emptied water from his lungs. He then mumbled something and fell back on the beach and closed his eyes. Somewhere in the distance, he thought he heard a wagon and some horses galloping up the road. Trying to rise again for a better view, but lacking distinctness he fell back on the beach and fainted. Unexpectedly, a wagon and two horses sped by. "Whoa!" called out a familiar voice of a neighbor. The horses neighed and came to a quick stop.

A young boy of about fourteen years of age sat next to his father. Turning around in the seat, the boy stood up and glared down to the bottom of the slope. "Pabbi . . . (Papa) isn't that Hallbera and Loftur down there?"

"It certainly is, that's why I stopped. But why in the world are they sleeping on all that sand and grass. Come on, son, let's find out," he stated excitedly. As they walked they sped up their gait.

"They don't seem to hear us, Pabbi."

"They must be sick, son."

"We better get them home. I wonder what happened?"

"And what are they doing way out here on a day like this?"

"Come on son, let's get them home, I have a feeling that we have less time then we thought. "Hallbera!" No response. "Hallbera! This is your next door neighbor, Herr Valdison." No response. "Hallbera do you think you can make it to the wagon with my son's and my help?" Mr. Valdison turned to his son. "We've got to get Hallbera home and get her some help. Come and help me get her up on my shoulders."

"Oh, look, Pabbi, Loftur is sitting up."

(Herr) Mr. Valdison smiled. "By Jove, he's going to be alright." As Loftur was assisted up the slope and into the vehicle, Valdison carried Hallbera to the wagon and placed her on the floor, then wrapped her up in an old saddle blanket.

Sigurun came to the door. "Oh, God, what happened!" She hurried to Loftur's bed and opened the covers as the man's son assisted Loftur into his bed, changed his wet clothes and covered him up. Glancing up at Mr. Valdison, Sigurun shook her neighbors hand. "Thank you so much, Herr, for bringing my mother and Loftur home—for saving their lives." Blotting the tears from her eyes, she glanced over at the neighbor's young son. "And thank you also for your help in saving two lives."

Mr. Valdison took Sigurun to the side. "I don't want the younger children to hear. But I think your mother is having a miscarriage—She is pregnant, isn't she?" Sigurun nodded. Mr. Vladimir spoke softer. "When we went by Johanna Jonsdottir home awhile ago, I noticed Dr. Barthason's carriage in front of her house. I am going over there immediately and ask Dr. Barthason to come and see Hallbera right away."

"Oh, thank you, Herr! Thank you!" Sigurun cried, wringing her hands.

Meeting Dr. Barthason at the door, she then crossed the room to her mother's bedside. She was awake and weeping. Hearing Dr. Barthason's voice she stretched out a hand to him. "Oh, Doctor, I lost my baby!"

"I'm so sorry, Hallbera," replied Dr. Barthason taking her small, cold, shaking hands in his.

After examining the fetus he shook his head despondently. "You are going to need a lot of rest, Hallbera. You have other children who need you. And thank God that you have Sigurun. She's a fine, young woman."

Hallbera touched the physician's arm. "I didn't want to look, Doctor. Was it a girl or boy?"

"A boy. Just what Olofur wanted—?" Hallbera nodded and burst into tears.

Two weeks had passed since the tragic incident. Sigurun sat at Hallbera's bedside brushing her long. reddish blonde hair. "Isn't life funny?" stated Sigurun starring out of the window at the beautiful, calm sea.

"Funny? What do you mean?" replied her mother.

"Just what happened two weeks ago."

"If you mean finding my son funny, I do not agree with you Sigurun. It was a miracle."

"What I mean, Mamma, is, that both you and I insisted that Loftur could not wear his white shirt. And through his stubbornness Loftur was saved. You would never have seen his dark shirt in that water."

"It was truly a miracle. And like you said, all because of Loftur's obstinate, unyielding nature to wear the white shirt." Pale and weak, Hallbera took the hairbrush out of Sigurun's hand. "That's enough, Sigurun. Brushing makes me nervous." She took a quick glance in the looking-glass at herself". And I think that I look nice enough for someone who will be spending the rest of her life in bed." Hallbera's intuition was correct. She never got out of bed again. Rising, Sigurun placed the hairbrush back on the bureau.

"It's about time to start supper," stated Sigurun spreading some fish on the counter to clean and cut.

"Sigurun, where are the children?"

"Porunn and Johanna are out in the back feeding the two sheep and the lamb. Loftur has to stay at school a little late today to make up what he missed when he was out those few days after that incident." All of a sudden the door flew open and Porunn came crying into the room.

"Mamma! Johanna spilled the baby lamb's milk all over the ground and now the baby doesn't have any milk."

Johanna followed her sister in. "I couldn't help it, Mamma. The nipple came off the bottle."

Unmoved, Hallbera lay back on her pillows. "Did the baby lamb's mother ever come back?" asked Hallbera.

"No," replied Sigurun reaching for a towel and wiping the milk off Porunn's sheepskin jacket.

All eyes rested on the door when the entrance opened and Loftur came in carrying the little lamb in his arms. "Who fed the baby lamb today? There's milk and broken glass all over the ground. And this tells me, the little lamb was not fed."

"Johanna wanted to try and feed the baby so I let her," replied Porunn, beginning to sob.

"The nipple slipped off the bottle," interjected Sigurun. "After all Johanna is only two years old, Loftur."

"Because Johanna is only two years old, the little animal goes without eating. True, Johanna is just a baby herself," "But that does not excuse you, Sigurun—or you, Porunn. The two of you could have at least cleaned up the mess."

Sigurun observed Loftur as he walked over to the cooler and took out a cup full of milk. "We don't have any milk, Loftur."

"Not now we don't," replied Loftur beginning to feed the lamb from the cup.

"That's the milk for our oatmeal in the morning, Loftur."

"WAS!" replied Loftur covered in milk from the small animal's inexperience of drinking from a cup instead of a nipple bottle or his mother's breast.

Hallbera rose weakly upon one elbow. "For heavens sake! Will you children stop arguing with each other? That lamb has been nothing but work since it was left here by the mother. Even the mother didn't want it. I hope she comes after it soon."

"Well, the mother isn't going to come back," stated Loftur. "Any mother who runs out on her own flesh and blood is not going to come back," he repeated. Patting the little animal on the head, he rubbed the soft, white wool on it's tiny neck. "No way is your mother going to get you even though she returns. Your mother dumped you so now you are mine."

Hallbera lay back again on her pillow. "And who do you think you are now that your father is gone, Loftur . . . . the manor of the house?"

"You could call it that. After all I am the only man here now."

"I am sorry, Manor, but the lamb is not yours. Last week I sold the baby lamb to Johanna Jonsdottir. She will pick up the baby lamb next Thursday." Burying his face in the animal's neck Loftur burst into tears. Raising his tearstained face he glanced over at his mother who lay unfeelingly gazing out of the window overlooking the sea.

Loftur glanced bitterly at her. "I love you, Mamma. But only because you are my mother . . . . your mean . . . . you've never had a heart." Sobbing again, he turned and with the lamb in his arms he ran out of the house into the cool, twilight evening. As he walked to the small sheepfold he thought about the enjoyable time helping his father enlarge the small sheepfold for the little stranger who apparently was going to make it's home here. He could feel winter in the air. His father had made the sheepfold warm by constructing it with cement and sod, using tarred skins for a roof during the winter months. The small enclosure now had three sheep . . . next Thursday, only two. He placed the lamb gently down into the fold, then strolled toward the sheepwalk, a meadow where the sheep were pastured. Abruptly, Loftur heard Sigurun calling him for supper.

Porunn and Johanna were seated at the table watching Sigurun fixing their mother's tray. "What's for supper Sigurun?" called out Loftur amicably.

"Skyr! the National food of Iceland! After all, you have worked hard to get on the honor roll and now you made it." Sigurun picked up Hallbera's tray and placed it in Loftur's hands. "Take Mamma's super to her please. I have to help Porunn and Johanna."

"What kind of fish are we having, Sigurun?" asked Porunn."

"Wait and see," she answered cheerfully.

Loftur placed a pillow at his mother's back, then positioned the tray in front of her. "Mamma, I didn't mean to speak to you the way I did last night. Please forgive me. We all know you love us and we all love you."

"Go eat your super," replied Hallbera coldly.

All seated at the table, except for Sigurun who stood at the cupboard placing the fish on a platter. "Here I come with some nice lax." (salmon)

Johanna covered her eyes with her soft, white hands. "Did you cut off the tail and head, Sigurun? Because if you didn't I won't look and I won't eat either."

Loftur removed Johanna's hands from her eyes. "Oh," exclaimed the two-year-old. "That's red lax."

"Baby," teased Loftur.

"No she is not. A lot of people serve lamb and fish that way. It would make me sick too, Johanna," replied Sigurun.

Darkness not quite completed, Sigurun began getting Porunn and Johanna ready for bed.

Johanna refused to go to bed until it was completely dark. Sigurun slipped Johanna's nightdress over her head. "Soon it will be summer, and it won't get dark all night." Johanna giggled and kissed Sigurun on the cheek. "I love you Sigurun sister."

Porunn moved over to Sigurun and turned her back. "Sigurun, will you button me up, I cannot reach the button in back?"

By now the late stages of evening shadows encompassed the room. Sigurun filled, then lighted the kerosene lamp on the kitchen table. After tucking Porunn and Johanna into bed she pulled out a large bottle of cod liver oil. "I don't want any . . . it's awful!" screamed Johanna, hiding under the bedclothes.

"Open your mouth, elskan." (love) Loftur sat quietly underneath the light of the kerosene lamp moving at short intervals to catch the light on his text book that he was studying for a test at school in the morning. Sweeping away a strand of blonde hair from his forehead, he glanced and grimaced at Johanna. "Take it! Then maybe we can have a little peace around here."

"Take it yourself!" screamed Johanna.

"I did. We all take cod liver oil. Even Sigurun, and she's fifteen years old. Mamma takes cod liver oil and our mother is thirty-five."

Johanna removing the bedclothes from her face, rose up in bed. "Thirty-five! Oh, that's old!" She closed her eyes and made a face, then accepted the bad tasting cod liver oil.

CHAPTER THREE

The small village lay in a dark shade of blue opaque and impervious to light. The tranquility was absent of disturbances with exclusion of the shore birds on the rocky beach nearby. Quietude was broken only by the shore birds lovely language lasting through the night

Morning dawned. Loftur hopped out of bed and began chopping kindling for a fire, while Sigurun reached on the shelf for a large black iron pot to cook the family's porridge.

Hallbera slid up in bed when she saw Loftur bringing her breakfast to her. "Thank you, Son," she smiled amicably. Loftur felt joy in his heart. It had been a long time since his mother had shown any warmth. As the rest of the family sat at the table finishing breakfast, Hallbera called out to her eldest child. "Sigurun!"

"Yes, Mamma," she replied rising from the table and moving to her mother's bedside.

"When you are through breakfast, I want you to bring the children to my bedside." Her features then grew cold and unemotional. "This means Loftur and you also."

"We are already through, Mamma, I'll tell them right away." Sigurun observed Hallbera's untouched tray. "Finish eating, Mamma."

"Take it away. I'm not hungry."

The puzzled group gathered around their mother's bed. Porunn placed her arms around her mother's neck. "You look so beautiful this morning, Mamma."

"Yes—well—well go sit down, Porunn." replied Hallbera in an ejaculated utter. Moving sprightly, Porunn hopped up on Hallbera's bed. "Not there, Porunn! You're sitting on my feet." Porunn slid quickly to the foot of the bed.

Sigurun hopping her mother had good news for them she dragged a chair to her mother's bed, then pulled the two year old up on her lap. Maybe they were moving to a better home. No that couldn't be it. There wasn't any money for that, even though Loftur would soon be graduating from school and would be looking for a job. Loftur stood in a corner stiff and formal, as if solidified in ice.

Hallbera scooted up in bed. "I have brought you children together to let you know that I cannot keep you anymore. You will all have to live with foster parents."

Loftur instantly unfroze. "Of course your little plan includes to keep Sigurun and me. After all we are almost grown-up and can be a lot of help to you."

"Sigurun I'll keep. I will need her to take care of me. But you Loftur I do not need."

Loftur's head dropped down on his chest. He then took control of his crushed emotions. "Where do you expect to find a home for all of us? Most people don't want three children. And they want children old enough to do all their work for them.".

"I have that all arranged. Dr. Barthason has found three homes who will take children temporarily," stated Hallbera.

"What do you mean three homes? Do you mean we are going to be separated?"

"Yes, the people Dr. Barthason interviewed for me only want one," She rested back on her pillows. "Dr Barthason has been so very kind."

"Yes, very kind, separating families!" cried Loftur bitterly raising his voice and running out of the house to the sheepfold

Sigurun rose from her chair and placed Johanna on the floor. "Mamma! There has to be another way," she pleaded with tears flowing down her cheeks.

"I haven't anything more to say, Sigurun." Johanna being just two years old and not understanding what was going on, reached over the bed and pulled Porunn's red curl giggling playfully. Breaking into tears, Porunn vaulted off the bed and threw her tiny arms around her mother's neck "Mamma please don't send us away!" she begged with heart-breaking sobs. "We won't be any bother we'll be good, Mamma, I promise." Seeing she was not making any progress with her mother Porunn ran to Sigurun and placed her head on her sister's lap. Instantaneously Porunn rose up, stopped crying and walked to the door. She turned back and glanced at Sigurun. "I will never cry again!" It was a promise she gave herself which she kept all through her hard life ahead.

Hallbera unmoved, called out to Porunn. "Sit down, Porunn! You are not excused until I say so." All eyes moved to the door when Loftur came back into the house again.

Porunn wiping her tears on the sleeves of her nightdress ran into Loftur's arms, and the two brokenhearted siblings stood waiting for their mother's decision of their future.

CHAPTER FOUR

"Tomorrow morning," continued Hallbera, "a couple who have a small farm near Bolunearvikur will come for Johanna."

"May I go with Johanna, Mamma?"

"No, Porunn these people want only one child. Somebody else will come and get you," answered Hallbera unfeelingly.

"Can Loftur come with me, Mamma?" asked Porunn, to persuade by advancing reasons. "No. Your brother will be picked up on Wednesday by some other people."

"Well, what about me, Mamma?" persisted Porunn continually and steadily applying herself with unrelaxed effort.

"I don't know exactly when these other folks are coming for you. They really were not too specific on the day you are to be picked up." Hallbera pushed a lock of hair away from her delicate features. "However, they did mention something about this week."

Johanna too young to know what was going on, ran straight into her mother's arms and kissed her. "I love you, Mamma."

The following day, a small black buggy driven by one horse stopped in front of the house, the large waves of the sea rolled up on the cliffs hiding the shanty from view. Sigurun stood watching as the man in the black buggy went by a couple of times. Sigurun opened the door and called out to the stranger. "This is the place, Herr." Looking again through the window, she saw a short fat farmer unshaven and wearing torn overalls. Porunn and Sigurun glanced quickly at each other, then returned their eyes to the window. When they saw the farmer hobbling on a lame leg up to the house. Sigurun ran to the entranceway and opened the door. "Good morning, Herr." With no response he dashed into the dwelling "Where's the kid, Ung Fru?" (unmarried) He then glanced down at Porunn. "Is this the kid?"

"No!" Porunn screamed. "And let go of my arm!" she cried, jerking away from him.

With a faint heart Sigurun ran out to the sheepfold and brought Johanna by the hand to the house. "Johanna this is Herr (Mr.) Bjornsson. And out there in front of the house is the horse and buggy that is going to take you for a ride."

"Oh, goody! I have never been in a buggy." Johanna then glanced innocently up at Sigurun. "Aren't you coming, Sigurun?"

"No, you are going with Herr Bjornsson and his wife who is waiting for you in the buggy, Elskan." (Love)

Johanna glanced curiously up at Sigurun for a moment, then put her tiny arms around Sigurun's neck and kissed her. "Oh alright, Sigurun. I'll be back soon."

Herr Bjarnsson took Johanna by the hand and led her to the horse and buggy where Hilda sat waiting for her husband and the child she had wanted all her life. However, being barren life had left her childless.

Happening unexpectedly, they heard Sigurun's voice calling faintly over the blatant sound of the ocean waves. In her hand was a paper bag. "Herr Bjornsson! Herr Bjornsson! Wait!" Breathlessly she ran up to the buggy. "Herr, I forgot to give you Johanna's clothes," she stated sobbing." handing him the bag.

Johanna jerked her hand free from the man's crude hand. "I don't need my clothes. I'm only going for a ride."

Sigurun kneeled down on the ground and placed her arms around her little sister's shoulders. "Johanna you are going for a ride, but you won't be coming home for awhile, Elskan." (Love) Sigurun stood up from the ground and ran down the path and with a broken heart disappeared into the lonely suffering home.

Johanna bewildered lay on the ground with heartbreaking, convulsive sobs. She then rose from the ground and started running for home. Hobbling after her Herr Bjornsson tripped her and she fell down on the path. He wrapped his good leg over her body, pinning her to the ground. Small, but crafty and sly, Johanna bit him on the leg making a severe lesion. "You little brat! Helga! Help me!

Helga sprang out of the buggy, grabbed the child in an insolent disorderly manor and threw her on the threadworn seat of the buggy. Sigurun and Porunn stood in the open doorway aghast. "We should have taken Johanna back into the house," stated Porunn.

"We couldn't, Porunn. Mamma would not have supported us on this."

"We could have tried."

Johanna's heartbreaking cries could be heard, then fade away as the small, black buggy disappeared around the curve of the sea.

Night fell. Sigurun, Porunn and Loftur sat around the table conversing after eating supper. Sigurun rose from the table. as partial darkness marked the room and spirit. Hallbera, half-asleep, lay listening. Lighting the kerosene lamp Sigurun slid onto a chair at the table. beginning to cry, she threw her head in her hands, then glanced down at Porunn's hard features as she fought to keep unmoved, determined not to break down.

"Well, Johanna is gone," Sigurun sobbed. "It is so lonely!"

"If you don't mind," said Lofter, I don't care to talk about it. I'm just glad I was at school." Rising from the table, Loftur's features dowered. "It's hard to believe that today was my last day. And of course the school would offer me a scholarship for college."

"You have really earned it, Loftur."

"Too late. Like everything in this rotten life, too late." cried Loftur.

Sigurun rose and lowered the flame on the lamp. "Goodnight, Loftur." Taking Porunn's hand she led Porunn to bed.

"Sigurun—Oh, nothing." stated Porunn sitting down on her bed.

"No, it is not nothing. What were you going to say?"

"May I sleep with you tonight?"

"Of course, Elskan." (Love).

The following morning a gray mist from the sea hung over the small village. Sigurun began to prepare breakfast. She fixed Hallbera's tray first, then set the table for Porunn, Loftur and herself. Standing up from the table, Loftur excused himself and began dressing hurriedly in a brown shirt and tan trousers. Hallbera pulled herself up in bed and pushed her breakfast tray aside. "When you get ready to pack, Loftur, you may take one of those flour sacks for your things."

"What things Hallbera?" he asked sarcastically. "I don't have anything to pack. The shirt and pants I have on, and of course my white shirt and one change of underwear plus a pair of socks. "That's about it, Hallbera." With tears dimming his eyes, Loftur placed his worldly possessions on the white shirt and tied the shirt in a geometrical necessity, then stuck a long stick in the center of the knot and slung it over a shoulder. Glancing at Sigurun and Porunn he called out to them. "I love you guys." Opening the door to his home for the last time, he walked sluggishmindedly toward a two horse driven wagon where a stranger awaited him. Loftur has never been heard of since.

The ensuing morning Porunn rose early. Her fatal day had come. Days with her mother were gone. Standing barefoot at her mother's bedside she glanced at the sleeping Hallbera. Sigurun with oblique movement tiptoed to the window over-looking the sea. "Today is the first day of spring!" she thought to herself gazing up at the pale blue sky over the ocean. The soft wind of the sea pushed the waves against particles of water moving up and down through the currents over the waves breaking, and the vast expanse gave a feeling of peace and security—"Security," Sigurun reflected on what was happening and formed her own opinion.

"It's a beautiful day, Elskan," Sigurun said to Porunn trying to conceal her feelings.

Moving to her bed depressed in spirit, Porunn sat down and began to dress. "You know, Sigurun, some people say this is an ugly world. Not true, it's the people in it that are ugly."

Spent and overstrained Sigurun nodded with tears streaming from her eyes.

Porunn combing her long, red hair in the mirror, glanced up from the looking-glass at Sigurun. "You don't have to curl my hair today. I'll just braid it. I'll have to get used to doing it myself. And I can't curl it so I'll have to get used to braids."

Over a solemn breakfast of oatmeal Hallbera sat in bed eating off her tray. Porunn hopped up from the table. "Excuse me, Sigurun, I better get my coat on before—what ever his name is comes."

"Herr Martinsson!" called out Hallbera.

A loud knock was sounded on the fore part of the entrance. Sigurun opened the door putting on a cheerful air. Herr Martinsson walked boldly in. "I hope my charge is ready. I have no time to waste, Ung Fru." (Ung unmarried)

"Yes, Herr, Porunn Olafsdottir is ready and waiting," replied Sigurun in a cold, unfriendly timber.

"I hope so" stated the rude, disorderly, insolent fellow. "If the charge is ready, where is she?"

"Here I am Herr," answered Porunn with a large lump in her throat trying not to spoil the promise made to herself not to cry ever again.

Sigurun glanced down at the bright flowered carpet bag that Porunn held in her hand. "I see Mamma gave you her old carpet bag. Take good care of it, won't you?" stated Sigurun, weeping and embarrassing Porunn for the last time with audible convulsive sobs and catching of her breath.

Dressed in her sheepskin coat and the colorful carpet bag in her hand Porunn felt an impelling force to leave the house immediately before she would break down. She opened the door and hurried without her overseer, down the path leading to the wagon and team of horses.

Herr Martinsson glancing out of the window with Sigurun shook his head. "An independent little witch!" he laughed,

When they reached Medallandi, Herr Martinsson continued on to a small homestead a broken-down dwelling of sod, covered with turf fitted closely and packed down to make an even surface. When the wagon stopped at the house Herr Martinsson's wife, Asa, hurried out of the shack to meet her new foster child. "Did ya get the chick, Marti?"

"Yep! I got her, and she's a real hell cat! Stubborn and independent."

"I'll take that out of her in a hurry. The last foster child tried that and I laid it right on her but good."

"That brat didn't stay very long, did she?"

"Long enough for me to train her for the next family who will take her. It seems after I get these misfits trained they leave."

"Oh, well, as long as it lasts it's good to have some help around. My gout ain't getting better. It seems to be spreadin' down my right arm," stated Marti lifting Porunn down from the wagon with grimacing pain. Asa peered down at the child's distressed features.

"She ain't very big, is she Marti? We won't get much work out of this chick. Well, at least it won't cost us a lot to feed her. The last one almost ate us out of our home," stated Asa taking Porunn by the arm and heading for the house.

Porunn pulled her arm from the woman's grasp. "I can walk by myself!" she uttered grimly, continuing ahead of the strangers.

"Well, I declare!" said Asa, seizing Marti by the hand and following closely behind Porunn to the house. Asa bent her head toward Marti and whispered. "You know, Marti, the chick acts a lot older than her years and has an intelligent mind. I believe she is going to work out all right."

"I hope you're right, Asa. An older girl would cost us too much to feed."

The shack inside was dark and shabby. In Porunn's confused disordered turmoil, she had forgotten all about Hallbera's carpet bag. "Where is my carpet bag, Herr Martinsson?"

"It must still be in the wagon, Boss," answered Herr Martinsson amusingly, admiring her grit.

Asa noted the change in her husband's demeanor.

"Don't ya be gettin' all soft and foolish, I'm still the boss here. It's the red hair that's gettin ta ya, ya simpleton." "Herr," said Porunn. Please go out to the wagon and get my carpet bag."

"I'll get the bag latter when I see to the horses."

"No, Herr, you'll get it right now. I need it—NOW."

"You women are all alike," he chuckled leaving the house.

Asa unbuttoning Porunn's sheepskin coat, yanked it off her and threw it on the woodpile. "You won't be needing this fancy coat tonight, missy." Porunn sat down on a stool by the window and gazed out of the broken window pane nervously waiting to see Herr Martinsson returning with her carpet bag. When he came into view she ran out to meet him and take her carpet bag from his hand.

"Thank you, Ung Fru. My arm was beginning to ache. You're a good, thoughtful girl."

Asa lighted the kerosene lamp in the corner of the kitchen. Porunn looked pleadingly up at her, "Could I go to my room now, Fru Jonsdottir?"

"What room, Missey? We have only one room beside this one and that's Marti's and mine." Porunn at loss of how to reply or what to do dropped her chin on her chest and twisted nervously the buttons on her dress. Picking up the carpet bag off the floor Asa moved across the kitchen to the back door. "I'll show you to your room, Missey." Porunn stood immobile, still twisting the buttons on her dress. "Well, move it kid! Follow me, your room is in the barn next to the house."

"Where does the horse sleep, Fru Jonsdottir?" asked Porunn puzzled.

"She sleeps in the barn with you Missey." Looking down at Porunn's languished features, the Fru with Hallbera's carpet bag in her hand opened the door. "Ya don't have to worry about poor old Gunna, she ain't goin' to harm ya none." She walked out of the house, Porunn trailing after her.

Porunn's pale—blue, beautiful eyes traveled over the interior of the barn which seemed larger than the house. It was clean, and the horse stall was far at the end of the stable. In a corner, Asa placed Hallbera's bag on a bale of hay. The floor was covered with a fresh thick carpet of straw. Asa smiled at Porunn in an amicable manner. "You'll be comfortable here, kid. The straw is warm and makes a nice mattress." Asa traversed afoot to the barn door. "I'm goin' to get ya a nice new blanket—Oh, and also a nice feather pillow that I made last week when I knew ya were comin'."

"Thank you, Fru Jonsdottir," answered Porunn praying that the dam which had harbored her heartbreaking tears for so long would not let go now.

Morning dawned. Streaks of the early sunrise could be seen through the cracks of the walls and small window. Hearing a rooster crowing in the barnyard Porunn vaulted off the straw And began dressing, remembering

Asa had informed her that her first chore was to feed the horse early in the morning before breakfast.

Thus in this quality of environment three years passed. Porunn now six years of age had accepted her life without complaints. Yet, in her subconscious mind and soul, there was a pain which never left her.

As she finished mopping the kitchen floor she dried her small, red undernourished hands, glancing at short intervals out of the window where she saw two reddish-blonde horses pulling a fancy black carriage. The vehicle then stopped at the impoverished dwelling. Porunn trying to get a better view put her face up to the window where she saw Herr Martinsson with a chain rake in his hands. Seeing the fine carriage in front of his house, Herr Martinsson threw down his rake and approached the carriage where a well dressed gentleman sat in the buggy. "Are ya comin' fer the kid, Herr?" (Mr.) asked Marti.

"Yes, Herr Martinsson." The gentleman pulled out a sheet of paper from his valise and glanced at it briefly. "I believe the young lady's name is, Porunn Olafsdottir. Is she ready?"

Asa came running down the rickety old steps of the house. "ya, Herr, the kid's ready. I'll tell the kid ya here." Porunn came out of the shanty in her sheepskin coat, now somewhat too tight and too short after wearing it for five years. Hallbera's carpet was in her hand, still clean and showing no wear. Unboarding his carriage, the gentleman removed his black silk derby, first styled in 1850. Bowing to Porunn he expressed pleasure. "I am Herr Christensson from Gladhfimun. We welcome you to join our family."

Porunn smiled and extended a hand. "I am Porunn Olafsdottir, Thank you Herr." she stated, stepping up into the carriage. She then glanced at the impoverished dwelling that she had learned to think of as her home. All at once she espied Asa and Marti standing in the yard waving. Porunn raised a hand and with a broad smile on her lips, she returned her last farewell to them, her heart aching for their poverty. "Thank you!" Porunn called out to them, as Herr Christensson touched the small, full-grown Icelandic horses with his whip and the two obedient animals started down the road.

It was a beautiful day. The sun was shinning brightly and warm on the many fosses they passed. When they glanced up at Detti Foss the current of water moved continually according to the nature of the region. Mount Hekla is the most active waterfall in the land. The rivers were full and flowing swiftly by. Porunn sat quietly drinking in their beauty. In her mind she was recalling when she had remarked to Sigurun: "It is not the world that is ugly . . . . it's the people."

"Our Iceland is a beautiful country," said Herr Christensson," taking his eyes off the road for a moment.

"Oh, yes." she uttered, in a state of being hindered. She was glad that Herr Christensson was not a talkative man as they traveled on, each with his own thoughts.

CHAPTER FIVE

It was a long ride. In the late afternoon the carriage turned off the mountain road and bent it's way toward a large estate. The horses then stopped at the carriage house where the caretaker hurried out and assisted the passengers down from the carriage and then saw to the horses. Herr Christensson took Porunn's carpet bag and they walked together to the large white house and climbed up the many, cement steps. leading to the entrance.

The Fru of the manor met them at the door. "Gunner! You know perfectly well, that we do not bring hired help through our front entrance."

"The child is only six years old. We can hardly call her hired help"

"Oh no? We'll see about that."

Herr Christensson handed Porunn her carpet bag. "Make yourself at home, Porunn, I'll see you at suppertime." he said kindly and left the parlor. Stepping into the room, his wife encountered Porunn. "Sit down, dear."

Porunn glanced pleadingly up at the Fru. "May I please go up to my room? I'm very tired."

"It's almost suppertime, and then we will have a nice talk. So, you better put your luggage in the kitchen, not in the parlor, and be sure you place it in a corner," she then left the room and climbed the long, wide stairway to discipline Gunner.

Porunn's eyes traveled across the lovely large room with it's rich carpets and furnishings. The huge mantle of the fireplace was in Ergonoma design laid with a Mèlange of silk flowers. Porunn stood mesmerized at the beauty, feeling that she was in a bounty of a heavenly garden. Hearing a footstep outside of the parlor Porunn quickly came out of her dream world and back to reality, locking her feelings back in her subconscious where they would be safe.

Herr Christensson came down from upstairs to check on his new member of his family. "We'll be having supper soon, Porunn. I'm sure you're hungry. I know I sure am."

"Thank you, Herr Christensson but I'm not hungry."

"Sure you are, Porunn—May I call you Porunn?"

"That's my name." They both turned their eyes when the Fru came down the stairs wearing a soft, green silk taffeta gown. Being of a fine, glossy fabric the Fru's gown rattled in swift succession of short sounds. "It is time to dine," she stated with arrogance, holding up her long skirt so as not to step on it.

"I don't feel like eating now, Fru."

"You will eat when we tell you to eat, and that means you will be having your meals in the kitchen with my housekeeper, Fru Svenson. She runs the house for me and you will take orders from her. Today she went to visit her sister but she will be back tomorrow and will clue you in on your duties and the rules of the house."

"Yes, Fru. I will follow orders. And now, will you show me to my room, I won't be long."

"Follow me. You will have the small room off the kitchen behind the scullery."

"What is a scullery?"

"It is a room where cooking utensils are cleaned and kept, A lot of your work will be in the scullery—plus kitchen chores."

They continued into the small darkled room. with rays of sunshine trying to filter through the cracks of the single pane of glass. "You see, this separates the hired help from the family bedrooms upstairs."

"But, Fru, I am not hired help I am just an orphan.

"Never mind being dramatic with me, orphan." Suddenly the front door opened and the two spoiled daughters of the estate age twelve and fourteen walked in dressed in the latest fashion.

Kicking off their shoes they flopped down on the luxurious sofa. Their eyes then found Porunn standing in the doorway. "Come here little girl," demanded Anna the eldest, assuming exercise of control. "What kind of a little waif did Pabbi (Papa) pick up this time?"

"Pabbi never did have any taste," laughed Dora, the youngest daughter. Afraid not to obey, Porunn stepped closer into the room.

Anna was secretly envious of Porunn's beautiful, red hair. "Where in the world did Pabbi pick THAT up! And look at that horrible hair. And in pigtails of all things." she laughed pulling on Porunn's long braid. "Don't you know, waif girl that pigtails are out of style?" asked Anna giggling into the palm of her hand.

"After all, Anna, what would a carrot top know about style?" asked Dora with exaggerated self-esteem.

Staying in control, Porunn bit her lower lip to keep from crying, then braced her emotions. "I can't fix my own hair," replied Porunn in ejaculated phrase.

The two sisters burst into a fit of laughter. "Oh, we have a beautician who comes to our home once a week to fix our hair and nails," stated Dora.

"__and what ever," interjected Anna with variedness. "It must be awful to be poor" added, Anna. "don't you think so Dora?"

"How would we know? We've always been rich." The two girls began laughing expressing merriment by convulsive sounds accompanied by opening their mouths and wrinkling their made-up faces. They then suddenly stopped laughing when an elderly man hobbled in the parlor on a cane.

"What's all the rumpus about—where is your mother?" he asked Anna.

"She went upstairs for a moment," Anna replied quietly.

His eyes rested on Porunn. "So, you are the new member of our family? Welcome!"

"Thank you, Herr," Porunn muttered in a low voice. Cognizant of Porunn's unhappy face and the expressions on his granddaughter's extorted features he knew Anna and Dora were up to their old tricks.

Drawing up a chair for Porunn, he called out to her. "Come here pretty little girl and have a seat beside an old man."

Anna and Dora rose haughtily and climbed the stairs. With flushed cheeks; Porunn slid slowly onto the chair beside him. "My, what beautiful, red hair you have, Porunn." He hooked the handle of his cane onto the arm of his chair. "I am the grandfather of these two unmannerly girls, Porunn. I am Gudmundur Jonsson, and I live here also. And, please, Porunn, if you ever need someone to talk to tell me and we'll have a chat."

"Thank you, Herr Jonsson for being so kind."

"Just call me, Gudmundur, young lady. No—I think Afi." (Grandfather)

Lying on the cot in her little room off the scullery behind the kitchen, Porunn watched the sun go down. The Fru of the house had ordered Porunn to retire early as her daughters were having a dinner dance in the ballroom that evening: that the housekeeper had hired another maid for the occasion who would take care of guests.

Several hours passed and the party had begun. Porunn was about to fall asleep when she heard loud blatant music from the hired orchestra in the ballroom. Sliding off her cot she opened her door slightly to get a small glimpse of the guests dancing passed the archway of the ballroom. She noted the guests were all young people dressed in formal attire. Porunn gasped at the beautiful gowns floating across the polished floor to the lovely music. How she had always wanted to learn to dance! Barefoot she began to move to the rhythm of the music. Suddenly the swinging kitchen doors opened and the maid came in with a shiny silver tray of empty glasses. So as not to be caught out of bed, Porunn closed her door quickly but soundlessly and hopped into bed.

The following morning she arose early. The first thing she saw was a pile of dirty dishes and glasses from the party, stacked high on the sideboard near the sink. Hearing a footstep, Porunn looked to the door and saw a tall, fat, fair-haired woman come into the kitchen. "I am Fru Svenson, the housekeeper here. I presume you are the new foster child." Porunn blushing, nodded her head. "You will be working with me and following my orders. Understood?" Again, Porunn nodded her head. "You will address me as Fru Svenson."

"Yes, Fru Svenson."

"To start with, Porunn, you can start washing your dishes while I prepare breakfast. The family won't be down for awhile. They always sleep in after staying up late."

"Yes, Fru Svenson."

Two hours went by. The dishes were washed and dried. Porunn wiped her red, swollen hands on a towel then climbed up on a chair trying to reach the high shelves to put the dishes away. She looked down from her roost when she saw Gudmundur come into the kitchen. "Let me help you down, Porunn, I'll put the dishes on the high shelves for you. These shelves are much too high for a little lady like you—and it's dangerous to stand so high upon a chair." Gudmundur lifted Porunn down and placed her on the floor. "You can put the glasses on that lower shelf."

Porunn smiled. "Thank you, Gudmundur."

"AFI!" he corrected.

Seven long years passed. Porunn now thirteen years of age lived by habit only. Gudmundur's support of compassion and his kindness made life for her more bearable. He protected her from the abuse of his granddaughters and Gudmundur was respected in the household of which was due because Gudmundur was the owner of the estate. It was his money that supported his son and his family, giving them all such a luxurious life.

Tonight more company was coming. Porunn was instructed to dust the house thoroughly. Standing with a feathered duster in her hand, she was interrupted when the Fru of the manor walked into the parlor.

"Porunn, put that thing down. Porunn, I have something to talk to you about. Tomorrow you will be leaving my service." Sitting down on the arm of the brocaded sofa, the Fru spread her pink satin dressing gown with eminence over her knees.

"But, Fru—I have been in your service for seven years. I would be lying if I say that I've been happy. But I have grown used to the work and I hope you have found it satisfactory."

"Oh, my dear child it has nothing to do with your work, you see, the orphan home needs help. And I am always there when someone needs assistance of any kind." She put on an artificial smile. "That's just the way I am."

"What time do I leave?" asked Porunn curtly.

"The orphan wagon will be here for you early tomorrow morning. And for heaven's sake get rid of that old sweater you've been wearing around here."

"It's all I have, Fru. I grew out of my sheepskin coat many years ago."

"Well, as I just said, being of a kind nature I will let you have Dora's old coat. She doesn't wear it any more anyway."

"Thank you Fru." Porunn looked askance at her. "Why does the home need help? I should think with all those orphans there they would have plenty of help."

"That's it. So many orphans but most of them are too young for certain jobs. The infant population there is growing and they need older orphans to take care of them. And that's where you com in."

"I am only thirteen. The older orphans working in the nursery must be at least sixteen or seventeen and will be leaving the home soon."

"That's right. And you will be making your home there for another five years. Besides, you are a very matured young lady."

"Where is the orphan home, Fru?"

"It is very near Vestmannheyjar. I don't know exactly but I understand it is situated on the outskirts of Reykjavik."

"What time will they come for me?"

"The ORPHAN HOME TRANSFER WAGON will be here at seven O'clock A.M."

"Thank you," replied Porunn in abated breath.

The following morning Porunn arose early. After dressing, she braided her hair, then removed Dora's old coat off the nail, shook out the wrinkles and laid it on the cot. Well, it was an expensive coat, long, black and had style. She then ran to the parlor window to see if the orphan wagon had arrived. And where was Gudmundur? Surely he would come downstairs and say goodbye. No—it was better this way. She would definitely break down an cry. Saying goodbye to Gudmundur would be much too painful. Slipping into her new long coat she picked up her carpet bag off of the floor and glanced out of the window again as a large white wagon driven by two horses stopped at the house. On top of the enclosed vehicle was a large sign reading: ORPHAN HOME TRANSFER WAGON. As Porunn opened the door, the Fru came down the stairway in a frilly negligee and slippers, yawning into her fingertips. "Good luck, darling," she called out and disappeared into the kitchen.

Approaching the wagon, Porunn saw a middle-aged man sitting on a very high seat holding the horses' reins. "Hurry up, young lady we don't have all day. I have to pick up another unwanted youngster in Eyfoed." Porunn jumped lively into the wagon and the horses galloped down the wet, murky road as rain began pelting down from the threatening sky.

The drive seemed endless as they drove over lava erosion where small, grazing horses could be seen stepping over wide cracks caused by volcanos. The animals had learned early after birth to step over the cracked earth. The country's rugged terrain was part of life here in Iceland. Passing rivers, glaciers and waterfalls, natures' beauty was masked in the dark, gloomy rain. When the sea came into view a strong wind blew off the ocean, spraying light mist over the wagon. Porunn pulled the collar of her new coat up around her neck. "My it's cold!" she stated to the driver, feeling comfortable with him.

"Sure is, Ung Fru. The next turn is where we pickup the child. Then we can head for the orphan home."

"How old is the child, Herr?"

"I understand she is three years old—just a baby," he replied," with a wry face. A pain crossed his features. "I sure remember my first day here. I was about this child's age."

"And why are you still here, Herr?"

"I never left."

"Why?"

"I had no place to go, and after all those years being my only home I felt comfortable here." And I guess it worked out a all right, they offered me a job driving the Orphan Home Transfer Wagon. I get my room and board—and a little change. I don't need much.' Porunn was remembering when she was just a child how Hallbera had given up duty being a mother. She swallowed the lump in her throat.

CHAPTER SIX

When the ORPHAN WAGON stopped at an old farmhouse, a woman came out to meet the wagon, pulling a small girl by the arm. The little child was crying and screaming refusing to leave her home. Jumping from the wagon, the driver picked up the little child into his arms and put her in the vehicle. As the heartbreaking sobs continued Porunn placed her arms around the child's shoulders and the girl responded favorably to Porunn's warm embrace.

The wagon was getting closer to the ocean now. Across the shore path road was the standing location of the Orphan home. The construction was a mixture of lime, clay and water, a substance used while soft, the essential part hardening. The cement was then cut in blocks but not cemented. "What kind of a building is that?" asked Porunn, "Oh I see, now," she added shifting her eyes to the top of the roof where a big sign read: ORPHAN HOME.

When the wagon parked in front of the institution, the door opened and middle-aged woman came out to the vehicle. She was very tall and thin. Her half-blonde-half gray hair was rolled into a small bun at the nape if her bony neck. Her long, thin feature emphasized a large protruding chin. A long, pleated, black skirt exposed her high-topped shoes. She approached the wagon. "I am the head mistress here at the home," she announced proudly to her two new charges.

"Good morning, Mistress," replied Porunn.

"You will please address me as Head Mistress."

"Yes, Head Mistress-I'm sorry," replied Porunn.

"You two get out of the wagon. Herr has work to do."

"Yes, Fru, I will tend to Sara."

"You will call me Ung Fru. I am Olga Arnidottir. Still a single girl you know," she smiled vainly.

Porunn glanced at the woman as thoughts were going around in her head—Ung Fru. The lady isn't married I guess. I think she said *UNG* Fru. But what else? What man could—No, that's not nice. The little girl in the wagon suddenly let out a scream. "I want to go home!"

The mistress reached into the wagon and dragged the screaming child from the vehicle and threw her onto the wet, soggy earth. "Listen here you little brat. Your mother don't want you, the foster home didn't want you and if you keep this up we won't want you neither."

Jumping from the wagon, Porunn wadded through the wet grass to the child's involuntary upheaval of contraction of muscles and tears, Kneeling down on her knees, Porunn pulled the child up from the ground. "What is your name, love?"

Her convulsive sobs then subsided. "Sa-Sara."

"That's a very pretty name Sara. Mine is Porunn. Now, you and I are friends and I will see that no one will ever hurt you. I'm going to be living here with you. Give me your hand, Love and we'll go inside with the HEAD Mistress." Porunn glanced up at the evil eyed mistress when she reached for Sara's hand. "HEAD Mistress, Please let me handle Sara."

"Let you handle her! And who are you but another helpless unwanted child. Now, the two of you get in the house!"

Inside, groups of children of all ages could be seen wearing uniforms all a like of thin burlap material. Off the long hall was a large room with many cribs which were occupied by infants being attended by the older orphans. The mistress ordered her two new charges to sit down so she could inform them of the rules of the house and their duties. "Porunn, you will be working with the older girls in the nursery. Of course most of the girls are older than you are. But you look like you can handle the job very nicely. A few of these girls are seventeen and will be leaving the home when they become eighteen. Now, you, have a long time yet being thirteen you have at least five years before you leave. Whatever—we'll take care of that when your time comes."

"Head Mistress, What hours do we go to school? Or, are the classes held here?"

"You are asking about classes when there's a scarcity of food? Wake up, sister—Iceland is in a famine situation. You children are lucky to be eating. Education indeed! The State cannot afford such luxury." Moving into a long corridor at the bottom of the stairway, the mistress picked up a large book from the hall table. "This is a dictionary and you older children are welcome to use it in any spare time you may have. and believe me, there's little spare time around here." Starting toward the dormitories upstairs, Porunn and

Sara followed closely behind. Porunn took Sara's hand and the threesome climbed the steps.

At the top of the stairway, the mistress stopped suddenly and turned to Porunn. "Now, to the right of the stairs is where the older girls sleep. To the left is the boys' dormitory. And at the end of the corridor is the small children's' dorm. And that's where you, Sara, will bunk." Unexpectedly, Sara let go of Porunn's hand and threw herself on the floor. "No, I want to go home!"

"Leave her alone, Porunn. She will have to learn herself how to cope with life." She headed down the steps and Porunn followed closely behind, crushed with sorrow for Sara.

The days passed. Porunn was now settled in another new, and erratic environment, straining to make all efforts to the conditions and influence under which she lived. One of the rules of the home was that all lights must be out by eight P.M. Tonight she was looking forward to going to bed. Fatigued as she was each night, she could never sleep until wee hours in the morning. How she wished she could read! Then she heard the mistress come up the stairs and blow out the kerosene lamps in the dormitories. A small glint shone from under the door of the main corridor. As Porunn lay in the dark she thought about her little friend Sara of whom she saw only at a distance with children her own age.

Then suddenly the dictionary came to her mind. How she would love to learn to read it . . . . maybe just hold it in her hand. However, there was not any time for leisure except a fifteen minute rest period. Usually the Head Mistress herself could be heard snoring in her room. But not long enough to steal a look at the dictionary. During rest period Porunn would run across the road to the ocean where two seals lay across a large rock basking in the sun. Familiar with her, they raised their heads and let out a deep sound, then closed their eyes again, paying no attention to their visitor.

Hopping up on the larger seal's back, Porunn embraced his large, fat neck and kissed him on the nose. His fine black fur shone in the sunshine like silk. (These European harbor seals) are either black or brown and are 3 to 5 ft. long. Thinking she heard the wakeup bell, Porunn jumped off the seals back and ran swiftly over the road to the home, careful not to make a sound when opening the door which she had purposely left unlocked.

It was almost ten thirty p.m. The orphan home had been retired for over two hours. Yet, as exhausted as Porunn was she could not sleep. Her mind was on the magic book on the hall table across from the nursery. She vaulted impulsively out of bed and carefully opened the dormitory door and peeked out. The long corridor lay in darkness She tiptoed back into her room and took out a candle and some matches from her carpet bag. She was remembering that the Head Mistress had informed Sara and her the first day, that she made sleep-checks every night at midnight. Well, hereafter she would wait until the grandfather's clock chimed. twelve 'O clock.

Lying in bed she thought about her seal friends. The only friends she had in the world. And she recalled when her father had told her that seals are found in abundance in cold regions. She then closed her mind to anything of the past. As different images came to her mind she heard the clock strike twelve, she sprang out of bed. Telling herself that she would have to wait awhile until the mistress had made her sleep-checks she crawled back in bed. Porunn closed her eyes quickly when she saw her door open. The mistress stood in the doorway with a small kerosene lamp in her hand holding it high in the air to get better light. Satisfied, the mistress left and went to her own room at the end of the corridor.

Porunn waiting nervously for the mistress to get settled for the night again, moved barefoot to the door. Her feet were cold from the wood floors so decided to take time to put on her lamb-skin slippers.

Not sure it was safe, Porunn decided to give it a little more time. About to return to her dormitory room, a loud blatant snore came from the mistress's room. Porunn lighted her candle and hurried down the stairs.

Setting her candle down beside the dictionary, Porunn flipped the pages, then started glancing at the many words. All at once she saw a light on the stairway. Knowing she had been caught she slipped behind the drape in the archway. Her heart was palpitating so fast she was certain the mistress could hear it from behind the drape. "Whose down here?" she screamed. "And what is this candle doing on the library table? This table is only for the dictionary and the Holy Bible," uttered the mistress espying around the room. "Come out where ever you are . . . and immediately!"

Porunn stepped out from behind the drape. "I'm sorry Head Mistress. I came down because I thought I heard one of the infants crying."

"I might have known it would be you. And if I forgot to tell you, we never pick up a crying infant day or night. Those little people aren't as dumb as they look. If they get used to being picked up every time they holler they'll pull this little trick all the time."

"Yes, Head Mistress, I won't do that again.". The woman adjusted her flannel sleeping cap, pulled up her long flannel nightdress so she would not trip on the stairs, and head up to her room.

Night after night after the mistress had made her round and had gone back to sleep, Porunn would sneak down to the dictionary. Working in the kitchen she would keep a leaf from the newspaper Which she rescued from the wastebasket and put it into her uniform pocket, so as to copy words to learn from the dictionary. The years had passed and Porunn's secret had not been discovered. Porunn was now able to read and write a little—but little was so gratifying—to not at all. The small confidence and satisfaction it gave her, was well worth the effort.

Five lonely years passed. Now having her eighteenth birthday tomorrow February 24th Porunn was expecting the mistress to discuss her discharge from the orphanage. Being nervous and afraid to go out into the world with no home and no work she glanced out of the window at the sea coming in strong and gray looking. With no sun her seal friends would not be out sunning themselves today.

As she lingered at the window, she had a recall flash through her mind. She saw herself as a three year old girl in her treasured sheepskin coat that her father had given her for her birthday, And now tomorrow it was February twenty-four—her eighteenth birthday. Depressed she left the window.

Night fell. The infants in the nursery had been fed and were ready for the night. On Porunn's way up to the dormitory she Glanced down the corridor and saw a group of little girls march in a straight line to their quarters. She was happy to get a small glimpse of Sara's happy face. Sara was laughing with the little girl marching beside her. Apparently Sara's home life with her mother could not have been good. In a short time the group disappeared into their sleeping quarters.

All at once the head mistress appeared at the top of the stairway. "Just a moment, dear." Her false face had changed tonight due to Porunn no longer being under her command.

"Yes, Head Mistress?"

"Oh, call me, Olga, Porunn. Why be so formal?" she grinned.

CHAPTER SEVEN

"Tomorrow is February twenty four—your eighteenth birthday. You will be discharged from the orphan home. Because I am of a caring nature, I have found a place for you to live and work as a domestic. I hope you appreciate my efforts because it is quite an honor to work for Sera Kartin. He is a fussy man," stated the mistress proudly.

"Do you mean the most famous clergyman in Iceland?"

"Yes. I know you will do me proud for recommending you to him. He was very unhappy with the last girl I recommended."

"Thank you Head—L mean Olga."

Ensuing night, morning dawned. The first appearance rise of the sun above the horizon flooded the dormitory window with effects of light and color. Porunn too excited and nervous to rest awhile before getting up, sprang out of bed and began to dress. "My last few hours, then I will be free!" Porunn thought to herself, feeling restless and weak. She crept down the stairway to the front window and gazed at the beautiful sea as the tide was going out. Heavy tossing swells on the water glistened in the early sunrise. She noted a sea breeze blowing inland from the sea. What a lovely day for one's birthday. Well, the weather-and a lovely seascape would have no affect on her life. Porunn walked wearily away from the window and climbed the stairs and began to dress. Hearing a footstep on the threshold, Porunn, turned toward the doorway. "Why are you getting up so early, Porunn? Sera Kartin won't be here for a couple of hours yet."

"Oh, I don't know, I guess I'm just too excited to sleep."

"It is a lovely day for the end of February. It's really more like spring,' stated the Head Mistress in a false sweet tone of voice.

"Then again, it's spring next month," replied Porunn putting on a cheerful act.

"This weather looks surely like an indication of an early spring," grinned the Head Mistress amicably.

In front of the orphan home, a black, large, fancy carriage stopped. Dressed immaculately in a black habit of Lutheran religious order, a suave looking gentleman of about fifty hurried out of the carriage and rapped at the orphan home door.

Porunn and the head mistress exchanged glances. "My word! That can't be the Reverend—or can it?" she asked herself all in a dither running down the stairs. "Sera Kartin!" she exclaimed. I didn't expect you so early," she exclaimed, agitated and embarrassed over her appearance in her flannel cap and gown. Snatching off her night cap she continued expressing herself orally. "It's indeed a surprise to see you so early."

"I am sorry, Head Mistress. but as you know, Sidanef is quite a drive to the orphanage, and it will be late when we get home."

"Yes, I know Sera Kartin. I imagine you have other performances scheduled for today."

"Oh, yes. Glancing around the small parlor, Sera Kartin inquired: "Where is Porunn Olafsdottir? Is she ready?"

"Probably not. You know how these young girls are, primping until the last moment, making everyone late . . . I'll go hurry her up."

All at once Porunn came walking down the stairs dressed in her long black coat that Dora had given her. She carried her carpet bag over her arm. Her beautiful red hair hung in curls down her back. "I have been ready and waiting for you since five O clock this morning, Sera Kartin" Porunn moved across the room and shook Sera Kartin's hand. "It is so nice to meet you, Sera Kartin. I feel like I know you. I have heard about so many things you have done for people. Thank you for taking me into your home. I will not disappoint you, if I can help it."

Impressed, Sera Kartin took her carpet bag from her hand and offered Porunn his arm. Smiling, she slipped her arm in his and they walked to the door. "Thank you, Head Mistress," said Sera Kartin."

"Goodbye, Head Mistress. And thank you for the many years you gave me a home," stated Porunn fighting back the tears.

Walking down the path to the carriage the beautiful, golden colored horse neighed restlessly, indicating to his driver that it was about time to get going. "This horse of mine is the impatient one," laughed Sera Kartin, placing the carpet bag in the back of the carriage, then assisting Porunn up into the front seat. He was about to board the carriage when Porunn sprang from the seat. "Excuse me, Sera Kartin, I forgot something." Thinking that the girl had forgotten something in the home, he smiled. "Take your time, Porunn." When she ran behind the carriage in the opposite direction his, features took on a puzzled stare.

She walked over the shore path to the beach where two seals basked in the sun on the large rock. Creeping up the rock she slid onto the seals back and wrapped her arms around his big, fat neck. He uttered a funny sound, she kissed his nose. "I'm here to say goodbye, my friends." We will never see each other again. You've been the only friends I have ever had. I will never forget you." The other seal paid no attention. He turned over and went back to sleep. Porunn leaving the shore, looked back over her shoulder for a last glimpse of her friends, then boarded the carriage.

As they rode Sera Kartin was feeling the loneliness Porunn was going through. "Not much of a change leaving from an orphanage to a stranger's home to work," he thought to himself. Well, he and his wife would do everything to make Porunn feel welcome and at home. He thought about their last maid also referred to them by the Head Mistress at the orphan home. Glancing over at Porunn for a moment, his eyes then returned to the road. "You are very quiet, Ung Fru . . . ." (single woman)

"I am sorry, Sera Kartin. I was just enjoying the beautiful scenery."

"I understand, Porunn. You do not have to explain your inner feelings to me. I was just thinking about the difference in you and our former maid . . . . the one you are replacing."

"I can imagine how difficult it is when someone fits in and you like, leaves."

"Quite the contrary, Porunn. I let her go."

"Why . . . ?"

"Well, she just did not work out. When I saw you I knew right away that you were our girl."

"Thank you," she smiled, letting out a big sigh. "My, Sidanefnd is really a long way. The scenery is very beautiful though."

"I am sure you have seen it many times, Ung Fru."

"Just the ocean. Oh, look, Sera Kartin, isn't that a tall mountain?" she stated trying to change the subject of the conversation in case he should ask her about her family.

Traveling through the country side, the carriage passed mountains and rivers, where farms were seen with small Icelandic horses grazing and stepping over seizures of cracked lava which had flowed from the volcanos cracking the earth. The beautiful, golden colored animals were used to Iceland's rugged terrain. Speckled here and there were white sheep resembling white cotton puffs.

Breaking the silence Porunn asked: "Do we have much farther to go Reverend?"

"No, dear. We are just about one mile from Sidanefnd."

A short period of time elapsed, then the red horse was slowed down and came to a stop. "Well, Porunn this is your new home. I hope you will be happy here with us."

"I cannot promise to be happy anywhere, Sera Kartin. But I am sure I will be more contented here than anywhere before, and that's a lot, Sera Kartin. And I thank you from the bottom of my heart."

"May God bless your life, Porunn."

The minister's wife came out of the house to greet the new girl from the orphanage. Going to the passenger's side she took Porunn's hand. "Welcome to your new home. Oh, my! What beautiful, red hair you have."

"You are very kind, Fru Kartin."

Upon entering the large house, Porunn's eyes moved around at the lovely rich furnishings and paintings of Icelandic artists. Sera Kartin holding Porunn's carpet bag placed it on the floor. and encircled his arms around his wife's waist. "Elskan, will you please take Porunn up to her room? I can see the girl is exhausted." The two women smiled at each other and climbed the long, winding stairs, Sera Kartin following closely behind with the carpet bag in his hand.

"Oh, Fru Kartin! This is a beautiful room," exclaimed Porunn as Sera Kartin placed the carpet bag on the floor in the pink and white bedroom.

Six months had passed since Porunn had left the orphanage. Happy she was not. But she was at ease and contented with the Martins. She worked hard all day and was anxious to go to bed early. And like most clergy the minister and his wife entertained frequently in their home and often attended church functions in the Icelandic Lutheran church. Porunn enjoyed her privacy during their absence. She was contented yes, but there seemed to be a void in her being which never left her free to enjoy the better life she now had.

(Mrs.) Fru Kartin entered the dining room were Porunn was polishing silverware. "Porunn, will you do me a favor?"

Porunn walked over to the buffet with her polished utensils, silver collectively. "You ask will I do you a favor. That's what I'm here for, isn't it?"

Fru Kartin placed her arms around Porunn affectionately. "Don't be bitter, dear."

"I was only joking, Fru Kartin. Icelanders are noted for poor jokes and I guess I'm one of them," laughed Porunn touching Fru Kartin's arm amicably.

"Will you go to the post office for me and get a package that I am expecting? Sera Kartin always picks up our post in the carriage but today he was called out of town to an important meeting in Reykjavik.

"Of course, Fru, but where is the post office?"

"It's across the river. Once you get on the other side, you can't miss it. There's a road that circles the river. Stay on the road and it will take you right to it."

"Sounds easy enough. How long do you think it will take me to walk it?"

"Oh, you cannot walk, dear, you'll have to ride one of our horses." Fru Kartin glanced curiously at Porunn. "You do know how to ride, don't you?"

"Of course I know how to ride. I often ran errands for the Orphan Home on horse back when the driver of the orphan home wagon was busy transferring orphans to foster homes when we got too crowded."

"Thank you so much for doing this for me Porunn. It's a real favor."

Leaving the dining room, Porunn washed and dried her hands then climbed the stairs for her old sweater and headed for the barn, sniffing in the cool summer air. She looked over the three horses hoping she would find the horse that had brought her away from the orphan home, Impatient one which Sera Kartin called him. Oh, yes, he was there with his eyes glued to Porunn's, daring her to choose him for her errand. Starring him down, Porunn reached for the bridoon where the snaffle bit and it's rein make a double bridle. Impatient had a mind of his own. Surprisingly Impatient walked cooperatively out with Porunn into the lovely August sunshine.

Unexpectedly, Porunn hopped upon Impatient's back without a saddle. Porunn had never ridden in a saddle, only bareback. Refusing to leave the premises. Impatient neighed and tramped around and around in small steps. "Come on now, Inpatient, you don't need a saddle lets go." Porunn being an excellent rider and a lover of horses, reached into her pocket and pulled out some loafsugar, leaned forward and slipped it into the horse's mouth. In an instant Inpatient began trotting down the driveway and on to the bridle path encircling the river.

"An enjoyable ride," thought Porunn to herself but a lot farther than she had expected. She could not have gotten lost, she was following the road straight to the post office like Fru Kartin had instructed. At a given moment,

The horse broke away from the road and galloped into the river with Porunn on his back. Knowing she could not swim she became frightened, so leaned forward and held him firmly around the neck with her fingers entwined in his red, blonde mane. Then all at once the horse threw her off his back into the deepest part of the river. Capable of being reflected, in an involuntary action in response to a nerve impulse as of a muscle, Porunn grabbed Inpatient's long, bushy tail and hung on it tightly with strong will and vigor. The animal continued across the river dragging Porunn by his tail through the rushing stream.

When they reached the other side of the river, the horse jerked. his tail from her hand and neighed. Porunn stood drenched shaking the water from her clothes then hopped up on Inpatient's back. Neighing again Inpatient trotted across the street to the post office. Now back home again the two tired, wet figures rode to the barn. After drying Inpatient off with a saddle cloth, Porunn went into the house shivering with cold. "Here is your package, Fru Kartin. I hope it's not too wet."

"God, Porunn! What happened?"

"I guess Inpatient thought I needed a bath."

"For heaven sake, Porunn, get off those wet clothes You'll catch pneumonia! And you'd better go straight to bed and warm up."

Helping Porunn out of her jacket, Fru Kartin shook her head. 'Now go up to your room and take the rest of your clothes off and I'll bring you up a hot water bottle."

"Thank you Fru, but I'm all right."

When Fru Kartin came up with the hot water bottle Porunn was sound asleep. "Oh, dear! Porunn must be ill! I'll call the doctor."

Fru Kartin cancelled her lecture at the church. It was almost dusk when the Fru noted Dr. Barthasson carriage stop in front of the house. Fru Kartin answered the door. "Oh, Doctor Barthasson, Thank you so much for coming. I know it is a long way."

Porunn awakened when she heard their voices in the parlor. "Did I hear the Fru say Dr. Barthasson?" she thought to herself. I hope she didn't mention my name. Dr. Barthasson attended my mother when she had the miscarriage and I was only three years old . . . well, he wouldn't remember me that long ago,", Porunn told herself. About to slip out of bed, Dr. Barthasson and Fru Kartin walked into the room.

"Well, young lady, I hear you took a little swim.

"No, Doctor, I don't know how to swim. I know that all Icelandic children must know how to swim before they are allowed to enter school, but I never went to school and I don't know how to swim," Þorunn replied in a bitter tone of voice.

Dr. Barthasson brought out his stethoscope and began vital signs. He picked up his little, black bag and moved to the door.

"Just a little cold, but you could have drowned."

CHAPTER EIGHT

Eight years passed. Porunn was now Twenty-six years old and still working for Sera Kartin. And although she was treated like one of the members of the family, she wanted more from life. Like a new environment away from Iceland where she could forget her past. Yet, it would be so difficult to leave her beloved land. Her pay from Sera Kartin was small therefore could not afford much of a change.

As she brushed out her long red hair, before going to bed, a thought crossed her mind. She would have a talk with Sera Kartin tonight. The Reverend always works in his study late at night. At eleven the minister's residence was usually dark, she told herself with deep emotion. She threw her hair brush down on the bed and flew down the stairs to Sera Kartin's study.

The door was closed. However, she could see a shaft of light under the bottom of the door. To make sure the Reverend was alone, Porunn lent an ear to the door. Then impulsively, she tapped lightly.

"Yes . . . ." he called out puzzled.

"It's me, Porunn. I'm sorry to disturb you Sera Kartin, but could I have a word with you?"

"Of course, child . . . anytime you should know that." he said rising from his desk and opening the door. "Sit here," he stated, pulling up a chair for her. Knowing it must be important for her to come to him like this he smiled. "Let me guess. You want a raise."

"No, Sera Kartin. I want a loan."

"A loan! What ever for?"

"I want to leave Iceland."

"Leave this beautiful country? There must be a very good reason, Porunn, But me being an inquisitive person I wont ask why."

"I am just not happy here, Sera Kartin. Yes, Iceland is a beautiful land . . . a magical land. But I will never find what I want here."

"Where are you planning on going, Porunn?" He looked at her and smiled." To America where the streets are paved in gold?" He stood up and walked to the window, and glanced out at the moon shining on the mountain. "Porunn, when you get as old as I am you will know, there are no streets paved in gold. He took in a deep sigh. "The only place you will find gold is in your heart."

"No. I am not going to America . . . . I am going across the ocean, but I am going to Canada."

"Canada . . . . ? That far? Do you know anyone there?" asked Sera Kartin.

"No, but I don't know anyone here either" except the Fru and you . . . and of course my seals that I won't ever see again."

Leaving the window, Sera Kartin sat down at his desk again and pulled out a checkbook and pen. "Of course I will give you a loan, Porunn. Any amount you want."

"Oh thank you Reverend! I will pay you something every month as soon as I get a job."

"Anyone would be proud to have you in their service." Shaking his head, he closed his eyes. "We are going to miss you, Porunn."

"You were the only person I could come to, Sera." Sera Kartin placed an arm around Porunn's shoulders. "When do you think you will be leaving, Porunn?"

"Probably in about a week or so."

"So soon!" he asked in abated breath. He opened the study door for her and they walked to the foot of the staircase. After saying goodnight, Sera Kartin climbed the steps to his room where Fru Kartin was in bed reading a book. She placed the book down and glanced up at him. My, you look tired, you worked too long in the study tonight."

"Well, we're loosing a daughter."

"A daughter? What in the world are you talking about? We don't have any daughter."

"Porunn is leaving our home."

"I wish Porunn was our daughter, she's a lovely girl."

"If we had only known that Porunn was up for adoption when she was three years old, she would have been perfect for us."

"You seem to forget, Elskan, that I have always told you that I would never adopt?"

"Yes, I remember. And I remember that I said getting older with out children is lonely."

"That's very true, Sera," agreed the minister's wife removing the hair pins from her long hair. "But you're like all the rest of the men. You've never carried a child or brought a little human being into the world. This is the important part of being a mother, not calling yourself mother because you bought somebody else's flesh and blood."

"How would you know, Elskan? You've never given birth to a child or ever carried a baby in your womb." She turned over in bed

"Because . . . . I am a woman." Indignant, she sat up again in a comfortable position. "You see, Sera, God has put into the realm of pregnancies a desire to be productive. And although some women are infertile, their hope never dies until their productive years have passed," Fru Kartin slid down in bed again. Yawning in her fingertips she mumbled drowsily "I can understand Elskan why it is easier for a man . . . . for a man . . . she was now fast asleep. Sera Kartin loosened his collar and habit, then sat down on the bed and removed his black shiny pumps. His mind was still on adoptions, not sure he agreed with his wife's theory. Porunn flashed through his thoughts. Yes, he agreed on the fact that environment was important when raising children. Porunn was raised like all the rest of the homeless children with not any permanence. These were the surroundings in which Porunn Olafsdottir was reared. Yet, she is dignified, intelligent and stands out from all the others. He told himself puzzled.

Sera Kartin slipping into bed, noted his wife had awakened. "How did Porunn get to be such a lady? Her bringing up in an orphanage wasn't any finishing school."

"Genes!" laughed the Fru.

"I think you have the answer elskan genes are not something one believes in, they are a fact," added the sera reaching for the bed lamp and turning off the light.

Time was passing and Porunn was getting more fearful yet, anxious to start her life in a strange land and language. Tonight the Fru was having a fund raiser at her home for the Icelandic Lutheran church. As Porunn dusted off the dining room table she glanced up at the doorway where Sera Kartin had just come in from going to the post office. "Porunn, could I see you for a moment in my study?"

Porunn placed the ostrich feathered duster on the staircase. "Certainly, Sera Kartin." Her face flushed as the idea came to mind that the minister had changed his mind about loaning her the money. With each step she made a private solemn address to God which she was remembering from her mother's prayer book when she was only three.

In the study Sera Kartin pulled out a chair for Porunn at the desk where he sat with a letter in his hand. "Sit down Porunn," he stated, opening the envelope of the letter.

"No . . . no thank you," Porunn replied coldly.

"I have never seen you this way before. I hope you are not ill. Your voyage is of considerable distance and we want you well."

Porunn's features broke into a smile. "Oh, I'm just nervous, Sera Kartin," she exclaimed dropping into the chair beside him.

"I understand, Porunn. Nervous but very excited." His face clouded. I received a strange letter today," he informed her, looking over his reading glasses at her.

Porunn knitted her brows. "But this letter is for you, Sera Kartin."

"Yes, but this woman claims to be your eldest sister"

Porunn's face flushed in a state of stimulation which worked upon her feelings. "What is the woman's name?"

"She signed only the name, Sigurun, but mentioned that she was Hallbera Eriksdottir eldest daughter. Sera Kartin paused for a moment then told himself, "There's the answer. Porunn has Hallbera Eiriksdottir's genes."

Porunn grimacing painfully stood like a statue gazing out of the study window. Noticing that the letter was upsetting her, Sera Kartin handed Porunn the script. "I think you had better read it yourself, Porunn."

"No. I don't want to read it," she replied with rancor Her mood then softened. "But I think Sera Kartin that it is only fair that I tell you that Sigurun is my eldest sister. So of course I also am Hallbera Eriksdottir daughter too. Becoming more interested now, she asked: "Is my mother still living, Sera Kartin?"

"I don't know, Porunn. Sigurun's letter was very brief. I can find out for you."

"No! I don't want to know. I don't need her now." With her features all aglow, Porunn glanced at Sera Kartin. "What does Sigurun want?"

"Read it for yourself," replied the minister handing Porunn the letter.

DEAR SERA KARTIN,
    I AM WRITTING TO YOU IN REGARDS to ONE OF MY SISTERS, Porunn Olafsdottir. I have not KNOWN OF HER WHEREABOUTS SENCE SHE WAS THREE YEARS OLD. I HAVE LOOKED FOR HER FOR YEARS BUT NO ONE WAS ABLE TO HELP ME. I FIGURED WHEN SHE BECAME

OF AGE AND WAS FREE, SHE WOULD FIND ME. BUT APPARENTLY she DOES NOT WANT TO SEE ME SO I STARTED SEARCHING FOR HER AGAIN. THEN ONE OF THE MEMBERS OF MY CHURCH suggested I CONTACT Sera KARTIN. HE SAID you were influential and had expiring powers effective TOWARD AN END. I HOPE YOU WILL BE ABLE TO HELP ME, SERA KARTIN.

ANXIOUS TO HEAR FROM YOU.

Sigurun

Porunn folded the letter and handed it back to Sera Kartin. "She's too late."

One week had passed since Sigurun's message, and tomorrow at 4.P.M. Porunn Would be leaving Iceland. She felt excited to leave and yet afraid of going to a strange land speaking a strange language. With tattered nerves she packed and unpacked her few belongings. She glanced up as Fru Kartin peeked into her room.

"Well, Porunn, tomorrow is your big day. Sera and I are really going to miss you."

"And I'm going to miss you and Sera Kartin so Porunn replied hugging her warmly.

After Fru Kartin left in her carriage for her meeting, Sera Kartin walked into the house. "Porunn!" he called out. Porunn came hurriedly into the kitchen. "You're late for lunch, Sera Kartin."

"Guess where I've been."

"I don't know. Church I suppose," she replied shrugging her shoulders.

"At your sister's house in Bolungar i vikur, much better than answering her letter; I wanted to meet her anyway. And as I figured, Sigurun is a fine woman."

"That was nice, Sera Kartin."

"Sigurun was very friendly, gave me coffee and ponnuk aur." (one of the native dishes of Iceland.)

"Well, I don't care to hear about it," replied Porunn coldly walking away.

"I wish you would hear me out, Porunn . . . . this message pertains to you," he stated with annoyance in his voice.

"I'm sorry, Sera Kartin. I'm so nervous about leaving tomorrow."

"I understand." He sat down at the table and pulled out some papers from his valise. "Sigurun wrote up some directions for you to follow tomorrow when you leave Iceland. Sigurun also said that all she asked was a glimpse of her little three year old sister. Then of course Sigurun began to cry."

"You may throw the message away, Sera Kartin, She will not get any glimpse of me."

"Sera Kartin glanced over his spectacles at her. "Would you mind letting me finish the work I started? Just listen to your sister's last plea that's all I ask."

"Go ahead. I still will not see her."

The minister unfolded a sheath of paper and began to read.

I am a happy married woman and we have a three month old baby, named Olofia. Thank you Sera Kartin for informing me that Porunn will be leaving Iceland tomorrow at 4 P.M. that she has a passage on the ship Laura. I have a plan. Tell her that the Ship Laura will pass the open field behind my house about 4:30 p.m. Tell her I will be standing in the open field on a hill holding Olofia in my arms. Porunn, please go out on deck with a white handkerchief in your hand. I will hold one of the baby's diapers and wave it as Laura passes. You will wave your white handkerchief. Will you please do this, Elskan?" pleaded Sigurun.

"You may tell Sigurun the answer is *no*. It's too late."

Shortly after noon the following day, Porunn came down the stairs dressed in a new, long, gray velvet suit, and wearing a wide brimmed matching hat with a large purple feather. Her long, red curls hung down her back. "About ready, Porunn?" Sera Kartin asked, noticing the carpet bag in her hand. He glanced again at Porunn. "My you look lovely, Porunn." He removed the carpet bag from her hand. "Shall we go?"

At the harbor, the carriages were lined up around the dock. "Good thing we came early," stated Sera Kartin. The Icelandic flags flew from each mast of the ships. The lights from the harbor were bright and glistening from the mist of the ocean. Reykjavik Harbor is so beautiful, stated Sera Kartin."

"Oh look Sera Kartin! There's the ship Laura!"

"That's your ship alright." He took her bag and held her arm as they started up the gang plank. All at once Porunn took her carpet bag from his hand suddenly stopped. "Sera Kartin, would you mind if I go by myself . . . I want to be alone.?"

"Of course, dear. I understand." He stood and watched her until she reached the entrance of the ship. Porunn looking over her shoulder waved, and blew him a kiss. "Bon Voyage!" he called out to her as she disappeared from view.

In her stateroom Porunn kept glancing at her tiny watch pinned to her white lace blouse. It was 4:20 P.M. How she longed to get just one little glimpse of Sigurun whom she loved dearly. No, she mustn't get soft. Sigurun would not be on the hill anyway, she had received the message, "No". Pulling the long gold chain on her watch so she could read the time, she picked up her carpet bag and removed a white handkerchief from it. She then hung the carpet bag on her wrist and ran to the upper deck of the ship facing the rail of the deck. Her beautiful, soft, gray eyes froze on an open field where a woman stood on a high-hill with a baby in her arms. Then all at once Sigurun saw the ship. LAURA come sailing from behind the bend of the mountain. and breaking from the straight line of the stream along the open field.

When Sigurun noted a young woman with her mother's carpet bag in her hand, she knew it was her sister. She began waving a diaper in the air as Porunn unfolded her white handkerchief and waved with great force. Sigurun broke into another lacrimal of tears and the Laura was gone.

One moment of excitement . . . . then two broken hearts lasting for a lifetime, the vessel, LAURA moved across the water propelled by wind and sail, disappearing from view.

The days on the ocean were lonely. Porunn not used to socializing she remained by herself except during the dining hours.

CHAPTER NINE

It was a lovely evening. A bright, pale-blue moon shone on the water as Porunn stood at the railing of the deck. The recall of her sister Sigurun filled her mind. Standing on a high hill with three months old, Olöfia in her arms. Billows of the sea threw great quantities of large rolling waves against the ship.

Hearing footsteps behind her, Porunn glanced over her shoulder.

"Good evening, Miss Olafsdottir."

"You called me Olafsdottir. How do you know my name?"

"I am the captain. I have everyone's' name on my list who are aboard my ship."

"Yes of course."

"I know you boarded in Reykjavik, Iceland. Anyone as beautiful as you must be Icelandic."

Porunn blushed. "Yes I am Icelandic." she replied observing his uniform, then adding in her broken English, "With your blond hair and blue eyes you sure look Icelandic."

"Oh yes, My ship LAURA and I live in Reykjavik."

"It was nice talking to you, Captain," stated Porunn moving away from the rail of the deck. "Good night, Captain."

"Oh, wait, Porunn, they're striking up the band. Will you dance one dance with me, Porunn?"

"No, Captain. I'm sorry I have to study my English book."

"Actually the broken English is cute. At least yours is

"To be honest with you, Captain, as I believe you have been with me, I don't know how to dance," she admitted blushing.

"I will teach you."

"Good night, Captain," she whispered, and disappeared down the stairs to her stateroom.

The long month of the voyage on LAURA finally came to an end. The passengers hurried out on deck screaming "Land! Land!"

Porunn calmly started gathering her few items and put them in her carpet bag. She could hear Laura's horn blowing as the vessel glided into the Canadian harbor. As Porunn walked down the garboard strake to leave the ship she began having mixed feelings having left her homeland. Trying to get confidence, she thought about the old expressions of the ancient Vikings. "If an Icelander still has one foot, he walks! Well, she was a Viking so she would walk! When she reached the sidewalk lines of the carriage trade were lined up waiting for passengers off the ship. Feeling depressed and alone, Porunn's eyes scanned for a hired carriage. Then her eyes caught a horse and carriage with a large sign reading: "For Let". A man in a long raincoat who was standing beside her asked. "Are you looking for someone, Miss?"

"Yes, Sir. Can you tell me what For LENT means?"

"Oh you are a foreigner" He then smiled. "It means it is available. Come with me," He let out a whistle and the horses brought the carriage to him. He assisted Porunn up into the vehicle and they headed for the city.

"Where to Miss?" asked the stranger.

"Well, what address?"

"No address, Herr. I'm looking for a place to stay"

Slowing down the horses, the driver scratched his head puzzled. "What do you mean no address?"

"I haven't found a home yet. I just got off the boat."

"You can say that again. But I won't let you off here Miss. This is a bad neighborhood. It wouldn't be safe for a fine lady like you."

"Please stop, Herr. I can only afford a cheap room until I find a job." The driver stopped his horses and Porunn stepped out of the carriage. "How much do I owe you?"

"Nothing, me lady. I was just passing time anyway."

She opened a handful of change. "Take what I owe you. I don't understand foreign money very well."

"And you take good care of yourself. Your a lovely lady," he repeated as he drove off in the carriage.

Dusk was falling and it was beginning to get dark. Depressed and lonely she walked on finding no vacancies. Glancing across the street she noted an old unkempt building with a sign in the window reading, BAKERY. Peering closer at the sign Porunn made out . . . ROOM FOR Let. I cannot live here she thought to herself. I'll have to for night. She would hunt for another place tomorrow.

Porunn ran across the street to the shabby dwelling. Opening the door she met with many stairs leading to different rooms. It was quiet and no one was seen around. Somewhat fearful, Porunn fled down the stairs. About to leave the premises, Porunn heard some voices in the bakery attached to the rooming house above the establishment where through the window she saw two women who appeared to be the woman of the bakery and a customer buying French bread. She hurried to the bakery and opened the door as the customer was leaving the store. "Thank you, madam," called out the proprietor to the customer, turning to Porunn. "Are you the pro-pro—?" Porunn asked in her broken English.

"Yes, dear, I am the proprietor. Kinda big word for a foreigner to say." The woman pulled out a basket of freshly baked French bread. "These are on sale today."

"I'm sorry, Ma'am" Porunn stated timidly, "I need a room, at least for tonight."

"I generally don't rent for just one night. But you look like an awful nice girl who is much in need of a break. Take it, the room is yours as long as you like. The rent is cheap, only two dollars a night."

"Oh thank you, Madam".

The room was small and dark with only one small window overlooking a busy street leading to a dance hall. Although the room was poorly furnished, it was tidy and clean. Yes, she would have to take it until she found a job.

Sleeping in a stupor all night, when Porunn awakened the following morning she glanced around the dingy room wondering where she was. After a few moments her mind cleared and her confusion was gone. How she wished to be back in her homeland. Well, when an Icelander still has one leg, he walks. Vaulting out of bed, Porunn began to dress. She would have to find a job today for most of the money Sera Kartin loaned her had been used for passage on the ship LAURA. She also had to send the minister a little bit of something each month.

Walking the streets without any job prospects she was beginning to feel weary and hungry. Pulling her long watch chain to where she could see what time it was, she glanced at it quickly. "Almost four P.M. and I haven't had anything to eat since five this morning," she told herself. Thinking about the aroma of the French bread Porunn reversed her steps and walked toward the bakery . . . and home.

As she went by the dance hall she noticed a small restaurant in back of the hall. Hastening her gait she turned the knob . . . It was locked. She then heard a man's voice call out. "Just a minute, Red and I'll let ya in." After arranging a lot of beer glasses on the bar, the short, fat, middle-aged man came and unlocked the door. "Come on in, Red. You're a little early for this type of restaurant. But sit down and I'll pour you a beer . . . . And by the way, sugar, my name is Tommy. What's yours?"

"Porunn," she replied, getting up from the stool. "Thank you, Tommy, but I really came in for a bowl of soup."

"The dining room is in the back. Go get yourself a table and I'll tell the cook to bring you in a bowl."

"Thank you, Tommy."

A few moments passed, then Tommy appeared with a bowl of soup for each of them. "You see, honey, this place doesn't open up until six o'clock. That's when the longshoremen get off work and come in to eat—and of course drink."

Porunn rose from the table. "How much for the soup?"

"Nothing, Red it was a pleasure."

"I was pretty tired when I came in. I've walked all day but still no job. Maybe it's because my English is so bad. But I have a lot of experience." she stated buttoning up her jacket as she crossed over to the front door to leave.

"Experience!" called out Tommy. "I hope you mean what I think you do," he said in a harsh, blatant tone of voice."

Porunn and Tommy looked toward the front entrance when a small. thin woman about fifty walked into the establishment. "Hi, Tommy, whose your friend?"

"Red. I want you to meet my better half as we longshoremen put it." His wife reached for Porunn's hand. "He means wife. My name is Liz honey. what's yours?"

"Porunn Olafsdottir," she replied with a forced smile Liz observed Porunn's innocent demeanor. "My husband is always joking around . . . and at the wrong time if you ask me," she stated giving Tommy a cold stare.

Tommy came out from behind the counter. "I'm sorry, Red. It's hard to understand your English. All I understood was that you wanted a job

"I do."

"Your hired, Porunn," stated Liz. "Be here tomorrow at six, we need a good waitress." said Liz.

"Wow! wait until the guys walk in the joint tomorrow and see this Icelandic doll."

Lia placed her arms around Porunn's shoulders. "Let's go back in the dining room where it's more comfortable and I'll give you a short run down of the job."

Porunn and Liz sat at the dining room table with a cup of coffee. "This, by no means is your type of place to work in, Porunn. But it's not easy to find work in a small town, let alone another country." Liz lighted a cigarette, took a puff, then put it out on a saucer. "I'm sorry, honey I didn't know that you don't smoke. "What country are you from, Porunn?"

"Iceland."

"Is your family still there?"

"I have no family."

Liz could feel that The young girl did not want to talk about her past. "As much as we like havin' you here, Porunn, I think as soon as you can save enough money to move to another town I think you should move on to a more decent town. These port towns are not for a nice girl like you. And now Porunn, the pay is not much, the tips are good."

"What does tips mean. Liz?"

"Tips means the money that the longshoremen and sailors—whatever, leave on your table If they like you. And I think you'll make a mint."

AT the first night working at Tommy's. Porunn was ready to quit. The customers were mostly men except for the few floozies who came to pick up men. The other waitress who worked with Porunn was the same type and fit in with the crowd. Liz was sympathetic toward Porunn and protected her from the rogues who forced pressure brought about and characterized by physical or mental powers. Liz was well aware that Porunn was only tolerating the job due to her situation.

Suddenly a longshoreman with a long, black beard grabbed Porunn's arm. Liz came to Porunn's rescue.

Porunn took off her apron. "I'm going home, Liz," stated Porunn. "This is not going to work out."

"No, honey it ain't. What are you going to do. I mean you need the money?"

"I'll just keep on looking."

"Why don't you look for a job on the other side of town. There's a few nice places there?"

Porunn placed her arms around Liz affectionately, "Thank you, Liz. You've helped me believe in humanity again." Slipping into her coat, she glanced at Liz. "I've worked four hours of my shift. Tell your husband to have my check ready by ??? tomorrow morning. I'll come by and get it."

"Listen to me, Porunn, there's a train leavin' for Brandon Manitoba tomorrow at 3 P.M. Now, that's a classy town. and I want you on that train."

"I have no money, Liz."

"I'm the one who takes care of all the checks and finances, Porunn. My old man has trouble adding two and two. Why he couldn't run this place if it were not for me, and he knows it." Liz picked up Porunn's apron off the table. "Come with me to my office, Porunn." Crossing the dark, narrow hall, they entered a small enclosure furnished with only a chair and a desk loaded with papers. Liz pulled out a drawer and removed a checkbook then began writing on a check. "You'll get your money tonight," stated Liz handing Porunn the check.

Glancing at the check Porunn handed the money back to her, "You've made a mistake, Liz," stated Porunn.

"I don't make mistakes when it's money, I've been at it too long Sweetie."

"Thank you Liz. I have your address I'll pay you as soon as I get a job," she exclaimed, kissing Liz on the check.

"Nope! It's a gift."

The next day was sunny and warm. Seated in the train by a window, Porunn feeling relaxed for the first time since her freedom, gazed out at the beautiful scenery flying past the train window. She had heard from Liz that Brandon was prospering. It was rich in minerals—copper gold and silver, though grain is the principal product. Liz spoke of Winnipeg being the chief city in Manitoba. When she mentioned a town called Portage la Prairie. The word Prarie dimmed her spirits. Never could she live on a prairie. Yes, she was going to Brandon Manitoba. If she were ever to have good luck. it would be here. She trusted Liz to steer her in the right direction. Porunn glanced over at the middle-aged woman and young boy who sat across the aisle from her. The compartment was small but comfortably held four people. Porunn observed from their conversation that the woman was his teacher. Feeling hungry, Porunn rose from her seat and reached up on the shelf for the carpet bag. Seated again she opened her lunch bag and took out a French bread sandwich which the bakery lady had made for her to eat on the train to save her money.

"Oh, that smells so good!" sighed the woman.

"Freshly baked French bread," smiled Porunn.

"Let me introduce myself, Mademoiselle I am an English tutor in Brandon, Manitoba. I am French, I came over from Paris. And this nice little gentleman is Claud Fortier, my student. I am Madam Dumond." Claud and I are just getting back from Winnipeg where esteem for Claud's literary works were honored."

"He doesn't have parents?" asked Porunn.

"Oh, yes! Very rich parents. So rich that they do not have any time for Claud, therefore stay in Paris with their friends and send Claud across the sea to Canada. It is a nice arrangement. It works out for everyone," smiled Madam Dumond.

"A fine arrangement-except for Claud", replied Porunn sarcastically.

Glancing amicably at Porunn, Claud smiled his appreciation. Holding her gaze, Claud asked: "Do you go to school Mademoiselle?" I am sorry I did not catch your name," added Claud.

"Don't be sorry I never give my name unless it's asked for. You asked, Claud . . . It's Porunn Olafsdóttir. And as for your question, I have never gone to school."

"Why was that, Porunn?"

"It's a long story. I don't care to go into it."

Madam Dumond who had been napping during her charges conversation awakened abruptly when the locomotive whistle blew.

"That is such a lonely sound. If it could only be my ship taking me back home," said Claude.

"I know what you mean, Ones home is very important . . . . especially for a child," replied Porunn.

Madam Dumond gave Porunn an icy stare. "What do you know about children . . . you do-not have any."

"I was once a child," stated Porunn.

Moving out of her seat the madam threw Claud his jacket. "Put on your coat. I believe Brandon, Manitoba is the next stop," she exclaimed nervously gathering up her gloves and gold beaded handbag. Porunn picked up her carpet bag and waited for the train to stop.

CHAPTER TEN

The train chugged up the tracks then the conductor strolled down the aisle calling, "Next stop Brandon, Manitoba." Walking through the cars the conductor proceeded calling, "Brandon, Manitoba." With her carpet bag holding all her worldly possessions, she left the locomotive and hastened into the waiting room of the train depot. Walking up to the clerk who sat in the glass encasement wearing a green visor, she noted two red garters around each of his arms holding up the sleeves of his freshly starched white shirt. He glanced through his visor at her as she approached the enclosure. "Can I help you little lady?"

"Oh., I sure hope so, sir. you see, I just got off the train but I don't live here."

"Yes, I noticed you when you got off the train. And you speak very little English."

"I am looking for a room for the night. Would you have a listing of a single room available?"

He glanced up on the wall where a sheet of paper was attached. "I have only two that I can recommend. Take your pick

"Only two . . . ?"

"yes. I only list first and second class hotels"

"Oh. Well, either one of those will be fine."

He scribbled an address on a scrap of paper and handed it to her. "Good luck, Miss".

"Thank you, Herr," she smiled, leaving the depot and heading for the busy street. She was beginning to learn the ways of city life as she hurried toward the sight where hired carriages were parked. She hastened her gait when she noted that there was only one left.

After finding herself a sleeping room in a middle-class section of Brandon, she went out again to find herself a job.

Now, early evening, she had still not found employment. Crossing the avenue to return to her room she espied an attractive building with a bright sign on the roof reading *COFFEE SHOP*. She walked timidly up to the door, peeked in, then turned the knob and walked in. Many small tables were scattered about the large room where the customers sat lingering over a cup of coffee and a doughnut. Porunn noted that the customers were all very well dressed. Having not eaten for many hours, she dropped down in a chair at a table. Instantly a pretty girl approached her table. "What kind of a doughnut would you like, Miss?"

"Oh I do not want a doughnut, I would like some soup, please."

"I am sorry. We do not serve soup here, Miss, just doughnuts. We're a coffee house."

Porunn rose from the table. "To be honest with you, Miss, I really did not come in for anything to eat, I came in looking for a job."

"Oh! Come here a minute . . . Do you see that glassed office in the corner over there? Well that girl sitting in there is the owner. Go see her. I heard this morning that she was thinking about hiring another girl. We get very busy when people go on their coffee break. There is a lot of enterprise in trade which calls for a lot of evening work too. And when the employees get off for their break they come here. The boss is very particular whom she hires but I think she will like you." Both girls turned to the door when a man and woman walked in and seated themselves at a table. The waitress smiled at Porunn and whispered . . . "Good luck!"

An attractive young woman sitting in the cashier's office glanced up as Porunn neared her open window. "Hello there! she called out. "Did you enjoy our new version of a doughnut?"

Porunn stepped closer to the window. "I did not have a doughnut, Miss. I am here looking for a job."

"Odd you should come here. I was just thinking about hiring another waitress." The woman glanced curiously at Porunn. But do you have any experience?"

"A lot of experience."

"You don't speak English very well. I like your appearance, but do you think you could handle the language?"

With new hope, Porunn stepped closer into the office. "Oh, yes, I will learn very quickly."

Picking up a pen from her desk the woman glanced at Porunn. "May I have your name and address, dear?"

"Porunn Olafsdottir. I do not know my address I only got the room an hour ago."

"Is it around here?"

"Yes, only a few blocks.'

"Fine . . . You can give it to me tomorrow when you come in."

"Tomorrow . . . ?"

"Yes. I will give you a try. You see father owns the coffee house I just run it for him. Father is involved in the enterprise in trade so I suppose that's why they patronize us on their coffee breaks."

"Well, this is a very nice restaurant."

"This isn't a restaurant. We actually only serve coffee with doughnuts or sweet rolls, especially at breakfast." The woman's face then doured. "I have to tell you, Miss, the pay is not much. The hours are from 10:am to 6:pm. Are you still interested?"

"Oh yes! Thank you very much! I will be back in the morning . . . and I won't be late."

Smiling the proprietor rose from her seat. "By the way, Porunn if I am not at my desk, just ask for Jill." Walking Porunn to the door, the proprietor paused. "Is Porunn Olafsdottir Icelandic?"

"Yes, how did you know?"

"Ordinarily I wouldn't know but we have quite a few Icelanders here in Manitoba."

"Oh I am so glad I thought I was the only Icelandic person in Canada."

"See you in the morning, Porunn."

With high hopes for a better future Porunn went to bed. Awakening early, she began to dress for her first day at work. Slipping into her pale-blue velvet suit she placed her matching hat with a purple feather over her soft red hair. She wanted to make a good impression she told herself as she was recalling that the waitresses were wearing black dresses with white ruffled aprons and ruffled forehead bands. With light spirit in every step she left her room and headed for the coffee house.

CHAPTER ELEVEN

The days passed swiftly by. Porunn loved her work and was becoming more comfortable in her new country. Jill helped her with her English and with any difficult matter pertaining to the coffee house. However, by the end of the month she had barley enough money to pay for her room and her loan in Iceland.

Inattentively the days went by for six months. This morning Porunn was placing a fresh bouquet of flowers on the white, linen tablecloth when the coffee house door opened and two very pretty young women entered the coffee house. They were very well dressed, laughing and talking. Porunn moved up to their table. "We have some freshly made doughnuts this morning," said Porunn.

"No thank you. I will just have coffee and a sweet roll," answered the girl with the light red hair.

"Pardon me Miss, but Er pu ekki Islensk?" asked Porunn with beating heart. (Are you not Icelandic)

"Ja Ja. And I believe you are also. Let me introduce myself. I am Rosenkranza Haflidadottir. But everyone calls me just Rosa."

Porunn's face flushed with excitement. "And I am Porunn Olafsdottir from Iceland."

Rosa moved her eyes to her companion. "I would like you to meet my best friend, Groa, also from Iceland."

When some customers walked in the coffee house, Porunn left abruptly and went to their table.

Several weeks passed. Each new day, Porunn watched the entranceway of the coffee house for a return of her new Icelandic friends but they had not come back. Then one day Rosa walked into the establishment. Porunn moved quickly over the floor to Rosa's table. "How nice to see you again. Where is Groa?"

"Oh Groa is at work. She is taking over for me for awhile. I came over here to invite you to my home for the Icelandic Pónnukokur I am going to make this coming Sunday."

"Oh that sounds wonderful!"

"You will come then?"

"Of course I will come. Thank you so much for inviting me . . . what time?"

"Two will be fine. Nobody works on Sunday." replied Rosa with a smile. and rising from her table. "I have to get back to work." Digging in her handbag, Rosa pulled out a card. "Here is my address" she stated handing Porunn her place of residence.

Sunday morning was a big day for Porunn. Never had she been invited out before. After she had washed her hair and shaken out the wrinkles in her velvet suit, she brushed out the feather on her hat. And soon the allotted hour had come. After leaving her room she hurried to the carriage lot where hired carriages were kept.

As Porunn rode in the carriage she was thinking how her life had become happier the last couple days. Perhaps her job was the main cause however her Icelandic friends had changed her thoughts about a dark future. Manitoba appeared to be a lovely city.

Suddenly the horse slowed down then stopped in front of a small gray house. It appeared to be a nice neighborhood with well-kept lawns and flowers. "Here we are, Miss," called out the driver. Porunn left the vehicle and walked to the door of the residence.

Rosa and Groa who were already there, came to the door.

"Welcome! Welcome!" cried Rosa giving Porunn a squeeze. Groa standing quietly by reached for Porunn's hand. "Come and sit down, Porunn" Groa was not one of the beautiful women in Iceland. However, her good personality and honorable character shinned through her features and her beautiful bright-blue eyes. Porunn and Groa glanced up when two children bounced into the room . . . age seven and ten. Rosa placed both her arms around them. "Porunn these are my children. I want you to meet my son and daughter," she announced proudly. "Children, this is the Icelandic girl we were telling you about." All responded in unison. "Kondu sael og blessud." (hello and bless you) Porunn smiled at Emily. "You have red hair like I have".

"Oh, yes. a true Icelander," interrupted Rosa.

"They're good looking children," replied Porunn.

"Yes, they're good looking enough, Porunn, but they've been a real handful since their father's death."

"I can imagine, working and raising children."

"Well, they are bigger now so it's getting easier."

After a wonderful meal and pönnukokurs, the national dessert of Iceland, the three women went into the living room and soon were active in serious conversation. Most of the dialogue was about why they had left their homeland and the hardships of starting life all over again in a strange country, not able to speak English. They all agreed those were difficult times. Porunn looked side ways at Rosa "Well, at least you had a good husband and a good job."

"I never worked when Jon was alive. I was a rich man's daughter in Iceland. After my husband passed away, I had to find work and I had no experience. So, for awhile I had to take in washing to support myself and two children." Glancing over at the two siblings she smiled. "It was all well worth it. It should be easy from now on. I have been promoted to manager of the restaurant, and the children are almost grown."

Porunn's eyes traveled across the room to where Groa sat quietly listening to the conversations going on. "Why did you come Groa?" Upps! She should not have asked anymore questions for she would be next to relieve her reason, and she had no idea of exposing her tragic past.

"Rosa and I were best friends in Iceland. When Rosa married Jon who was a shepherd boy up in the Icelandic mountains' Rosa's father, disowned her. Rosa asked me to come to visit her in Canada where she and Jon had gone to live their own lives."

"Have I regretted it . . . ? Never." cut in Rosa.

"What is your last name, Rosa?" asked Porunn. "Who are your people?"

"My full name is Rosenkranza Haflidadottir. We are from Hrafnabjorgum. Later on our family moved to Bolungarvikur where my father bought a large, fashionable clothing store." Rosa's eyes dampened. "Oh, no, a poor shepherd boy was not good enough for a Haflida Helgason's daughter." Sighing deeply, Rosa went to the kitchen for some more coffee and cups and set them on the coffee table. "My family are all snobs. Of course my siblings are all grown now . . . even Sigudur the baby of the family should be about twenty eight or more by now."

"Is your little brother still home . . . ? Of course you would not know that." stated Porunn.

"Yes. When my parents passed away some years ago, Sigudur wrote me a letter and said he wanted to see me, so he is coming to Canada for a visit one of these days. am so excited!"

"He is a sea captain, isn't he?" asked Groa.

"Oh, yes," replied Rosa, "He graduated from the major academy in Reykjavik." Passing a cup of coffee to Porunn she grinned. "Nothing could keep Sigudur away from the sea." Glancing over the rim of her coffee cup Rosa smiled at Porunn. "And what about you, Porunn?" we have not heard why you left our wonderful land."

"No reason really. Just wanted a change." She glanced quickly at her gold watch pinned to her soft frilly blouse. "I have a carriage picking me up in about ten minutes. Do you want to share my carriage with me, Porunn?"

Scrambling for her suit jacket Porunn slipped it on. "Thank you Groa. This is great."

"Next Wednesday I have a day off." stated Groa. "I remember your telling Rosa and me that you were off every Wednesday. Would you like to go shopping with me . . . say about one o'clock?" stated Groa.

"I do not have much money to spend."

"There is a very inexpensive dress shop on Bolton Street."

"Well, I sure do need some clothes," replied Porunn thoughtfully. "I can hold my loan money up one week. No . . . that won't be so bad. I will meet you on Bolton Street at one o'clock," replied Porunn dashing out of the door with Groa when the carriage drove up to the little gray house. "Pak fyrir unadslegur daginn," Porunn cried out over her shoulder as they hurried down the sidewalk and boarded the carriage awaiting them.

The day was warm for being only May. Groa and Porunn hurried excitedly into the dress shop. Racks of very pretty dresses met their eyes. Oh, what beautiful summer dresses!" said Porunn removing a pale yellow cotton dress trimmed in white braid. "I would love this one, but I am sure it is too expensive for me." Still holding it in her arms she moved it up across her chest and examined herself in the long mirror next to the racks. "Oh, I just love it! Well I'll find something. They have a lot to choose from," said Porunn dejectedly. placing the garment back on the bar of the rack.

Groa moved to the bar and removed the yellow dress again. "Porunn did you read the price tag on the dress?"

"What is a price tag, Groa?"

"It is a little paper tag stating how much you have to pay for something you want to buy. Here, let me see," stated Groa retrieving the dress. "Oh, Porunn! Only $2.00! I am going to buy me a couple for that price."

Porunn's eyes traveled to the rack again and her eyes rested on a pale blue full skirted voile. "I love this one also I think full skirts are so feminine." she whispered to Groa as a group of women flocked into the dress shop.

"Porunn, why don't you take both of them?"

"I cannot afford both dresses. No, I think I will just take the yellow one . . . maybe later."

"Porunn, this rack is a sale for three days. I will tell you what, Porunn, I will buy three dresses, one for you and two for me, and you are going to take the yellow dress so that will be two each."

"Thank you, Groa, but I cannot let you do that."

"At this price?" Groa took the three dresses up to the clerk as Porunn followed with the pale yellow dress draped over her arm.

On the following Sunday Rosa, Groa, children, Jani and Emily stuffing themselves with cotton candy, and Porunn dressed in her new attire strolled through the park.

Monday at the restaurant where Rosa and Groa worked the cook came out from the kitchen. "Since when has Rosa been taking Mondays off?' he asked Groa.

"Rosa does not take Mondays off Jake. She is always the first one here in the mornings . . . Where is she?"

"ya got me," replied Jake shaking his head and returning to the kitchen. "I can tell you one thing Groa, if Rosa Isn't here by eight O' clock I am going to get a carriage and go out to her house." stated the cook.

"What do you mean, Jake . . . close-up? Sorry Jake, you cannot do that."

"Watch me."

"I can sure see why you have never made boss," stated Groa walking away.

CHAPTER TWELVE

The morning crowd had come and gone. And even with Jake's help Groa was exhausted. Time flew by but no sign of Rosa.

It was almost noon when the bell sounded at the front entrance and Rosa walked in the coffee house. "Oh my God! What a morning!" she cried dropping down on a chair at a table. "Anyone here?" she asked glancing around the room. "No, I guess not. I am so glad you had it quiet

"Quiet!" exclaimed Groa. "Hardly quiet for one person to service. I couldn't have done it without Jake. Thank you Jake." Groa focused her eyes on Rosa. "Now that the ten o' clock crowd has gone would you mind telling me Rosa why you did this to me."

Jake stepped closer to the kitchen door and lent an ear to the dining area. Rosa began to sob. "It was so heartbreaking!"

"What happened Rosa?" asked Groa. "No, forget it Rosa it's not important. The important part is that you're safe. Forget it. it's over."

"No it is not over. And it's important that you hear this Groa".

Rosa let out a long sigh. "Please don't criticize me for doing what I did. We all have to follow our own hearts."

"We will not criticize you, Rosa. However, I believe the contrary. It has been my belief to follow my head. Hearts are too softhearted and actually blind reality. No, I'll depend on my head for advise," repeated Groa.

"I was not asking my heart for advise. I did what I felt was right," cried Rosa.

"What your heart thought was right, not your head." Groa placed an arm around Rosa's shoulders. "Right or wrong, you will always have my support."

Rosa returned her eyes to Groa's gaze. "Oh Groa, he is so small and helpless," she sobbed picking up her uniform and blotted her tears on the apron. "Well, I was all ready to leave for work when I heard someone on my porch. I listened for a moment but I didn't hear a sound. So I continued into my sweater picked up my handbag and left for work. When I came out on the porch, I heard a cat mew. I looked around and my eyes caught a white straw laundry basket on the veranda. Right away, I thought someone I had once done laundry for was leaving me some more clothes to wash and not knowing that I no longer do laundry. Then suddenly I heard a baby cry! This was not a cat but alive little human being!"

"A baby . . . !" cried out Jake forgetting his hiding place.

"Yes, a baby!" replied Rosa, breaking into more tears. "The infant was wrapped up in a white, clean blanket but I could not see it's face, so I picked up the basket and brought it into the house and put it on the kitchen table. Removing the blanket I saw the most beautiful baby I have ever seen . . . an Indian baby."

"An Indian baby!" gasped Jake and Groa in unison.

"Oh, Rosa you will never find the infants mother. There are no Indians around here." informed Groa.

"That is what I thought at first, then I knew who the mother was and where I would find her." All eyes were glued to Rosa's features anxious to learn the ending of the story about the Indian boy. "Your right, Groa we do not have any Indians in our neighborhood. But up and over that steep hill are a few Indian families/ Every day when Jon was living, I used to see this beautiful Indian girl pass our house. Then one day she did not come. Several years went by, Jon had passed away and the Indian girl was forgotten. My heart tells me she is the baby's mother. If not, then maybe the Indian girl can tell me who is. So, I wrapped the infant up in his blanket again, picked up the basket and started up the long, steep hill."

"Good for you," said Groa. You don't need to start raising children again now that yours are almost grown. And it wasn't easy." Groa dropped down on a chair by a table to rest her tired legs. "Did you find her house?"

"Not right away. The houses looked like huts and it appeared that several families lived in the same dwelling. So I just had to knock on every door. Different Indians answered my rap except one which kindled my suspicion."

"So, what did you do?" asked Jake.

"I just kept knocking . . . louder and louder!

"I then began pounding the door with my fists. "Open this door, young lady! If you don't I will break your door down! I have your little son with me." The door flew open. I walked in.

Holding her hands over her face, the Indian girl fell to her knees. "Oh, please keep me Cheko an raise him to be a good man."

"Cheko . . . ?" I asked.

She nodded. "I name him, Cheko." Smiling through her tears she glanced lovingly at her infant "See, him all ready know him name an him only two day old'". Then digging into a broken red pottery of clay, she pulled out a scrap of paper and pinned it onto the baby's blanket. "For me Cheko."

Curious, I read the words."

INDIAN PRAYER
GREAT SPIRIT

"GRANT THAT I MAY NOT CRITICIZE MY NEIGHBOR UNTIL I HAVE WALKED A MILE IN HIS MOCCASINS." I was very touched but did not know what to do.

Bursting into a fresh break of tears, the beautiful Indian mother took my arm. "Please help me!"

"Yes, I will help you. I will get someone to find a family who take in foster children." I walked to the door with my eyes resting on the helpless little human being whose future was being decided by a stranger and a good mother but one who was not able to care for the child because of the evil word . . . poverty.

"No! No1" the mother screamed. "No white people will be good to my Cheko. No white folks like color of our skin."

"If you believe that, why did you leave your baby with a white woman?' I asked.

"I have heard for many years how good you have been to people in trouble. An to people of all color too. Great Spirit him tell me you be good to Cheko and me son someday will repay you," she sobbed throwing herself on the floor to her knees at Rosa's feet.

Rosa glanced at Groa. "How could I turn my back on this tragic situation, Groa? I cannot help how I am. Call it softhearted call it anything you want, but I picked up the basket and ran out of the hut with the baby crying and most likely from hunger."

"Well, where's the kid now?" asked Jake.

"I left the baby with my next door neighbor. The woman is an elderly lady who lost her husband a couple of months ago and living alone in her fine house is very lonely." Picking up her purse from the table she let out a sigh of relief for having told them. She felt better now. "I must get my uniform on. It's almost time for the lunch crowd."

"Just a moment, Rosa, why would Mrs. Cox, at her age take a foster child to raise? She's all ready had four of her own now grown and married?" asked Groa.

"She isn't going to. Mrs. Cox is going to look after Cheko for me when I am working. She said she would love to have the company and for something to do. Said she wouldn't even charge me. Of course I will pay her. She suggested if I insist on paying her that she had another plan. I could do her laundry every two weeks for her, that it would be a small amount for only one person."

"That's a good deal, Rosa."

"You see. Great Spirit is helping me already." When the bell on the restaurant door buzzed, Jake hurried to his kitchen. Standing at her post, Groa smiled amicably to the customers as they filled in for lunch. Sitting at her desk in the cashier's office, Rosa was thankful for a few moments to think. it had been a hard day.

Thus the days passed. Cheko was the joy and love of Rosa's home. Her children, Jani and Emily idolized the little Indian boy and called him their little brother. The woman living next door was now called by Cheko, Grandmother. Even though the youngster was hard to understand in his baby English, the woman loved it. The boy was now beginning to learn how to walk, and everyone took part in instructing the child how to balance. Much laughter imbued the air.

June brought abundance of red roses to Rosa's flower beds. With Porunn and Groa coming for dinner this Sunday evening she cut a nice bouquet for her table.

Sunday after dinner more coffee was served in the living room as Rosa put the baby to bed. The house was quiet And lifeless. "My it's so quiet!" announced Groa sitting down on the sofa in the living room. She turned to Porunn seated beside her. "How many children do you want when you get married."

"I am not getting married, Groa. What about you?"

"Oh, Id' like a full house of children."

"I have always wanted to be a writer . . . maybe an actress," added Porunn . . . but married, no thanks."

"You can do both, Porunn. Most writers are married."

"Yes, and most writers are divorced. That is not the kind of marriage I want. Say nothing of what this does to children."

"Things are changing, Porunn. Today people can have the best of two worlds."

"Do not believe everything you hear, Groa. No one can have the best of two worlds. One world will suffer and most likely both. And it is generally the children. But the parents enjoying their two worlds do not think about that," stated Porunn.

"Mothers were mothers in the olden days," said Groa. I'm glad our mothers stuck with their marriage through thick and thin. My parents did not get along but we children always came first. I used to hear her say, "Skoli, if it were not for the children I would leave you." "I think they loved each other though. I could see it in their eyes when they were on good terms."

Porunn's featured dowered. as she thought of how Hallbera had given all her children away. She came quickly out of the past when Rosa came into the living room. Groa arose from the sofa. "I think we are going to leave now. Rosa it is getting late. Don't forget there's work in the morning," stated Groa picking up her cape on the arm of the sofa.

"Sit down for a moment I have some important news from Iceland I want you girls to hear," replied Rosa.

"Iceland!" cried Porunn with a faint heart. Groa placed her cape back onto the arm of the sofa and sat down again.

Smiling, Rosa pulled out a letter from her youngest sibling, Sigudur. The first word she had ever received since leaving Iceland.

"Sigudur is coming to Brandon Manitoba to visit me. Says he will most likely stay almost a month. Isn't that wonderful news?"

"Yes," Groa glanced at Rosa puzzlingly. "Isn't this the first word you have received from your family since you left Iceland?" asked Porunn.

"I have never had a word from any of them. Not even my mother." replied Rosa somberly.

"You were disowned, you know'" replied Groa. "What else does little brother say?"

"He informed me that both my parents are gone. They passed away but no one bothered to let me know." said Rosa somberly.

"Well, there is your answer. He's his own free man now."

"Maybe he is a little different from our family."

"I don't think so, Rosa. Don't forget you and I grew up together so I know a little bit about the snobbishness of you Haflidason," Groa looked over at Porunn as she sat quietly listening to Rosa's and Groa's conversation.

Rosa glanced at her letter again and reread it's contents. "I am so excited!"

"Well, does he say when he is coming?" asked Groa.

"Oh, yes! He says he will be arriving by steamer across the ocean to Canada at four thirty our time. He will then aboard a train to Brandon Manitoba.

He asks me to meet him about seven P.M. at the train station in Brandon. I am so nervous!" she looked at Groa and Porunn. "You girls will have to go with me to meet Sigudur. I am much to emotional to go alone."

"Sure, Rosa. It will be fun." smiled Groa.

"You go with her, Groa. I am not very good at meeting strangers. Sigudur probably remembers you," stated Porunn.

"Oh I don't think so Porunn. He was pretty young then."

"Oh, please come, Porunn. I would be so proud of my two Icelandic friends." Rosa folded up the letter again and placed it in the pocket of her sweater. Smiling, she added, "You girls better doll up. Sigudur is used to beautiful women."

"No problem, Rosa. Porunn and I will outshine all the women in Brandon, Manitoba."

" . . . And don't forget Sigudur is used to beautiful, fashionable Icelandic girls," stressed Rosa seriously.

"Well, what are we, Rosa . . . Chinese? Did our nationality change because we crossed the ocean to Canada?"

"Don't pay any attention to me," replied Rosa. "I'm a nervous wreck!".

"Sigudur is still single isn't he, Rosa?" asked Groa.

"I suppose so. But he is still young. This March 3rd he was about twenty-nine years old."

"Sigudur is coming this month . . . ?" asked Groa.

"Yes, June fifteen he will get off the train in Brandon Manitoba about seven P.M."

Groa picked up her cape. "Let's go Porunn. And it looks like we have more shopping to do if we are going to meet the Prince Of Iceland."

"We already have two dresses." replied Porunn following her out of the house to a carriage awaiting them.

"Hats, this time. And for hats a lot more expensive than our dresses were," informed Groa.

"Well, I suppose for once I could splurge. Our appearance seems to mean a lot to Rosa."

Dressed in her only suit, Porunn stood waiting for Groa at a big store window dressed in gorgeous hats. Suddenly she heard Groa's voice behind her. "Come on Porunn let's go in."

Picking up a white leghorn hat, Porunn turned to Groa "Wow! These are expensive."

"I can loan you for the hat."

"I do not want this one, I want something to go with my pale yellow dress."

"You mean perhaps like a pale fine straw . . . ?"

"Yes, here is one," stated Porunn excitingly. "And look at the beautiful white flower on the brim. It will match the white braid on my yellow dress." They glanced up as a young clerk approached the counter of hats.

"May I help you young ladies with something?"

"Oh, we just love these hats but they are very expensive!" said Porunn.

"Well, those are our most expensive ones, Miss. You see they are all originals. We never put these on sale." The clerk moved to another counter of hats. "While these hats are very chic, they often get marked down."

"How much do the hats sell for?" asked Groa.

"$35.00 a hat."

" . . . and the originals . . . ?" asked Porunn still holding on to her light straw hat from the original table.

"From seventy-five dollars and up."

"Thank you, madam," she exclaimed dropping the pale, light straw original back on the table and moving back to the less expensive hats. Picking up a light silk yellow hat she placed it on her head and glanced into the mirror above the table.

"That hat looks so chic with your beautiful red hair." said the clerk.

"No flower," said Porunn removing the hat and throwing it down on the table again. She turned to Groa who was standing beside her with a original hat in her hand. "I see you found a hat," said Porunn.

"Yes, isn't it beautiful?" exclaimed Groa placing it on her head and twirling around.

"I guess we can go then," replied Porunn.

"Aren't you going to buy one?" Groa asked puzzlingly.

"No. I don't like any of those cheaper hats and I cannot afford the price of the originals. Come on, Groa, Let's go."

"No, Porunn you will take the one you wanted. I'll pay half and you pay half. That won't be too bad. The two girls moved to the original table again.

"I am happy to see you have changed your mind." stated the clerk following the two young women to the expensive table again.

Picking up the soft natural straw hat with the white flower on the brim, Porunn glanced at the clerk. "How much is this one?"

"That one, Miss is $75.00."

"We'll take it," said Groa.

"I will pack your beautiful purchases in our lovely hat boxes . . . they come with the hats," said the clerk reaching down on a shelf of colored boxes.

"No thank you, Madame, I am going to wear mine," replied Porunn.

"So am I," said Groa cheerfully, moving to the big mirror and placing her hat on her head.

It was a warm beautiful day as Groa and Porunn strolled down the busy street of Brandon. Then a photograph studio attracted their attention. "Let's go in and have our picture taken," exclaimed Groa jovially tugging Porunn by the arm.

"I have never had my picture taken Groa. Well, not since I was a child."

"We should have a picture of us in these beautiful hats . . . come on!" said Groa pulling Porunn by the sleeve into the photo studio.

"Good day, ladies," exclaimed the cameraman. "Which one of you young ladies want to be first?"

"We are going to have our picture taken together," replied Groa smiling.

After the shoot Porunn went to her little room and addressed a letter to Sera Kartin with a small payment for his loan.

As the days flew by today was now June fifteen, the exciting day of Sigudur Rosenkar Haflidason's arrival from Iceland.

Rosa picked up Cheko in her arms and crossed the lawn to her neighbor's house. "Cheko! Cheko!" cried the woman. "You have come to spend the night with grandmother."

"Gra!" called Chico reaching out for Mrs. Cox.

The little child knew the routine.

"I believe Cheko would rather be with you than me." said Rosa solemnly.

"That is only natural. Mothers do not spend much time with their children when they work. He loves you, Rosa I see it in his eyes each night when you pick him up from work."

"Hope you do not mind keeping the baby over night, but I hate to disturb his sleep to take him home. We don't meet my brother until six thirty when he gets off the train in Brandon."

"What time does your brother's steamer dock?"

"At four-thirty P.M."

"Cheko loves his little bed I bought him for his naps. We'll get along just fine. Now go and get prettied up for your brother." She then instructed the child to give his mother a goodbye kiss. Slipping into a pale blue dress with a matching feathered hat which accentuated her pretty features and pale blonde hair' She dashed out to the carriage that had just driven up to the house with her friends dressed in their finest array. The three young women made an attractive picture as they deboarded the hired carriage at the railroad station and bustled out of the vehicle into the depot waiting room.

"I think we are early," announced Rosa nervously.

Groa broke away from Rosa's tight grasp and approached the ticket agent. "Will the train be in on time, sir?"

"The old gal is due in a few minutes, Miss."

"And what time is that . . . ?"

"In about two minutes, Miss."

"And what time is that," persisted Groa her natural Icelandic, stubborn streak surfacing.

"At six-thirty. The old gal is never late she'll be blowing anytime," said the clerk in an annoying timber.

"Thank you," she replied. She then called out to her friends. "Come over here girls. the locomotive will stop about here." Sudden a train whistle blew around the corner, slowed and then stopped near the platform closest to the waiting room where Groa was waiting.

Excited and nervous, Rosa let out a sigh. "Oh I hope we haven't missed him!" she mumbled when the passengers filed quickly out of the locomotive. Walking into the crowd, Rosa ran ahead of Groa and Porunn to the steps of the train where a conductor stood balancing himself on the steps of the train. "Brandon! Brandon!" he called out. "Last call for Brandon Manitoba".

Groa took Porunn's hand. "Come on, Porunn let's wait for them over here", "she said, leading to the rafters of the waiting room. "They certainly don't need us. I doubt Rosa even gives it a thought that we are here." When they leaned against the depot building, they saw a handsome young man come out of the train. He was dressed in a very expensive suit and wore a white, hard straw flat crowned hat with a small brim. "That is Sigudur alright, son of the owner of the most exclusive men's clothing store in Iceland. And look at the spats would you. they match his hat," exclaimed Groa.

"That kind of a fashion plate has never attracted me", said Porunn dryly. "Oh, look, Groa, Rosa has spotted the prince of Iceland."

Running toward him, Rosa threw her arms around her brother and broke into sobs when Sigudur endeared her to him and kissed her lovingly on the check. "You look wonderful big sister. You do not look one day older than when I saw you last." He took her by the hand. "where can we get a carriage, or do you have your own?"

"No, we have a hired carriage behind the depot." Then grimacing Rosa glanced toward the waiting room where Porunn and Groa waited for them to come over for them. "Oh Sigudur I forgot my friends that came with me." Rosa took her brother's arm and led him over to the rafters of the depot. "Girls, I want you to meet my brother, Sigudur. Of course you already know Groa." Groa nodded.

"That was a long time ago. It's nice to see you again, Groa. You have certainly been a loyal friend to my sister. And I want you to know I really appreciate it." His deep dark blue eyes rested on Porunn's serious features. "You must be visiting from Iceland," stated Sigudur shaking Porunn's hand. "Huz dottir ert pu?" (Whose daughter are you)

"Olafsdottir," Porunn replied timidly, her heart skipping a beat. His beautiful eyes seemed to penetrate hers. She told herself to get hold of her senses. "I am Porunn Olafsdottir from Iceland, a new friend of Rosa's and Groa's."

"I love your red hair, Tòta. And your hat is beautiful."

Porunn smiled. "I have not heard the name, Tòta sense I was in Iceland . . . and then only once or twice."

"That seems very strange. It is commonly used for all Porunns. And of course the masculine name for Porunn is Por, and the pet name for Por is Toti. Sigudur grinned. "Tòta, are you sure you were brought up in Iceland?" The group all laughed at Sigudur's humor.

Sigudur assisted Porunn into the carriage then climbed in beside her. Groa stepping up into the carriage behind them whispered to Rosa. "I think your brother has found what he has always been looking for. Beauty with brains."

Sound of horses hoofs could be heard up the dusty road leading to Rosa's house. "What a pretty little, home," said Sigudur when the carriage stopped by a rose garden gracing the front entrance.

Gathering up her handbag from the seat Porunn turned to Sigudur. "I've enjoyed meeting Rosa's brother from Iceland and perhaps we'll meet again. Bless! as we Icelanders say at partings."

Snatching up her hand Sigudur tightened his grip. "Tota, are you not coming in?"

"No, I have to go home."

"Porunn! You certainly are coming in," interrupted Rosa. "I have made some Icelandic dishes for us."

"May I intercede here a moment.?" asked Groa. "Of course we are coming in. Get the coffee pot on Rosa. The group went into the house.

Over the rim of his coffee cup, Sigudur rested his eyes on Porunn's beautiful features. And he was realizing right away that it was not her beauty that attracted her to him. He was used to Iceland's beautiful women. No, it was her innocent ladylike demeanor.

Feeling Sigudur's dark, navy-blue inset eyes on her, she glanced into his stare . . . and her pale, gray eyes locked with his.

Rosa and Groa looked on unbelievably. realizing that Sigudur and Porunn had fallen in love at first sight.

CHAPTER THIRTEEN

The summer was waning. And signs of an early winter etched the paths and walks with an abundance of Autumn leaves.

Strolling arm in arm, Sigudur and Porunn turned up the walk leading to where Porunn resided. "Goda note, Tota," whispered Sigudur in Porunn's ear. (Goodnight) "Don't go in, Tota. It is really still early."

Porunn freeing herself from his arms placed her house key in the lock. "I have to go to work in the morning, Sigudur."

"I know, Tota. I should be back in Iceland. It looks like I have abandoned my ship. I have already stayed a month longer than I should have."

"Do you have any idea when you will be going back to Iceland Sigudur?"

"I do not want to think about it, Tota, unless you have changed your mind and are going with me."

"No. I have told you I am never going back." she exclaimed, her features coloring and grimacing. "Goodnight then . . . until tomorrow."

Tonight the Harvest moon hung low and mysterious in the sky. High up on a hill Sigudur parked the carriage as horses could be seen grazing peacefully in the valley below. "When will you be going home, Sigudur?" Porunn asked, afraid to hear his reply.

"Can you be ready by Sunday, Tota?"

Porunn glanced at Sigudur with a wry face. "I have told you many times that I will never be ready to go back to Iceland. And I have told you that I am never getting married."

"But I know you love me, Tota . . ."

"Yes I love you very much, and if I were to get married you would be the one man in my life. There never has been one and I intend to leave it that way. You love children, I do not. Marriage is the union of a man and woman as husband and wife. And the union of matrimony without children is not a home, it is a couple only living together," stated Porunn with a faint heart. When a cold breeze blew against the carriage, Sigudur slipped his arm around Porunn's shoulders. "Well, Tota I believe you have just answered your own question . . . . When am I going home? I will never be ready to go back to Iceland without you Tota."

"I do not understand," replied Porunn curiously.

"Easy to understand. I am not going back and leave you here, Tota."

"I am still not marrying you, Sigudur."

"I am going to resign at the academy."

"I cannot let you do this, Sigudur."

"You are not doing it, Tota, I am," he whispered enwreathing her to his breast and kissing her warmly.

The sound of the horse's hoofs resounded up the dusty road to the outskirts of Brandon.

Tonight sleep would not come.

She lay in her bed staring into dark abyss of space. Imagining her life without Sigudur was unbearable to think about. Then a thought passed her mind. She would write to her sister Sigurun. She would give her honest advise.

Scrambling out of bed, Porunn went to the closet and from Hallbera's carpet bag, removed a pen and paper for her to write her sister. Kara Syster Sigurun,

This will be a short letter but I have run into a problem. Not really a problem but something very important to me. Elsku, sister, I have met a wonderful man who has asked me to marry him. I love him, Sigurun, but there is one thing that is holding me back. He is from Iceland and likes to take a drink once in awhile. His name is Sigudur Rosenkar Haflidason. You have probably heard of his family. Sigudur is such an honest man and so gentle and thoughtful of me. And very handsome. Please answer as soon as you can. I miss and love you, Sigurun. Pinn sister, Porunn Olafsdottir.

The Winter solstice between June 22 and December 22 was fading. Gone was the beauty of the flowerbeds and sun. Regions of treeless tundra added to the cheerless scene.

Sigudur and Porunn with fingers entwined walked quickly up the walk to Porunn's residence. Slipping her key into the lock of her room she glanced up at Sigudur with a wry face. "My it is cold! Much too cold to walk any farther." With chattering teeth and an oblique movement of her eyes she rested them on Sigudur's features. "Aren't you cold, Sigudur?"

"Oh, yes. It is certainly colder in Manitoba than Iceland."

"Most people have the wrong impression of Iceland. They think because it is named Iceland there's nothing but ice and snow," replied Porunn.

"Yes, Iceland was really misnamed. Greenland should be called Iceland."

"Of course Iceland is not the original name of our country. It's original name was Isafold," stated Porunn. Wrapping her arms tightly around her body and shivering she opened the door. "Goodnight, Sigudur. It's too cold to stay out here."

"May I come in for just a moment to warm my hands? It will be a long walk if I don't get a carriage."

Stepping aside Porunn gave Sigudur a quick look. "Just for a moment."

Sigudur was gone. Porunn concentrated on a letter from Iceland. The allotted time it took from Europe had passed. Each day after work she would run up the walk to meet the postman to see if he had brought the important letter she was so impatiently waiting for. Well, maybe tomorrow.

This evening the weather was much warmer. Sigudur and Porunn had taken a walk through a large grain field." "I hear grain is a leading product here in Brandon as well as in Winnipeg and other providences of Canada," stated Porunn.

"Yes, and wheat," added Sigudur. "And of course cattle and mixed farming." He stopped walking suddenly and took Porunn in his arms. "Lock at the moon up there, Tota".

"Yes it is beautiful. But not as pretty as the one in Iceland."

"I think it is prettier," replied Sigudur jokingly.

Heading for Porunn's rooming house, they walked unspoken, each with their own thoughts.

When Sigudur came home, his sister Rosa sat at the table drinking a cup of coffee. Reaching into the cabinets she brought out another cup and filled it with coffee.

Smiling, Sigudur drew up a seat to the table beside her and picked up his cup. "You do not have to wait up for me, big sister. I'm a grown man now."

Glancing over the rim of her cup, Rosa grinned. "There is not many men who can boast about planting a beautiful virgin's first kiss on her lips," she teased.

"I have never kissed Tota . . . She won't let me," he replied sullenly.

"Oh, then it isn't going to well."

Rosa took another sip of coffee. "You must keep in mind, Sigudur, Porunn is an old fashion woman. And you know that is why you fell in love with her at first sight. God knows you have had enough of the other kind."

"Tota is not a woman . . . she is an angel."

A cold brisk wind blew through the cracks around the windows and door of the rooming house where Porunn sat on the bed writing to Sera Kartin along with the last payment of the loan. At the bottom of the letter she scribbled a short note.

> P.S. I want to thank you and Fru Kartin for all your kindness and
> for your loan which has given me another start in life
> > gratefully, Porunn Olafsdottir.

Leaving her work place, Porunn hurried home to see if the postman had brought the letter from Sigurun. She put her hand in the box but it was empty. Then suddenly she espied the mailman coming up the path. She ran out to meet him. "Anything for me?" she cried out.

He handed Porunn a letter. "Looks like a foreign address . . . it is Iceland! It must really be cold over there to day!"

Slipping the letter in her pocket she noted the postman's curious stare: "Well, aren't ya going to read it. Ya been bugging me a whole week about this letter."

"Thank you postman," she called over her shoulder and disappeared into the rooming house.

Seating herself down on the bed, Porunn removed her letter from her pocket and began to read her letter from her sister Sigurun.

Elsku sister Porunn,

You can never know how happy I was to learn that you have met a wonderful man. And . . . he has asked you to marry him. Yes, I know his family. I do not know his family but I have heard and read about the Haflidi Helgasons. I read in the newspaper once that Sigudur Rosenkranz Haflidason was the youngest child out of eight children. Sigudur's mother was Johanna Jonsdottir. The family was originally from Hrafnabjorg in Ogurhreppi where Sigudur was born on March 3, 1873. Sometime later, Haflidi Helgason moved his family to Bolungar . . . Efstadal where he bought a sport clothing store. Sigudur studied at the Sjomen's academy and in no time was captain of his own ship.

You ask me if you should marry him, My advise to you Porunn is to get married right away before someone else snatches him from you. You are a very lucky girl, Porunn. Grab happiness when you can. You have had so little of it in your life. Good luck, Elsku Porunn. (dear) Keep me posted.

Sigurun sister.

Full of emotion, Porunn stood up from the bed and opened the closet for Hallbera's carpet bag where she threw Sigurun's letter in and closed the closet door.

Covering her face with her hands in deep emotion her heart felt light . . . for this time her response to stimuli was joy.

December brought colder weather to Brandon. Parked on a small hill by the wheat field, Porunn and Sigudur sat in a hired carriage with a fur lap robe thrown over their knees. "Is the horse tied up?" asked Porunn rattling in her handbag for a lump of sugar which she had brought with her for the faithful, patient animal standing out in the cold.

"Yes, Tota. I tied her to the field gate."

"You sound kind of downhearted, Sigudur."

"No, I am always happy when I am with you, Tota. I just wish you could love me half as much as I love you."

Opening the carriage door Porunn held the lump of sugar in her hand. "I will be right back, Sigudur."

He removed the sugar from her hand and closed the vehicle door again. "You are not going out there. I will give it to the horse," he stated, jumping lively from the carriage and rolling up the collar of his sheep skin coat. "Burr! It's cold out there. I wish I was in Iceland," he exclaimed jovially, heading for the field gate with the sugar in his hand.

Back in the carriage Sigudur Placed his arm around Porunn's shoulder. "Tota, are you warm enough?"

"No. I am freezing! But can you imagine how the horse outside feels?"

"I was thinking that when I took the sugar out to the mare. At first she would not even take it. I believe we should go. It's just too cold for man or beast as the old expression goes."

"Yes, let's go. But before you hitch up the horse again I have something to tell you," she whispered bashfully. "Sigudur . . ."

Clasping both hands over his ears, he glanced at her with a metallic luster. "Tota, I do not want to hear any bad news to night," he stated removing his hands from his ears and taking Porunn's hand in his. "I was not entirely honest with you when I told you I was not downhearted this evening. Tomorrow will be better, Tota. Tell me then."

"How about better tonight?"

Sigudur stared with an oblique movement of his eye. "I do not understand you this evening. You seem different Tota. Do not tell me you do not want me to come for you anymore."

Porunn broke out into a large smile. "You won't have to Sigudur, we will be married."

"Did you say married Tota?" Porunn grinning bashfully nodded her head.

"Oh, Tota!" he exclaimed drawing her to his breast, and the weather was forgotten. "When can we get married, Tota? Of course it takes a lot of time to plan a wedding—even a small wedding,"

"Yes, but I do not want any guests except Groa, Rosa and the children. You and I have no friends and our families are in Iceland."

"Yes, I can see what you mean. Suits me, we have our love Tota that is all we need." Looking deep into her pale blue eyes, Sigudur kissed her hand. "Could I ask one favor of you, Tota?" She glanced curiously at him. "Will you wear a white dress for our wedding? Virgins wear white. However, the prostitutes of today are also wearing white. Looks like all decency has gone with the wind."

Pulling her lap-robe up closer around her knees she began to shiver. "Let's go, Sigudur. We will make plans tomorrow evening."

There was still a light in Rosa's small gray home. Sigudur jumped boyishly from the carriage and hurried into the house. "Rosa! Rosa! Why are you not waiting up for little brother?"

Coming out of the bedroom half asleep she peered blurry-eyed out of her pale gray ones. "You told me you were a big boy now. What did you do shrink since the last time I saw you today?"

"Got some hot coffee on the stove to warm me up?" he asked with his voice trembling.

"For goodness sake, Sigudur, you're catching a cold," she stated hurrying to the cooking range and heating water for coffee.

Slipping out of his sheep skin coat he placed his arm around her. "I am not getting a cold big sister. I'm experiencing a psychological stimuli from the thought of finally getting married."

"You two only met about five months ago . . . are you sure?"

"I was sure the first day I saw her at the railroad station. Oh, Rosa I have never been so happy in my whole life!"

"I am very happy for you both. Porunn is a wonderful woman."

"Tota is not a woman. She's an angel."

Groa and Porunn turned the knob of the wedding shop door and walked in. "Oh, this looks expensive!" Porunn whispered to Groa.

"Well this is an expensive store."

"Why did you bring me here then, Groa? I cannot afford these prices."

"Because we're going down to the basement where the mark downs are." Hunting through the rack of beautiful wedding gowns, Groa suddenly stopped and removed a dress from it's hanger. "Oh, look Porunn. Isn't this one beautiful?"

Taking the gown and holding it up to her Porunn glanced into the mirror. "Oh, Yes. it is lovely," she replied, stroking the rich white satin. "And so plain. I want something very simple to match my simple wedding."

"Aren't you going to fit it on, Porunn?"

"No. I do not want it," she replied continuing to hunt through the rack of mark-downs. Her eyes finally focused on a white chiffon frock. cape sleeves with a sweetheart neck. The wide full skirt fell in ripples to the floor. Smiling, Porunn turned. to Groa with the gown over her arm, "Look no farther . . . I have found my gown "It's lovely. Porunn. Your kind of dress," smiled Groa.

One of the sales ladies entered the fitting room where Porunn and Groa were examining the gown. "Do you girls need any help? I'm so sorry, girls, I would have been in here much sooner but one of our old customers cane in crying and all excited because the wedding gown we sold her a few weeks ago is too tight . . . she can't even get into it."

"And of course she blamed you?" said Groa.

"Of course. I then asked her if she was pregnant. She started to sob again and nodded her head."

"What did you do?" asked Porunn.

"We offered her the money for the dress back. She didn't want it. Said she loved this dress and she was going to have it let out if possible. We called in the seamstress, she looked it over and because it was an expensive gown there was more material used therefore there would be plenty of room. And, our customer left light hearted.

"I hope this kind of thing doesn't happen often," said Groa.

"More often than one would think. For instance, I belong to the catholic church and I sing in the choir. We have a very nice choir director, a woman about forty-two years of age. She announced her engagement Sunday morning after the service. Everyone was surprised for this was her first marriage. Naturally she asked me to help her find a beautiful wedding dress. She was a wealthy spinster and her first wedding so was having quite an elaborate affair.

About two months went by and one day she came in sobbing like they all do. I always say these girls aren't sorry, they are sorry they got caught."

"Were you able to help her?" asked Porunn with a wry face.

"We couldn't give her the same dress. She had bought it from the sale rack and there was no extra material the seamstress could use to let it out. After browsing awhile the woman found a gown exactly like the one that got too small for her. I noticed she took a size three times larger than the first dress. When I questioned her about it being too big, she said, "'Virgil wants to wait until this summer to be married.'"

Holding hands Groa and Porunn sauntered down the street to a coffee house. Sitting at the table with two coffees and some doughnuts they relaxed and spoke about Sigudur and Porunn's wedding.

"I'm going to miss you, Porunn."

"Not for awhile, you won't. Rosa has offered Sigudur and me to stay with her until we find our own place."

"Oh, wonderful! Leave it to Rosa with already a house full of children. Well, I have to get back to work. I only took the morning off because I knew you had Wednesday off. See you Friday . . . . that's your big day."

"And as you know Lutherans usually marry by candle light in the evening." said Porunn nervously. "Sigudur has made arrangements with the minister for seven P.M. Friday evening," she added.

"Rosa and the children and of course Sigudur and I will meet you at the church."

With an arm full of soiled linen Porunn tripped down the stairs to the basement and washed her laundry. She glanced up when the landlady came in and confronted her. "My, Miss Olafsdottir, I haven't seen you for a long time. Is everything alright?"

"Oh yes fine. It's funny how we should meet today . . . I was just about to come to your room and talk to you."

"Is that pipe still leaking, dear?"

"No, every thing is fine. I was coming because I want you to know that tomorrow is my last day here."

"You've found a better place."

"No. I have been very comfortable here . . . no, I am getting married this coming Friday."

"Married! My lans! Aren't you the lucky one. Lighting a cigarette, the landlady took a puff and blew a gust of gray-purple smoke into the air. "You know, that's what I used to tell my girls when they got down. 'If ya can't make it on your own hop on someone else's wagon who has."

Porunn forced a smile. "I want to thank you for taking me in that first night. I was so tired and depressed," said Porunn starting to hang her washing on the clothes line.

"I'm going to miss ya kid. Ya always pay me on time".

"I generally pay you on Friday but I will be down with the rent Thursday night . . . that is tomorrow. And thank you again for your kindness.," stated Porunn climbing the stairs and disappearing in her room.

Friday's dusk covered the early evening with dark shadows commingled with saffron colored streaks across the horizon. Porunn dressed in her wedding dress, pinned her long, red curls up in back with the exception of two shiny locks which she hung over her left shoulder.

Opening the closet door Porunn removed the old coat which had been given to her so many years ago. It was cold outside. She would wear it to the church and slip it off and leave it in the carriage.

She was about to leave the closet when her eyes fell to Hallbera's carpet bag in the corner on the floor. For one second a flash of nostalgia swept over her. It had never happened before. How she wanted her mother! And how she missed their little home in luvatn. They were all so happy there before her father's death. Where was her little sister Johanna, a grown woman now? And her brother Loftur? Staring at the lonely carpet bag she then closed her eyes and made a cross over it.

Porunn left the closet and the carpet bag forever.

When Sigudur, Groa Rosa and children's carriage arrived at the Lutheran church, the premises appeared dark. "Oh, I see a light!" said Jani in a loud voice. "It looks like a candle," added Rosa's son.

As they advanced closer to the church they noted the parish was lighted only in the chapel where small weddings were held. "It looks beautiful," commented Sigudur. "So soft and peaceful".

The church vestibule was warm and cozy. "Is Tota here yet, Rosa?" asked the nervous groom to be.

"She's probably on her way over, Sigudur".

At the rooming house Porunn stood at the window her eyes searching for the carriage Sigudur was sending for her and thinking . . . "The driver is late and I will be too if he doesn't come pretty soon." Still glancing out of the window she finally saw a horse and carriage stop in front of the dwelling.

The horse galloped lively to the church. When the carriage stopped, Porunn pulled off her old coat and hurried up the path to the entrance. She pushed hard on the two swinging doors, too heavy for her to open. Sigudur hastened to the entrance and drew her in, placing a dozen white roses in her arms. "You look beautiful Tota. So is your dress."

Rosa stepped between them. "Come on you two, the minister is already in the pulpit waiting." The small wedding party moved to the pulpit where the minister stood with a Bible in his hands. He was dressed in his vestments, a red satin robe with a high, white, starched lace collar.

Groa standing beside Porunn suddenly opened her evening bag and removed a small, white net veil from her purse and slipped it over Porunn's head, the veil fell over Porunn's face to her shoulders. She glanced quickly at Groa and murmured, "Thank you." Everyone smiled. Sigudur and Rosa stood like they were frozen in ice. Then the minister opened the Bible and began the wedding ceremony. Sigudur felt better when the minister came to the part, "You are now husband and wife." Removing his glasses the minister glanced at the happy groom and bride, then focusing his eyes to the groom he added, "You may now kiss the bride." Lifting the veil up from his wife's face, Sigudur kissed her for the first time.

With their fingers entwined Sigudur and Porunn hurried down the path to the awaiting horse and carriage with Groa and Rosa with her children following closely behind. Sigudur lifted Porunn off the ground and Placed her into the carriage. "Better put your coat on Tóta It's very cold."

"I didn't bring a coat, Sigudur."

"Yes you did. I'm giving it to the horse,' he stated, grabbing the coat from the seat and throwing it over the mare.

"Sigudur!" she cried that's my good coat."

"Not anymore it isn't. You'll find your good coat in that package on the seat. An early wedding present from me. I would have given it to you a long time ago but I knew you would not except a present from just some man." Sigudur opened the box and removed a beautiful camel hair coat and placed it on her shoulders.

"oh, thank you Sigudur. We are married now I can except it." She placed her arms around him and kissed him warmly on the lips.

Giving the horse the signal to start moving the mare refused to go. The animal shook himself all over trying to remove the coat. All at once a bitter, cold wind came to the horses rescue and blew it off. The mare let out a deep sounding 'nay' and began moving briskly down the road. Rosa and family, with

Groa stood and watched the nuptial carriage leave the church and disappear from view. Groa dried her tears with a hand. "Weddings are so sad."

"Oh, yes. and my brother is the youngest and the last of the Haflidasons to marry."

"He waited until your mother . . . and father were gone, didn't he, Rosa?"

"One would think so Groa. but I do not. Sigudur was waiting for the right girl and having a good time in the meantime."

"Well, it certainly worked out well for him. Porunn is a wonderful woman. And like Sigudur always reminds people. 'Tota is not a woman she's an angel.'" Groa wrapped her arms around her chest and shivered. "When is the carriage going to pick us up, Rosa?"

"I asked the driver to have the carriage back in one hour. He should be here anytime."

"Here comes a horse up the road!" cried Jani with his hat in his pocket and his jacket flopping open in the strong wind.

"Jani!" called out Rosa. "Button up your jacket and put your hat back on. You'll catch pneumonia in this blizzard."

All the wedding guests sat quietly and unspoken as their carriage headed for the little gray house in the west.

"Hurry up and open the door, Mamma . . . I'm cold." complained Jani.

"Open it for him, Emily. I'm going over to get Cheko."

CHAPTER FOURTEEN

A week honeymoon in Winnipeg. Porunn and Sigudur were back at Rosa's. Here they would stay until they found a place of their own. Winter had passed, spring was almost over and extremely warm heat from the summer solstice was near.

Sitting on the back screened porch at Rosa's, Porunn and Sigudur sat at a table sipping a cup of coffee, and enjoying ponnukokur's (one of Iceland's national dishes.)

"I appreciate your sister's hospitality, Sigudur, but I am so anxious to get our own place."

"It's tough on Rosa also to have so many people in the house."

"Oh, I know it. And how she finds time to bake these fancy desserts is more than I know."

"She couldn't do it if it were not for your wonderful help."

"Not and working every day . . . and then there is Cheko." Children are a lot of work and responsibility," replied Porunn knitting her brows.

"Excuse me, elskan," said Sigudur standing up from the table and picking up the dishes. "I'm going to give Emily a few more dishes to wash. She could do more around here than she does. Emily is just getting to the lunch dishes and it is almost supper time."

"That's part of raising children. One has to take the bad with the good." Porunn's thoughts wandered to the time when she and Sigudur would have children. It was clear that he believed in unconditional love.

Yes, her husband was a man of distinctive individuality. And although kind and gentle he had strong likes and dislikes which no one could change.

It was now the middle of summer. The heat was unbearable. Sigudur came home from being in town most of the day. Enwreathing Porunn in his arms he kissed her. "It's good to be home. It's hot out there."

Setting a pitcher of cool lemonade on the table, she reached into the cupboard for some glasses and poured them a drink.

"Thank you, Tota. Do we have any ice?"

"No. The ice box is empty. Looks like the ice man isn't coming today."

"It tastes good anyway, may I have more?"

Refilling Sigudur's glass, Porunn examined his features carefully. His face took on an expression of nervousness exhibiting that the man was ready to present a statement.

Picking up the glasses from the table, Porunn began washing the goblets. When Sigudur remained at the table unspoken she averted her eyes from her work. "Well, how did everything go today in Branford? Any luck in finding us a house?"

"Oh, a house . . . I want to talk about that, Tota. You don't have to say yes just to please me, what ever you want I go along with your decision."

"You make it sound complicated. We are just looking for a house."

"Very few houses are for rent. Lots of them for sale. But we should not strap ourselves down until we're sure in making Brandon, Manitoba our permanent home. Ideas change when the children come."

With the mention of children, Porunn took a deep breath remembering her vow to have children. Not just a house where a couple lived together. Yes, Sigudur was keeping his promise of not drinking anymore, and she would have to do the same. Replacing the glasses back to the cupboard, she let out a deep sigh.

"What was that for, Tota? Are you alright? You look so very white today."

"I am always white, Sigudur. I am an Icelander . . . remember?"

"No, you have a pallor, an unnatural white."

"It's the heat, I'm getting a migraine headache."

"Get to bed and rest for awhile." He glanced curiously at her. "I have never known you to have any kind of a headache before. but I have read in the Lögberg paper that migraines are torture . . . and no medications have been found for them," stated Sigudur." "My experience with migraines is that they are definitely caused by psychological problems." Glancing blurry eyed at Sigudur, Porunn stated, "Will you bring me a hot water bottle for my head and neck and pull down the shade," she added in a weak voice, rising and moving into their bedroom. Sigudur's statement was forgotten as Porunn twisted and turned with severe pain in her eyes, head and neck. The new groom came into the room with the hot water bottle and put it gently on his wife' forehead. Her eyes closed as she whispered, "Thank you Sigudur."

It was a long afternoon waiting for Porunn to wakeup from a convulsive sleep. When Rosa and Cheko came in Sigudur began setting the table for supper. "Where is Porunn?" asked Rosa.

"She is in bed with a migraine headache. I never knew that Tota had migraines," said Sigudur with a worried expression on his face.

"It's the first time I knew it. However, one day before you two were married, we were discussing genes. And she casually said she hopped she wouldn't get her mother's gene of migraines. I had never heard her speak her mother's name nor did she ever again, said Rosa. "Her life in Iceland seems to be a closed chapter of her life so who am I to pry?"

"well, i have learned not to inquire about her past When she is ready I am sure she will confide in me."

"Can you think of anything you said to upset Porunn Sigudur?"

"No. I just came in after house hunting in Branford. I told her I wanted to discuss what I accomplished and said what ever she decided would be what we would do."

"That doesn't sound like anything to get upset about.'

"Well, I did mention something about when we would have children."

"Ah! That's it, Sigudur. Children!" replied Rosa.

Morning brought cooler weather, and fresh red roses to the flower beds. Porunn and Sigudur were out doors planting Bleeding hearts. Porunn had recovered from her migraine but was feeling in a weakened condition. "How are you feeling, Tota? Don't you think you should go in and rest awhile?"

"No. I feel fine. The sun feels so good."

'Do you think you feel well enough to hear about my adventure into town yesterday?"

"Of course, Sigudur. I am very anxious to hear what you found. But let's go sit on the back porch where the sun is screened it seems to be getting stronger and my eyes get weak with migraines."

They pulled up some chairs to the table and sat down. Rising, Sigudur moved to the kitchen door. "I'm going to get us some coffee, Tota. I'll be right back." With the coffee cups on the table he kissed Porunn on the back of her neck. "We already mentioned how buying would not be the time now. renting almost impossible with people coming into Manitoba to work the wheat fields." The broker was very helpful. Said this would all change. Of course we can not wait for that. The man informed me of an act which helped immigrants get started in a new land. There is a law called the Homestead

Act of 1862. It's a law that exempts a homestead owner from attachments or sale of payment of the owners debts. Any law giving special privileges to the owner of the homestead. I would say that is a pretty good deal. What do you think Tota? It's your decision."

"I do not know, Sigudur, I did not understand one word of it. Your the educated one, you explain to me."

"I studied ships and the sea, not how to purchase a house."

"What ever you decide, Sigudur is fine with me. I am happy where ever I am with you."

Standing up from the table he pulled her up and drew her in his arms. "I love you, Tota." He glanced into her pale gray eyes. "These homesteads are nothing but a broken down farm. The new owners duty is to work it into an attractive piece of land. It will take time and a lot of work. I believe one is given two years to accomplish this toilsome job. In two years if we have achieved putting the farm like it was when it was new we will be the owners."

Porunn stood up from the table grimacing. "it sounds good, but everything that shines is not gold. How much land will we have?"

"About fifty acres."

"That does not sound like a lot but for one man to work I do not see how he can do it in two years."

"You forget, elskan, I was brought up on one of the richest and largest farms in Iceland."

"I think you are the one who is forgetting Sigudur. You and your father and all the rest of the Haflidi Helgasons were gentlemen farmers. The more unfortunates toiled the fields while your family indulged in luxury." She jumped up from the table, picked up the coffee cups and disappeared into the house.

Shocked at Porunn's behavior he hurried into the kitchen where she was rinsing out the coffee cups. Her face was flushed and she appeared to have a raise in body temperature.

"Tota! What is the matter?" No response.

"Tota! Speak to me. What have I done?"

"You have done plenty!" Sigudur touched her hand affectionately. "Do not touch me!" she screamed.

Confused and broken hearted Sigudur left the room. In her bed Porunn lay staring up in the ceiling. When Sigudur came in she would close her eyes and pretend that she was sleeping.

The hours passed and soon Rosa and Cheko came home. When Sigudur slept on the sofa that night Rosa was very concerned but because she was not an inquisitive person she pretended not to notice.

Morning dawned with prospects of a better day. Sunday breakfast was already on the table as the family gathered to eat.

Sunday was quiet. Rosa had taken all the children to the park. Leaving the living room, Porunn went to Sigudur's and her room to write her sister Sigurun a letter.

The family gathered around the dining room table for Sunday super of a red, baked salmon which Rosa had cooked. "Rosa! I didn't know that you could still cook fish. I was hoping I would never see another fish once I left Iceland. This is delicious . . . best fish I have ever eaten."

"You are just trying to butter me up little brother."

"No, Rosa Sigudur doesn't really like fish," added Porunn to the conversation.

"Thank God!." Whispered Sigudur to himself. "She's forgiven . . . for what I have done . . . whatever it is."

Super was over. Rosa was busy bathing and getting the children ready for school in the morning. Knocking at Porunn's closed door, Sigudur asked. "May I come in, Tota"? She stepped out of the doorway and hugged him affectionately.

"I have been crazy with worry, Tota. What have I done . . . What have I done,?" he pleaded.

"You made me pregnant I am going to have a baby."

"Oh, Tota I am so happy!"

"Well, I am not happy but I guess I will have to make the best of it."

Moving into the bedroom, Sigudur picked Porunn up in his arms and placed her gently on the bed. "Don't move, elskan, I'll be waiting on you now."

"Waiting on me? I am only two months pregnant."

"Yes, from today on. I am sorry that we can not find an Icelandic woman to live with us about a month after the baby comes." Grimacing, Sigudur placed a blanket over her. "Having an English speaking woman will be difficult for you."

"Quite fussing with me, Sigudur. I am not the only woman in the world having a baby."

"No. But you are the only one in the world having my, baby. And I sure hope that it will be a girl."

"No. I want a boy." All of a sudden Porunn scrambled out of bed. "I am sick I have to throw-up," she cried rushing from the room. Upon return she took Sigudur's hand. "Do you mind if I go to bed now. It is early but I feel like resting."

"I will rest with you."

"No, Sigudur, I'd rather rest alone."

His features dowered. "Well, there's a homestead about fifteen miles from here. When the realtor broker took me out here the other day to show me some homesteads I saw a young woman out in the yard planting flowers. I thought nothing of it at the time, but now that a baby is coming I thought this woman might take a housekeeping job for a month or so." He rose from the bed and put on his sheepskin coat. "I think I will go out there and let you rest."

When Sigudur's carriage stopped at the homestead he hoped the woman would be home. Suddenly he saw her come from behind the house with a rake in her hand. Looking alarmed Sigudur cried out to her. "I'm your neighbor, or will be . . . I hope."

She dropped her rake to the ground and came walking to meet him. She offered a hand. "I'm Mr. Martin's daughter."

"So nice to meet you, Ma'am."

"My father owns the farm to speak, and I have lived here since mother died." She glanced at him and smiled. "My name is Clara. And I am so happy we are going to have nice neighbors. The people who lived there before didn't do a thing. Just sat around and drank beer all day."

"That's pretty obvious," replied Sigudur. Extending a hand again, he tipped his hat. "I am Sigudur Haflidason from Iceland. My wife is with child and is expecting the baby in the spring. Do you think you could stay with us for a month or so after the baby comes, Clara? And have you had any experience with newborns?"

Clara laughed. "Oh, yes real newborns. I am the neighborhood midwife."

"Good. That's an excellent reference, Clata. But I have a doctor for the delivery." Knitting his brows he added. "My wife speaks little English . . ."

"No problem, Mr. Haflidason. This section of Brandon farmers are almost all immigrants. We are used to broken English."

"Well, the part that you have blonde hair will make her comfortable with you, Clara."

For a moment she glanced curiously at him. She then burst into laughter. "Oh, I get it! Iceland has mostly blonde or red haired pimple." Clara's features became more serious now. "Yes. Sir, I will except your offer of a job, and thank you."

Arriving home again Sigudur found the house dark in the semi shadowy twilight. When he walked in the vestibule he noted a light under Porunn's door. His heart leaped with joy noting that his wife was waiting up for him. "Are you awake, Tota?" he asked happily, advancing into their chamber.

"Yes, Sigudur. I am happy that you are home." Hanging up his sheepskin coat, he moved to the bed and kissed her. "I found a hired girl for us when the baby comes."

"Found her . . . ?found her where?" asked Porunn sitting up in bed.

"Out at a homestead farm on the outskirts of Brandon." Changing into pajamas he slipped into bed beside her.

"I think Sigudur we should be hunting for a house not a hired girl that we will not need for many months."

"I am real proud of myself, Tota, I found both. Now with a family started we have to have a home. I told the realtor I would be in Monday . . . that's tomorrow to sign the title if i decided.

"I remember you telling me about it but I cannot remember for how long?"

"Two years."

"A lot of hard work for one man."

"Please let me try, elskan."

The next two weeks were busy. Shopping to set up housekeeping was a difficult chore. Summer was almost over which brought cooler weather and some relief to Porunn's delicate condition and threatening migraine headaches. Rosa was of great help. After supper she and Porunn would pack the new household purchases in a box. Breathing in a deep sigh, Rosa stopped packing and placed an arm around Porunn's waist. "I hate to see you and Sigudur leave."

"Not that far, Rosa. Sigudur has already bought a team of horses and a wagon. Soon, Sigudur will get us a small buggy, and we can visit."

"When are you expecting, Porunn?"

"I think sometime in March," replied Porunn placing he hands over her abdomen. Grimacing, she asked, "Am I showing? Oh, I hope not. Being pregnant is so embarrassing, especially in front of men. It is very awkward for a man to be looking at another man's wife who is with child. I better start wearing an apron, that would help some. I've seen pregnant women on the street covered up in a coat on a real hot summer day," stated Porunn seriously.

"I do not know what is happening to the world in 1906. Women have no pride today. And they are getting what they deserve. They certainly are not respected by men like they used to be." agreed Rosa.

Bending over and kissing Porunn on the cheek she whispered softly. "Good night Porunn I am going to bed."

Walking into the kitchen Sigudur smiled happily. "You girls better go to bed." Placing his arms around his wife he guided her from the room.

CHAPTER FIFTEEN

Six months had passed since Sigudur and Porunn had moved into their new home. February came in cold and bitter. Unable to work the hard frozen field Sigudur spent the winter inside painting the rooms. Porunn was very happy with Sigudur's artistic flair and good taste in colors. Striding through the rooms of the homestead she picked up her pace to the kitchen. "Don't forget I want this room white . . . real white."

"But you told me that I could choose the colors."

"All but the kitchen."

"And why is that, elskan?"

"Because I am going to sew some white muslin curtains with small, yellow polka dots. Oh, yes and I am going to make some matching chair pads. Won't that be pretty?" exclaimed Porunn happily.

"A beautiful combination, Tota." His features then dowered. "Tota, have you forgotten that it is March next week. You're not going to have time to do all that sewing before you go into labor."

"Kitchen curtains are very simple. They won't take long. Of course I am going to make several flannel kimonos for the baby first."

"What color, elskan? Maybe pink. Tota?"

"Oh, no, Sigudur. One never dresses a baby under a year old in anything but white."

"Has your material that you ordered from the Mount Gomery catalogue come yet?"

"It came yesterday and it is beautiful! So soft and fluffy. The muslin for the kitchen should be here soon."

"I hope you will like your new sewing machine, Tota. It should be good it's a Singer."

"I will let you know tomorrow."

Sigudur embraced and kissed her gently. "This kiss was for you and the little one."

"You are a good husband, Sigudur and I can see you will be a good father," stated Porunn kissing him on the cheek.

"I wish I could deliver the baby for you, elskan but that's not the way God designed it."

Grimacing, Porunn bit down on her lower lip. "I have to admit it Sigudur I'm afraid!"

"You have me, Tota."

"Will the doctor let you stay with me?"

"No of course not elskan. Men are naturally not allowed in the sick room with his wife. Child birth is a matter of life or death . . . not a sideshow."

"Yes, that's true. And probably I'll be asleep and won't know what is going on anyway."

"I wish it were that easy elskan, but you will not be asleep nor receive any medication. You will be expected to help bring this little life into our world. It will be tough and painful. I hate to scare you Tota. But I just cannot lie to you."

"Oh, why should women have to go through such hell?"

"Someday women will be sedated but that's not going to help you now . . . maybe the next one."

"The next one! No thank you once is enough for me."

"I really think that sedation will be common in several years up the road. There's an anesthetic which was founded in eighteen forty eight. It is called, Trichloremetrane . . . or chloroform." said Sigudur. "Who invented it?" asked Porunn with interest.

"An Englishman named, Sir James Simpson."

"Well then, why can I not have it.?"

"It isn't used much yet."

"It is for pain isn't it Sigudur?"

"Yes, but it is almost priceless it is so expensive and also very dangerous! The anesthesia yields gas which dulls pain and causes unconsciousness . . . very dangerous!"

March came in with brisk, blustering wind. Porunn glanced out of the kitchen window of the homestead and her eyes traveled over the frozen field searching for a sight of Sigudur who was out on the property repairing an old fence. There he was! Dressed in an old jacket he had found in one of the barns. Could this be her Prince of Iceland? He was loosing weight. Gone was his round, healthy attractive features. And what about the field work that faced him for a couple years. She could not let him do this. Walking away from the window a sharp pain pierced her side. Her first thought was to run out and call Sigudur. The pain appeared to be gone. No, it was too early in March. Not her time yet.

As the days slipped by the weather became warmer and taxing on Porunn's health. The days she had migraine headache she would pull the shade down with a hot water bottle at the stem of her neck. Toward the end of March the month refused to give up winter to spring. Sigudur strolling through his field with a heavy stick inserted it into the wet earth to see how frozen the ground was. "Not bad," he told himself anxious to get working the field. All at once he heard Porunn's voice calling. "Sigudur!! Sigudur!!"

"Oh, God that's Tota", he cried dropping the stick and running across the field and into the house.

Opening the door he saw Porunn lying on the floor. "Get the doctor! Quick! Get the doctor! It's coming!" Assisting her to her feet he picked Porunn up and carried her to their room.

Harnessing one of the mares to their small buggy he headed the horse toward the city of Branford. When he approached the outskirts of the busy town he looked carefully for the address Clara had given him. He then spied a small white cottage with a sign in the window reading, "Dr. Morgan" Jumping out of the buggy he tied his horse to a railing on the porch. Sigudur pounded forcibly on the door. No response. After repeating the knock several times a short, middle-aged man with gray hair opened the door. "What's your hurry, son?. You have a very bad temper. Don't you know that's bad for your heart?"

"We have no time for chat-chat, Doctor. My wife is having a baby, probably as we speak. Follow my buggy I live in the homestead vicinity . . . just follow me."

"If this is your wife's first child there is no sense in hurrying. The first baby takes the longest."

Throwing open the door, Sigudur noticed a hat thrown carelessly over a black medical bag on the sofa. Picking up the hat he placed it on the doctor's head. "Come on, were leaving!"

The two buggies clamored up the road in full speed. When they reached the homestead Porunn's cries could be heard from outside. Springing from the buggy, Sigudur walked with leaps into the house. "Tota," he called out, "The doctor is here. I'm going after Clara I will be right back." Exhausted, Porunn had fallen in a comatose sleep.

Advancing to the white and yellow kitchen the physician placed a pot of water on the cooking range. "We'll need to boil some water. What did you say your name was?" he asked, glancing at Sigudur.

"Sigudur Rosenkranz Haflidason . . . from Iceland."

"Are all the people in Iceland as independent as you are, Sig?"

"We are called the independent people. But I just call it honesty. And if you will stop this chit-chat I will go and bring our hired girl. Clara will be of great help. She's a mid-wife."

"A mid-wife, eh? Well then I am going home and get some sleep. You won't need me."

"You will stay here. I hired a doctor not a mid-wife. Clara is our hired girl to take care of the baby when it comes and care for my wife for at least a month." Springing out of the door, Sigudur untied the mare from the hitching post he had constructed and leaped into the buggy.

When Sigudur and Clara entered the barn Porunn's tortured voice could be heard all the way to the house.

When they hurried to the sickroom, Porunn lay on the bed unconscious and still. Sigudur averted his eyes to Clara. "I cannot understand. Her screams have been utterly inhuman. And now she appears to be resting and comfortable."

"What you are seeing here Mr. Haflidason is one of God's miracles which are missed by most people." Sigudur glanced curiously at her. She then continued. "God knew that Mrs. Haflidason's pain was too severe for such a delicate woman. He knew that she needed relief for awhile. This is God's way to give her rest."

Dr. Morgan sat in the kitchen eating some fruit. He rose from his chair and moved into the sickroom. With his stethoscope in his black bag he began taking vital signs. Porunn slept on.

Suddenly Porunn awakened with a blood curdling scream. "Might as well make our selves comfortable folks, we have a long day ahead of us." stated the physician."

Giving Dr. Morgan a distasteful stare, Sigudur asked, "How much longer?"

"These women who are delivering a baby for the first time take as long as fourteen to sixteen hours of labor sometime."

Clara stood at Porunn's bed and wiped the perspiration from Porunn's face and neck. With a large fan which she had brought from home she stood fanning her at long intervals.

The hours dragged but soon it was nine thirty in the evening. Dark shadows flooded the sick room as Sigudur came in. Dr. Morgan snoozed on the sofa, his snores drifting through the rooms.

With pains coming more often and more severe all had happier prospects of the infant coming soon.

The silence did not last. Porunn's cry brought Sigudur to his feet from the easy chair in the chamber to Porunn's bedside. "Oh, "Tota! It will only be a little longer!"

Standing in the doorway Clara, followed by the doctor, entered the sickroom. "You can get out Mr. Haflidason," stated the doctor. "This is no longer a labor room. It is now the delivery."

"I would like to stay," replied Sigudur.

"Get out!" screamed the doctor. "Time is of essence." Moving sluggardly out of the door, Sigudur glanced at Clara.

"Sorry. You have to leave, Mr. Haflidason. Husbands are not allowed in the delivery room. Men should certainly understand, this is very personal time for a women and they have earned it.

Leaving the room, Sigudur glanced at Clara and whispered, "Thanks." Porunn's tortured cry continued, then she fell into a unconscious state.

Dr. Morgan slapped Porunn lightly on the cheek. "No sleeping on the job. You have to stay awake and help deliver this infant." With no response Clara and the physician continued.

Walking aimlessly over the kitchen floor, Sigudur stopped all at once when he thought he heard a baby cry. There it went again! "Oh, my God! It is a baby's voice!"

Clara came in with an infant wrapped in a white soft blanket. "Look what I have for you . . . a beautiful boy!" Sigudur's features clouded. "Yes, he is beautiful. But I was hoping for a girl." Clara placed the infant in Sigudur's arms for a moment. "He's too good-looking for a boy." Clara retrieved the baby from Sigudur's arms. "I have to take him back to the sickroom. Don't worry Mr. Haflidason you will be seeing plenty of this little fellow at night when you and Mrs. Haflidason want to sleep."

Peeking gently into the blanket to look at the baby again, Sigudur rested his eyes on Clara's features. "May I go in and see my wife now?"

"Only for a couple of minutes, sir. Mrs. Haflidason is very tired and weak. She will probably sleep the whole night."

"Thank you, Clara. You will mind the baby?"

"yes. I'm settled in the room across the hall. And I'm going to keep the baby's cradle in my room for tonight . . . and of course keep your wife's and my door ajar also in case she awakens."

"Goodnight, Clara."

Little Johann was now one month old. He was an especially beautiful child with set-in navy-blue eyes and long eyelashes sweeping his cheeks.

When Sigudur came into the chamber, Johann lay nursing at Porunn's breast. He bent over the bed and kissed Porunn, then the baby. "Oh, Sigudur! I love him so much!" exclaimed Porunn.

"Smiling, Sigudur sat down on the edge of the bed. "Tell me something, Tota. Shall we trade our son in for a writing career?" he asked her teasingly"

Porunn smiled weakly. "Not for all the money in the world. Johann is worth all the pain I suffered, but I would never go through it again."

"Sorry elskan, you owe me one."

"Owe you one?

"Yes, a girl . . . at least one."

May brought flowers and the bright sunshine brought warmth to their hearts. Never had Porunn been so happy. She spent hours rocking Johann in the rocking chair which Sigudur had bought at Porunn's request. Each night she would rock Johann to sleep for the night. Sigudur accused her of spoiling the baby which she never paid any attention to. Yet, through all Porunn's new found happiness, she worried about Sigudur's health. He was now out in the field working eight and nine hours a day. Coming in from the field in the evening his steps were slow and sluggish. Large beads of sweat flooded his face and neck. When he greeted her she noticed that his enthusiasm was gone. Porunn ran to the door and opened it when she saw him approaching the kitchen. "You are just in time for supper, Sigudur," said Porunn forcing an amicable smile.

"Thank you Tota but I am not hungry. I think I will just go to bed."

"Don't do this to me Sigudur. I worked hard in making your favorite dish."

"What favorite dish . . . fish?"

"No. Sauðakjöt." (mutton)

Drying his face on a towel, Sigudur drew her in his arms. "I'm sorry Tota, I am so tired! Let's sit down and eat before the baby wakes up for his feeding."

Six months had passed. Johann could sit up now if braced with a pillow. Yes, he was growing fast and loved more each day. Sitting in his crib he held a new white and blue rattle in his tiny hand. "Look how smart he is Sigudur. He dropped his rattle and picked it up again," exclaimed Porunn. Sigudur observed with interest. Sliding down in his crib The little boy closed his eyes.

"What is Johann doing that for?" asked Sigudur approaching the crib with Porunn closely behind.

"I don't think Johann feels well, Sigudur. Last night he coughed several times which I have never heard him do. Oh, Sigudur we have to get the doctor!"

"Calm yourself, elskan. I think he will be alright. We must keep a close watch on him."

"I would feel much better, Sigudur if Dr. Morgan would take a look at him."

"Alright, Tota I'll go into Branford and ask him to come out here as soon as he can."

Two days passed. The infant lay in Porunn's and Sigudur's bed Lethargic and with fevered brows the little boys' shallow breathing was barley audible. "I'm going in Branford and bring that quack back by the hair . . . except he doesn't have any," stated Sigudur hurrying out to the barn. In a short time Porunn saw Sigudur ride past the window on horseback in full speed to Branford.

As Porunn waited for the doctor she was certain that the physician had not been in, that Sigudur was waiting for him. Picking up Johann in her arms she rocked him in the rocker. His muffled cries continued. She then put him to her breast and the infant with closed eyes contentedly began to eat. Afraid to awaken him she kept him to her breast and waited.

It was almost noon when she heard a horse prance past the kitchen window and she knew that Sigudur had come home. "I hope this won't take too long, Mr. Haflidason. I have a baby to deliver today. The woman's seventh offspring. This one should come in no time." stated Dr. Morgan, throwing his medical bag on the floor.

Porunn stood up from the rocker. "I think the baby is more comfortable. But I appreciate your coming Dr. Morgan."

Porunn placed the baby into the crib and the doctor picked up his medical bag from the floor and began taking vital signs with his stethoscope. Throwing his stethoscope into the bag he glanced at Porunn. "More comfortable . . . eh? He averted himself toward Sigudur. "Your little son has pneumonia."

"Oh, my God! Sigudur!" she cried taking her husband's hand.

"You must have something with you to give him." said Sigudur.

"Nothing potent enough for pneumonia. But I can give your wife some advise. Take the baby off breast feeding. a bottle of milk will be just as good."

Dr. Morgan was gone. Dark ghostly shadows draped the homestead. Johann slept most of the day. After three days the child became more listless and unaware of his parents and environment. Porunn sat in the rocker with

Johann in her arms, She held up his bottle of milk. "He hasn't touched it," she said grimly."

Sigudur took the bottle from Porunn's hand. "He cannot live without eating." Removing his sheepskin coat from the closet he hurried into his wrap. "I'm going into Brandon, Tota. I'll be back as soon as I can."

Understanding his errand she nodded her assent and pressed the baby close to her heart.

After several hours had elapsed, Porunn would run to the window to see if there was any sigh of Sigudur and the physician.

The day was waning. It was now almost dark. Suddenly the back door opened and Sigudur leaped in, the physician following far behind. "I'm sorry I was so long Tota. But there was not anything else I could do . . . is Johann any better? Where is he?"

Porunn shook her head. "I have him in our room."

Sigudur and Dr. Morgan stood by the large bed as the doctor took vital signs. Dr. Morgan then threw his stethoscope down on the bed. "Your little son just expired . . . I'm sorry, exclaimed Dr. Morgan picking up his stethoscope.

"You are sorry! You killed our son! Murderer! Murderer! Weaning an infant from breast milk. Get out!"

Coming into the death room, Porunn glanced at her baby. "Johann is not . . . is he.?" She asked resting her eyes on Dr. Morgan scrambling for his hat. "Your little son expired a few minutes ago."

"What is expired? What does it mean."

"It means dead." Dropping into the rocking chair, Porunn placed her head on the back of the rocker and closed her eyes. She was definitely in a catatonic phase. "Tota!" called out Sigudur. "Tota!" he repeated. With no response he picked up a blanket off the sofa and spread it over his wife's unconscious body. Staring at Porunn's pallid features, he was remembering Johann's birth. When Porunn could not endure anymore, God had his way to give her rest. God was being merciful again. She was no longer subjected to conscious control. Porunn had now entered the seat of repression the impelling force of libido.

Opening her eyes the following day Porunn came back to the real world. "I have taken care of everything, elskan," stated Sigudur.

Porunn took in a deep breath. "It is a good thing we had Johann christened."

"Yes, no one knows what can happen," replied Sigudur.

Dawn was breaking. Pellets of rain flooded the earth. Streaks of lightening flashed across the horizon. Dressed in dark clothing, Porunn and Sigudur boarded their small buggy and the horse headed for the small churchyard behind the Lutheran chapel built recently for the homeowners of the homesteads. Already in the center of the cemetery Rosa, Groa and children stood under one umbrella in the dripping rain. Groa moved over to Porunn and kissed her. "Oh, Porunn, I am so sorry!" she cried, breaking into a convulsive sob. Hugging Sigudur, Rosa caught her breath in a spasmodic contraction.

When the tiny casket was placed in front of the minister Porunn closed her eyes and muttered a short prayer. Suddenly an ample quantity of rain poured from the sky into the open casket. The minister recited the famous words: "Ashes to Ashes . . . dust to dust." Sigudur thought to himself. "Here comes the painful part." The coffin was picked up to bury in the ground. As the casket started sinking into the earth Porunn seemed to defrost. "Wait!" she cried out running to the coffin and tearing off a genuine silver plaque reading . . . JOHANN attached to the side. She dropped it in her purse. At home she put it where she held her worldly possessions. Johann's plaque remained there her whole existence.

Life was now very lonely and empty. Like a couple living together as they used to say, not a family.

Summer was here. The extreme heat was taxing to Sigudur's health. When he came from Iceland and married he weighed one hundred and sixty pounds. Now, one hundred and twenty. Leaving the field early Sigudur dragged himself into the house.

"Is that you, Sigudur? You are early."

"Yes elskan. Is supper ready?" he asked, hyperventilating at intervals.

"Just about. I knew you could not stay out long today," replied Porunn.

"Beside the heat outside I want to talk to you about something. Please don't hold what I have decided against me, Tota. I love you and I know how hard we both have worked at the homestead. But I must leave here," he stated firmly.

"You don't think that I see you come in at sundown every day exhausted and barley walking. Oh, God, Sigudur! What do I care about material things. And as I have always said, as long as I am with you I am happy."

Moving to her side Sigudur took her in his arms. "Thank you, Tota. You are wonderful."

At the supper table Sigudur glanced over the rim of his coffee cup. "I am going to Winnipeg in the morning. On horseback will be quicker."

"Where is Winnipeg I have often heard it mentioned."

"Winnipeg is the capital of Manitoba. It is a very active city. In fact, we get the Löberg newspaper in Iceland mailed to us from Winnipeg."

"I know I will come back with a job, Tota. Not a fancy job but a job." He kissed her tenderly. "You are a wonderful wife and I love you dearly." He glanced sheepishly at her. "You were right, Tota, I am not a farmer . . . Nor was my father we were gentlemen farmers while our laborers did our work."

Morning dawned. Sigudur leaped out of bed and dressed hurriedly to get on his way to Winnipeg. Barley eating breakfast he put on his best suit jacket in case he would be fortunate enough to get an interview for a job. Porunn awakened as she heard a horse gallop past the bedroom chamber window. She felt lonely with Sigudur gone. She knew she could never let her husband recede from her life.

After eating breakfast Porunn sat down at the Singer sewing machine and began to stitch some flannel sheets for next winter.

It was now midnight. Sigudur had not come home. Running to the window to see if she could see him coming she then disappointedly returned to bed. Involuntarily she fell in a deep sleep.

At three a.m. Sigudur's horse galloped into the barn.

He tiptoed into the bedroom and after undressing slipped carefully into bed beside her so as not to awaken her. To himself he thought: 'Tota is not a woman . . . she's an angel.'

Awakening early Porunn glanced over at her husband. Yes he was awake also. Both too excited to sleep they arose out of bed and went to the kitchen for breakfast. "Did you get a job, Sigudur?" inquired Porunn.

"Yes elskan and a pretty good one I think . . . I hope. There is a large feed store in Winnipeg and the man who owns it is retiring and going to Europe to live. He does not want to go out of business because it is doing too well and he needs the money to live on in Europe."

"What will you be doing?"

"He offered me to take over his job as manager. I think he was very impressed with my education at the academy in Reykjavik. He said I should go back to Iceland where I had prestige."

"I am very proud of you, Sigudur. You go after what you want and usually get it." Beginning to wash the dishes Porunn looked askance at him. "What about a house?"

"I found a rented house and placed a down payment on it. It's located in town. I hope you will like it. If not we can find another one. But I do not want to loose this job so I think we had better get packing."

"Hadn't you better sell the wagon . . . just keep the buggy?"

"No elskan, I am going to get rid of the buggy. We need the wagon to transfer our belongings to Winnipeg. You have your sewing machine and we have quite a lot of furniture now. There will be things you will have to leave, Tota. I am sorry elskan. The wagon only holds so much. I have to be on the job in two weeks."

One week had gone by. Porunn stood at the kitchen table wrapping dishes in newspaper and putting them into a box.

Sigudur coming in from the wagon for another box, picked up the container then placed the box back on the table. "You are taking too much, Tota. You will have to leave the rest of the dishes . . . only the essentials."

"But I just love these dishes, Sigudur."

"The Montgomery Ward catalog has a lot of them," he replied, picking up Porunn's sewing machine and proceeding to the wagon.

Returning to the kitchen Sigudur took off his sweater. "It is going to be hot today. Let's have some coffee. We have another week here so we will have to take the rest with us when we leave."

Placing two cups on the table Porunn poured the coffee and sat down. "This is really going to be a hot day. Fine thing for a migraine."

Another busy week passed by. The following Monday Sigudur was starting his first day as manager of the large feed store in Winnipeg.

CHAPTER SIXTEEN

The long journey to Winnipeg was over. Porunn was delighted with the house and right away began placing things in the correct places. Sigudur was outdoors in the horse stall feeding the mare. Upon returning to the house his eyes traveled through the small five room house. "It looks like home already, Tota," he exclaimed. "But where ever you are, elskan is home to me."

Six months passed. Sigudur was happy with his job and the establishment was pleased with their new manager. He often spent a lot of his own time out at a customer's home helping the customer with something he did not understand. Sigudur was always the first one to give assistance.

Autumn came in fresh and balmy. Sitting one evening on the veranda drinking lemonade. Porunn feeling extra warm slipped off her sweater.

"Better put that sweater back on Tota. It's not that warm yet," stated Sigudur slipping her sweater back on for her.

Picking up the Lögberg newspaper she fanned herself. "I found out yesterday why I get these flashes of heat. Now I'm with child again."

"Pregnant? Oh, my God, Tota! I'm so sorry!"

She looked curiously at him. "You mean you do not want anymore children?"

"Not at your expense. Not even for a little girl," he added.

"I will love which ever God wants me to have," said Porunn. When a star burst in the sky Porunn arose from her chair. "My the heavens look so magical. Winnipeg is a beautiful town. With grain being the chief product here the countryside must be lovely."

"Yes lovely to look at, not so lovely to work in the fields . . . . How far along do you think you are in your pregnancy, Tota?" asked Sigudur.

"Not far. We probably have until spring." Grimacing, Sigudur left the veranda and went indoors.

The winter came in cold and bitter. Porunn's pregnancy was taxing on her health forcing her to spend many hours in bed resting offering little conversation. However, the days went by and it was now spring. Tiny blossoms could be seen hopping up here and there and homeowners were planting flowers in their gardens and flowerbeds, the temperature was coming in higher degrees. Porunn and Sigudur sat at the kitchen table eating breakfast. Sigudur reached across the table and took Porunn's hand. "I have something to tell you and I do not want you to get up set or do anything you don't want to do."

Glancing at him she looked at him closely.

Clearing his throat, Sigurdur's features became serious and she knew he was about to present a serious statement. "Tota, if our baby should happen to be a girl, you said you would name her Groa . . ."

"Yes. Groa was a wonderful friend to me when I first came to this strange land," interrupted Porunn placing her cup down on the table.

"I agreed with you. Groa is a wonderful person and it's a lovely name. But I must tell you, we cannot name this baby Groa." He rose and brought a hot cup of coffee to the table and sat down again. "Tota, my dead mother came to me last night in my dream. I saw her so clearly. She stood under a large naked tree with long spiderlike branches. Then my mother called out to me. "Sigudur! Do not name the baby Groa!" She then faded away from my sight."

"We have to abide with our dreams. As an Icelander you know that. Your mother's name is Johanna, is it not?" asked Porunn.

"Yes.

"If the child is a girl we shall name her Johanna after your mother Johanna." added Porunn. Sigudur smiled his appreciation.

On May 22nd 1908 after hours of agony and pain Porunn gave birth to a beautiful baby girl. Sigudur was elated beyond reasoning. After the hired girl had gone home Sigudur would hurry home from work to hold and rock the infant to sleep. Porunn was still too weak to get out of bed except for short intervals. Time passed and she was now feeling stronger. She picked up Johanna and sat down in the rocking chair to breast feed the infant until she would awaken for her 2 am feeding. Arrangements for the child's christening had been made for the following Sunday at the St. Paul's Lutheran church.

The years passed. Little Johannz was now two years old. Sigudur was not working this weekend so was taking Johanna into the city for some shopping. Dressing Johanna in a pale green dress the child glimpsed into the mirror on the wall. "Take it off, mamma. pabbi does not like this dress."

Porunn looked askance at the two year old. "Did he say he did not like it?"

"No! I just know he doesn't like it," replied the two-year-old in baby talk.

"Leave it on Johanna until he comes in and we'll ask him."

"No, mamma. I want to wear my pink dress that pabbi bought for me. you bought this one," she cried pulling the dress off a shoulder.

Opening the closet door, Porunn took a pink dress from the hanger and assisted the child into the frock. Sigudur came smiling into the room. "My, doesn't my blonde princess look beautiful!" When Porunn did not reply Sigudur figured the two year old and the mother must of had some words. But who could talk against such a beautiful small child? Having ordered a carriage for the occasion, Porunn glanced out of the window. "Your carriage is here, Sigudur."

"Goodbye, Tota," said Sigudur kissing her quickly on the lips.

The quietude of the atmosphere felt good, She slipped into bed and fell into an unrested slumber. Still asleep when Sigudur and Johanna came home they looked for her in the chamber.

"Mamma! Mamma!" cried Johanna. "Look what pabbi bought for me." She held up a small gold mesh handbag which she had twisted on her wrist by a long gold chain. "Isn't it beautiful?"

"Yes, Johanna it is lovely."

Taking her father's hand she looked up at him with her pretty bluish-green eyes. "Come and read me a story, pabbi."

"I cannot read English very well but I'm learning."

"When I go to school, pabbi I will teach you," said Johanna

"That will be a long time, elskan. You are only two. In Iceland children are not allowed to attend school until they are nine. It's probably the same here."

Porunn smiled. "And don't forget, Sigudur, Children have to learn how to swim, read, and write before they can enter first grade."

Johanna made a face. "We are not talking to you, mamma. Pabbi and I are talking."

"I'll go make supper," said Porunn quietly. As she prepared their meal she was getting up enough courage to tell Sigudur that she was pregnant again.

Well, another day won't matter. "Supper is ready," she called out to her little family. Sigudur slipped a couple cushions on to a chair and placed Johanna down to eat. She now refused to sit in her high chair, that high chairs were for babies. "There will be another baby soon who will need a high chair. We'll save it until then, Johanna," said Porunn.

"Baby . . . ? We don't have any baby." said Johanna wrinkling up her nose at her mother.

"We are getting a brother or sister for you to play with. It isn't good to have only one child." stated Sigudur, aware that Porunn's conversation was meant for him.

Standing up from the table he moved to Porunn's chair and kissed her. "Oh, Tota! You don't know how happy I am. When are you expecting, elskan?"

"I think in the middle of August."

"I hope when you go into labor this one won't take so long." said Sigudur.

Spring turned into summer. Johanna was a delightful child. Porunn took time from her busy schedule to fix Johanna's beautiful blonde hair into long curls. "Sit here, Hanna," said Porunn lifting Johanna up on the cushioned chair. "No, mamma. I don't want any curls to day."

"Alright, Hanna how shall I comb it?"

"I'll just let it hang." Johanna climbed down off the chair and ran outdoors to the horse stall where Sigudur was feeding the mare. After a few moments passed Porunn heard Johanna's voice crying. She glanced out of the window and saw Sigudur holding Johanna by the hand coming toward the house. "Tota! he cried. "What have you done to Hanna's hair?" he shouted entering the kitchen.

"Nothing!"

"Nothing is right. She tells me she asked you to put her hair in curls as always, that you refused to do it. You can see Hanna is not lying, the proof is right in front of you."

"Yes, true I did not curl her hair because Hanna asked me not to." Enraged, Porunn paced the floor. "She is lying, Sigudur. I have nothing more to say . . . Hanna is lying."

Summer solstice was waning. Taking notice to the changes in nature, the birds and all the small creatures began to hunt and store food for the cold bitter winter ahead. Sigudur came home from work with a downcast expression on his face. Opening the icebox he glanced over his shoulder as Porunn came into the kitchen. "Where is all the ice? Didn't the iceman deliver any ice?"

"No, he didn't come today." she replied quietly.

"Pabbi . . . pabbi!" screamed Johanna leaping into her father" open arms.

Although exhausted from working long hours Sigudur could not sleep. How he dreaded telling Porunn that he had lost his job . . . and with another member of the family added. Well, tomorrow was his last day, he would have to let her know by then. He placed his arm around her waist and closed his eyes. Porunn raised herself up on one elbow. "I'm awake, Sigudur. I cannot sleep when I detect there is something bothering you."

"It can wait until tomorrow, Tota."

"No, I want to hear the bad news tonight."

"Alright elskan. I lost my job. And now we have another member of the family to worry about."

"God will see us through." She slid down in bed. "Good night, Sigudur." In the darkness he stared into the night. What could he do? Look for another job of course. In Manitoba . . . ? No, he would move to Saskatchewan which has been a Province of Canada since 1905 and is also the capital of Canada. Feeling better now his tired eyes began to close and he fell into a deep repose.

Morning dawned with new hopes for the future. Sitting at the breakfast table Sigudur asked, "Is Hanna still asleep?"

"Yes. Let her sleep. It would be nice if I could get a word in once in awhile."

"So you are picking on the poor child. Hanna told me you were."

"There is a big difference in picking on someone and discipline. Something you apparently do not believe in."

Pulling his watch out of his vest pocket Sigudur pushed his chair back from the table. "Time for me to go to work, Tota. Try to get plenty of rest today."

"I cannot rest until I have heard why you lost your job," replied Porunn remaining at the table.

"Oh, it wasn't my fault. The owner of the feed store is coming out of retirement already. He doesn't like living in Europe and he needs something to do."

"Well, it is his store." She glanced proudly at him. "I just knew you had never done anything. Goodbye, Sigudur Don't be late on your last day."

Porunn spent the day packing their essentials in boxes for Sigudur to take out to the buggy. The wagon was sold due to no barn and only one horse stall. The second set of Montgomery Ward dishes were left behind much to Porunn's dismay.

"Let's get going Tota. I want to get to Holar before the real estate offices close."

"We cannot make it that fast, Sigudur. Saskatchewan is just too far. We better get a room for tonight and hunt for a house to rent tomorrow." Porunn locked the house up for the last time with a painful heart. "Where is Hanna?" asked Porunn?"

"She is already in the waiting for us." replied Sigudur laughing.

"How did she get into the buggy herself?" questioned Porunn?"

"She didn't. I lifted her up into the seat. Hanna refused to get in the back. So I figured it wouldn't do any harm until we came out." Sigudur opened the rear door of the buggy. "Come on Hannah, you're going to ride in the back seat." he picked her up screaming and crying. "Your mother rides with me," he stated firmly. lifting Porunn up in his arms and placing her down on the front seat beside him. When the buggy began slowly moving, Johanna jumped up and stood up behind her father and placed her small arms around his neck. "Pabbi you always take mamma's side You love mamma more than you love me."

Glancing back over the front seat Porunn turned and looked at Johanna with a long drawn out expression. "Sit down Hanna and behave yourself."

The first town they came to was called Holar. Tired and worn, Sigudur decided to make their home here. It was a small town, moreover appeared to be very active for it's size. "Whoa!" he called out to the exhausted horse. Before going into the rooming house Porunn took a piece of cube sugar and put it in the mare's mouth. "After we get settled Tota I will look after the mare."

This time Sigudur bought a small cottage with a nice yard for Johanna to play in. There was a small stable and a woodshed on the property. He found work in a large boat company as foreman. And the nature of the job dealing with old ships and boats, he adjusted to his new work in no time.

Sitting on the veranda one warm evening, Porunn fanned the perspiration from her brows with the Lögberg newspaper. She then rested her eyes on Sigudur's serious expression as he came out for a drink of lemonade. "This month of August is almost gone." stated Sigudur.

"Yes. Has your dead mother come back again in your dreams?"

"No, Tota. If it is a girl we will be safe to name the infant Groa."

Smiling pleasingly, Porunn touched him gently on the arm. "You probably would like another girl".

"I would love a whole house of them."

On August 18, 1910 another beautiful blonde girl was born.

Sigudur picked up the infant and kissed her. He then placed Groa on her mother's breast where an infant does not need to be shown the duties of a mother. Nature provides all instructions. Nature does not change . . . man changes many things.

The years rolled by. Johanna idolized Groa. And although Johanna would not assist Porunn in the house she made the work for Porunn ever so much lighter looking after Groa. Porunn had great faith in Johanna's gentle, patient care. Johanna was extremely matured for her age. However the beautiful little girl continued to be a threat to Porunn's marriage with Johanna's complaints to her father that her mother was picking on her when ever Porunn had to correct her His answer to Porunn was 'Well, Hanna has been known to stretch the truth to fit her gain when she has to, but there is always two sides to every story,' would be his answer.

Two years past. Groa was now walking and getting a lot of help from Johanna who was almost five years old now.

Summer was fading and in October, Porunn was expecting another child. Sigudur came in from work and kissed Porunn affectionately. "It is the first of September next week. October is almost here. What if the new baby is another girl? You said you wanted to name this child after an old man who was good to you when you were a child."

"Yes . . . Gudmundur. If it is another girl I will call her Gudmundina after him."

"We are all set with names then?" Smiling Porunn nodded.

October blew in with a strong gale. The days rolled by. On October 16, 1912 Sigudur was presented with a beautiful blonde girl. Sigudur came into the room and sat on the edge of Porunn's bed. "Three beautiful girls and all blonde." Encircling Porunn in his arms he kissed her gently. "Looks like I am getting my house full of girls After all. You've made me a proud man Tota. I know how hard it has been for you and you never complain."

"I hope this is the last one," she mumbled in ejaculated phrases. The hired girl came into the chamber. "You will have to leave the room Mr. Haflidason. Your wife is falling asleep she is much too exhausted to respond to you."

A month passed. The hired girl had left. Johanna was delighted with her new charge. Porunn forbade Johanna to left or carry the infant yet. She could drop the baby and injure Gudmundina for life. With her father excepting this rule Johanna was satisfied. It was a happy little family. Porunn spent hours at the sewing machine making dresses for her three girls. Johanna asked her mother not to make her dress like Gudmundina's and Groa's. For they were babies, so Porunn made her a plain white pleated skirt with a long, white jacket and a navy blue, sailor collar and red tie.

Porunn was now up and enjoying normal health. Sigudur and Porunn lay in bed discussing the girls and their future. Looking firmly at her husband she uttered. "Three children are enough."

"I'm sure that's not your decision, elskan."

"You are right, Sigudur. It is yours."

"No, not mine . . . God's."

"Don't fluff it off on God. You are like all of the men you're all too selfish to use the practice of abstinence."

"I have never heard you so bitter, Tota."

"I am just getting all worn out, I suppose." exclaimed Porunn tearfully.

"You are still young and beautiful, Tota . . . one or two more girls ought to do it," he said teasingly kissing her

Coming home from work the following day, Sigudur went directly to his chest of drawers in the chamber. Returning to the kitchen he held up a small package. "Hanna's birthday present. Today is the twenty second of May you know . . . Hanna's birthday."

"Yes, I know. I baked her a cake," replied Porunn.

"I saw the girls in the back yard when I came in. I think I will go out and bring them in."

"No, Hanna knows when she wants to bring them in."

She looked askance at her husband. "Aren't you going to show me what we got for Hanna's birthday? . . . I hope you included me on the gift."

"Oh, yes. You can see it when she receives the bracelet."

"Why are you so secretive? It's just a bracelet, Sigudur, actually I bought myself one the other day at the five and dime store for only ninety nine cents. I love it."

"We Haflidasons do not buy junk. The bracelet is fourteen karat gold with a small diamond and a ruby in the center," stated Sigudur with a wry face.

"Don't you think Johanna is a little young for expensive jewelry?"

All at once a scramble of little feet could be heard on the back porch. Running to the chamber with the bracelet he whispered over his shoulder. "I don't want Hanna to see it yet, I want it to be a surprise."

After a special meal and a pink strawberry birthday cake, the treasured bracelet was given. "Oh, pabbi, did you buy it for me? It is so beautiful and expensive looking. I don't like the one mamma bought for herself it looks cheap."

"This bracelet is from both your mother and me."

"But you bought it." Porunn arose and collected the dishes.

Gudmundina was now one year old. She was a beautiful child, however appeared very cold. She loved her sisters but always remained a little distance from them. at the table for meals she always pulled her chair away from the chair next to her and would remark. "I do not like anyone sitting so close to me." Then she would slide her chair where there was more room. Gudmundina adored her mother and spent a lot of time with Porunn when everyone else was outdoors.

Coming home from work one late afternoon, Sigudur was confronted with Johanna crying. She told her father that the little girl next door had stolen her bracelet. In full speed Sigudur threw his lunch pail down on the ground and hopped over the fence. After pounding on the neighbor's door a middle aged man opened the vestibule entrance. "Yes?"

"Your young daughter today stole my little girl's gold bracelet."

"Not my daughter. She wouldn't do that." Coming to the door his little girl held the bracelet up by the chain. "Take your old bracelet."

"Thank you. And thank you for being so honest. You must take after your mother," stated Sigudur leaving the premises.

With a fresh cool breeze blowing in from the open window, Johanna seated the girls around the table for breakfast. Gudmundina being the baby of the family now was still in a highchair beside her mother. Johanna's eyes rested on Groa eating an egg. "Groa!" exclaimed Johanna, "Use your fork, not your spoon. Only babies use a spoon."

Groa leaped off the chair and ran crying to her mother. "Mamma, I'm not a baby! I'm not a baby . . . am I mamma?"

Porunn pulled Groa up on her lap and kissed her. "No you are not a baby you eat by yourself very well. And Hanna used to use a spoon too when she was only two like you. Now, go back and finish your breakfast elskan." (love) Porunn's eyes traveled to Johanna. "And hereafter, Hanna try to remember that you do not discipline the children when I am present." Johanna jumped up from her chair and moved to Sigudur's side. "See, Pabbi, how mamma picks on me.?"

"You go back and finish your breakfast, Hanna." With a grim face Johanna gave her father a cold stare and returned to her place setting. Porunn noting that Groa was still eating with her fork and with a struggle she removed the fork from the child's tiny hand. "You are not ready for a fork yet. Use your spoon." Groa smiled her appreciation.

Sigudur took in a deep long breath. "Now if I can get a word in with all you women complaining I would like to let you know we are leaving this country . . . eight years is long enough. Are you with me, girls . . . ?" Although they did not know what they were agreeing to their little heads nodded. Porunn already having received the news smiled at her happy family. She was reluctant to make this big change but wives never had much to say in important matters.

Sigudur glanced at Porunn's disinterested features. "We have an appointment with immigration tomorrow at ten a.m."

"Can't just you go and sign the papers or whatever?" asked Porunn.

"It's not that easy, Tota. Coming into another country is not child's play. It is serious business. Immigration wants to see every face and probably take pictures."

"I'll help you get the girls ready, mamma," chimed in Johanna.

"Thank you, Hanna" replied Porunn patting affectionately her daughter's arm.

On the following morning Sigudur and his family arrived at the Immigration Headquarters. Sitting in the office at a large mahogany desk was an immigration official. "Do you people have an appointment with me?" he asked espying over his spectacles.

Sigudur rose and approached the desk. "Oh, yes, sir. At ten o'clock, sir." Glancing over at the mahogany bench against the wall with Porunn and her family sitting nervously, the officer glued his eyes on each face. "Are you with these people, Mr. Haflidason?"

"Oh, yes, sir. This is my wife Porunn Olafsdottir and daughters." replied Sigudur proudly.

"You certainly have a beautiful family. And all girls except one." added the officer. "Which one is the boy?" I don't believe in long haired boys.".

"We have all girls now. Our first child over eight years ago was a boy. He expired from pneumonia in Manitoba," replied Sigudur.

Hunting through a stack of papers the officer pulled out a document from Sigudur's file. He scanned the paper then glanced up at Sigudur. "Something is wrong. It says here that you have three daughters and one son, Olaf."

Porunn hopped off the bench and moved to the officer's desk. Gudmundina started climbing off the bench and following her mother. Johanna's alert mind held Gudmundina down and sat back on the bench.

"I beg your pardon sir. I believe I understand the mistake that has been made here," interrupted Porunn nervously.

"What would you know about mistakes in this office?"

"Well, sir, as you know my husband and I do not speak very good English. When my husband gave all our children's names he must have given the officer the name, Olaf which of course is masculine." What the officer did not know was that my husband said her name was Olöf a feminine gender of Olaf. My husband always calls Gudmundina by her middle name, which is Olöf . . . "Not Olaf."

"I am sorry, officer. I forget that names are different in other countries," stated Sigudur.

"I have heard a lot of names in this kind of a business but you Icelanders have the most Godforsaken names I have ever heard." You and this lady are married I hope. After all you have three children," he stated suspiciously. "So, what are your children's last names?"

"Let me explain to you, officer. You see in Iceland when a woman marries she never takes her husband's name. She keeps her blood name her whole life. This way she does not loose her identity. And when their children are born the children take the father's first name and add to it dottir or son. My father's first name was Haflidi I added son. Had I been a female child I would have added dottir to my father's first name." (dottir-daughter Sigudur smiled amicably up at the officer. "It's as simple as that."

"Simple! Oh, my God! I don't want to hear anymore." Stacking his papers in a neat pile on his desk he glanced at Sigudur, "Now, where in the United States do you want to visit?"

"Oh, this is not a vacation, officer. We are moving to the United States."

"I see. you and your family are going to be permanent residents. Well, I am going to have to make a few changes on your immigration papers. On your way out a clerk will take all your finger prints . . . it won't hurt it only takes a second." He rose from his desk and shook Sigudur's hand. "Good luck to you and your beautiful little family. You will receive your permission pass in about a week after everything has been checked out. If everything is factual that you have told me I will make you a reservation for you and your family on the 9:30 train arriving in the first town across the border . . . the United States of America."

"What is the name of this town, officer ?" asked Sigudur.

"Blaine . . . Blaine Washington."

"How long will all this take, officer ?" asked Sigudur.

"Like I said, Mr. Haflidason, if every thing checks out you should be on that train in two weeks."

Johanna, Groa and Gudmundina hopped up from the bench. "Goodbye!" they called out in unison and slipped out the door, one holding her mother's hand and the other grabbing on to her mother's skirt.

Having lunch at their kitchen table, Porunn glanced up at her husband. "You know Sigudur, I still feel we are making a mistake leaving Canada. We have a nice home now, the girls seem happy and you don't mind your job." Rising and filling her cup with hot coffee, she returned to the table and sat down. "What do you expect to accomplish by tearing up our lives again, Sigudur?"

"My dear Tota, You are not thinking of the future. The United States is where all the opportunities are. As one has always heard said, 'anyone can become a president in the United States Of America.'"

"Oh, yes, and all the streets are paved in gold." added Porunn.

"I am not thinking of gold, Tota, I am thinking of our daughters' future."

"I have not looked at it that way. But that sounds reasonable . . . " She rose and took Gudmundina out of the highchair and put her down on Sigudur's lap. "Here you hold the baby. I'm going to start the dishes." Gudmundina now one year old gurgled and pulled Sigudur's red mustache. "She's such a tiny little thing," said Sigudur kissing the child on the cheek.

"It won't be long until Gudmundina won't be the baby anymore . . . I'm with child."

"What a time! Won't this trip be hard on you, elskan!"

"I'm only a couple of months . . . mostly morning sickness."

"Tomorrow is Saturday. I am going into town and see if I can get a buyer for our house. And I'm going to sell the mare and buggy." said Sigudur placing the baby in her playpen. "Now the furniture, I am going to sell the house furnished and that will take care of that."

"What about your appointment with the photographer, I believe you told me you had an appointment with the photo shop next Monday to have your picture taken with Hanna, Groa and Gudmundina," stated Porunn.

"Oh, Yes, Tota don't let me forget it. Of course Olöf is just a baby so she should still wear white. Don't worry about Hanna she'll choose her own dress and Groa is such a good child she will leave it up to you Tota."

Arriving early at the photo studio Porunn removed her childrens' coats, then pulled a comb from her handbag and re-did their hair for the picture. Sigudur stood dressed up in his expensive tailored made suit from his father's fashionable men's store in Iceland. His red mustache was trimmed and Porunn thought about how handsome Sigudur looked.

Soon a heavy curtain was drawn open and Mr. Bradford the Owner of the studio came out to greet them. "I hear you people are from Iceland. I am from Iceland also." He placed a black sheet over his head, adjusted the camera then came out from under the sheet.

"Mr. Haflidason you can come over here and sit in this chair and Mrs. Haflidason you can stand behind your husband's chair."

"Oh, Mr. Bradford, I am not going to be in the pictures. Just my husband and our girls." She moved to a sofa in front of the studio and sat down. When his eyes returned to the photo shoot he saw Johanna standing beside her father with her hand posed on Sigudur's knee. She was wearing her gold expensive bracelet which Sigudur gave her. Groa who sat quietly by rose when

Mr. Bradford told her to stand on the other side of her father and put her hand on his knee. Groa was wearing a ivory bracelet which matched the white braiding on her brown dress. Gudmundina, age one was in all white and was placed into Sigudur's arms. The baby was not walking yet. She pushed her tiny hand into Sigudur's pocket and left it their during the shoot.

Ten days passed Then one day there was an important letter in the mail box which Johanna said must be their immigration papers. and started opening the letter.

Sigudur grabbed it from Johanna's hand, "This is addressed to me, Hanna . . . not you. You do not open other peoples mail."

The following day Sigudur and his family deboarded a carriage at the railroad station to catch the 9:30 P.M. train for The United States of America.

Excitement imbued the air as the old heavy locomotive labored up the tracks to the railroad station. When the horn blew in loud blows, Groa let go of her mother's hand and ran ahead to her father's side. "Pabbi, what is that noise. It scares me."

Carrying Gudmundina and a shopping bag he glanced down quickly at Groa. "Go back to your mother Groa. That noise is just a train whistle to let us know they are coming."

Now on the train Sigudur took the many bags and threw them up on the rack, then shoved the basket of food under the seat. Sigudur instructed Johanna and Groa to occupy the seat in front of their parents. When Porunn went to the rest room and returned, she found Johanna sitting in her place with Sigudur. "Get out of my seat Johanna . . . Sigudur! tell her!" Porunn exclaimed.

"Hanna is just playing with you, Tota. "That's enough Hanna"

"Gudmundina is heavy on my arm, Hanna. Now move!"

"Why can't you sit with Groa?" argued Johanna. When the train curved around the mountain Johanna stumbled into her assigned seat.

CHAPTER SEVENTEEN

Year Nineteen Thirteen

The long journey was almost over. The family enjoyed their lunch then tried to sleep in their seats as comfortable as possible. Suddenly the locomotive stopped and Sigudur hopped up from his seat and accosted the conductor who was walking down the aisle of the train. "What is the problem, conductor? Why are we stopping here?"

"Nothing to worry about. We had to stop for a cow that was on the track." The train whistle began blowing in short intervals, then started juggling down the tracks once more.

It was almost dusk when the Conductor strolled down the aisle again swinging a loud speaker in his hand. He then started speaking in it and announced: "We are now approaching the United States Of America. Our next stop will be Blaine, Washington . . . the border town between two big nations . . . Canada and the United States Of America"

Scrambling off the train Sigudur and his family walked to the center of the small, quiet town of Blaine Washington. "We will have to find a rooming house for at least one night," informed Sigudur. His eyes focused on to old ill kept buildings. "They don't look too inviting," added Sigudur. "Well, there isn't anything else to choose from and as long as the room is clean."

"It looks like there is no new building in this town." said Porunn.

"They get all the trade with out fancy buildings, being a border town." replied Sigudur. "Actually I think their wise."

"There is something old fashioned about this little town," said Porunn, "I feel at home here." With Sigudur carrying Gudmundina and a large shopping bag Porunn took his arm as they crossed the street to the rooming house.

Several horses, buggies and carriages trotted up the street past them, but the traffic was light.

In a small but very clean room they settled for the night. They all went to bed early and fell into involuntary sleep.

The following morning looked brighter as the sunrise spread it's rays. After dressing they went down stairs to a small restaurant adjoining the rooming house for breakfast. The food was excellent.

Up in their room again Sigudur then left to hunt a real estate office. Porunn exhausted, rested in her bed with Johanna's offer to look after the baby Gudmundina now a year old and Groa promised to help Johanna.

It was four p.m. when Sigudur returned from the real estate broker. He had requested a rented house which was furnished. There was only one who rented with furniture and utilities and that was way out of the town. It was in the Birch Bay area A lovely section and a lovely house.

"It's a beautiful spot with the ocean near by," stated Sigudur.

"We have to be practical Sigudur, You'll be working and it will be much too far even in a horse and buggy to travel to and fro every day," replied Porunn with a heavy weight expression on her face.

"We'll stay another day at the rooming house. Tomorrow there is another house coming on the market. The broker told me if I didn't take the rent out at Birch Bay to come back tomorrow. They have new prospects every day."

"One more day here will not hurt us!" replied Porunn.

Johanna watched out of the window for her father's return from the broker's. When she saw him coming down the walk of the rooming house she ran out to meet him. "Pabbi, did you get us a house?" she asked anxiously.

"Indeed I did. Hanna,"

Everyone was excited and very happy when he told them he had discovered today that there was an Icelandic settlement in Blaine. And it was here where he found a house for them. A house right next door to a middle aged woman from Iceland. Her husband had passed away and her grown son lives with her. His name is Einer Ottson . . . hers Ingibjorg Ottson."

"Can we go now?" asked Johanna."

"No, Hanna. It is too late. We will have our dinner down at the restaurant then go to bed early and get a fresh start tomorrow."

Life was beginning to look up for the Haflidason family.

Ingibjorg was a delight and a helpful neighbor. She and Porunn in no time became close friends. Einer Ottson, Ingibjorg's boy was a well brought up son and helpful also like his mother. Porunn making new curtains for the

kitchen, rose from her sewing machine when she heard a light rap at the back
door. "Oh. Einer come in. I was just about to make some coffee."

"Is Mr. Haflidason home?"

"No, he is out looking for a job." replied Porunn placing the coffee pot
on the cooking range. "Just call my husband Sigudur."

They pulled their chairs up to the kitchen table. then Porunn poured
fresh made coffee into their cups and sat down. "Where do you work, Einer?"
she asked.

"I work where everyone in Blaine seem to work. At the saw mill in town."
He glanced over the rim of his cup. "Funny you should ask that. I came over
to see if Sigudur would care about working there. I have a good track record
over at the mill and I would give him an excellent reference."

"Oh, Thank you Einer. When he comes home I'll have him come and
see you."

Sigudur was informed to go to the Morrison Shingle Mill in down town
Blaine. It was a large corporation, the president's name was Mr. Taylor. He
was a British gentleman. Not very friendly but was honest and just with his
employees. "Be sure to ask for Mr. Taylor and tell him I sent you," stated Einer.
"But be sure you call me, Mr. Ottson. He does. "Oh, yes he's all British."

One afternoon Ingibjorg and Porunn were having coffee and Icelandic
doughnuts. "Ingibjorg I want to tell you that I am with child again."

"That's wonderful, Porunn. Maybe the next one will be A boy."

"Sigudur is very happy about it."

"And you Porunn, would you like a boy or a girl?"

"I do not want anymore children, Ingibjorg. I love my three little girls
very much but I do not want anymore. Childbearing is hard on me. And my
migraine headaches are getting worse."

"How far along are you, Porunn?"

"I believe about seven months."

"Sigudur must be delighted hoping to finally maybe getting a son."

"Strangely enough, Ingibjorg, he still hopes for another girl. What ever
the baby happens to be Sigudur is a wonderful husband and a wonderful
father."

"That helps so much. I had two boys, and then my husband passed away.
Those were difficult years raising two children alone."

Ingibjorg helped herself to another Icelandic doughnut. "These are
really good, Porunn," she exclaimed. She then began to laugh. "Funny thing
happened to my eldest son's wife. My daughter in law is a lovely woman. She
is from Iceland and has red hair which has darkened since she has been in the

States. a year a go she gave birth to a beautiful red hair baby. My daughter-in-law was so upset and ashamed of the baby's hair that she crotchet a white cap for the baby to wear all day so nobody would know she had red hair. When she took her to the photographer she told with him to leave the cap on. I feel so sorry for the child when we have a warm season." The two women began to laugh and helped themselves to some more hot coffee.

April 11, 1914 . . . Rain pelted the earth, filling the atmosphere with gloom. Then the sun came out and warmed the yellow daffodils with sun. Outside the chamber window a small baby wren broke into a song where Sigudur and Porunn were sleeping. Suddenly Porunn raised up in bed and let out a blood curdling scream. Oh, my God, Sigudur! The baby is coming! Quick! Get the doctor!"

Sigudur springing out of bed pulled on his trousers and harnessed the horse to the buggy and headed into the small town doctor. He rapped frantically on the door. When a young women answered the door Sigudur called out. "Where is the doctor' miss?"

"He ain't here sir, He left to deliver a baby hours ago." The young woman looked askance at Sigudur. "You're welcome to wait."

"Thank you, miss but I cannot wait. I have to get home to my wife."

"Would you like for me to go home with you sir?" asked the young woman.

"what could you do?" asked Sigudur.

"I am a nurse there are many things I can do." She looked warmly at him. "Maybe just a little moral support."

"Yes, please come home with me. You are very kind." He glanced askance at her. "Are you the doctor's daughter?" asked Sigudur.

"No, his wife. I'll leave him a note so he can come out as soon as he gets home. All at once the trotting of a horse was heard in the back yard. "Oh here is the doctor now." Running out to meet the physician, his wife called out to him. "Leave the mare hitched to the buggy we have to hurry out to Mr. Haflidason's. His wife is in labor." The nurse hopped into her husband's buggy and the two vehicles jogged a run to the Icelandic settlement.

After the two horses were tied to the hitching posts on the back porch the threesome entered the house. Ingibjorg Ottson met the group at the door. "I had Johanna take the girls to my house. Einer will look after them until I get home then he can go to work. I better go now and stay with the girls. They should not hear their mother's screams."

"It seems very quiet now," stated Sigudur dashing into the chamber.

Ingibjorg picked up her shawl and wrapped it around her shoulders.

"A pain is pretty severe to cause unconsciousness. And I understand that's God's way to give a human being relief if just for a few minuets . . . yes, God works in strange ways. Ingibjorg Ottson slipped through the outside entrance into the beautiful fragrant day, April 11 nineteen hundred fourteen.

The doctor was young and fresh out of medical school.

He had the looks and personality for a good future. He was polite and appeared to care for human beings which now is missing in today's physicians. The young Dr. Murdock smiled up at Sigudur. "I'm afraid I will have to ask you to leave this room, sir. Your wife is about to deliver."

"Thank God! And thank you for informing me Doctor." The screams started up again . . . then everything was quiet . . .

When the chamber door opened, the physician's wife walked into the kitchen with a small white bundle in her arms.

"Sorry, Mr. Haflidason it's another girl," stated Mrs. Murdock placing the infant in Sigudur's arms.

"Just what I wanted," he exclaimed, peeking into the soft, white blanket.

Coming out of the chamber, the physician's wife approached Sigudur. "Will you be having help after we leave? If not I will try and get you some."

"Thank you for your concern, Mrs. Murdock, but I have a hired girl coming today," replied Sigudur moving in quick gait into the chamber. Porunn lay still and pale with her eyes closed. "Tota!" he cried. "Are you alright?" Receiving no response from her knew she was asleep and unaware of the new born infant feeding at her breast. Exhausted, Sigudur fell sound asleep in the rocking chair. As he slumbered he heard through his sleep light knocks at the kitchen door. Half asleep he stumbled to the exit. A young girl stood on the porch with a small knap sack on her shoulder. "Mr. Haflidason?"

"Yes. Oh I am sorry you are the new hired girl. Come in Helen. I believe that is your name."

"Well, my friends call me Buzzy."

"Well, I'll call you Helen. "Bring your bag and I'll show you to your room." stated Sigudur leading to the spare chamber. He glanced curiously at her. "The agency sent you . . . right?"

"Oh yes. I work out of the agency all the time."

"Could I see your reference, Helen?"

"The agency says we don't need a reference. That their sending us out on a job is all the reference we need."

"Alright. Please have supper ready around five o'clock."

Dusk was closing in on daylight. Helen came out to the kitchen and began preparing supper. All at once the door opened and Ingibjorg Ottson walked in. "How are things going, Sigudur?" she asked.

"We're making out." She detected a dissatisfied timber in his voice. "Well, keep me posted if I can do anything for you."

"Thank you Ingibjorg, we'll do just fine."

Days passed. The girls appeared to like Helen because she played with them hours at a time instead of minding the new infant. Johanna took notice and reported this to her father. But if the children liked the new girl then he was going to try and put up with Helen's shortcomings Was his reply.

Sigudur coming home from work hurried into the chamber to see Porunn. "How are you elskan?"

"Much better now that you are home," she smiled reaching for his hand.

"How are the girls taking their new little sister?"

"They simply adore little Ingibjorg. They fight all the time to hold her. I get up in the rocker for an hour each day and that is when I supervise them in holding Ingibjorg."

"I am so happy that you decided to name the baby Ingibjorg after Mrs. Ottson. She has been a wonderful friend," stated Sigudur.

"Yes, she is very pleased. Have you made a date with the Lutheran minister yet for the christening?"

"No but I will when you get feeling better, Tota."

"Isn't it wonderful that the Lutheran church here is an Icelandic Lutheran church?"

"Unbelievable!"

It was almost the first of May. Helen would soon be leaving. Today the hired girl was cutting out pictures from an old magazine and putting them in an old book. Groa standing close by asked Helen if she might have one, "No, you can't have one you brat! Get out of here!" Breaking into tears Groa placed her head on Johanna's lap.

It was almost five o' clock, an hour before Sigudur would be home from work. All of a sudden Gudmundina's voice was heard from the out-house in convulsive sobs. Johanna ran outside to the out-house and found it locked. Then all at once Helen came out with a switch in her hand which she had beaten Gudmundina with. "You little brat, if you ever wet your pants again I'll really give you a beating.!" The door of the out-house opened and Gudmundina with heart breaking sobs ran into her mother's room.

At five P.M. Johanna stood at the kitchen window waiting for her father to come home. Stirring a stew on the kitchen range, Helen eyed Johanna suspiciously. "Go sit down and get out of my face." Suddenly Johanna left the window and ran out to greet her father who was coming up the path. "Pabbi!" called out Johanna. "Helen beat Gudmundina with a switch and she is crying."

"Where is Olof now?"

"Gudmundina is in mamma's room."

"Thank you Hanna. But I don't need your help I'll take care of it," he stated with choleric temper and hurried toward the house. Sitting down on the stoop Johanna could hear Helen's and Sigudur's high pitched voices. Then all was quiet. Tiptoeing into the house Johanna went to Helen's room and found it vacant . . . she was gone. Coming from Porunn's chamber Sigudur came out of the room with Gudmundina in his arms.

At the supper table Sigudur hurried through his meal, then went over to talk to Einer Ottson who just finished his supper. "I hate to bother you at this hour Einer but I had to let my hired girl go today."

"No problem, Sigudur I have just the girl. I was going to get her in the first place but you had already hired one from the agency. She is Icelandic and a very serious young lady. Well, she isn't good looking but a first class young woman." His brows wrinkled suddenly. "In fact Sigudur, her mother was a friend of Porunn's mother in Iceland."

"What is her name Einer?"

"Lena."

"Thank you so much, Einer and I hope she will take the job and come over tonight."

It was almost seven o' clock p.m. when a light rap was sounded on the front door. Hurrying to answer the call, Sigudur in fast gait walked to the entranceway. When he opened the door a young girl about seventeen years of age stood on the veranda holding a large straw suitcase in her hand. "Hello . . . Mr. Haflidason?"

"Yes, I presume you are Lena? Come in!"

Leading the way to the guest room, Sigudur took her suitcase from her hand and carried it to her room. "I hope you will be comfortable Lena. Any complaints about anything come to me."

"Thanks, Mr. Haflidason. Einer speaks very highly of you and your wife."

"Would you like some coffee, Lena?"

"No thank you sir. I just had a cup before I left home."

"Let me hang up your coat then you can meet Porunn. What a wonderful surprise she will have when she finds you can speak Icelandic."

"Oh, yes, we speak it at home all the time. Mamma says anyone can learn to speak two languages."

May brought flowers to the yards and gardens. Lena was a God send to the Haflidason household. Porunn was delighted with the way she so gently handled little Ingibjorg. Lena drying her hands on a towel in the kitchen glanced over at Porunn sitting with Ingibjorg in her arms rocking the infant to sleep. "If there isn't anything else I can do right now, I think I will take a little rest."

"That will do you good, Lena. You're so busy all the time."

Entering her room one day Lena noticed some torn and wrinkled chewing gum wrappers on her bedroom floor, and that her suitcase was pulled out from under the bed and open. Just as she thought the thief was after gum. Lena passed Johanna in the small hall. "Johanna you stole my chewing gum. I had three packages and now I don't have any!"

"I did not take your old gum!" shouted Johanna tightening her lips. "I know who did though because I saw her . . . it was Groa."

"Groa did not do it, and you did not see her do it. Groa never touches anything and I have never seen her in my room. Shame on you Johanna for lying on an innocent girl. And never mind telling your father I will tell him myself." Johanna hurried outdoors to enjoy her gum.

November blew in cold and windy. Ingibjorg was now almost seven months old. She was a wonderful baby. Seldom fussed or cried without cause. Johanna spent hours with Ingibjorg teaching her to take her first step. It was now almost the Christmas holidays and at twelve months she took her first step without falling.

The four little sisters were taken to Bible class every Sunday to the Icelandic Lutheran Church in the town of Blaine. Here they expanded their Icelandic and Sigudur hired an Icelandic tutor a Mrs. Benson for Ingibjorg and a man named Christion Davis for Johanna. American schooling would take care of the English language.

The years rolled by. Johanna was now six years old. Groa age four and Gudmundina age two. Ingibjorg one year. Sigudur noted one day that Gudmundina had a very beautiful singing voice. He mentioned this to one of the Sunday school teachers at the Icelandic Lutheran Church. "Do you think the child would give a solo on Christmas?" asked the choir director."

Laughing, Sigudur shook his head. "Gudmundina is a very odd child. I can't speak for her. But I will ask her. If she consents I will be very proud. If she says no, then so be it."

Lena had gone. Þorunn was feeling well again. Stepping up to the supper table she glanced at her husband. "Thank God Ingibjorg is the last one," she stated sitting in the chair her husband had pulled out from the table for her.

"I'd say about one more, elskan." he remarked teasingly.

"Don't forget, Sigudur, I am almost fifty years old!"

"And don't forget you are Icelandic. Icelandic people have very lengthy longevity."

"We were not talking about longevity, Sigudur, we were speaking about child bearing . . . menopause." Þorunn helped herself to some boiled fish, then returned her attention back to her husband. "You know, God made a mistake letting children twelve and younger in Latin countries, able to have a baby. I was eighteen years of age before I knew what a period was all about. And becoming a woman so late I can see where i can get pregnant again." Looking over the rim of her cup Þorunn continued. "Where I was working in Manitoba one of the waitress who was married with children, told me she had been married since she was a nine year old child.

Listening attentively, Sigudur asked: "How old was her husband when he married her?"

"He told her fifty, but she said he looked a lot older." Taking a sip of coffee Þorunn added. "Naturally to a child he would."

"Are they still married?" asked Sigudur.

"No," replied Þorunn. "When she became nineteen he did not want her anymore. She was too old. So he found another nine year old."

December blew in cold and bitter. Sigudur jumped on his bicycle and with his bill—bird cap pulled it tightly over his ears.

During supper the conversation was mostly about Christmas. "It certainly is getting to look like Christmas everywhere," stated Sigudur, glancing down at Gudmundina and getting ready to ask her about singing two songs in the Icelandic Lutheran Church.

Johanna rose from her chair and placed her arms around her father's neck. "Pabbi, Are we going to get new dresses to wear to church Christmas Eve?"

"What ever your mother decides for you girls to wear."

"I don't care what mamma says. I want a new dress."

"Go back to the table, Hanna. Your mother will attend to all that." Ingibjorg sitting in the highchair imbued the air with baby talk. Groa as usual did not offer any conversation.

"Olöf," began Sigudur. "I have been asked by the Icelandic Lutheran Church if you would sing two solos on Christmas Eve. One in Icelandic and one in English."

Gudmundina age two glanced askance at her father. "What did you tell them, pabbi?"

"That I would have to ask you. I would be very proud Olöf, but it is up to you to decide." Sigudur waited with abated breath.

"No I don't want to sing."

"If I give you twenty five cents will you sing?"

"No.

"Fifty cents or a dollar . . . five dollars?"

"No, pabbi I am not going to sing."

"I was just thinking, Olöf, your English song is entitled ROCK A'BYE BABY, What if I buy you a new doll. Will you sing then?'

"Yes, I will sing."

Christmas Eve, Sigudur hopped off his bicycle and hastened into the house. "We'll have to hurry girls. We have to be at the church at Seven P.M."

After a quick meal Porunn and the girls packed white, bleached sugar sacks with Christmas gifts to bring to the church. After the girls were dressed in their new dresses, Sigudur lighted two lanterns. Handing one to Johanna and keeping one for himself. "I'll walk with you and your lantern?" announced Johanna to her father.

"No. You take your mother's light. She'll be carrying Ingibjorg most of the time, and Gudmundina and Groa can walk with me."

Stepping over mud puddles, they walked with measured steps with their heavy sacks. No snow for Christmas in Blaine Washington, only rain.

Passing through the black leather swinging doors of the vestibule, Sigudur and his family slid exhausted on the mahogany benches.

Groups of people were coming in and soon the pews were all taken. The only light seen was the hundreds of small candles on the enormous Christmas tree standing on the platform. Soft strains of beautiful piano music playing Heinsom Bol, Heilgërda Jol. (Silent Night Holy night.) echoed through the church.

Groa leaned toward her father's ear. "Pabbi, how can that man light candles with a stick.?"

Sigudur bent his head and whispered in Groa's ear. "That long stick Groa, has another lighted candle attached to it. The candles are too high up to light if he did not have the stick or pointer as this stick is called."

"Oh, I see, pabbi. Thank you." Groa replied in a wee voice.

Porunn nudged Sigudur and whispered, "Stop talking the minister is getting in the pulpit." Pulling out their hymnals the choir began to sing the Icelandic Anthem of Iceland Gud vors land, Land vors Gud", to the tune of, My Country Tis Of Thee."

All was quiet, then the accompanist began playing the first line of Silent Night. "That's your cue, Olof," said Sigudur in a low voice.

Gudmundina with a hard serious face rose and picked up her new doll from the bench and walked slowly across the polished church floor to the large platform hugging the doll all the way.

Loud clapping and cheering came from the audience. as the small girl, aged two climbed the steps to the platform. The accompanist started the piece, "Silent Night," and the beautiful voice of a child brought tears to many eyes. When the song ended, Gudmundina repositioned her doll in her arms and burst forth in the English lullaby which Porunn had taught her. "Go to sleep dollie my dear, when I am with you there is nothing to fear. Go to sleep, Go to sleep dollie my dear." She ran off the platform into Sigudur's arms smiling. The ovation was endless but she would not sing again.

Upon reaching home with their lanterns Porunn and Sigudur joked about Gudmundina's not willing to give such a nice audience another song and Porunn remarked, "Well, maybe she would Sigudur if you bought her another new doll."

CHAPTER EIGHTEEN

Three years passed. Johanna now age ten had started school by Sigudur's Icelandic standard of age nine. Ingibjorg the baby of the family was four years old and waiting excitedly for her sixth birthday so she could be with her sisters at school.

It was now summer vacation which brought children outdoors and the flower beds and yards flourished with color.

Sitting on the back porch on a lawn swing Porunn and Sigudur relaxed drinking lemonade. "Where are the girls, Tota?" asked Sigudur.

"Hanna took them to the park. I told her to have them back in an hour."

"To the park alone! My how they are growing, Tota."

"Yes. All in school except Ingibjorg," replied Porunn.

"Well, probably not all of them for awhile, elskan. You'll be giving me another girl one of these days," stated Sigudur teasingly.

"You're forgetting Sigudur I was fifty years old on my last birthday February twenty-four."

"And you're forgetting that you haven't even started menopause yet."

"Well, what will be will be," declared Porunn seriously.

Moving closer to Porunn, Sigudur endeared her waist. "Thank you, Tota for being so understanding and patient with me." He rose from the swing. "I feel for a walk. Let's go and bring the children home."

In the park dusk was creeping through the wrought-iron fence. Johanna and Groa sat near by where Ingibjorg and Gudmundina squatted down beside a small pond of gold fish. Johanna called out, "You kids stay close by. We are going home now." Gudmundina's eyes rested on a shiny black limousine parking outside the fence. Then a middle-aged woman came out of the vehicle and walked to the enclosure working a hand through the lattice opening and extended a hand. "I am Priscilla Taylor. What is your name, little girl?"

"My name is Gudmundina Haflidason." And placing her arms around Ingibjorg, she added, "And this is Ingibjorg my baby sister."

"You have a wonderful family. Any boys?" asked the stranger?"

"No. I'm six years old and my baby sister is four but I'm intelligent for my age."

Mrs. Taylor grinned. "Oh I can see that." Then on a more serious note she added. "I had a little girl once who would be just your age now. Her name was Linie. Oh, I miss her so!" cried the woman breaking into sobs. "Could you visit me sometime? I live close by here?"

"I do not know. I will have to ask my mother." replied Gudmundina.

"Gudmundina!" called out Johanna. "Where are you? We're going home!"

Sigudur met them at the door. "Oh, you're back." The table was set for supper and the happy family seated themselves around for a delicious meal of fish. No highchair at the table any more. Ingibjorg was one of the 'little women' sitting on a chair like her sisters.

Porunn examined Gudmundina's features as she sat quietly in deep thought.

"Mamma, why do you think a grown woman would come to a park and talk to one of the children playing there. Doesn't it seem strange to you?" asked Gudmundina.

"Yes, very. Unless of course she had a reason." Porunn thought about this for a moment, then interrupted. "You say the woman invited you to visit her in her home?"

"Yes. She is a very nice lady, mamma. And I really would like to see her again."

"I am going to the park with you tomorrow, Gudmundina, and get this straightened out. But I doubt very much that this lady of yours will ever show up again."

"Please don't tell her I cannot come, mamma. I want to go to her home and visit. I know she is very rich, and she is certainly pretty. She looks a lot like me and has dark-blue eyes like mine."

"How would you know that she's rich?"

"I can tell I am very observant. That's why I am going to be such a wonderful writer when I grow up." replied Gudmundina with arrogance.

Porunn chuckled. "You'll change your mind about being a writer many times by then." In deep thought she began to set the table for supper.

Heading for the park the following day daughter and mother walked briskly together. Crossing over the street to the park, Porunn took Gudmundina's hand. "I don't think your mystery woman will show up today." said Porunn.

"She'll be here, mamma. The lady has very trusting eyes. In fact, her eyes look a lot like mine—very dark blue." As they reached the gate a black, shiny limousine drove slowly past them. "Mamma!" cried Gudmundina. That's her!" They hastened their gait and hurriedly entered the enclosure of the high wrought-iron fence as the vehicle stopped and parked. "You are right, Gudmundina. Anyone with a chauffeur has to be rich." When the woman reached the fence Porunn walked over to her and offered a hand through the lattice work. "I am Porunn Olafsdottir Haflidason, Gudmundina's mother."

"And I am Priscilla Taylor. I suppose your daughter has told you she is the image of the girl we lost. When I first saw Gudmundina I thought it was my daughter, Linie.

"I am very sorry Mrs. Taylor. I know what it is to loose a child. I lost my son at six months old. Johann was my first child." stated Porunn. "Do you live close by here, Mrs. Taylor?"

"Yes, very close. I have asked Gudmundina if she could visit me once a week. Something to look forward to," she added with tears in her pretty dark-blue eyes. She wiped her tears away with a hand. "Gudmundina said she would have to ask her mother." Smiling through her sorrow Mrs. Taylor touched Porunn's arm. "We will take good care of her, Mrs. Haflidason. We will pick her up at school every Wednesday and we will bring her home safely."

"Mamma, Please! I want to mamma, please say yes/" cried Gudmundina.

In the weeks to come Gudmundina looked forward to every Wednesday. She was given a new dress each visit and all the beautiful frocks were pink—Linie always wore pink.

Summer was waning. Gudmundina today was visiting at the Taylor residence. Carrying a big box with Gudmundina's new dress in it, the chauffeur placed the dress box on the rear seat, then assisted Gudmundina into the limousine. Gudmundina was extremely impressed.

As the limousine was about to leave, Mrs. Taylor came running out of her house with a sweater in her hand. "Here, honey your sweater. You left it on the sofa." she stated wrapping the sweater around Gudmundina's shoulders. "And don't forget, this coming Friday, we will be going to our summer home in Birch Bay for a two week vacation. I have arranged with your mother for you to come with us."

"Yes, mamma told me. I am very excited. I simply love the ocean."

"Good! My chauffeur will pick you up at your home about five forty p.m." stated Mrs. Taylor.

Friday after school was busy at the household of the Haflidason family getting Gudmundina ready for her two week vacation out at Birch Bay with the Taylors. At five forty p.m. the limousine appeared in the driveway. When backing out on the main throughway to leave, the vehicle passed a man on a bicycle turning into the Haflidason driveway. Paying no attention, the chauffeur sped up and headed toward the main street. Sigudur's eyes traveled with the limousine. The vehicle then turned a corner and disappeared in a trail of dust. Sigudur hopped off his bicycle and put it in the barn. "That was Mr. Taylor's car!" he mumbled to himself. "No, that didn't look like Taylor. And this man was in uniform. But why should Mr. Taylor's vehicle be in my driveway?" Tired and confused, Sigudur went into the house.

Holding out his arms he embraced Ingibjorg, Johanna, and Groa. "Only three little girls tonight," stated Sigudur jovially. "Gudmundina gone for two weeks, eh?"

"Pabbi" called out Johanna. "Did you save part of your lunch for us today?"

"Oh, yes, Hanna. Look in my lunch pail."

Johanna opened the container and divided the extra sandwich which Porunn made each day for the girls. "Well . . . I see Olöf got off on her vacation," said Sigudur with a heavy heart, eyeing Porunn.

"Yes, she was so proud to be picked up by a chauffeur," replied Porrun laughing.

"I saw them leave, Tota." Glancing curiously at her he added. "This family Olof is vacationing with, are they also Taylors"

"What do you mean, also—?" asked Porunn.

"The Morrison Shingle Mill's president whom I work for is named Taylor. Of course a lot of people have the same name. Just tell me that it's just a coincident."

"I have never asked Priscilla where her husband works, or am I going to, Sigudur. It would be nosey and impolite."

Stretching across the table, Sigudur stroke her hand. "As long as Olof is happy so be it, as you always say." Refilling the coffee cups with fresh hot coffee Sigudur grinned. "It sure is going to be boring around here without Olaf telling us how beautiful and intelligent she is."

"That's right! chimed in Ingibjorg. Near by Groa sat quietly listening to the conversation but offering no input. Groa was a strange child. She kept to herself, never complained or criticized. However, when she heard the down-trod attached she was on the unfortunates side. She had an uncontrollable temper, if anyone touched her personal things. Sigudur had given all the girls a large trunk where each child held her worldly possessions. This is an old Icelandic custom. In Groa's trunk was a large doll given to her by Sigudur years ago. It was very beautiful with long, black hair. She was dressed in a pretty green velvet coat. Once in awhile Groa would let her sisters look at her doll but they were not allowed to touch or hold the doll. Also, inside the trunk was a small well-known figurine of the three monkeys. One monkey holds his ears—symbolic of not listening to gossip—another holds his mouth—symbolic of not spreading gossip—and the third covers his eyes so as not to see any evil. When Groa felt sleepy would lie down on the parlor floor beside the living room heater. Later Sigudur would assisted her to bed.

Porunn placed a large platter of lamb on the table. Jumping to her feet Ingibjorg pulled out her mother's chair. "Sit here, mamma. I'll set the table for you. You've been working all day."

At the saw mill the main conversation was that the boss would be returning a week from next Monday. Sigudur became disturbed with the news. My how the time had flown! He was expecting this of course, but how could he face the president now who was beginning to display his true feelings about having Gudmundina as his own child.

Each morning Sigudur walked heedfully through the back door so as not to run into Mr. Taylor. The president never used the rear entrance.

Time went by. The escapade continued. Noting a young worker at the assembly line, Sigudur was hoping that the president was not planning on letting him go for this kid. A weird, strange feeling passed through his being. Suddenly a middle-aged man from the office approached the youth's bench. "You are wanted in President Taylor's office, young man. "In a very short time, the young worker returned and walked to Sigudur's bench. "Here comes the ax!" thought Sigudur to himself. Taking off his work goggles, he pulled off his bill bird cap and threw it on a bundle of shingles. Knocking lightly and only once Mr. Taylor called out. "The door is open, Mr. Haflidason."

Tense and with heavy heart Sigudur crossed the floor to his elaborate mahogany desk and sat on the edge of the assigned chair. "You sent for me, sir?" asked Sigudur. "What have I done?"

"Oh, this is not about your job, Mr. Haflidason, this is strictly personal", replied Mr. Taylor forcing a smile. "No, Mr. Haflidason your work is impeccable." He picked up a pencil and whirled it nervously in the air. Clearing his throat he grinned a amicable smile. "As you are aware of Mr. Haflidason, your daughter, Gudmundina has been spending a lot of time with our family and we all have grown to love her as our own."

"You have three children of your own, do you not?" asked Sigudur.

"Yes, our eldest, Ada is a school teacher. And we have a grown son and a twelve year old boy." Mr. Taylor scanned Sigudur's features, then continued. "I want you to let us adopted Gudmundina."

"Give my child away?" retorted Sigudur hopping off the chair.

"Gudmundina has a lot to offer the world and I have the means to help her."

"Yes, you have the means but you do not have anything else. I have envied you, Mr. Taylor, but not anymore. Keep your means, President Taylor. I'll rely on our families love to get us through."

"Your answer then, Mr. Haflidason is what . . . ?"

"Do you want to get rid of your little boy, George? Your answer is the same as mine!" Enraged, Sigudur moved to the door.

Glancing back over his shoulder at Mr. Taylor, he cried out angrily. "Please, accept my resignation as of now, Mr. President!"

Flustered and depressed, Sigudur wheeled his bicycle and lunch pail up his driveway, then went into the house.

Ingibjorg washing off spinach in a big bucket Looked up when her father came in. "Oh, pabbi you are home early."

"Yes Ingibjorg, but we will talk about that later. Where is your mother?"

"Mamma is sick today, pabbi. I told her to go to bed for awhile and I would get supper started."

"I heard Gudmundina come home last night, why isn't she in here helping you?" asked Sigudur curtly.

"I asked Gudmundina but she said I could do it myself."

Leaving the kitchen, Sigudur went into the chamber where Porunn lay in bed pale and listless. "Oh, Sigudur, you're home early. Is everything alright?"

"I hope so." He bent over and kissed her gently. "Is it a migraine, Tota?"

"No, I went to the doctor, and like we thought, I am pregnant. And I have been with child since January. Diagnosed wrong because the doctor believed it was the beginning of menopause."

"How did the doctor find out he had diagnosed you wrong?" inquired Sigudur?"

I believed all along I was pregnant, my clothes were getting tighter and I had morning sickness several times. He based his theory on the fact that I had not even started menopause. I told him anyone who has been pregnant as often as I have, should know the symptoms." Raising up on an elbow Porunn looked curiously at Sigudur. "What are you doing home?"

"I'll talk to you about that later when the children are not around. But how did you get the physician to see his mistake?"

"I insisted on a rabbit test," whispered Porunn.

Coming into the kitchen, Gudmundina approached Ingibjorg at the cooking range boiling spinach. "Did I hear pabbi's voice?" asked Gudmundina with a new dress in her hand.

"Yes, he came home early today.," replied Ingibjorg running to pull off the boiling-over spinach pot on the stove.

Hearing Gudmundina's voice Sigudur left the chamber and approached her in the kitchen. He hugged her with both arms. "I'm so happy to have you back, elskan!"

"I missed you too, pabbi," she exclaimed, kissing him on the cheek. She then looked up at her father and grinned. "Guess what, pabbi. I now have a grandmother! And she is real pretty, not ugly like most old people. And she is so nice to me."

"Well, where did you get this grandmother?"

"She came from London England to live with her daughter forever—Mrs. Taylor is grandmother's daughter.

"What is the grandmother's name—Taylor.?"

"No, pabbi. It's Mrs. Cokeroft. Grandmother is going to buy me a lot of things."

"Um—" replied Sigudur in deep thought.

Supper was over. Gudmundina and Ingibjorg washed and dried the dishes together then went out to relax. Sigudur and Porunn sitting on the lawn swing felt tense as they waited for the children to retire for the night and Sigudur could inform his wife of his day.

Night dropped her curtain. All members of the household were in bed for the night. Sigudur and Porunn lay quietly in their chamber. Porunn looked at Sugurdur inquisitively. "Well, Sigudur, it can't be that bad."

Turning over and facing the wall he took her hand. "Would you mind elskan if I tell you tomorrow morning. I am so tired!"

"No, Sigudur. You cannot sleep with problems on your mind." And besides you won't have time before going to work in the morning."

He sat up in bed and looked firmly into Porunn's beautiful gray—bluish eyes. "I won't be going to the mill anymore, Tota."

"That is bad, Sigudur—real bad."

"I am sorry, Tota, but that's the good part of the story." Hopping out of bed he blurred out with rancor. "Your wonderful Taylors are asking for permission to take Gudmundina away from us legally."

"Through adoption—?"

"Yes," he replied with tears running down his face.

"I know Gudmundina will miss seeing them—" began Porunn.

"—especially their presents," interrupted Sigudur with choleric timber in his voice.

"I dread telling Gudmundina that her visitations are over." said Porunn.

"You won't have to tell her anything, Tota. We're moving."

"I can't lie to her, Sigudur."

"No the truth is better. We leave here in two weeks."

Porunn's features paled. "Oh Sigudur! I cannot think of moving again especially now that I am with child. We own our own home and even have some Icelandic neighbors."

"I realize that, Tota. But where will the money come from if I don't have work?"

Almost two weeks had passed. The girls and Porunn were busy packing in boxes for the long Montana run. Sigudur had left for the country to look for a large wagon for their travel. Johanna let out a cry when she saw her father drive into the backyard in a big wagon drawn by two horses. Unhitching the team he then walked the horses to the small barn in back of the house. "How do you like the wagon, girls? Isn't she a beauty?" asked Sigudur cheerfully.

"Yes! When can we get in it?" asked Groa happily.

"This wagon will be able to take most of our things," said Sigudur with satisfaction. "We can leave tomorrow, Groa."

So I'm ready "I think it's ugly, pabbi. But I'm dying to see Montana, so I'm ready to leave now," said Gudmundina.

"We will be leaving by first light tomorrow morning. It will be a long slow trip but we'll make it. Montana is rough country." He glanced over at Porunn as she placed a box of cooking utensils in the wagon. You forgot the dishpan"

"Let it go, mamma I'll go get it for you." called out Ingibjorg running back into the house her, flaxen hair blowing in the breeze over her black velvet cape.

Johanna wrinkled her nose and glanced at Sigudur. "What do you mean first light?" asked Johanna puzzled.

"Jo doesn't even know it means first beep of light in the early morning." said Gudmundina shaking her head. "Jo could never be a writer."

"We all cannot be writers, Olof. And Hanna can do many things that you can't do." said Porunn curtly.

Leaning against the wagon, Gudmundina asked. "Is Montana a big city?"

Sigudur grinned. "Montana is not a city Olof it's a state."

"See, mamma. Gudmundina doesn't even know that Montana is a state. You're right mamma there are things I know which Gudmundina knows nothing about."

Sigudur placing four small chairs on the floor in back of the wagon, positioned himself in an animated stance, getting ready to present a statement. "Listen here Hanna and Olof. I don't want to hear anymore arguing from either one of you or anyone else in this family. We all love each other, right?"

"Yes . . . !" they all shouted in unison.

"Then show it—talk is cheap let's eat our supper and go to bed early. Remember by first light we're off." Sigudur glanced toward the house where Porunn was tidying up the house for the last time. Advancing to the wagon Sigudur rested his eyes on her worried features. "It's going to be a long rough journey for you Tota, but nothing could be as rugged as Iceland."

"I wasn't pregnant in Iceland," she responded dully.

"We can take it Tota we are Vikings! I say Hurrah for the Montana run! Are you with me girls?"

"Yes! Hurrah for the Montana Run," shouted the group from the wagon. where all except Johanna were picking out their seat for the dawn's first light.

At the crack of day-break Sigudur and Porunn went into the girls' rooms to awaken them for the journey. They were all up, dressed and excited to leave. Groa and Gudmundina climbed up into the wagon and sat down in their assigned chairs. Sigudur and Porunn were in the front seat and Porunn held the youngest child, Ingibjorg on her lap. Noticing Johanna still standing in the driveway, Sigudur called out to her. "Come on Hanna! What is the matter with you?"

"I have no place to sit. Mamma took my seat in front with you."

"What do you mean your seat? You know perfectly well your mother always sits with me. Now, get into the back of the wagon where you belong." Pouting and stomping a foot on the ground, Johanna climbed into the vehicle and sat in the vacant chair. Smiling to himself, Sigudur called out. "Are we already to go?"

"Yes, Hurrah for the Montana Run pabbi.!" shouted Gudmundina followed by Groa's, Johanna's, and Ingibjorg's youthful voices.

CHAPTER NINETEEN

The trek was slow. Still in Washington state they found a hotel for the night, then Sigudur saw to the hungry, tired horses.

Too tense and tired they could not sleep. At daybreak the family was up and back in the wagon. Several days past and they were now starting to climb the mountain surface of the Rockies. "Are we in the Rocky mountains pabbi?" asked Johanna who had always been interested in geography. After eight thirty P.M. she use a flashlight from under the bedding to hide the light from her mother who had made a house rule. (No light after eight thirty P.M.)

"Yes these are the Rockies. How will you like living close to the mountains, Hanna

"I wouldn't like to live here very long," replied Johanna. The surface becoming taller, the wagon kept climbing. "Pabbi what purpose do mountains have asked Johanna.

"Well, Hanna, the Rocky mountains exist of extensive plains that rise gradually to heights of four thousand feet. And trees bound on the mountain, nature is a wonderful phenomena Hanna."

"You said we were going to live on a prairie when we get to Montana," said Johanna stretching her neck to the back of Sigudur's seat to hear what he was saying over the blatant screeching of the wagon wheels she asked, "What is a prairie pabbi?"

"I don't know too much about a prairie, Hanna, But the little I have read it is an extensive track of slightly undulating land, without trees and covered with tall, course grass."

"That sounds terrible! Why are you coming here pabbi?" asked Johanna.

"Only one reason, Hanna—money. This cattleman pays a terrific salary."

"What is the name of the town where we will be living pabbi?"

"Windon. It is a very small town, one store one post office and I believe a feed store. Now Great Falls is the largest city in Montana. And Helena is a pretty good size also if I remember right Helena is the capital city."

"Pabbi you are so smart."

"No, Hanna I am not smart, just an avid reader."

Now high in the mountains the air was changing. All at once Groa began having labored breathing from the high altitude which was not enough to compensate her persistent oxygen shortage. And with Porunn, mountain sickness had brought on a migraine headache. The mountain sickness appeared to be the result from a accumulation of fluid in the brain causing pressure inside the cranium. Some people are not effected. Sigudur shifted his eyes on Porunn. "Are you alright, Tota?"

"Yes, Sigudur. I am fine," she replied in a weak voice. "I'll be better when we get down to a lower level."

"Pabbi! Pabbi!" cried Johanna. "Groa has fainted!"

Porunn rose on her knees, and turning to the back seat reached for a dishpan off the floor and placed it on Groa's head. Time passed and the tired group had reached the lower level.

Groa's breathing was still short but improving. and her head was clearing. Smiling, she sat up. More relaxed now Sigudur picked up speed. All of a sudden the horses came to a dead stop neighing wildly and attempting to break away from the harnesses. "Oh my God!" cried Sigudur, "We've lost a wheel!" He jumped out of the wagon and ceased the frightened animals' by their reins and held them firmly. In a short time they were calm again and eating grass along the roadside.

Johanna vaulted out of the wagon and went to where her father was settling the horses down. "Pabbi shall we go get the wheel now?"

"We have to find it first Hanna." stated Sigudur. anxiously

"I know where it is Pabbi." Grinning he followed Johanna down the small hill where it had rolled.

Back to the wagon with the wheel Sigudur called out. "Now, everyone out! I can't lift the wagon up with all this weight," he cried out, becoming tense and nervous. Johanna was the first one out. "I'll help you, pabbi."

"No Hanna. Get out of my way." Porunn lifted Ingibjorg out of the wagon and set her on the ground with Groa and Gudmundina following after. Taking a wagon travel kit from the wagon, Sigudur hunted through the tool box for something to fasten the wheel again. The group strolled together back down the trail, happy to be able to stretch their legs. After an extended time, Sigudur's voice was heard over the wind. "All Aboard!" The family climbed back in and the wagon made a quick run for the other side of the mountain where the terrain boarded a large vegetable field.

"We are out of the mountains ladies," announced Sigudur pridefully.

"Thank God!" replied Porunn, taking in a deep breath.

"Are you alright?" asked Sigudur?"

"I hope so," she replied in a faint wan voice.

It was almost dusk. Sigudur pulled up the horses to the side of the road. "We will have to find lodging before it gets too dark." Resting his eyes on Porunn he asked, "Do you think you can go a little farther, Tota?"

"Yes Sigudur, stop worrying about me."

Suddenly Johanna jumped up in her seat and placed her arms around the back of her father's seat. "Look, pabbi there's a field or a garden or something over there."

"Good girl, Hanna! I'll tell you what we'll do. I'll set up our tent at the far end of the field. It's dark and the owner won't even know we are there. We'll clear out before it gets light." The tent was up and the blankets made into beds on the ground. Taking Porunn in his arms, Sigudur drew her closely to him "Tota, I have to leave you over night. I must go further into town and find a livery stable where I can get fresh horses for these poor worn-out animals,"

"We'll be fine after a good nights sleep," stated Porunn.

The long night passed. The dawn was peeping through the tent. Suddenly a big rush of water washed over the tent, the strong force of the water pulling the tent to the ground, the blankets, the children and Porunn were soaking wet and drenched to the skin. "Oh, my God! What happened?" cried Porunn vaulting to her feet.

"The farmer must have seen us when it started getting light and knew how to get us out alright." said Porunn. "Come on everybody, let's go up to the road where it is dry." She picked up Ingibjorg and the water-soaked group moved to cold but dry earth. Soon they saw a green wagon and a team of horses galloping up the road toward them. Johanna leaped off the ground and into Sigudur's arms as he hopped out and led her back to Porunn Ingibjorg, Groa and Gudmundina.

"What are you all doing here?" asked Sigudur, "And why are you all wet?" Pulling off his jacket he wrapped his coat around Porunn's shoulders. "Tota, be careful not to catch a cold, elskan."

"The owner must have seen us. He had a clever way of getting us out. when it became light the farmer saw our tent. So he turned on his irrigation system and flooded the field—and us."

"You weren't flooded out during the night then?" asked Sigudur.

"No, replied Porunn grimacing, "Not until about an hour ago. Thank God you came back early."

Sigudur wadding back into the field, picked up the wringing wet tent and the soaked blankets and threw them in back of the wagon to dry. "All Aboard!" Sigudur called out, and the group hopped into the wagon and continued on their way.

"Oh," sighed Porunn, "It's so good to be out of the mountains."

"Maybe we are getting close to Winden," said Groa, resting her big gray eyes on her mother.

"Could be, elskan," replied Porunn.

"What are you talking about, Groa—Whose ever heard of Winden?" stated Gudmundina laughing.

"Apparently you haven't Olof. But Groa remembers Winden is where we are going to live," said Porunn interjecting into the conversation.

Johanna rose on an elbow—"Will you people shut up I'm trying to sleep!"

"Hush up you two. If you girls would sit up and keep an eye out for the mountains you might see some wild animals," stated Sigudur.

"What kind of animals pabbi?" asked Johanna

"Way up in the hills there are, bears, wolves, pumas, moose, elk, and there are deers here also. The one that comes down to the ranch is the coyote who kills the cows. And very difficult to catch."

"I don't see any animals, pabbi," said Groa glancing toward the hills.

"They are not likely to come down here, Groa. And especially in daylight." replied Sigudur. All at once a large flat plot of ground came into view. "You're right Groa, this must be winden. And that large white house inside the high steel gate is the ranch." He bent his tracks to a tall gate and stopped the horses and the wagon, to open the high, steel enclosure. As they drove closer a small brown house constructed behind the main dwelling was seen. "Were home!" cheered Sigudur stopping his vehicle behind the main house and jumping from the wagon. A large sign on the roof read. LAZY RANCH.

"Are you sure Sigudur that we are in the right place?" asked Porunn.

"Yes, Tota, this is the house that goes with the job. Pretty nice place for free. Seems like the rancher has a hard time getting cowboys to work here. The duties aren't difficult but tedious so Mr. Baker has to have some initiative for people to take a job like this. And I hear none of the cowboys stay very long—Oh, look! there is someone coming out of the back door of the main house."

A tall distinguished man of about forty years of age approached their wagon. "Good evening folks. I am Mr. Baker, the owner of LAZY RANCH. Welcome!"

"Good evening, Mr. Baker. I am Sigudur Rosenkranz Haflidason and this is my family."

"Hello—", called out the girls together. as Porunn smiled and nodded.

"You have quite a spread here, Mr. Baker."

"Yes, and it takes a lot of hands to run it."

"Where do you sleep the cowhands, Mr. Baker?"

"Down at the far end of the field I have bunk houses for about eight men. You'll be eating your meals down at the mess hall with the cowboys except for your dinner where you will eat at home with your family." Mr. Baker took Ingibjorg from Porunn's lap and helped her out of the wagon. "Are you with child, Mrs. Haflidason?"

"Yes," replied Porunn quietly.

The group followed Mr. Baker up the path of the brown house. As they climbed the steps Porunn glanced quickly up at Mr. Baker. "I hope there won't be any night work."

"Not unless there is an emergency, Mrs. Haflidason."

The interior was spotless. There were four rooms, one large which served as a living room and kitchen. Three small rooms served as bedrooms. Johanna and Groa shared one of the sleeping rooms and Gudmundina and Ingibjork were room mates. Mr. Baker looked seriously down at Porunn. "Will you be alright here do you think?"

"Oh, yes, Mr. Baker everything is just fine." she muttered breathlessly. "I am just very tired and would like to go to bed."

"Not before you eat. Come on over to the main house my daughter Nina has made you a little lunch."

"That is very kind of her. We will be right over."

CHAPTER TWENTY

Thus was their new life.

Sigudur was gone all day out on the ridge wrestling up stray horses and cows. Around six 'o clock in the evening the girls would listen for the sound of a lone galloping horse with one rider—their father had come home. Jumping off the horse Sigudur tied the animal to the veranda as Gudmundina, Johanna Groa and Ingibjorg were waiting to greet their father. He embraced them all with open arms. Porunn standing at the cooking range making dinner, put down her spoon as Sigudur crossed the floor and endeared her to him. "It's been a long day, Sigudur," she stated, placing her head on his shoulder. It was a happy household as they all sat down to eat. "What did you have for lunch, Sigudur?" asked Porunn.

"It could hardly be called lunch, Tota. The workers have their main meal at noon." Sigudur smiled. "That Mr. Baker is a funny person. He supervises in the mess hall and a delicious dinner is served. In the middle of the long table is a large tray with a huge roasted beef. After one serving he removes the meat and returns it to the kitchen to the cook. Then he comes back to the table and announces. "Have some more potatoes boys." The cowhands and I always laugh at his declaration for we want more meat. "And now the family joke with each other when some one wants another helping of something, one of them call out. "Have some more potatoes, girls."

This evening was a Saturday night. Porunn was heating a big vessel of hot water to give her children each a bath in the living room by the heater where a pot-belly stove heated the bulk of the dwelling. In the center of the large room Porunn placed a big washtub filled with the water for the baths. As she finished bathing each child she wrapped a large Turkish towel around their nude body. Resting on the bed in his and Porunn's room Sigudur could hear the children bickering, laughing and splashing water at each other. Porunn glanced over at Gudmundina who was hiding in a corner behind a chair. "You're next, Olof." Gudmundina hesitated a moment, then stepped into the washtub. All at once a loud steady rap at the door sounded.

Gudmundina let out a blood curdling scream and dashed out on the floor, falling against the heater burning a thigh! Then realizing that she was nude she cried out, "Mamma! Get me a towel before some one sees me naked!"

Sigudur hurrying to answer the door found one of the cowboys from the bunk-house dressed in boots and spurs. "I am so sorry to barge in like this, Siggi. But you'll have to ride with us tonight. There are thieves stealing our horses. They rode off just a few moments ago with three of our steers."

"Thanks, Jake. I'll be right behind you." The cowhand hopped back on his horse and hit the trail. After pulling on his boots and spurs, Sigudur jumped into his sheep-skin jacket and galloped to the ridge where the cowboys stood waiting for orders from Sigudur whom Mr. Baker had put in charge because of Sigudur's expertise with horses.

It was now morning. The tired cowhands returned to the ranch. "I don't understand how they got away so fast," said Jake.

"Oh. yes they can, Jake. These devils really ride and before you know it they have disappeared in the hills."

At midnight, Sigudur came home. Porunn half asleep sat up and rubbed her eyes. "Did you catch up with the thieves, Sigudur?"

"No, Tota it was a useless trip." He hung up his jacket and pulled off his spurrs and boots. "I cannot understand why Mr. Baker hasn't had these animals branded. Even though we could have confronted the thieves there was no way we could prove they were ours." Exhausted, Sigudur crawled into bed.

"Go to sleep Sigudur think about it in the morning," stated Porunn sliding down in bed again. He had not heard her, he was sound asleep.

There was a change in the weather. Nature made the switch in occurrence according to the season Groa and Ingibjorg were in the back yard picking the last of the berries for the season. "Where is Gudmundina?" asked Groa. "She came out with us."

"Yes, she came out with us but she said she was going over to the main house and sit on the steps," replied Ingibjorg, filling her full skirt with blossoms. "I don't think Gudmundina likes flowers," she added.

"Gudmundina likes flowers. But she likes the ones that are sold in floral shops-like roses," said Groa.

"Oh, I love wild flowers best because they're God's nature," said Ingibjorg dropping wild violets in the full fold of her dress. "I can't carry any more. Let's go in and make a wreath." The girls strolled to the front of their house where they saw Gudmundina sitting on the steps of the Baker house glancing up at the two story window where Nina Baker, the boss's daughter sat putting on make-up. Nina was a beautiful blonde girl who had lived with her father since her mother passed away. Gudmundina was very impressed with Nina's beauty and lovely clothes. All at once Nina looked out of the window and saw Gudmundina sitting on their steps. "Oh, hello there!" she called out. "Come on up."

With excited emotions Gudmundina ran through the back door and up the winding stairs to Nina's room where she sat in front of the large mirror attached to her dressing table. "Oh, hello, honey. What is your name?"

"My name is Gudmundina. I live behind your house."

Nina smiled. "Yes, I know. And you have some beautiful sisters too." She rose and slipped into a pale blue dress. "Come over here, Gudmundina and sit at the vanity. You may try some of my make-up if you like."

Gudmundina slipped on to a chair at the dressing table. "Thank you, Nina. when I grow up I want to look just like you.

You must be going somewhere very special," said Gudmundina.

"Not really. I am going out to lunch today with a friend of my father's. John is an older man and very rich. I believe my father would like me to marry him but I would never marry anyone for their money."

"I don't want to get married. I'm going to be a writer. And I want to be rich—and have a chauffeur," she added, when Taylors flashed across her mind. Glancing around the pretty room her eyes focused on a large vase of red roses. "Oh those are beautiful!"

"Would you like one, Gudmundina?"

"Oh, yes. I love flowers, especially roses," replied Gudmundina, pulling a rose from the vase. All at once a shrill cry was heard from the window looking out on the barren field beside the house. Gudmundina ran to the window and looked out. A small animal lay sprawled out on it's back and was held down by two cowhands who had a burning hot iron pressed to the helpless animal's groin. Breaking into tears, Gudmundina called out to Nina. "These men are torturing a little animal!"

"Gudmundina, get away from that window!" called out Nina in a blatant tone of voice.

"But the men are hurting the poor animal!", cried out Gudmundina sobbing in her hands. Nina moved to Gudmundina and placing her arms around Gudmundina's delicate form guided her to the dressing table and sat her down. "It has to be done Gudmundina, but we do not have to watch. I have been exposed to this since I was a little girl and I have never gotten used to it. In a little while the baby colt will be fine." From the back window they heard a trotting sound of a horse and carriage. "That's John Gudmundina I have to go."

Back at home Gudmundina put her rose into a vase of water. Porunn gathering soiled laundry to wash, looked up at Gudmundina when she took her rose and placed it on the table. "Did you have a nice visit with Nina Baker?"

"Nina is a very nice young lady. I like her mamma and she said I could come again."

Night dropped her dark curtain and all the Haflidason members were asleep in their beds. Far away in the hills the coyotes' howling could be heard loud and clear. "I can't sleep," complained Porunn nervously sitting up in bed.

"I have never heard them so aggressive as tonight," said Sigudur getting up. Something must be going on. I am going to the bunk house and gather up the men."

"Not tonight, Sigudur it is only three in the morning."

"It is my duty to check". Pulling on his boots and spurs, he grabbed his sheep skin coat and disappeared out of the house.

It was five o'clock in the morning when Sigudur returned. Porunn began washing and boiling on the cooking stove as the girls ate breakfast near by.

Coming into the kitchen Sigudur gulped hurriedly some coffee and gave Porunn a quick kiss on the cheek. "I am sorry, but I have to leave again."

He hopped on his horse and in full speed galloped across the prairie.

Taking some tad-dried animal droppings for fuel out of the wood-box Porunn noticed the box was empty. "Groa will you and Gudmundina go out to the shed and bring in some more tad?" asked Porunn, "I have to wash."

"Let Ingibjorg help her. I don't like that stuff," stated Gudmundina.

"Come on Groa I'll help you," said Ingibjorg heading for the back door.

The two small girls advanced to the shed. When they tried to open the old leaky structure they found it locked. "I wonder why the door is locked," said Groa rattling the lock. "Oh, something stinks in there." cried Groa holding her nose.

"I smelled something bad when we came out here," replied Ingibjorg.

Groa found a crack where a shingle had fallen out of the structure. She lent an eye through the opening and let out a scream. "There's an animal in there chained!" The poor thing is probably hungry and afraid. What will we do?"

"Let's go tell mamma. She will know what to do," replied Ingibjorg.

Standing on her toes she peered in the opening. "It looks like a dog, Groa". stated Ingibjorg.

"No that's no dog. It must be a coyote he looks very dangerous. Let's go in," stated Groa. The sisters clasped hands and ran back into the house.

"My you girls were long to fire is just about out." said Porunn.

"Mamma," said Groa, who locked a poor, helpless animal in our shed last night?"

"Animal—? Let the fuel go. I will talk to your father tonight."

The day wore on and around five o'clock a trotting of horse's hoofs could be heard at the back entrance. Sigudur was home.

Porunn waiting for him at the back entry, called out to him. "Sigudur, can you tell me why you have an animal chained and locked up in our shed?"

"It's a coyote, Tota. He has killed many cows and a young colt and now we have caught him. I will remove him from the shed tonight."

"The poor animal is hungry, Sigudur." cried Porunn, running to their room

"I don't think so Tota," he said grimacing. "He won't need any food after tonight."

"What is that supposed to mean? Are you going to kill him?" called out Porunn.

"I don't want you to worry about such things, Tota. The boys and I will take care of the coyote tonight. I'll go over to Bakers and borrow some tad so we can cook dinner. Maybe you and the girls can go over to the mountain in the morning and gather some."

The following morning Ingibjorg and Groa went out and peeked into the open door of the shed. The coyote was gone. Johanna came into the kitchen with a bundle of gunny sacks. "Here are some sacks for the tad," she started throwing them each a bag.

"I don't need one Jo. I am not going," stated Gudmundina firmly, throwing her bag back at Johanna.

"What do you mean, you're not going?" asked Porunn with temper.

"Alright I'm going!" called out Gudmundina picking up her bag from the floor.

It was a lovely day the sun spread long rays of light and warmth when the group bent their steps toward the mountain. As they climbed they came across patches of cattle and horse droppings which had become dry and hard. They filled their gunny sacks and headed down the mountain.

Starting her washing Porunn glanced out of the window. "My, we are lucky to have such nice weather to dry our clothes."

"Pabbi says you can't always tell in Winden. In one second there can be a big blizzard. And it is very dangerous to be out," stated Gudmundina.

"Well we better get our washing out on the lines while were ahead," replied Porunn hastily placing some wet laundry into a straw basket. Ingibjorg wiggled into a coat and reached for the straw basket. "No, Ingibjorg you stay. Gudmundina, Groa and I can handle it." The sun was going down and dark shadows enveloped the atmosphere.

"It looks like rain," stated Porunn reaching for a clothespin.

"It's too cold for rain," replied Groa.

"I'm cold," said Gudmundina. "My hands are frozen."

"We only have a few more clothes to hang up. Let's hurry and get into the house," stated Porunn picking up the wash basket and going inside. In the late afternoon when Porunn looked out of the window all the clothes were gone off the line, some were flying in the air miles away. "We will have to hunt for our washing," said Porunn. "Hard telling where it has blown". Large thistles flew over their heads in the gale. and hail dropped down on their heads. As they walked now and then they found a garment or some part of their laundry.

"My hands are frozen, mamma I can't go another step," cried Gudmundina.

"We have to go back home, Groa Gudmundina is right."

Inside of their home Porunn tried to rub and bring life to Gudmundina's hands which looked definitely frozen. After several hours her hands were normal.

August was dying. Porunn counting the days on the calendar glanced over at Sigudur eating breakfast. "Do you realize the summer is gone. It will be September in a few weeks."

"I know what you are referring to Tota. We have to start thinking about the new baby coming."

"Not another one!" exclaimed Johanna."

Sigudur grinned. "Yes, Hanna, another girl."

"Oh, I can't wait," chimed in Ingibjorg.

"I hope it will be a boy this time," said Groa.

"What ever we will love it," replied Porunn.

Sigudur pushed back his chair from the table. "Sorry to leave you lovely ladies but I have to get to work." He paused a moment and glanced at Porunn. "I forgot to mention, Elskan, I am expecting an important letter in the mail. I know I always pick up the mail on my way home, but I'll be working late tonight and the post office closes at five. Do you think the girls could get the mail today. It is only a stone's throw away."

"Of course, Sigudur, don't worry about it we will get the mail."

The afternoon was cloudy with patches of sun shinning at intervals then disappearing in a dark cloud. "Johanna," said Porunn. "Will you go to the post office for your father?"

"Sure. It's not far."

"I'll go with you," said Groa.

"No, Groa I'm going with Jo," stated Gudmundina.

"All three of you can go. And you better get started so you can get home before the weather changes. And I'm pleased you're going with the girls, Johanna."

"May we take Sheppy, mamma?" asked Groa.

"You mean that ugly matted old dog that's been hanging around here ever since we moved in?" asked Gudmundina.

"Sheppy is a wonderful dog. He just doesn't have a home." replied Groa. "Can we take him with us, mamma?"

Porunn's features grew serious. "You know Groa, I think you have a very good idea. If there happens to be a cyclone of some kind Sheppy could protect you from the storm. He is heavy, large and has thick long hair. So if a wind storm of any kind, throw him down on the ground and you, Hanna and Gudmundina sit down beside Sheppy and hold on to his long fur until the violent storm passes."

"Sounds kinda stupid to me, but let's get going," exclaimed Gudmundina. Sheppy sitting by the back door rose and followed the girls down the long, thick grassy path.

All at once it began to rain. Thunder and lightning with a violent storm impelling to act in haste. Johanna threw Sheppy to the ground. "Get down you two," shouted Johanna, her voice barely heard over the howling wind. She then dropped down be beside the dog and held on to his fur tightly. The storm then with a slow retard was finished. "You girls go home", said Johanna to Gudmundina and Groa. "The storm may not be over. I'll continue on to the post office in case pabbi received a letter."

"No, Jo, we are going with you," replied Gudmundina.

"No you are not—now go!" Sheppy's eyes traveled from Gudmundina and Groa to Johanna who was already on her way to the post office. Hurriedly Sheppy caught up with her and she stopped instantly in her tracks. "No, Sheppy! Go back!" The dog glances at her with big honest eyes and turned back, following Gudmundina and Groa home.

Porunn opened the door. "Oh, I am so glad you are back—where is Hanna?"

"She made us go home after the storm let up."

"She is going to get pabbi's letter," added Groa.

"Good. I hope this is the last of the hurricane."

When a sound of footsteps was heard on the back porch, Porunn opened the door. "I am so happy you are back, Hanna."

"Yes I am back," stated Johanna downheartedly. "but I lost pabbi's letter! the wind took it right out of my hand!. I couldn't help it, mamma."

"That's alright, Hanna. You were a brave girl to go on. Your father will understand. At least he will know that he did get a letter."

Sitting around the supper table, Sigudur was the first one to break the silence. "Don't feel badly about the letter, Hanna. I am just thankful that the wind took just the letter, not you." All the girls laughed. He glanced at his children's happy faces. "Your mother has been told about a position at the Ethridge Railroad which I have applied for. I should have heard from them some time ago. However, thanks to Hanna we know I have received it. What I don't know are the contents, did I or did I not get the job." Sigudur rose from the table. "Excuse me ladies, but I am going to ride to Ethridge to night. Probably won't get there until morning."

"Is Ethridge far pabbi" asked Johanna?"

"Not far to speak but I would say an all night ride."

"Anything will be better than here," stated Porunn grimacing.

"It won't much different, Tota. Ethridge is also a prairie or plain." replied Sigudur.

"What is a prairie or a plain pabbi?" asked Groa.

"Well, Ethridge is very flat, no trees, same windstorms. But the job is good paying. Not like what Mr. Baker pays but I cannot take the hours or the rough riding of a cowpuncher." Sigudur slipped on his sheepskin coat and placed his birdbill cap on his head. Hurriedly buttoning his jacket he took Porunn in his arms and kissed her. "I'm going to miss you elskan. If the letter stated that I got the job I will not be back for a few days. I have to find a house to rent. If I do not get the position I will be back sometime late tomorrow."

Kissing each child goodbye, he then fled out the door and mounted his horse.

Several days passed. Sigudur had not returned. Porunn went out to the shed for boxes. When the girls came out to see what she was doing, Porunn glanced at them. "Bring in some boxes, we might as well start packing. We have our answer."

At dusk Sigudur walked into the house. "Wow!. We are all ready packed!" Two days latter the family was back in the wagon and on their way to Ethridge.

CHAPTER TWENTY ONE

As they headed toward the mountain, Gudmundina asked. "Do we have to go over the mountain again, pabbi?"

"No Olöf I am going to take the long way this time. We can't take a chance on the thin mountain air with Groa."

The day was long. They stopped along the way once or twice and ate some lunch that Porunn had put up for them in the large laundry basket. The miles seemed to get longer as cold air swept over the open wagon.

It was now beginning to get dark. long gray shadows were stretching over the vehicle. Sigudur pulled up on the side of the road. "Whoa!" he called out to the team of horses. They instantly stopped and stood in abeyance. "We have to find a place to pitch our tent. And not too close to the road," stated Sigudur.

"We just passed a small house sitting back from the road pabbi," said Johanna.

"We just can't barge into someone's home Hanna"

"I don't think anyone is living in it pabbi. The windows are all broken."

"Broken—! The house must be vacant then. A few broken windows wouldn't matter. We have our blankets." Sigudur lashed the horses and turned them back down the road. "There it is pabbi. Don't go back any farther."

Sigudur parked the wagon in back of the shack and tied the team to the back porch. The tired travellers fell asleep and were quite comfortable through the night.

Morning dawned. and they were now ready to travel again. As the group headed for the wagon Gudmundina went in the opposite direction. "Olöf!" called out Sigudur, "where are you going?"

"I'll be right back pabbi. I'm going to go up to that little mountain and pick some flowers to take home. I won't be long."

"Flowers! What are you talking about?" called out Sigudur.

"There are some very pretty flowers on top of this little mountain."

"How would you know, Olof? You have never been here before. Now get into the wagon and stop talking foolish." Breaking into tears, she came back and climbed into the wagon.

Porunn took Sigudur to the side. "Don't make too much of this Sigudur. I have heard of similar cases where people swear they have been there before and they haven't. Just another phenomenon none of us understand."

"You're right Tota. You are always right. We are going to have to find a livery stable and see to the horses." They traveled on but nothing came into view. Johanna stood up behind Sigudur's seat and placed her arms around his neck. "What about that house along side the road we just past?" asked Johanna.

"I'm looking for a livery stable for horses, not people."

"Why don't we stop and ask them where there is one?".

"Whoa!" he called out to the horses. "I'll be right back Johanna," he said, jumping out of the wagon and handing her the horses' reins. He then hustled back on foot to the small house on the road.

As Sigudur approached the shanty, a middle-aged man came out to greet him. "Can I help you, sir?"

"Oh I hope so. I have my family with me in a wagon. We have come from Winden and we are moving to Ethridge, but the horses need food and water."

"You are already in Ethridge. Another two miles and you will see a livery stable and the little town of Ethridge too." The man shook hands with Sigudur "You won't have to pitch a tent tonight. I hear there is another storm coming."

"Well, we were lucky last night. We found an old shack with broken windows so we slept there all night."

"Broken windows! My God, man! There was a big robbery and murder, an hour before you folks got there. The owners were murdered and everything worthwhile stolen. That was God's good timing that you didn't arrive at that time. Good luck in Ethridge sir." said the man. "And may God Bless you and your family."

"Thank you. You have been very helpful," replied Sigudur tipping his bill-bird cap. Hurrying back to the wagon he leaped in and took the reins.

"Hurrah! We are in Ethridge. Only two more miles."

They were now in their house. After unpacking the vehicle, Porunn cooked a nice meal for her family then all went to bed for the night.

Two weeks passed. Sigudur reported at his job. At the end of the day he returned pleased with his position and his fellow workers. Porunn was busy getting the children ready for school that would be starting in a few weeks. August was slowly dying, September was arriving fast, and plans for the new baby was the essential topic. "What are we going to name our new girl, Tota" asked Sigudur good-humoredly.

"You mean what are we going to name our little son," smiled Porunn.

It was almost five o'clock p.m. Waiting for their father to come home from the railroad station, the girls would look through the back window for the bicycle. About to leave the window Ingibjorg cried out. "Look . . . pabbi has a new motorcycle!" She ran outdoors with Johanna, Groa, and Gudmundina following closely behind her.

Sigudur drove inside of the gate on a brand new motorcycle. "How do you like her, girls? Isn't she a beauty?" he asked jumping off and shinning the fender with a sleeve of his sheep-skin coat.

"Where did you get it, pabbi?" asked Johanna.

"The boss decided that my bicycle is too slow. He said I can keep the motorcycle home for my use when I am not working."

"Well, what about us, pabbi? Where are we going to ride?" asked Ingibjorg.

"I am going to get a small buggy for the family."

"I want to ride on the motorcycle pabbi. Just once," said Gudmundina.

"I'll give you all a ride when I have the time." He rested his eyes on Gudmundina's features. "I think you, Olof will be glad to hear that I plan on buying an automobile for the family. I can't afford it now, but the next time I build I will buy a Maxwell touring or a Franklin. I have read that automobiles are making great strides and in 1920 the Maxwell and Franklin will be available. How do you like that Olof?"

"Oh, good pabbi I cannot wait," smiled Gudmundina.

All was quiet on the weekend. Porunn cooked a special breakfast and the family lingered at the table conversing together with happy faces. Sigudur then rose from the table and excused himself. After a short time he came into the kitchen clean shaven and wearing his best clothes. Ingibjorg pulled on his sleeve. "Pabbi this is Sunday. Where are you going?"

"I know it is Sunday, elskan. I am going to take a ride to the other side of the mountain. I was told by a fellow worker that there are two Icelandic families living there. He gave me their address and said I should get acquainted with them."

"Oh, Sigudur that would be nice." exclaimed Porunn.

"Can I go with you, pabbi?" asked Groa quietly. Gudmundina gave her a stare. "No you can't. I'm going with pabbi." interjected Gudmundina.

"No Olof you aren't going either," answered Sigudur.

"Please pabbi take me with you," insisted Gudmundina.

"Take Gudmundina, it seems to mean so much to her," said Porunn Grinning, Sigudur looked at Gudmundina. "Let's go Olof."

Everyone tripped out and gathered around the motorcycle. "Lift Olof on," said Sigudur to Johanna. "Your mother should not do it in her delicate condition." Seating her in the seat in back of her father, Johanna then strapped a belt around Gudmundina's waist. The blatant sound of the motorcycle imbued the air, and soon disappeared from view. The mountain breeze was cold and uncomfortable. However in a short period of time they reached the little town. After hunting for the address they could not find it. When Sigudur saw a large white house without an address he stopped the motorcycle. "We will ask these people about Annika Sidurson's dress. Ranveig Westman's residence we will save until later," he stated lifting Gudmundina from the motorcycle.

Holding Gudmundina's hand Sigudur and his little daughter climbed the steps and knocked lightly on the door. "No answer. Maybe the family have gone to church."

"Can we go home pabbi?" asked Gudmundina. "I'm cold." Suddenly the door opened.

A middle-aged blonde woman answered the door. "I've been expecting you. One of your co-workers told me about the nice Icelandic family who have moved into Ethridge and that the husband was working at the railroad company." Annika stood back from the door. "Come in—Come in." She dropped her eyes down at Gudmundina. "My, you have a beautiful daughter Mr. Haflidason." Annika glanced curiously up at Sigudur. "Any relation to the wealthy Haflidason family in Iceland?"

"Yes, I am the Haflidason's youngest child." The back door opened and two pretty girls age six and ten entered the house.

Annika placed her arms around the children. "This is Asa and Dora my children. Glancing at Gudmundina she exclaimed, "Oh, and this Mr. Haflidason's daughter, Gudmundina."

"Hello,"

"Do you want to come out and play, Gudmundina?" asked the younger girl Asa. Gudmundina nodded and the three girls went outdoors.

Annika tied a fresh ruffled apron around her waist and smiled. "How about a cup of coffee and Icelandic pönukokurs?"

"Sounds good to me," replied Sigudur smiling. "We Icelanders must have our coffee."

Sitting at the kitchen table Sigudur glanced over the rim of his cup. "Do your children speak Icelandic or have they dropped their Icelandic heritage?"

"Oh no they have kept their mother's tongue. They speak English all day at school".

"Where do the girls go to school Annika?"

"We have a school near by which makes it handy. It's a one room. The teacher's name is Miss Brent. She is very nice and a very good teacher also."

"Of course the woman is single," he stated. "Married women are not allowed to teach school."

"Oh yes. And a pretty little thing too."

"Is Miss Brent Icelandic?" inquired Sigudur.

"Oh, no, she is English," stated Annika, rising and filling the cups with fresh hot coffee. "I liked the way you called me Annika a few moments ago. May I call you Sigudur?"

"Please do."

The hours passed quickly as the two Icelanders spoke of Iceland. Why did they come to a strange land and was it a mistake? Annika had become a widow after Asa was born, six years ago. It had been a hard life for her raising her children alone. She looked closely at him. "Have you ever thought about returning to Iceland?" asked Annika.

"When I first came to this country but my wife refused to return." I believe My wife, whom I call Tota as most Porunns are called in Iceland, must have had a bad childhood. I know her heart is in Iceland but she finds it easier to cope with in another land. I never question her."

"Thank you for telling me, Sigudur. I will not mention her past." A dark shadow came over her features. "You know, Sigudur I often wonder if we foreigners don't make a mistake when we leave our homeland."

"I believe that if we can prosper in a new country that it's good. But giving up my profession taking menial jobs has not been easy. Here in America I am nothing." He took a deep breath then a sip of coffee. "I have never complained to her, nor has she complained to me about her hard life with me."

"Porunn must be a wonderful woman."

"Tota is not a woman—she's an angel." He glanced up at her. "And now Tota is with child."

"That's nice, maybe this time you will get a son."

"No, I think it will be another girl."

"What ever, a child is a blessing." She paused, then added. "Do you think you could bring your family here to dinner next Sunday? And we can go over to Ranveig Westman's. She is a lovely lady and her husband, Jon Westman is a wonderful man also. They have three children, two boys, Eyther and Hannis, and a daughter Domhilder."

"That sounds great. Thank you very much, Annika." Sigudur rose from the table. "I think we better go home, Annika. It has been wonderful visiting with you."

"No, no. You and Gudmundina are staying for supper."

All at once Asa, Dora and Gudmundina came into the house. Approaching her father, Gudmundina placed her arms around Sigudur's neck. "Pabbi, I want to go home. I feel sick."

Placing her hand on Gudmundina's forehead, Annika's features changed expression. "Gudmundina has a fever. Her face is so warm and very flushed," she stated leaving the room to get a thermometer. She placed it in Gudmundina's mouth. "Yes, she has an elevation of 103, degrees. Not too bad for a child but enough to worry about." She called out to the youngest girl. "Asa, you will sleep in Dora's room tonight. I am going to keep Gudmundina in your room."

Gudmundina let out a cry. "No, I want to go home."

"I think it would be better if I get her home, Annika. But thank you for your concern," stated Sigudur.

"I'm sorry, Sigudur, I will not allow you to take a sick child over that mountain on a motorcycle," replied Annika firmly.

Gudmundina's head was dropped down on the dinner table and her eyes were closed. Annika pulling her up from the table guided her to Asa's room and put her to bed. Too ill to resist, the child fell asleep in a deep slumber. "Oh, dear I hope she doesn't doze long, I have to get some medicine in her to get the temperature down." Almost instantly Gudmundina opened her eyes. "No1 I am not going to take any medicine."

Moving closer to the bed, Sigudur sat down on the edge of the bed. "Olof, you have to take it if you want to get well and go home. If I give you a quarter will you take it?"

"No!"

"Fifty cents—a dollar?"

"No1"

"Gudmundina,", said Annika, "if Asa gives you her new doll will you take the medicine?"

"Yes." Asa came in with her new doll with an unhappy expression on her face. "Here, you can have my new doll," she said placing it on a pillow beside Gudmundina.

Gulping down the medication Gudmundina slid down in bed with her arms snuggly around the doll and fell asleep.

The old grandfather's clock struck twelve midnight. Annika awakened and bent her ears to Asa's room where Gudmundina lay sleeping. Satisfied that Gudmundina was asleep she turned over in bed. Suddenly Gudmundina's screams awashed the darkened room. Annika scrambled out of bed where Gudmundina sat perched against the head of the bed screaming. "The men are laughing at me! Oh, take them away!"

"Gudmundina there are no men in here. Lie down and go to sleep." Another scream. "They are up in the ceiling and laughing at me. Can't you see them? They have big, round fat faces. Make them go! Make them go!"

Turning on more light Annika assisted Gudmundina down in her bed again. "See, honey there are no men in the ceiling. now go back to sleep I'll stay with you for awhile."

It was now daybreak. Annika jumped out of bed and went to Gudmundina's room. She was sitting up in bed with her doll in her arms. "Good morning, Mrs. Sidursson. Is my father here yet?" she asked.

"It's a little early, dear. How do you feel?"

"Fine. I want to go home."

CHAPTER TWENTY TWO

By the end of a few weeks, Annika, Ranveig and Porunn were close friends. The days passed by and it was now the first of September. The households were busy preparing the children for school. Porunn's migraine headaches continued and because of Johanna's help with the younger children, she was able to rest in bed.

On September third, Porunn awoke with scrutinizing pain. "Sigudur!" she cried. "Get the doctor! I'm going into labor!."

Two hours went by. Sigudur had not returned from the small town of Ethridge. Johanna closing Porunn's door to block out the screams, stepped into the room. "Pabbi will be back soon mamma."

"Hanna where is Groa, Gudmundina and Ingibjorg?", asked her mother.

"They're here. Don't worry about them. They're with me," replied Johanna leaving the room. Suddenly Sigudur and the physician walked into the kitchen.

Following Sigudur into the sickroom, the doctor glanced askance at him. "No emergency here. Looks like your wife is sleeping comfortably," stated the physician.

"Make yourself comfortable, doctor We may have a long wait. I'm just thankful that you are here," said Sigudur, moving quietly out of the room with the impatient physician following behind him. Glancing around the room Sigudur approached Johanna putting hot water on the range. "Hanna, where are the other girls?"

"They are next door at Boga Thompson's house. She made some lemonade and baked them some cookies."

"Thank you, Hanna they have no business seeing and hearing their mother in such agony."

The doctor picked up his medical bag. "There isn't anything I can do here" said the doctor. "I'm going back to town I have another baby to deliver there."

"Oh no, doctor. You're not walking out of here until you have done your job," stated Sigudur.

"That could be all day—all night, and where would I sleep. You have no room for me here."

"I have a bed in the shed I'll bring in for you—wait here."

Returning to the house, Sigudur brought a spring and a mattress with him. "Where's the bed," asked the doctor.

"You'll see," replied Sigudur pulling four chairs out from the kitchen table. "Come on doctor give me a hand." The spring and mattress were placed upon the chairs. "How's that?" asked Sigudur.

"You tell me, Mr. Haflidason after you have slept in it tonight."

Several hours went by. Johanna served some sandwiches and coffee the doctor lay upon the mattress and took a nap as Sigudur tiptoed into the sickroom. She was still asleep. Dropping into an easy chair he closed his eyes.

After a light supper the doctor pushed away from the table. "I don't believe your wife is in labor, Mr. Haflidason. Many women think after their first pain that they're in labor. I might just as well go home and come back tomorrow."

"No, you will finish out the night now that you are here. My wife couldn't be off that far, after all this is her sixth child."

"Well we might as well retire for the night," stated the doctor taking off his shirt and tie.

As everyone lay in deep slumber, the clock struck eleven. Sigudur sleeping in the easy chair sprang up and moved to the bed to check Porunn. She turned over and let out a faint cry.

He glanced up at the door when he heard a soft footstep. "Is mamma still asleep pabbi?" whispered Johanna.

"Yes Hanna. Thank God! The doctor thinks that your mother miss-counted her days. Go back to bed Hanna. You've been very helpful."

September 4, 1917. Morning dawned. At the break of day a loud scream penetrated through the partitions of the bedroom. Sigudur leaped up from his chair and awakened the doctor. Gudmundina and Ingibjorg came out of their room. "Is mamma alright?" asked Ingibjorg sobbing. Groa coming out of her room placed her arms comforting around her youngest sister.

"Your mother is alright, Ingibjorg, Hanna is going to take you girls to Boga Thompson's house," said Sigudur.

"Again?" asked Gudmundina. Not answering her Sigudur walked away.

Porunn's agonizing screams continued. Johanna, Groa and Ingibjorg moved to the back entrance. Following far behind them Gudmundina opened her mother's door and glanced in. When she saw her mother pushed against the headboard on her knees biting and chewing at the end of a long sheet, she froze. Porunn tugged with her teeth and pulled on the sheet to be able to bear the pain. Standing in a catatonic stupor she heard Johanna shout at her. "Gudmundina! Get away from that door!" Gudmundina's emotionalism response lasted through her whole life. In the bedroom delivery room, the doctor accosted Sigudur standing petrified by Porunn's bedside. "You will have to get out of this room Mr. Haflidason." stated the physician in an authoritative timber.

After a prolonged time waiting in the kitchen, the sickroom door finally opened. The doctor came out carrying a soft white blanket in his arms. "Here is another daughter for you, Mr. Haflidason. Sorry it's not a boy but this baby is exceptionally beautiful

Good luck with your harem," said the doctor placing the infant in Sigudur's arms. "I have to get back to town."

"May I see my wife, doctor?"

"Just for a moment. The woman is exhausted!" replied the physician.

The doctor was gone. The house lay in silence. Sigudur took the baby into Porunn's room where she lay unaware of her environment. He lay the infant on her breasts and the new member of the family instantly found it's forte. He came out of the room when he heard the back entrance open and the voices were music to his ears.

Boga Thompson approached him. "I have brought your family home, Sigudur. Let us guess. It's a boy!"

"Wrong, Boga it's another girl And a very beautiful one I must add."

"May we see her?' asked Gudmundina.

"Not now," replied Sigudur. "Your mother and little sister are both asleep."

Boga Thompson took a long glance at Groa, Johanna and Ingibjorg. "Did your father tell you that I will be working here for a month?"

"Yes Mrs. Thompson, we are all very happy. We never liked those other hired girls. Mamma is happy about you staying with us too." stated Johanna.

"Your mother speaks a little Danish as most Icelanders do. And of course my being Danish we can converse together."

It was almost dusk when Sigudur heard Porunn call out to him. He hurried to her bedside. "It's over elskan. Thank God!" He kissed her gently, then kissed the baby. "Have you decided on a name for this beauty?"

"Yes," she smiled weakly. "I'm going to name her, Annika Ranveig."

"Those are lovely names and the names of two lovely ladies. Annika Sigursson and Ranveig Westman."

"I'll be up soon and the christening is all ready arranged at the Lutheran church."

Winter was settling in on the prairie. The bitter winds blew large thistles across the flat terrain whirling spirally in unbelievable fury. Porunn bending over a washboard doing the family laundry glanced up at Johanna when she entered the kitchen. "Your father is working late tonight. We might as well start supper." said Porunn. Sitting around the table eating their evening meal the happy group chattered together. Gudmundina smiled. "I had a dream last night mamma."

"What did you dream?" asked Porunn. "Tell us about it. Was it a good dream, Olof?"

"Yes, mamma, very good. But tell me your dream first".

"I dreamed that we moved back to Washington state—Blaine. I think we were happiest there."

"Oh my dream was wonderful! I dreamed that a handsome prince came to our house. The prince was searching for the most beautiful girl in the world."

"So he didn't find one," laughed Porunn.

"Of course he did—me."

"That's hard to believe, Olof, your sisters give you a lot of competition. And now beautiful Annika will grow up. I don't know, Olof your sisters are all as pretty as you are. And some people think even prettier."

"You're just saying that mamma."

Ingibjorg wrinkled up her nose. "Gudmundina is making it up." Porunn rose from the table and gathered the dishes. "I'll wash the dishes for you mamma," stated Ingibjorg getting up from the table."

The following day was quiet. Gudmundina, Johanna and Groa were in school. Taking a nap, Ingibjorg and Annika now three months old were tucked in their beds. Glancing out of the window Porunn noticed that the skies were darkening. "Looks like another storm," she thought to herself as high winds of a cyclone blew about in circles. She sat down on her bed and removed a letter three days old from her apron pocket. She was about to read her sister's letter when Johanna and Groa came in from school. Quickly pushing the letter back in her pocket. she hopped off the bed. Sigurun's letters were private. "Hello girls how is school?" asked their mother

"I enjoy school" stated Groa. "But Jo hates it and says she isn't going anymore."

"We'll see about that. Twice this week the truant officer has come here to see if you were sick. I am not going to lie for you again, Hanna." Putting up her nose Johanna went to her room.

On the following morning Sigudur and Porunn awakened hearing the baby's cry for her five A.M. feeding. "Let me get up Tota. I have to get up to go to work anyway. Stay in bed and I will bring your lump sugar and coffee."

"Thank you, Sigudur." He left the room, then brought Annika in and lay her to feed on Porunn's breast. "I want to talk to you about something when I get home tonight, Tota. I don't have time now."

Supper was over. He glanced over at Porunn at the other end of the table. "I think it is time that we leave Montana. I believe Washington state is the one for us."

"I hope you are telling me you want to go back to Blaine Washington," said Porunn, her beautiful gray eyes starring a blank.

"No, elskan," interrupted Sigudur, "Yakima, Washington. It is larger than Blaine. As you know the large cities have more advantages."

"I will just be happy to leave Montana, Sigudur. Life here has not been easy for any of us."

"I know that Tota. That's why I've been inquiring about Yakima. There is an Icelandic man living there who helps Icelandic immigrants get started in all unknown country. His name is Sali Petersson."

He owns a big peach farm. There is only one thing you may not agree to. You will have to travel to Yakima alone with the children. I will come later, in about two weeks."

"I don't understand. We have always traveled together," replied Porunn.

"We won't be going by wagon this time. We will go by train," stated Sigudur. Groa sat listening attentively with her big, gray mother's eyes on her father. "Train?" she asked.

"Yes, Groa."

"Oh, I've never been on a train. When can we go, pabbi?" asked Ingibjorg.

"In about one week."

"I don't know Sigudur. This is going to take a lot of money." replied Porunn in deep thought.

"Yes, and the reason you will be going alone with the children. Let me explain Tota. I was informed awhile ago that my whole family and I are entitled to free railroad passes on the train. They are good for any place in the United States. After checking them out the manager and I noticed a railroad member would have to have worked another two weeks, and I am a little short. So he suggested you go ahead with the children and that I follow in two weeks. It will save us a lot of money, Tota. I know it will be difficult for you traveling with five children, and especially with a three month old baby. Thank God Annika is not on a bottle that would be hard."

"It's all settled then," said Porunn. "We will start getting ready to leave." She then glanced at her husband curiously. "What do we do when we get to Yakima—where do we go?"

"Sali Petersson's oldest son will pick you up at the station. The son will take you to the peach farm, and you and the children will stay with them until I arrive and rent a house during the time I'm building our home."

"It seems like an imposition for Mrs. Petersson to have so many strangers in her home," said Porunn.

"I think the Peterssons considers us more like friends rather than strangers. Sali found out that he was a friend of my fathers when he lived in Iceland. He is doing very well financially. They have a large home and of course the peach orchards," stated Sigudur. He pulled Porunn up from the table and kissed her. "I know this won't be easy for you Tota. Not speaking English and all."

"I can speak English for her," said Johanna.

"We'll be just fine, Sigudur," replied Porunn picking up the dishes from the table, trying to conceal her tension and fear from her children and husband.

A week passed. The excited day had come. Dressed and waiting for Sigudur to come home to take them to the railroad station, her tension mounted. Groa entered the room. "Pabbi should be home pretty soon with a hack. What is a hack mamma?"

"It's a small vehicle that came out in 1912. The railroads have what they call a depot hack to transfer baggage to different railroad stations. It will be a tight squeeze. They are very small, but it will get us to the train depot." All at once Gudmundina cried out, "Pabbi is back with the hack." She ran out of the house with Johanna, Groa and Ingibjorg following after her to the driveway. Sigudur pulled out his watch. "Is everyone ready? The train will be coming in at 4 P.M."

As they sat in the waiting room Sigudur kissed each one goodbye. Then clasping Porunn in his arms he released her and removed a sheet of paper from his pocket. "Oh! I almost forgot elskan. You won't get far with out this", he stated giving Porunn the paper. "Put it in your handbag, Tota, and don't loose it. This is your train pass." Shifting the baby to one side, she pushed the document into her bag. Suddenly a loud, shrill whistle imbued the air and the brilliant lights of a locomotive pulled up to the station. The group rushed up the steps of the train and found a seat. "I'll sit with you, mamma," said Johanna.

"Thank you, Hanna."

In a short period of time, a conductor stood on the steps of the train and shouted. "All Aboard! All Aboard!" He then shut the train door and the locomotive started down the tracks. "Mamma!" called out Ingibjorg. "I have to go to the bathroom"

"Not now, Ingibjorg," stated Porunn. "Why didn't you go before?"

"I didn't have to go then," she said, grimacing and twisting in her seat. Johanna scrambled to her feet and took Ingibjorg by the hand up the long swaying corridor to the rest room.

"I have to go too," sighed Groa.

"Why in the world didn't you say so", exclaimed Porunn. "Go on then." Back in their places they settled and enjoyed the train ride. When a black conductor came walking down the corridor, Porunn noted that he was checking each passenger for tickets and passes.

Gudmundina rested her eyes on the conductor, then bent over the back of her seat to confront her mother. "Mamma," she whispered, "Why does the conductor have a black face?"

"The conductor is a black man, Olof." whispered Porunn in a soft voice. The officer stopped at Porunn's seat. "My what a lovely family. And all girls. May I see your train pass or ticket or whatever?" he asked pleasantly putting on his glasses.

"Yes sir," said Porunn nervously hunting in her handbag.

"Look mamma," stated Johanna. "let me help you," she said, pulling the document out of Porunn's bag and handing it to the conductor.

His eyes traveled over the list of names, then read aloud: "Porunn Haflidason, wife, Johanna, daughter; Groa, daughter, Olaf, son, Ingibjorg, daughter, Annika Ranveig, daughter three months old." Glancing at Porunn the conductor asked: "Are these all your children?"

"Yes, officer. Oh, yes, sir. all these girls are mine."

"It is documented here that you have one son, named Olaf."

"There must be some mistake," replied Porunn with her nerves on end. Her eyes then brightened. "Oh, I see where the mistake is, officer The name on the pass is no doubt spelled with an (a) which is masculine as Olaf. The feminine gender is spelled with an (o) like Olof. My husband should have given her first name. But he is so used to calling Gudmundina Olof. Sorry officer."

"Oh I get it, foreigners have very funny names."

Listening to the conversation, Gudmundina glanced up at him. "Well, we think you Americans have funny names too. Pabbi says Americans name their cats and dogs the same names as humans."

"You're a spunky little thing. I like that in a female," he said, laughingly pinching her nose playfully then continuing down the corridor.

Gudmundina let out a scream. "Mamma! mamma! the conductor made my nose black!"

"He did not. For heavens sake control yourself," stated Porunn.

"Yes he did with his black fingers. Can we wash it off?" she asked desperately.

Porunn dug into her handbag for a small mirror and handed it to Gudmundina. "See for yourself."

Scanning the mirror for a look at her black nose, she smiled. "My nose is not black, mamma. You were right."

Porunn looked over at Johanna. "Will you get our food container from under the seat Hanna? Annika is asleep and I don't want to disturb her."

"Is it dinner time already?" asked Johanna on bent knees. "That fried chicken and salad really look good." After their meal, Porunn and the children settled down for the night.

After a long uncomfortable night morning dawned. Suddenly the overhead lights came on and a conductor walked down the aisle speaking in a large horn. "We are now approaching the state of Washington. In forty-five minutes we will be in Spokane, Washington. Passengers going on to Yakima have to change trains here. There will be no train going until tomorrow morning at seven 'o clock." Moving down the aisle he added. "You folks will have to sleep in the waiting room the best you can." Repeating his words he advanced ahead through the many cars.

Porunn looked over at Johanna. "What's this all about, Hanna?" asked Porunn through blurry tired eyes.

"In forty-five minutes we have to get off the train and wait for the connecting train to Yakima."

"Will we have to wait long, Hanna?"

"Yes, mamma, all night. We'll have to sleep in the waiting room."

"Waiting room!" exclaimed Gudmundina. Time passed. Johanna stretched over the back of her seat. "You and Groa, and you too, Ingibjorg get your coats on and your bags ready. We have to change trains."

"Will you carry the food container Hanna?" asked Porunn.

"I can't mamma. I have the big suitcase to carry," stated Johanna reaching up on the rack and pulling the suitcase down on the floor. "Let Groa do it. She has only one little bag."

"Give it to me," said Ingibjorg, "My bag is much smaller than Groa's."

The Spokane railroad station was large and filled with passengers who had come to board the train for oncoming cities. Soon the locomotive still sitting on the track, huffed and puffed and moved slowly up the tracks and disappeared around the bend.

In the waiting room Porunn espied a large easy chair and sat down with Annika in her arms. The children were exhausted and becoming restless running aimlessly around the waiting room. Porunn rose from her chair and took the baby to the lavatory to change her diaper and wash up the infant as well as possible. Returning to the waiting room she sat in the easy chair, and with a diaper spread over her shoulder and the baby's face, she was shielded and indisposed from the traffic of passengers going through the waiting room as the baby breast fed. "Why don't we eat early this evening Hanna so we can get settled for the night? I'm sure everyone is exhausted."

"How much chicken and salad will we have left?" inquired Johanna.

"Enough to last us for breakfast and tomorrow's lunch. That ought to do us. "We should be in Yakima by late afternoon," said Porunn, resting the sleeping infant on her knees.

After a long miserable night it was daylight. Johanna stretched over the seat and glanced at Gudmundina and Ingibjorg crowded on two chairs together. Groa lay on the floor with her coat draped over her. "Time to get up, everyone. Our train will be here in less than an hour." At quarter to seven, the group left the waiting room and went outdoors to the passenger's loading zone. "We're a little early," said Porunn. "But we certainly don't want to miss it. I'd hate to spend another night in a waiting room."

It was five to seven. When a loud whistle of a train imbrued the air and groups of passengers came filing out of the waiting room to the platform. The blatant sound became louder and soon the locomotive stopped at the Spokane railroad station.

Porunn hurried into a seat with her girls close by. "I certainly hope Sali's son won't forget us." she said her features douring with abated breath.

"I hope he's good-looking," said Johanna jokingly.

"Don't worry about it, Hanna. "You are much too young for him." replied Porunn.

Now settled in the train, Porunn and the girls became more relaxed. Groa and Gudmundina sharing a seat gazed out of the window and watched the landscape fly by as Ingibjorg curled up in the seat she occupied by herself and fell asleep.

It was almost 4 P.M. when the conductor came down the aisles speaking in his horn. "Yakima! Yakima!" he called out advancing down the aisle to the other cars. In a short period of time the train slowed down and drew up to the Yakima railroad station. When they got off the train, they stood on the platform and glanced around for Helgi Petersson who was suppose to meet them here. "I hope Sali Petersson didn't forget to ask his son to pick us up," stated Porunn nervously. Suddenly Gudmundina espied an elderly man with a long white beard. "That's Soloman!" she cried. "Pabbi said Soloman had white hair and a long white beard. Helgi must have brought his father with him. Look mamma! They're coming over here." Noticing Porunn and the baby with the small girls gathered around her, the two men hurried to the platform. Gudmundina looked up at the older man. "Are you Soloman?" she asked.

"Yes I am Soloman Petersson—most people call me Sali," he stated glancing over the group of pretty girls standing by their mother in a bashful huddle. He looked at the young man beside him. "This is my son Helgi. I am glad that he talked me into coming along with him to the station," he smiled amicably.

Porunn shook his hand. "I am so happy to meet you and your father. How nice of you to pick us up."

"My pleasure," said Helgi. Johanna took in Helgi's good looks but decided he was much too sophisticated for her. And seventeen was certainly too old.

Sali Petersson stepped toward Porunn. "Let me carry the little one, Mrs. Haflidason. You must be exhausted. "My automobile is parked in the passenger slot behind the station." They boarded a long, black vehicle, a Briscoe with shiny spoke wheels and a bi-folded hood. Gudmundina was speechless.

"It's a beautiful automobile," said Gudmundina. "Do you have a chauffeur?"

Sali laughed. "I'm afraid not."

"I'm going to have an automobile like this someday." she stated. "But I'm going to have a chauffeur too".

"Those are big dreams for a little girl, Gudmundina. But keep dreaming. Who can tell, they just might come true."

Driving out to the country, they passed orchards of ripe fruit where farmhands were picking and putting them in baskets and crates. As they drove they soon came to a peach farm of extended length. "Here we are, folks," called out Sali when Helgi turned the vehicle through a wide wooden gate. On the fence was a large sign reading, SALI's PEACH ORCHARDS.

After the automobile parked, Mrs. Petersson came out of the house and placed her arms around Porunn and kissed her. "You poor child, you must be ready to drop carrying a baby on the whole trip. Here, let me have the little thing." Mrs. Petersson walked to the house with the baby in her arms, the group following close behind.

After a special dinner cooked in the traveler's honor there was coffee and Icelandic ponakukur. The main topic of conversation was Iceland. The Petersson's youngest son, Harold glanced over at Groa who sat in the living room quiet and unspoken. He came into the parlor and smiled at her. "Is your name Groa?"

"Yes," she replied, her features flushing.

"I'm Harold. Have you ever had a pigeon?"

"I don't think so. What is that?"

"Come on out and I'll show you."

The two children went outdoors and strolled to the barn. The building had a high loft where four or five pigeons sat on a perch.

"Oh, look at the birds," exclaimed Groa.

"Those are pigeons. Come on up to the loft and you can hold one. They're very tame."

Up in the loft, Harold picked up a pigeon and put it on Groa's arm.

"Is this the pigeon who delivers messages?" asked Groa. "Or do they all do it?"

"No, this is the only one that I have trained. And when I train another one I am going to give it to you."

"I hope I will be able to send you a message, Harold."

"I heard your father is going to build a house. And then we can send messages to each other. And while you're here you might as well come up to the loft and I can teach you how to send messages back with the pigeon."

When they returned to the house Johanna greeted them. "Groa, do you know where Gudmundina is?"

"She was here a little while ago, Jo."

Ingibjorg came out of the kitchen with a dishtowel in her hand. "Gudmundina is down in the orchard helping Sali crate some peaches for freight," replied Ingibjorg, hurrying back into the kitchen to help Mrs. Petersson with the dishes.

Two weeks passed. No sign of Sigudur. Then one morning a 1920 Maxwell automobile drove up the road leading to the house and stopped. "Who can that be?" asked Mrs. Petersson as Porunn came into the kitchen with the baby in her arms. Johanna glanced through the window. "That's pabbi!" she cried hurrying out to the road and running straight into his open arms. "Pabbi, where did you get the automobile. It's beautiful!"

"Where is Gudmundina, Hanna?" asked Sigudur. "I promised her some time ago that when I could afford an automobile I would get the family one. And now she isn't even here."

Brushing her hand over the shiny engine, Johanna asked! "Is this a new automobile, pabbi?"

"This years—1920," replied Sigudur proudly. When he heard voices on the road he called out. "Tota! I am home. I've brought a family present with me." Enduring Porunn in his arms he glanced over at the lady of the house. "You must be Mrs. Petersson, Sali's wife."

"Yes Mr. Haflidason."

"Please call me Sigudur," he stated.

"And my name is, Anna." She rested her eyes on the automobile. "A Maxwell is a very fine vehicle I hear. Lots of room in them which you need. I am glad you are here Sigudur and now I have to get back in the house. Before I came out I put the baby down for her nap."

Seated at the supper table Sali averted his attention to Sigudur. "Now that we're in December, the weather will be getting colder. Yakima has cold winters and very hot summers. There is no way you can start building until spring," stated Sali.

"I have thought about that, Sali. I think I'm going to wait until March. I will rent a house for the winter and start looking for a job."

"I saw in the newspaper the other day that the Cascade Ice cream Company was advertising for help there," said Sali unfolding his napkin and spreading it over his lap.

"Oh, I think I will go there tomorrow. Thank you, Sali."

Gudmundina rested her eyes on her father. "I love our automobile pabbi. When will we be leaving here?"

"Probably Wednesday," replied Sigudur.

"That soon? I want to stay until I've helped Salomon finish packing the freight peaches."

Sali grinned. "So Gudmundina, that gives us just two more days."

CHAPTER TWENTY THREE

Arising early, Sigudur boarded his new Maxwell and headed to the country to find a house to rent for one year. He also found a piece of property near by to build in the spring. It appeared to be a family area. A high mountain could be seen not far from the neighborhood where groups of cows were grazing. It began to snow. By the time he was back to the peach orchard farm the ground was carpeted in ice and snow. Coming out of the house, Johanna went out to meet him. "Isn't the snow beautiful pabbi?" she asked.

"Not when one has to drive in it." replied Sigudur. "I hope it lets up by tomorrow. I'm going into town and apply for a job at the Cascade Creamery."

"When will we be moving into our rented house, pabbi? Is it far from the school?" asked Johanna.

"It's about five miles I think. Farther than I thought it would be," he replied taking her hand as they headed for the house. "Nothing is perfect. We have to take the bad with the good."

"Well, we have an automobile now can't you take us?"

"Yes I'll drive you to school on my way to work. But when school lets out you children will have to walk home."

Hearing voices Porunn opened the door. "I'm glad you are back Sigudur. I was worried about you."

"No need Tota I'm a Viking."

Gudmundina, Groa and Ingibjorg came out to the kitchen. "Isn't the snow beautiful pabbi?" sighed Ingibjorg.

"If you don't have to drive in it," replied Sigudur shaking the snow off his clothes.

"It must be fun to drive an automobile," said Groa.

"Oh yes Groa, automobiles have come a long ways since 1895 when they ran by electricity."

"Today they use a gasoline motor, operated by means of internal combustion," said Sigudur. When a baby's cry was heard from his and Porunn's bedroom, he hurried in and picked Annika up in his arms.

Night fell and the storm continued. At dawn Sigudur rose from his bed and dressed for an interview at Cascade Creamery. Porunn accosted her girls. "Start getting your things together. We will be leaving Sali's Peach Farm bright and early tomorrow morning," stated Porunn eyeing Groa who was opening the back door. "Where do you think you're going, Groa?" she asked.

"I'm going out to the barn mamma. Harold is up there and I won't see the pigeons for awhile."

"I told you to gather up your bags. We are leaving in the morning."

"I already have packed my bags." Porunn smiled and nodded and Groa left for the barn.

Gudmundina entered the kitchen with her traveling bag. "I'm all packed too. may I go out to the packing sheds and say goodbye to Salomon? He is closing up the warehouse for the winter."

"Yes of course Olof."

It was now noon. A sound of a motor car imbued the air. The girls ran out as their father drove up the driveway and parked. "Did you get a job?" asked Ingibjorg.

"Indeed I did Ingibjorg. And I believe a good one too." he replied spreading his arms for a hug. When they entered the house Porunn came in the kitchen.

"Did you get some work Sigudur?" she asked.

"Yes Tota, after the personnel manager saw my track record up in Iceland he offered me the position of foreman at the creamery." He glanced at her and smiled. "Naturally I took it."

In the morning the family anxiously climbed into the new automobile with excitement and vigor. Sali and Anna Petersson stood by waving until the vehicle was out of sight. Sigudur headed toward the country. Before long there was another snow squall covering the earth with a blanket of white. Soon they came to the house in the small village. "Oh look pabbi," exclaimed Johanna, "there's a mountain."

"Yes, and our house is only a short distance from those hills," stated Sigudur.

"Are we almost there?" asked Gudmundina.

"Yes Olof, it's that little brown house with the fence."

Now settled in their new home the family thought about Christmas. Porunn came into the kitchen and placed a pot on the cooking range. "Your father will be home from the creamery pretty soon. Groa, will you set the table for supper?"

"Yes mamma." replied Groa quietly.

"When will we be going to our new school mamma?" asked Gudmundina.

"The schools are closed for Christmas vacation. After the new year your father will take Johanna, Groa you and now Ingibjorg, to be admitted."

At five '0 clock p.m. Sigudur blew in the door. "Whew!" he exclaimed, "There's blizzard out there!" Walking into the house with his feet covered in ice and snow, he dropped a large package on a chair.

"What is that pabbi?" asked Gudmundina.

"I don't know Olof it was in our mail at the post office."

Porunn picked up the package. "It's from Blaine Washington!" she exclaimed. "And addressed to the Haflidason family."

"Open it up," said Gudmundina.

"No, we have to eat first. Everything is getting cold," replied Porunn placing the package back on the chair.

After the family had finished supper Ingibjorg and Porunn washed the dishes. All eyes were on the package.

Gathering around the mystery package, Porunn untied the string and pulled it off, exposing individual gifts wrapped in bright Christmas paper. "My what pretty paper," said Porunn lifting one of the packages out of the box. Handing the gift to Gudmundina, she smiled. "This one is for you, Olof. It has your name on it."

Gudmundina removed the paper and read the tag: From Grandma Cockroft. "Look!" she cried. "Grandma sent me Linnie's doll."

"Isn't Linnie Mrs. Taylor's daughter who passed away?" asked Porunn.

"Yes. Mrs. Taylor used to let me play with this doll." Holding the doll lovingly Gudmundina glanced at her mother. "Isn't she beautiful mamma? When I grow up I want to look just like her."

"You both have the long blonde hair. What did Linnie name her doll?"

"I don't know. I'm going to call her Gloria."

"Gloria—stated Porunn.

"Yes, after Gloria Swanson the beautiful actress that's so popular now." Groa, Johanna and Ingibjorg loved the books which Grandma Cohroft had made for them from gold cotton material, sewed on machine. She had cut out pictures in a magazine and pasted them through each leaf of the book, suitable for the individual age of the child. Porunn picked up the box to put in the trash when a small package fell from the corner of the wrapping paper. The tiny tag read: To baby. "Wasn't that thoughtful?" said Porunn opening up Annika's gift. It was another gold cloth book, small in size and pictures of infants and young children pasted on the pages.

The holidays were over. Johanna, Groa, Gudmundina and Ingibjorg were dressed for their first day at their new school. As they drove up the long gravel road, several children were walking to school. Sigudur stopped his automobile and offered them a ride. The day wore on, it was now time to go home. The group headed down the gravel road toward the mountain. They were half-way home when Johanna instantly stopped and listened. A roaring sound filled the air, Johanna saw hundreds of cattle running up the road in their direction. "Come on!" she screamed. "That's a stampede!"

She hustled the group through a fence and ran up on the porch, the children following close behind. In no time the thundering noise of hoofs became louder and soon the cattle came in droves past the fence and gate. As the herd stampeded on the clamorous sound gradually faded. Johanna scrambled off the porch. "Come on let's go. They might just come back."

When they reached home Porunn opened the door. "I hope you children did not get caught in that stampede."

"Yes we did," said Ingibjorg. "I was so scared!"

"What in the world did you do Hanna?" asked Porunn.

"It's nothing to be concerned about mamma. I just told my sisters to run up on someone's porch until the stampede passed."

"That was quick thinking Hanna. I am so glad that you were with them."

"I can't always be with them mamma."

"I know that Hanna. But they will know what to do next time."

Winter was ebbing. All the children were looking forward to spring vacation. Sigudur was drawing plans for the new house he would soon start building. Annika was growing and now sitting in a highchair at the table. She was a beautiful child and had a pleasant nature.

Today was the last day of February and the weather was mild and sunny. With all the children in school except for Annika the house seemed peaceful and quiet. Looking out of the window, Porunn focused her eyes over the long gravel road where the girls would be coming from school. She then espied Groa and Johanna with Gudmundina and Ingibjorg walking behind them. They entered the house and threw their books on the table. "I'll be glad when spring vacation starts", said Johanna.

"I'd just as soon go to school there's nothing to do." said Ingibjorg.

"I'm going to make Gloria a new dress," said Gudmundina.

"Gloria—? Whose Gloria?" asked Groa.

"That's Gudmundina's new doll that Mrs. Taylor gave her," stated Ingibjorg.

"Sure sounds boring," chimed in Johanna removing her coat. "I'm not going back after vacation. I hate school!"

"Oh, you'll be going back all right," said Porunn interjecting into the conversation. "I am sure you remember how the truant officer used to come to our other home to see why you were not in school."

"Well, I got away with it because you told hooky bull I was sick."

"I'm not going to lie for you anymore, Hanna. Your father can handle it." picking up Johanna's coat Porunn rested her eyes on Groa. "What are your plans for vacation?"

"I don't have any mamma. Harold said his parents were coming over and that he could come with them and bring his pigeon."

Looking over at her children she paused, then smiled. "I think it is only fair that I tell you all that I have made an appointment with Dr. Kelly to have your tonsils out. I figured during vacation you wouldn't loose any school."

"Ohh, mamma!" they all cried out.

"I can see I was wrong interfering with your vacation plans. I am going to change our appointment to next week." She rested her eyes on Gudmundina. "You have to have your adnoise removed also Olof."

"Why me?" asked Gudmundina.

"Because Dr. Kelly said so. The other girls are all right."

It was a busy time for Porunn with five children sick in bed. Sigudur brought large containers of ice cream home for the children's sore throats. A week passed. Johanna, Groa and Ingibjorg returned to school. Gudmundina was ill and too weak. Her abnormally high body heat was of great concern. Another week past and Gudmundina's temperature was normal.

As time passed vacation was over and the girls were back in school. Each day the children in the small village would look for Sigudur's automobile for a ride to school. He never failed to give anyone a ride who was walking up the long gravel road into the city. Porunn ironing glanced up when her children came in from school. "How was school today Hanna?" asked Porunn. Shrugging her shoulders Johanna made a face. A light rap was heard on the back entry. Both exchanged glances. Porunn opened the door. Standing on the porch was a pretty young girl. She smiled and asked, "Are you Mrs. Haflidason?"

"Yes," replied Porunn curiously.

"Did your husband find my pants in his car last night? I forgot my pants in his back seat."

"I will ask him when he comes home from work tonight." replied Porunn, showing no emotion.

"Thank you," called out the girl running down the steps and down the gravel road.

Johanna accosted her mother. "You sure handled that calmly."

"What do you mean Hanna what is there to get excited about?"

"A beautiful young girl comes to your house and tells you she forgot her pants in the back of your husband's automobile last night. And all you could say was that you would ask him when he got home from work tonight. I think pabbi needs watching mamma. After all he is just a man."

"And I think Hanna that you have a pretty warped mind for a twelve year old child."

Spring was taking over winter. A soft breeze blew through the naked tree branches. Sigudur left the creamery and headed toward the mountain and home. Hearing his Maxwell drive up Johanna, Groa, and Gudmundina ran out to meet him. He removed a sandwich out of his lunch box and gave it to Johanna. "Here," he stated, "is the usual sandwich I save. You can divide it Hanna." Suddenly he inquired. "Where is Ingibjorg?"

"She is helping mamma in the kitchen with supper."

Moving to Porunn's side, Sigudur kissed her. Porunn edged away from him and looked at Ingibjorg. "Elskan will you put Annika in her high chair. We are ready to eat." Lifting Annika in the chair Ingibjorg rested her eyes on her mother's features. "You know mamma I think Annika should be sitting in a regular chair. She is almost four years old now." Porunn did not respond.

Sigudur sat down at the table . . . "You must have one of your migraines today, Tota."

"No Sigudur, I feel fine." A pause, then she added, "We had a visitor this afternoon."

"A visitor? Who . . . ?"

"A very pretty young girl. She wanted to know if you found her pants in the back seat of your car."

"Yes, I found her pants on the back seat floor. She came out of the high school next door to the creamery the same time I left work. I gave them to her. She told me she plays basket ball every Tuesday so needs her gym bloomers."

Gudmundina smiled. "Bloomers in gym! I understand that swimsuits are also showing bloomers." Grandma Cockroft pasted a real pretty girl in my book she made with a model in bloomers."

"I'd like a pair of gym bloomers," said Groa.

"I don't think so Groa. You don't play basket ball or swim," said Porunn.

"You're probably right," replied Groa.

Porunn stood at her bedroom window and observed the dark, gray shadows stretching over the hills. Glancing on the wall her eyes traveled to the calendar for today's date. Yes, as she thought it was February 24. A recall of her third birthday flashed across her mind. Her father Olafur was holding her in his arms. She could hear his voice. "Gledileg Amaleg, Porunn." She came out of the past remembering she had requested Sigudur and her family to disregard her birthdays.

March blew in sunny and mild. Sigudur was now starting construction on the new house. He spent most of his time down at the construction lot carrying on where Helgi Peterson who was helping Sigudur with the project left the job on weekends.

At home Porunn kept busy with the children. Johanna came into the kitchen and filled up a bowl of oatmeal then sat down at the table. "Mamma did you remember that this is pabbi's birthday?"

"Of course I did Hanna—this is the third of March. I baked him a nice birthday cake this morning."

"Oh, you would. I wanted to bake it for him," said Johanna grimacing.

"I'm sorry, maybe next year."

Time passed. April 11 Ingibjorg bounced into the room as Sigudur walked into the house from the creamery. "Pabbi, did you remember today I am seven years old?"

"Of course elskan. Look in my vest pocket."

"Where is your vest pocket pabbi?" she asked, hunting through the whole coat. "Oh I found it," she laughed pulling out a blue velvet box. A beautiful ivory bracelet met her eyes. "Oh, pabbi! It's beautiful!" she cried throwing her arms around him and kissing him on the cheek. "How did you know pabbi that I wanted a bracelet"

"Because I heard you tell your mother the other night that you wanted a white bracelet to go with the trimming on your new brown dress."

It was now May 22. Coming home from the construction sight Sigurdur's eyes traveled around the room where Johanna sat hemming a dress. "Where is your mother?" asked Sigudur.

"In her room. She has a migraine," replied Johanna standing up from the table and pouring her father some coffee. "How is the house coming, pabbi?"

"Great! Helgi and I have only been working three months on it and already it looks like we may have it finished in three more months."

"So about September we can plan on moving into our new home?"

"I should think so Hanna." He looked askance at her and smiled. "I am sure you know what this day is."

"If you're referring to my birthday yes. I am now thirteen years old—an adult."

"Not quite an adult yet Hanna." He picked up his jacket and pulled out a maroon velvet jewel case and handed Johanna the box. "Happy Birthday Hanna!"

Opening the case she saw a beautiful gold wristwatch. "Oh pabbi, a Bulova!"

"Nothing but the best for my Hanna," exclaimed Sigudur giving her a hug. He rose from his chair and crossed to the threshold of the bedroom. "I'm going in to see your mother. I hope she isn't asleep."

It was now the day before school was closing for the summer solstice. Porunn stood filling five oatmeal bowls for breakfast. Gudmundina entering the kitchen helped herself to the cereal. "What are you doing in your good dress Olof? That's the dress you keep for Sunday school."

"Today the school is taking pictures of our class. I want to look pretty," she replied saucily, dropping down on her chair.

"Oh I see," stated her mother. "But be sure you take it off as soon as you get home."

In the late afternoon Porunn peered through the window to see if her daughters could be seen coming home from school.

Then she saw Johanna, Groa and Ingibjorg walking together with Gudmundina dragging behind them. Upon entering the house Gudmundina threw a manila envelope down on the kitchen table. "I don't want this stupid picture!" she cried with choleric temper.

"What is the matter Gudmundina?" asked Porunn coming into the kitchen.

"Those large horsy girls spoiled my picture! No one can even see me. The photographer should have had them stand in back of a small girl like me."

Porunn picked up the envelope and took out the picture. "You look quite small compared to some of the other students, but you look very nice in that soft pink dress with the low, black pattern leather belt." Placing the picture back on the table, Porunn gave her a hug. "It is no federal case, Gudmundins—just a picture."

School was now out for the summer. By June and July the weather was unbearable. Today was Saturday. Sigudur was working late on the house and would not be home for supper. As the girls finished supper Porunn rose from the table. "Now that your father is working late this evening I thought we might visit an old lady who lives alone in a small shack at the foot of the mountain."

"I'm not going," stated Johanna.

"I'm not either," said Groa."

"I'll go with you mamma," said Ingibjorg gathering up the dishes off the supper table.

Porunn smiled. "Thank you elskan."

"Is she a nice lady mamma?" asked Ingibjorg.

"I don't know Ingibjorg. I have never met her."

"Then why do you want to visit someone you don't know?" asked Groa.

"Because she must be lonely being the only black person in the neighborhood."

"A colored lady—?" asked Gudmundina.

"Yes. Black people get lonely too."

"Well if no one visits her why should we." asked Johanna.

"Because no one visits her," replied Porunn, her features douring. "I want you girls to promise not to tell your father where we went today."

"Why not mamma? Because he doesn't want you being friendly with a nigger?" said Johanna.

"Don't use that word in this house, Hanna," exclaimed Porunn.

"I think I will go with you, mamma. It may be an interesting story to write when I grow up and become an author," said Gudmundina.

"I hope Annika will be able to walk that far. Go get her bonnet Groa." Returning with a pink silk cap with long streamers, Groa placed the bonnet over Annika's long, blonde silky hair. "I want to bring the woman some ice cream. Gudmundina so bring up that little red wagon down there. I don't know who the wagon belonged to. It was there when we came."

Porunn, Gudmundina, Ingibjorg and Annika set out for the mountain stopping at short intervals to rest. "I think you should take a turn hauling that gallon of ice cream Gudmundina," stated Porunn. "Ingibjorg has pulled that wagon all the way from home."

"That's alright mamma I don't mind," stated Ingibjorg. Gudmundina grabbed the handle of the wagon and started up the long dusty road leading to the foot of the mountain.

"Look!" cried out Ingibjorg. "That tiny unpainted house must be the old woman's!"

Stopping and squinting her eyes, Porunn replied, "I think you must be right Ingibjorg. "Let's knock at the door and see," said Porunn shading her eyes with her hand from the sinking sun.

They walked softly up the steps of the shanty and knocked. They paused for a moment then knocked again and waited. No answer. "Maybe she went to church," whispered Gudmundina. About to leave then a small crack in the door opened with a squeak.

"What do you folks want?" the woman bellowed in an angry tone of voice.

"We have brought you some ice cream."

"Go away and take your ice cream with you. I don't want any charity from white trash!"

"We are here as friends. Please, may we come in?" said Porunn.

"Why do you want to be friends with a black woman. The neighbors around here poke fun at me and throw stones at my house."

"You should not hold against us what others have done." All of a sudden Annika let out a scream from the bottom of the steps where she sat resting, "Mamma!", she cried. "I want to go home!"

"Whose that screaming?" asked the black woman throwing the door open and coming out on the small porch.

"My little daughter is resting on the bottom step. She has never walked this far before and is tired and wants to go home," replied Porunn.

"Bless her heart," said the woman, moving with measured steps to where Annika was sitting. Taking Annika by the hand she led her up the porch. "You come right in with Mrs. Cutbank darlin,' She has a nice piece of rock candy for you in her cupboard." Annika glanced up at her and smiled.

"Your name is Mrs. Cutbank?" asked Porunn. She nodded and led Annika into the house with Porunn following after them.

Picking up the ice cream Ingibjorg called out to Gudmundina. "Leave the wagon out here. Gudmundina," called Ingibjorg over her shoulder. "Annika can ride home in it."

The one room was comfortable and spotlessly clean. A pot belly stove sent off a welcoming warmth throughout the structure.

Placing a jar of hard candy on the kitchen table, Mrs. Cutbank lifted Annika on a chair. "Take all you like darlin'"

"Thank you Mrs. Cutbank," replied Annika smiling.

"What a sweet child. And with unusual beauty also." She glanced at Ingibjorg and Gudmundina. "All your children are beautiful and I am sure they are beautiful inside too or they would not come to visit a black woman. If all mothers would raise their children as you are there would not be such hatred among the blacks and whites." Mrs. Cutbank crossed over to the cooking range. "I'm going to make me and you a cup of coffee. Please sit down. It will only take a minute."

Pulling out a chair from the table Porunn sat down next to Annika and smiled. "She's a nice lady mamma," said Annika.

Mrs. Cutbank came back to the table with hot coffee and cinnamon rolls. Pouring Porunn some coffee she glanced at Porunn curiously. "I don't believe you gave me your name."

"I'm sorry Mrs. Cutbank, my name is Mrs. Haflidason. But you can just call me by my first name, Porunn."

"Sounds like a foreign name?"

"Yes my husband and I are both from Iceland."

"They must have nice people in Iceland," stated Mrs. Cutbank.

"Well I'm of the opinion that there is good and bad people everywhere. It is the character and heart that count." The two women spent their time in deep conversation, drinking coffee and eating cinnamon rolls with ice cream.

Gudmundina gazed around the room and her eyes focused on an old trunk sitting on the floor in a corner under the eaves. She took Ingibjorg to the side and whispered in her ear. "Do you see that old trunk over there?"

"No I don't see any trunk."

"Well, you're not as observing as I am."

"What do you think it is, a trunk?" asked Ingibjorg with her eyes fastened to the lower border of an eave which overhung a wall.

"I haven't a clue, Inga." whispered Gudmundina.

"I think it could be most anything," said Ingibjorg. "She could even have tools in there."

Noticing the girls taking interest in the old trunk Mrs. Cutbank called out to them. "Would you girls like to see inside of the trunk?"

"Oh Yes1 Could we?" exclaimed Gudmundina.

"Certainly. Go ahead and open it."

Gudmundina tried lifting the lid but it would not open. "It's locked, Mrs. Cutbank."

"Oh I'm sorry. I forgot to give you the key." She reached down her dress and pulled out a long chain from her neck. Removing a small key she gave it to Gudmundina. When the lid flew open a flame of brilliant satin and silk pieces of about four by four inches of every color met their eyes. The trunk was filled to the brim. Mrs. Cutbank then left the girls and returned to the table.

"Oh they're beautiful!" exclaimed Gudmundina fingering the silk gently. "We have to find out what they are for," stated Gudmundina curiously.

"We shouldn't ask her Gudmundina. It wouldn't be polite. It's plain to see that the pieces are important to her. They are probably an old wonderful memory of her past."

"Maybe you're right Ingibjorg. We have no right to pry."

Mrs. Cutbank stood up from her chair and brought some more coffee to the table. "Let me warm up your coffee Mrs. Haflidason."

"No more for me, Mrs. Cutbank. You make very good coffee, but my husband will be coming home soon."

"I understand, Mrs. Haflidason. Thanks so much for coming and for the ice cream. I hope you and the girls will come back real soon."

The sinking sun was going down behind the mountain. With Annika in the little red wagon, Ingibjorg and Gudmundina headed for home with Porunn by their side.

Johanna and Groa came to the door to meet them. "How was the visit?" asked Johanna.

"We had an awful good time Jo,' stated Gudmundina.

"You of all people had a good time," cut in Groa.

"Gudmundina is going to write a story about Mrs. Cutbank when she grows up," stated Ingibjorg removing Annika's bonnet. "And she already knows a word, observant."

"I'm so excited I have the plot already," smiled Gudmundina. The back door opened and Sigudur walked in the door.

June and July's hot weather continued through August. Johanna making lemonade in the kitchen glanced up when Groa came in drying the sweat from her face. "Oh I am so hot!" she exclaimed. "I'm glad you're making lemonade Jo, did the iceman leave any ice yesterday?"

"Yes it's in the icebox." Johanna filled several glasses of lemonade and placed them on a tray. Picking it up she moved to the dining room threshold and glanced over her shoulder at Groa. "We better get out of the kitchen. Mamma is coming in to bake your cake. We don't want to be in her way."

"Oh my birthday cake!" exclaimed Groa smiling. "I'm getting so old I can't remember my birthdays anymore."

"Yea, real old eleven birthdays. I was two years old when you were born and I remember it was August 18th."

"Oh come on Jo mamma told you the date of my birthday." When Porunn came in they went to the dining room for lemonade.

CHAPTER TWENTY FOUR

It was now fall. The fourth of September was Annika's 4th birthday. Her present was a white straw doll buggy for her many cherished dolls.

Autumn brought cool winds blowing through the tree branches and leaves that were beginning to fall to the earth. Today was moving day. The new home was now finished. All children were back in school. Waiting impatiently for the dismissal of the school bell to ring, Johanna sat at her desk and glanced at her Bulova wristwatch at short intervals. With the first sound of the bell she was gone. Ingibjorg hurrying down the hall to Johanna's room, found it vacant except for the teacher correcting papers. "Hello Miss Brent. Has Johanna gone home?"

"Yes she was kind of in a hurry." The teacher placed her pen down on the desk and smiled. "Are you Johanna's sister?"

"Yes I have two more sisters who go to school here, Groa and Gudmundina. My sister Gudmundina is going to be a writer when she grows up."

"Ohh!"

"Gudmundina is very smart. She says writers have to be because they use big words like observant. Do you ever use that word Miss Brent?"

"Oh yes."

"Well be sure you spell it with a va instead of ve. Gudmundina said she had a hard time remembering whether it ended in ve or va."

"Oh I will try and remember," said Miss Brent chuckling to herself.

"I have to go now Miss Brent. Maybe I can catch up with Johanna."

October's weather gave great comfort and relief after the hot summer. "October had a party leaves by hundreds came." On October 16 Gudmundina had her ninth birthday. Sigudur presented her with a beautiful six foot concert grand piano. It was a used four leg square antique piano in perfect condition. He engaged a music teacher, a Mrs. Murphy who came to the house once a week to give Gudmundina piano lessons. The novelty lasted about three years then Gudmundina refused to practice.

It was a beautiful autumn day. Eating breakfast, Gudmundina glanced over the table at Ingibjorg. "Let's go for a walk."

"I want to do the dishes first," said Ingibjorg.

"I think I'll go put on my new red dress." said Gudmundina.

"I'm just going to wear my old skirt and blouse," replied Ingibjorg rising from the table and picking up the dishes to wash.

As they walked Gudmundina lead the direction to the large field and climbed the fence. Ingibjorg followed her. "Oh, Oh,!" the bull is out there today."

"The bull is out there every day come on let's go!"

"Look Gudmundina! He's looking at you and he's coming over!", cried Ingibjorg climbing back over the fence.

"You're such a baby!", stated Gudmundina continuing across the field. The bull picking up speed got ready to charge with a steady eye on Gudmundina's red dress. She let out a scream and ran back and climbed over the fence. Stepping up his gait he paused for a moment, then moved slowly back to the end of the field to his usual spot.

"Let's go down to the creek and cool off," said Gudmundina, dobbing the sweat from her face.

"I'm not that warm," said Ingibjorg. "You've been running. Do you think it will be safe to go through the field?"

"Sure. The bull is way down at the other end of the field. He generally doesn't notice us."

"Of course not. It's that red dress you insisted on wearing."

They hopped over the fence and walked in the direction of the large creek at the far end of the field.

Sitting on the bank of the creek they swished their feet in the cool water. "The water is cold," stated Ingibjorg drawing her feet out of the creek.

"Cold!" exclaimed Gudmundina. "I'm still hot."

"Pull your dress up higher and cool your legs. I'm real comfortable," said Ingibjorg. Glancing around the water, her eyes caught a tall tree growing on the edge of the creek. "Oh look at the tree. It's half way in the water."

"And look at the red apples on it. Oh let's get some apples," exclaimed Gudmundina hopping up on her feet.

"There are only two apples that we can reach from the bank," said Ingibjorg.

Pointing a finger up at a couple of small apples hanging on a loose branch Gudmundina grimaced. "Surely you don't mean those shriveled up apples over there. Look above those logs, Ingibjorg. Those are beautiful."

"We can't get those, Gudmundina. We can't reach them from the bank."

"No we can't. But you can. I'm afraid of heights. The least thing you can do Ingibjorg is try."

"All right I'll try." Ingibjorg stood up. "You're taller than I am why don't you try and reach it?"

"Because I might fall. Go ahead and climb the tree."

Starting up the trunk of the apple tree, Ingibjorg began stretching for the pretty red apple hanging from a branch over the deepest part of the creek where logs were kept floating in the water.

Gudmundina standing barefoot on the bank watched with her eyes on the red apple. "You almost got it that time Ingibjorg. Stretch a little farther and I think you'll have it."

Ingibjorg took in a deep sigh and repositioned herself closer to the end of the branch. All of a sudden a large splash in the water was heard, the aged limb had cracked and fallen in six foot water deep, and Ingibjorg with it. Slipping between the logs she panicked but tried to work herself up on a log. Luckily the day before some logs had been delivered here.

Pushing herself up on top of the floating logs she worked her way to the edge of the bank. Gudmundina came running over and reached for Ingibjorg's hand and hoisted her up the bank. "Don't you tell mamma that I asked you to get me that apple."

"No I won't. But mamma will see that I'm all wet."

"Tell her you were wadding at the edge of the creek and you lost your balance."

When they arrived home they dreaded to go in. Porunn busy in the kitchen glanced up as they tried to sneak behind her. "Ingibjorg! What happened to you? You're all wet!"

"Nothing mamma. I was wadding in the creek and I lost my balance and fell in the creek."

"You could have drown."

"No. I was only at the edge of the creek."

"Thank heavens! Hurry now and get some dry clothes on."

November brought snow and ice and a bitter wind blew through the naked tree branches. Christmas day the earth was carpeted in snow. A bright sun warmed the atmosphere as neighborhood children, Johanna and Groa were out making snowmen.

Gudmundina came out of her room dressed in her heavy parka. "I'm going out to make a snowman too mamma."

"Where are your mittens Olof?" asked Porunn.

"They're in my pocket. I'll put them on."

Standing at the window Annika looked out at the lively activity in front of the house. She left the window and came into the kitchen. "May I go out with you Gudmundina?" asked Annika.

"No," said Gudmundina. "You're too small." She pulled on her mittens and dashed out of the door.

Sigudur came into the kitchen and kissed Annika on the cheek. "Pabbi," said Annika, "Am I too small to go out and play with the other children?"

"Of course not elskan. I'll tell you what we'll do. Your mother will put you in your snow suit and boots then you and I will go out with the other children and make a snow man."

"Oh thank you pabbi," smiled Annika blotting her moistened eyes with a hand.

Christmas bells were ringing a message of yuletide at the village church where the town folk gathered for the Christmas service. Sigudur and Annika walked over to Johanna and Groa who were almost finished making their snow man. "They look great but wait until you see Annika's and my snow man," said Sigudur picking up a large hunk of snow and starting the base for Annika. She rolled several pieces and Sigudur placed them on the figure. Laughter imbued the air as the children worked.

"I think the snow man is beautiful," said Annika. "But could we go into the house pabbi? My hands are cold."

"Yes the sun is going down and it is getting colder."

Thus the months passed by. Spring came, then summer took over. School closed for the season and all the happy children in the neighborhood were out doors playing most of the day trying to keep cool. One morning when the neighborhood children and Johanna, Groa, Ingibjorg and Gudmundina came out to play, Johanna noted a large irrigation troup right inside the field against the fence next to where they were playing. Her eyes traveled across the long field where several troughs had been installed against the fence also filled with water. After hours of sitting in the sun the water had gotten warm. "Look!" cried Johanna. pointing to the field. "There's enough troughs for all of us and they're filled with water." The group of children hopped over the fence and into a trough fully dressed. "Oh this feels so cool" said Gudmundina stretching out full length in the long but narrow trough. Apparently the owner of the field used the irrigation troughs to cool and give his animals water to drink during this crucial heat wave.

Several hours passed. Johanna hopped out of her trough in her wringing wet clothes. "Let's go home. It must be almost five 'o clock. Pabbi will be coming home from work and he will be mad if he sees us in our wet clothes." The drenched group of children jumped out of the trough and they all headed for home.

Porunn opened the back door when she heard her children's voices on the porch. "My heavens! What happened?"

"Nothing," said Gudmundina brushing past her into her room.

"Hanna, what is the meaning of all this?" Groa slipped by her and hurried to change her clothes.

"Nothing mamma. It's nothing to get excited about. The owner of the field now has irrigation troughs for the animals so we all can now be cool in this hot weather."

"You all went in the water with your clothes on?"

"Well this came on suddenly—sort of a nice surprise for us." Ingibjorg standing saturated in water glanced up at her mother. "We're going to wear an old blouse and pants tomorrow." All at once foot steps sounded on the back porch. "That's your father! Go to your room and put on some dry clothes."

Endearing Porunn in his arms he kissed her warmly. "It's good to be home Tota. It must be a hundred out there!"

"Another hot day," said Groa on the following morning.

"We won't have to worry now that we have a swimming hole of our own," laughed Ingibjorg. She glanced at Johanna. "Where is Gudmundina?"

"When I went to her room to see why she hadn't come to breakfast, she was sound asleep. I woke her up and she told me she was sick."

"Does mamma know?" asked Ingibjorg.

"Yes I told her and she said she would check on her as soon as she got Annika up."

Placing a bowl of oatmeal on the table Porunn set Annika up to the kitchen table. "I'll be right back, Annika. Try to finish your breakfast," she said leaving hurriedly for Gudmundina's room.

Lying flushed and still with her eyes closed. Gudmundina then opened them. And with fevered lips she murmured, "Mamma!" Porunn fled from the room to the kitchen where Ingibjorg was eating oatmeal with Annika. "Is Gudmundina very sick. mamma?" asked Ingibjorg.

"Very! Your father will have to go and get the doctor. It's going to be a long day until he gets home."

"Where does she seem to be sick?" inquired Ingibjorg.

"I couldn't talk to her she was like she was in a coma. But one thing clear, she is burning with fever! I'll have to keep her as cool as I can until your father gets home and can get a doctor."

"I'll help you. I won't go to the field."

It was a long day. Porunn and Ingibjorg worked together placing cold wet towels on Gudmundina's forehead. Johanna and Groa spent the day in the irrigation troughs.

The day finally ended. Sigudur arriving home noted Porunn was not in the kitchen cooking supper as usual. Shortly ensuing, Ingibjorg came out to greet him. "Oh you're home Ingibjorg," said Sigudur removing his white Panama hat.

"Mamma needed help. Gudmundina is very sick!" said Ingibjorg.

Sigudur hurried to the sickroom. "Olof!" he called out placing his hand on her feverish brow as she lay in a comatose slumber. Noting Porunn's devastating features he moved to the entry. "Olof is going to be alright Tota. I'll get the doctor."

Two hours elapsed. Sigudur had not returned.

When a 1921 model ford followed Sigudur in the yard Johanna and Groa home from the field left the room when Sigudur and the doctor came in. At Gudmundina's bedside the physician took out the stethoscope from his little black bag and began taking the patient's vital signs. He then picked up a thermometer. "I cannot check the elevation of her temperature by mouth. She still is not aware of her environment," stated the doctor placing the thermometer in the armpit of one of Gudmundina's arms.

When the allotted time was up the physician adjusted his horn-rimmed glasses. and retook the temperature. "It is up to the danger zone. Get her ready Mr. Haflidason. I'm taking this nine year old child to the hospital!"

"Just a moment, Dr. Bates. No way are you going to take my daughter to a hospital. What ever she needs she will get right here at home," said Sigudur.

"She will need a lot of care. Care which a lay person cannot handle," stated Dr. Bates. "The child should have a nurse."

"Then get us a nurse!" Sigudur blurted out with temper.

"Mr. Haflidason, I cannot force you to put your child in a hospital but she will die if not given the proper care."

"I told you, Dr. Bates, then get us a nurse."

"It will cost a lot of money, Mr. Haflidason. And if Gudmundina has what I think, she will need nursing care for more than a year—after that who knows?"

Sigudur's dark blue inset eyes looked steadily in Dr. Bates's face. "What are you trying to tell me Dr. Bates?"

"I am trying to have you realize that if not treated properly typhoid fever could be fatal . . . and could become an epidemic."

"Oh my God!' cried Sigudur burying his face in his hands as he broke into a sob. "Whatever, Dr. Bates I refuse to let her go to a hospital. If she dies she will do so at home. I know how these nurses keep opening up windows all the time even at night. Half of the people who die in hospitals is from pneumonia."

"This is a pretty big problem for a person to handle himself," stated Dr, Bates. "But I am sure the Red Cross will investigate this. They are used to disasters and are very helpful." Throwing his stethoscope into his bag he rested his eyes on Sigudur's worried features. "Tomorrow all the little girls will have to be inoculated for typhoid fever and probably the whole family. Tomorrow morning the health officer will come and quarantine your home."

"How does he do that?" asked Sigudur.

"By posting a large sign on your house reading, KEEP OUT . . . TYPHOID FEVER."

"What about my other girls. Can they attend school?" questioned Sigudur.

"Yes, after they have been inoculated which will be tomorrow. And until then no one can enter this house or leave." Dr. Bates looked thoughtfully at Sigudur. "You'll get your nurse Mr. Haflidason. She'll be here at seven tomorrow morning."

"What causes typhoid fever, doctor?" asked Sigudur.

"As a rule polluted water. When Gudmundina was soaking in the irrigation water she probably swallowed some with out being aware of it. As you know the other children didn't get it." stated Dr. Bates.

Sigudur shook the physician's hand. "Please except my apology for my bad temper I wasn't myself."

"I understand, Mr. Haflidason. Your a good father. And I'm sure with Gudmundina's parent's loving care she is going to come out of this just fine."

Porunn and Sigudur stood and waved goodbye at the physician as he stepped into his ford and headed for the gravel road leading to the city.

Placing his arms around Porunn's shoulders Sigudur held her close. "I want you to go to bed and sleep, Tota. I will keep check on Olof through the night."

Bright and early the following morning a knock on the door was sounded. Porunn and Sigudur exchanged glances. "Must be the health officer," said Porunn with her nerves all on edge.

"No Tota. That's a woman's knock. It's too light for a man." He rushed to the door and saw a small slender nurse standing on the porch. "Good morning! I am Mrs. King, your daughter's nurse," she smiled amicably.

Noticing the red cross on her cap, Porunn stepped back from the doorstep. "Oh I am so happy you are here. Come in Mrs. King." As they were to advance into the living room an official van drove into the yard. "That's the health officer," stated the nurse, moving into the house and shutting the door. Removing a long ladder from the van and with a large sign and a hammer, the official climbed up on the roof and posted the bright red sign reading, KEEP OUT . . . Typhoid FEVER.

It was a long day. Mrs. King worked endlessly at Gudmundina's bedside. At the close of day Mrs. King took Porunn to the side. "I don't mean to come in here and change your home all around, however We have to make a few changes here. I want your husband to buy a small bed and I suggest a Junior child's bed with rails. Gudmundina is having hallucinations and she has to be restricted for her own safety." She slipped her navy colored cape over her uniform. "Also her bed will have to be completely covered in mosquito netting and put in the living room."

"Will you be having Gudmundina on a diet?" asked Porunn.

"What she eats is very important. The wrong food could bring on a convulsion. And absolutely no bread. Only graham crackers. Also she is not to have any solid food only puddings and ice cream or Jell-O, things like that . . . and cocoa will be all right."

"Now that the other girls have had their inoculation can they go back to school?" added Porunn.

"Yes. Tomorrow will be just fine," replied Mrs. King hurrying down the steps to her vehicle.

Thus time passed. Gudmundina remained in a semi-conscious state, waking up at short intervals then dropping off in a deep slumber. Coming home from school Johanna went into the sick room to see her sick sister. "Gudmundina! I'm home!" she called out. With no response Johanna left the room. Porunn stood in the kitchen baking bread. "Did Olof recognize you Hanna?"

"No. She didn't even open her eyes," replied Johanna. "Something smells awfully good mamma," said Johanna. "Don't tell me you are making bread?"

"I bake all the bread we eat."

"Gudmundina can't eat it."

"Yes I know. But we have other mouths around here that have to be fed."

"It sure smells good," said Johanna leaving the kitchen and going to Groa's and her room.

"Did you stop and see Gudmundina when you got home." asked Groa.

"Of course but it didn't do any good. She's still sort of in a coma."

"They say people who are unconscious often know more what's going on than we think. So visitors have to be careful what they say in a sick room," stated Groa leaving the chamber. In the kitchen Groa noticed a rack of freshly baked bread. Johanna entered the room. "Does that smell good!" said Johanna slipping a small paper bag in her pocket. Groa glanced at her curiously then left the room to join Mrs. King who was preparing the night medications.

With a small paper bag hidden in the folds of her full pleated skirt, Johanna dashed to Gudmundina's bedside. "Wake up Gudmundina I have some nice bread for you." No response.

Moving slightly her eyes half opened. "Br . . . ead?"

"Yes. Mamma baked it for you."

With Johanna's assistance Gudmundina nibbled on a corner of the bread then fell asleep again. Groa was suspicious that Johanna had done this before but knowing this was only Johanna's pity and genuine concern about her sick sister whom she loved very much, decided to let it pass as she had previous done.

Mrs. King was a devoted nurse. And she had become very fond of Gudmundina, spending hours spoonfeeding her with the utmost patience. During Gudmundina's waking hours it was in her eyes the closeness she felt to her nurse. Gudmundina's fever was going down but not yet stable.

It was three in the morning, Porunn and Sigudur awakened to a blood-curdling scream! Running to Gudmundina's bedside they found her crawling to the head of the bed on her knees. "Mamma! Mamma!" she cried desperately, "the ceiling is falling down and it's going to fall on my head!" She threw her arms up in the air then covered her face with her hands for protection. "Mamma hold the ceiling up!"

"You go back to our room Tota I'll take care of this. Gudmundina is hallucinating!"

"I'm not going back! She's calling for me to help her." Porunn lifted the mosquito net and placed her arms around her underweight body. "Mamma is here elskan. The ceiling is not falling down. Go back to sleep and I will stay with you for awhile." After kissing Gudmundina good night Porunn replaced the mosquito netting and dropped down in an easy chair by the bed.

It was now almost December. Gudmundina was able to sit up in bed. She was now lucid with the fever gone. Gudmundina's beautiful long, blonde hair had fallen out and all mirrors were kept away from her as long as possible. Her lethargy took over her whole body preventing her from being able to get out of bed or walk. Her sisters were devoted to her visiting in her room after school Gudmundina looked forward to time of day. Johanna was the most frequent of Gudmundina's visitors. And she usually brought off-limited food to her sick sister hidden in the fold of her skirts.

Spring brought sunshine and flowers. Unable to walk Gudmundina was still on bed rest. She could hear her sisters' voices talking and laughing outside her window. "Oh look! There's some daffodils growing under the steps," cried Groa. Annika playing with her doll buggy outside called out, "Pick it for me Groa, I want it."

"No. Annika it will just die," replied Groa.

"I'll pick you some of those pretty poinsettias Annika, They're prettier anyway", said Johanna plucking a few golden flowers and putting them in Annika's doll carriage. "Thank you Jo," said Annika smiling.

Coming out of the house, Porunn looked under the step. "Those daffodils are beautiful. And they have all ready worked themselves away from the steps."

'That's mamma's voice,' thought Gudmundina, 'I can't go outside but if I get up and look out the window I will be able to see the daffodils.' She unfastened her mosquito net and crawled from underneath her bedding. As her feet reached the plane level of the room, she was too weak and fell in a heap on the floor. Unhurt but embarrassed she tried to hurry to her feet. Too weak . . . too late. They had heard a thump and suspected what had happened.

Christmas morning 1921. Mrs. King walked in at her usual time. She was carrying a package wrapped in Christmas paper. When she entered Gudmundina's room she kissed her on the cheek. "Merry Christmas Gudmundina." said the nurse handing Gudmundina her gift.

"For me?" asked Gudmundina.

"Yes. And I have another surprise for you. Next week I am getting you up for a couple of hours. Dr. Bates reports that your fever is all gone. It is just the matter of time now to get your strength back."

"Oh I'm going to miss you Mrs. King!"

"Don't think about that now Gudmundina. It will take two or three weeks before you will be completely mobile.

Go ahead Gudmundina. Open your present."

After untying the string with the utmost care, she opened up the box. "Oh Mrs. King! A baby doll!. And look at Baby Ella's eyes. Aren't they beautiful?" exclaimed Gudmundina.

"Have you named her all ready?" asked Mrs. King.

"Yes. Is Baby Ella all right Mrs. King?"

"It's perfect." The nurse collected the paper and debris from the bed and threw it in the wastebasket. "After your bed is made I'll put Baby Ella at the foot of the bed where you can see her. Now, don't you have another doll Gudmundina—a grownup doll? I think you called her Gloria Swanson."

"Yes the famous movie star. This one has long blonde hair and pretty blue eyes just like me. Or at least I hope I will look just like her when I grow up." Gudmundina glanced curiously at her. "Would you mind if we put Gloria on my bed with Baby Ella?"

"I think that would be lovely. Where do you keep her?" asked Mrs. King.

"In the third drawer of that dresser," replied Gudmundina pointing a finger at the chest of drawers.

Advancing toward the bed with Gloria in her arms she gave her to Gudmundina. "She does look like you," smiled Mrs. King.

One month had passed. Gudmundina's new routine had started and she looked forward to each ensuing day as she progressed. Ingibjorg was happy to have Gudmundina as a room mate again, and once more she was able to go out and play with her sisters. It had been a difficult year for Gudmundina and for everyone.

Autumn took over summer. And tonight a haunting Hunter's moon was shining through the windows. Sigudur took Porunn in his arms and kissed her. "Thank God we can maybe have some peace in our lives for awhile Tota." They went to their chamber and were soon in a contented deep slumber.

Now almost three o'clock in the morning, Sigudur was awakened by the timber of excited voices at his door. "Wake up Tota something must have happened! The yard is full of people!" He slipped into his robe and answered the heavy pounding at the front door. With buckets of water and a lawn hose the group broke into the living room. "Get your family out of the house! Your house is on fire!." said a man.

"On fire!"

"Your roof is almost gone! Get your family out. Look up Mr. Haflidason the fire has all ready reached the attic.!" Sigudur then saw Johanna and Groa standing in the living room. "I can smell smoke!" said Johanna, looking at the doorway as Porunn and Annika came out carrying their pillows and running frantically from the burning house! Ingibjorg and Gudmundina followed closely behind them. "We have to save the piano!' cried Sigudur.

"It's starting to burn also," said his next door neighbor.

"Get over here then, neighbor, and give me a hand." stated Sigudur with choleric temper. "It will take four men to carry it outdoors. Any volunteers?" Four men advanced to the heavy, four legged concert grand piano. He glanced over at his next door neighbor. "We won't need you my friend. This is a man's job," said Sigudur with his nerves beginning to fray.

Outside on the grass from an extended way to the burning house, Porunn sat with Annika on her lap, Groa, Johanna, Gudmundina and Ingibjorg at her side watching with heavy heart their treasures turning into ashes . . . all except Gloria and baby Ella who were cradled on Ingibjorg's and Gudmundina's laps. Gudmundina and Ingibjorg were invited to spend the night with the two girls who lived close by. Still in night attire Sigudur took Porunn, Annika Johanna and Groa to a rooming house in town.

On the ensuing morning, the neighbor girls gave them some clothes to wear being the same size, and had oatmeal and tea for breakfast. Ingibjorg wrinkled her nose. "What is this? I can't drink it. I've never had any before."

Gudmundina picked up her cup and poured her tea on the ground. All at once Gudmundina let out a cry. "Look, Ingibjorg! Isn't that pabbi's Maxwell coming up the road?"

"I see it! I see it! That's pabbi coming for us," exclaimed Ingibjorg scrambling up from the ground.

At a small cafe in downtown Yakima, Sigudur sat having lunch with his family. Noting their devastated features he put on a happy demeanor. "Your mother and I last night made plans for our next step. I believe it will make you all happy when you hear what we have to say."

"We all know what you are going to say pabbi. And I am sure we all disagree." stated Groa.

"I know what pabbi is going to tell us, he's going to build us another house where the one that burned down used to be," said Ingibjorg.

"That's a good idea Ingibjorg," he teased. "But hear my plan first."

"I am not going to build anymore houses. There are too many homes one can rent."

"I have never seen one for rent around here," chimed in Johanna.

"Did not say around here, Hanna. We are leaving Yakima the day after tomorrow for Blaine, Washington."

"I was born in Blaine, Washington, wasn't I mamma?" asked Ingibjorg.

Porunn breaking into a smile replied, "Yes, elskan."

"I was born in Blaine too wasn't I mamma?" asked Annika.

"No Annika, you were born in Montana."

"Don't remind me," said Gudmundina grimacing.

"Does mamma agree to this change again, pabbi?" asked Johanna.

"Oh, yes, Hanna," exclaimed Sigudur, drawing Porunn in his arms.

"Yes I am very happy to go back to Blaine Washington again where we had made many Icelandic friends," stated Porunn smiling.

"Today is our last day in Yakima, so why don't we do a little shopping?" asked Sigudur.

"We bought the girls new dresses yesterday," It can wait until we get to Blaine," stated Porunn.

"I don't think so Tota. I want to get some coveralls for the girls to wear over their new dresses to keep them clean for when we arrive at Ingibjorg Otson's house. If we leave early tomorrow we should get to the camping grounds by dusk where we can set up camp for the night."

"Where can we eat?" asked Annika.

"I understand this camp has many cooking stoves." replied Sigudur.

It had been a long, busy day.

At dawn the following morning the family was up preparing for the long journey ahead. By eight A.M. Sigudur and Johanna had boarded the Maxwell and headed for the city. Porunn stood at the window and waved as the vehicle left and disappeared at the turn of the road.

"Where are they going?" asked Gudmundina, wrinkling her brows.

"Your father has some last minute business to attend to."

It was almost noon when Sigudur arrived home alone. "Where is Jo?" asked Groa."

"Hanna is gone. She is not coming back," replied Sigudur with grimacing features. "Hanna was married today. She is now on the train on her way to Seattle Washington."

"Married!" exclaimed Groa. "Johanna is a fifteen year old child."

"I know Groa. We are all broken hearted," stated Sigudur blotting the tears from his cheeks.

"Blame yourself, Sigudur," said Porunn. "Hanna was married with your consent. And to a young man she does not love . . . will never love. Well, we cannot change yesterday. But you did not do Hanna any favors."

"What could I do . . . ? What could I do, Tota . . . ?" Sigudur took in a long, drawn-out sigh. "We have to cancel our trip until tomorrow. After lunch I will telegram Ingibjorg Otson that we will be a day late. I see they have a special lunch at the cafe today." Forcing a smile he added: "Let's go down and try it."

"I'm not hungry," stated Groa. "You can go to the cafe without me."

"I'm not hungry either," said Ingibjorg breaking into a sob.

"Now listen here girls. We are all going to quit this foolishness. We are still a family, are we not? And we all love each other, do we not?"

Placing their arms around each other they called out in unison . . . "Yes!"

"You girls are growing up and there will be a lot of changes in our lives. Some successful some failures. And I as the Digger Indians believe' "In the beginning God gave to every people a cup of clay and from this clay man drank his life." The unhappy group went down to the cafe.

The long solemn day past.

After a restless sleep, dawn peeped through the windows as the brilliant sun flashed into the room. "Time to get up," stated Sigudur vaulting out of bed. With the Maxwell packed they were now ready to travel up the highway to their future.

CHAPTER TWENTY-FIVE

Groa, Gudmundina and Ingibjorg occupied the back seat of the vehicle. Sitting in the front seat of the Maxwell was Annika beside Porunn. As Sigudur drove on he noted the group had not conversed with each other since they had left. All of a sudden Sigudur burst into a song. "When your smiling when you're smiling the whole world smiles with you . . . "when you're laughing" the group chimed in, "the whole world laughs with you . . . but when you're crying you bring on the rain so keep on smiling and the whole world smiles with you." After the song, the group permeated the atmosphere with laughter. "That was fun," stated Ingibjorg bouncing up and down on the rich velour, upholstered seats.

"Sure beats a horse and wagon," laughed Sigudur.

"Pabbi will we be going over the same mountain that we went over when we went to Montana?" asked Groa.

"No elskan. We are going the opposite direction. This time to the Cascade Range South East of Seattle, Washington." stated Sigudur.

Groa laughed. "Thank heavens I won't have to sleep with a dishpan over my head." she stated jovially.

"Did I have to sleep with a dishpan over my head?" asked Annika placing her head on Porunn's shoulder.

"No, Annika you were not born yet."

"Will we be in Blaine soon?" asked Annika yawning.

"No, elskan. Washington is quite a large state. And a very pretty state with tall, evergreen trees, rivers and many dams," explained Sigudur noting his children's mood swing was more cheerful now.

"I hear Mt Rainier is a very popular ski resort," stated Gudmundina.

"Yes, replied her father. "Especially for the Seattle area. We should reach Snoqualmie Pass by sundown," Sigudur informed his passengers.

"What is a pass, pabbi?" asked Gudmundina.

"A pass is a narrowing way between mountains where we will set up a camp near by."

"Where do we eat, pabbi?" asked Ingibjorg.

"I hear the camping sights have many cooking stoves all set up for campers. Your mother brought plenty of food which we will heat up."

The tired travellers pushed on and soon they reached Snoquqlmie Pass.

At six A.M. they were once more on the road heading for Bellingham and then Blaine.

It was nightfall when they arrived at Mrs. Otson's home. She ran out to meet them. She glanced at Annika, then at Ingibjorg. "So this is my namesake, Ingibjorg!" she exclaimed. "How you have grown."

After sitting down to a delicious meal the exhausted group retired for the night.

The ensuing morning the family moved into the rented house beside the Icelandic Lutheran church. The summer solace was coming to an end and school would soon be resuming. Sigudur escorted his children to enroll at the Central grade school. Groa age thirteen would be going to high school next year. She was an excellent student, an honor pupil since the first grade. Sigudur was given his old job back at the saw mill with no questions asked, but avoided Mr. Taylor as much as possible.

Thus life went on.

Porunn was content for having made the change in their lives. and her Icelandic friends gave her many hours of relaxation. Sigudur did not care about socializing with his neighbors or with friends. However, everyone called Sigudur if they needed help of some kind. He was the first to offer assistance. This morning his next door neighbor asked Sigudur for help to fix his broken gate. Sigudur had it mended in no time. His neighbor called out to him. "Come on in, Siggi, and have a cup of coffee."

"No thank you. I can afford to buy my own coffee." was Sigudur's reply.

After supper the family sat in the living room around a cozy fire in the parlor heater. All appeared to be in deep thought. "What do you say girls," stated Sigudur, "that we do our Kveding."

"Kveding . . . !" called out Annika. "what is that?"

"You're too young to know how to kved," said Groa.

"I am not," cried out Annika . . . am I mamma?"

"Of course not elskan. Your sisters were about your age when we taught them to kved," said Porunn.

"It's an old Icelandic game of us Vikings," explained Sigudur taking Annika on his lap. "One person in the group starts making up a verse . . .

generally nonsense. and sings the words in a monotone tune . . . kind of a dull voice. And your verse can only be eight words long. Then the next person continues with the verse in the same fashion until everyone has had his turn. Then they all laugh at their nonsensical tune and words they had created." Sigudur glanced down at Annika. Bored, she had fallen asleep. He carried his youngest child to her bed. Groa, Gudmundina and Ingibjorg rose in their long, flannel nightgowns and also retired.

The summer was pleasant in spite of Blaine's rainy climate. As days passed it was now autumn. Sigudur and Porunn sat in the kitchen having a cup of coffee before retiring. Suddenly a light knock was sounded on the back door. They exchanged glances. "Who can that be?" whispered Porunn, rising from her chair and opening the door. "Oh, Ole! How nice to see you. Come on in. You're just in time for a cup of coffee."

"Ole Byron!" Sigudur called out in an amicable manner. Porunn reached for one of her pretty China cups in the cupboard and filled it with coffee. "A pretty fancy cup for someone like me." stated Ole. When he had been a young man a group of hypnotists came to town and with Ole's consent, used Ole Byron for their subject. All went well until the hypnotists were unable to get their subject out of the trance. Frightened, they left town. Those who do not know the story find Ole odd.

"You make good coffee, Porunn," stated Ole. "Sigudur is a lucky man to have such a wonderful woman."

"Tota is not a woman, Ole. she's an angel." Sigudur handed Ole his coffee cup drained of coffee grounds. "See what you find in there, Ole. I never let anyone read my cup except you. You, I believe can foretell the future. You have for me many times."

"I cannot read in a cup all painted with red roses. Get me a plain white cup." Porunn dashed to the sideboard and handed Ole a plain white cup. "Give it to Siggi, Porunn. He has to drink from it so I can read the grounds."

"Sigudur glanced at Porunn. "Would you mind leaving the room Tota? A man's future is private." She did not reply. Rising from the table Porunn paddled Ole on the shoulder. "Good night, Ole. Come again soon."

Ole still sitting in his cap, tilted the bird beaked brim over one eye and sliding down in his chair held the cup in an upward position and began to read, Sigudur noticed Ole's eyes were over the brim of the cup and starring directly into the abyss of space. "Well my friend, I see you are going to build another house . . . but not in Blaine, you will build in a large city this time. And this pretty, white house will be your last home I assure you, Siggi."

Ole Byron, his American friend, was gone. Sigudur went to the chamber and sat wearily down on the edge of the bed where Porunn lay sleeping. "How was the fortune?" she asked.

"Oh, I don't know elskan. I know Ole is no faker. What he says he sees . . . he sees. but that does not mean we laymen have to believe in it. But it's good entertainment."

Porunn could feel Sigudur was hurting. That was generally the case anything about building another house here in Blaine?"

"As you know Tota we decided to just rent from now on. And remember I promised we would hold to that."

"I have not complained to you, Sigudur, but I am not happy living in a rented house. It doesn't feel like we belong in it. If you want to build again I will be very happy. It would seem more like home."

"Thank you, Tota I believe that's what I need right now. I'll start looking for some property."

"I have all ready found a vacant lot across from the school where the girls go to Central grade school," she said.

"You never told me about that Tota."

"No, I was afraid you did not want to build again and I had no intentions of breaking our promise." she added.

"It would be handy for the girls," stated Sigudur. In lighter spirits Sigudur fell asleep in a restful slumber.

Six months passed. the house was now finished. The day after they moved in Gudmundina walking home from school, saw a large moving van stop in front of her new residence. She hastened her gait, "Sir!" she called out "you have the wrong house. We moved in yesterday."

The driver scanned his invoice sheet, then glanced down at her. "Is your name Gudmundina Haflidason?"

"Yes," she replied.

"Do you own a piano?"

"Yes!" she exclaimed. "Oh pabbi must have shipped my piano from Yakima. I thought he had sold it, junked it, or something." Running ahead of him she threw open the door.

"Where do you want this monster?" Suddenly another mover hopped out of the van. "Let me help you, Sam."

"Put it in the parlor," said Gudmundina hopping up and down with excitement.

The next day Gudmundina went to the dime store to buy some sheet music for piano. In the evening the family gathered around the concert grand

and sang, with Gudmundina's beautiful voice standing out from the other voices.

One year had passed since Ole Byron's visit to Sigudur's home. Yet, his call had left a mark on Sigudur soul. At night he could not sleep. When he dozed nightmares of his trying to build a house and the structure crumbling to the ground time after time. He awakened exhausted to face the day at the mill. As the months passed the memory of Ole's future telling was still vivid.

Yet in his heart he felt the family would have more opportunities in a big city. Yes, a small town was very comfortable and lovely for raising small children, however his were nearly grown now. Yes. Tota and he had made a grave mistake by moving back to Blaine. Well, it was too late now. His mother always told him it was never too late to correct a mistake if a mistake can be corrected. Sigudur was fully aware that Porunn would sacrifice her comfort of a small Icelandic community for their daughters' successful future.

Coming from their chamber, Porunn glanced quickly out of the window. "Where are the children playing? I don't see them out there and it is beginning to rain."

"Oh, they are out on the front porch playing chess."

"Tell them to come in, it's getting cold."

"No, Tota leave them out there for awhile. I have something to discuss with you and I don't want them to hear our discussion."

"Can't it wait until tonight when they have gone to bed?"

"No Tota. I have been waiting almost one year to reveal my utmost thoughts to you. Please, Tota hear me out and then it will be your decision."

"I am sorry, Sigudur I had no idea you were struggling with a problem by yourself." She pulled out a chair from the kitchen table and sat down with a cup of coffee.

Sigudur dropped down on a chair beside her. Rising from the table again Porunn poured a cup of coffee for Sigudur then resumed in the conversation. Looking deep and seriously into his faded, dark blue eyes she stated, "I have a feeling we have been through this before."

"Same story, the same mistake I have dragged you through all of our married life. Look at your hair, Tota. All the beautiful red has turned gray!" He broke into a sob. "Do you know Who put the silver there, elskan? Your children and I," he sighed, wiping his tears on his hands.

Porunn rose and placed her arms around his shoulders. "Sigudur you have been a wonderful husband and father. We have all had a very happy life together because we had love. I don't need to hear what you had intended to tell me, Sigudur, I know. You want to leave Blaine. And of coarse that would mean building again." Porunn moved back to her chair and sat down. Sipping her coffee her eyes looked at him over the rim of her cup. "How soon can you start building? And by the way where are we moving to?"

"Seattle," he replied tearfully.

"That far!" exclaimed Porunn.

"It's not that far. Tota" he smiled. "It's only about a three hour drive from Blaine."

"How will you manage two jobs?"

"I will drive to Seattle every weekend. and go home Sunday nights."

"It will be very taxing for you. Sigurdur but knowing you, you'll make it."

With Sigurdur in Seattle on weekends the days were long and lonely. It was now early spring. March winds blew the naked branches as Groa and Ingibjorg hurried home from school. As they walked into the house Sigurdur had just come home from the saw mill. "Where is Gudmundina? Doesn't she get out the same time as you girls?"

"Yes," replied Groa placing her homework on the kitchen table, "but Mrs. Kyle is keeping Gudmundina after school."

"Is she behind in her lessons?" asked Sigurdur.

"No pabbi," said Ingibjorg, "Gudmundina sassed the teacher." Sigurdur put his coat back on and dashed out of the door. In no time he was across the street and in the Central grade school building. The halls seemed vacant and lonely. Glancing up at the numbers of the class rooms he remembered Gudmundina's room number was fifteen. There it was. The door was open and he saw an elderly spinster sitting at her desk dabbing rouge on her cheeks. The students benches were all empty. Every one had gone home except Mrs. Kyle and Gudmundina. But where was Gudmundina? Sigurdur rushed up to the desk. "Where is my daughter, Gudmundina?"

"Oh she's here, Mr. Haflidason. I have her in the cloak room where she will stay until she apologizes to me. It may be a long wait for you Mr. Haflidason. Gudmundina is a very stubborn little girl."

"Pabbi! Is that you?" called out Gudmundina.

"Yes, Olof. Get your coat! . . . and for you Lady Spinster if you ever shut up any of my daughters in a cloak room again, You will deal with me."

Saturday the following morning Sigurdur rose early to pack a small bag for Seattle. Annika still half asleep rubbed her pretty green eyes and climbed up on her father's lap. "Do you have to go, Pabbi?" she wailed beginning to sob.

"Yes elskan today I have to go. But in about four to five weeks our home will be finished and we will all go to Seattle." He kissed her soft white forehead. "Won't that be nice?"

She hopped off his lap. "You better go now pabbi so you can finish the house and we can all go to Seattle."

Groa came out to the kitchen. "Goodbye pabbi, we'll see you Sunday evening."

"Do you have any plans for today elskan?"

"Not really I'm just going to stay home and answer Harold Peterson's last letter." replied Groa blushing.

"Oh Sali's boy . . . the one who has pigeons."

"That's right," she laughed.

"Where is Gudmundina and Ingibjorg . . . and your mother? Oh here they are," he smiled picking up his traveling bag and placing it on his shoulder. Drawing Porunn in his arms he kissed her warmly. "I'll be counting the hours until Sunday evening." Gudmundina glanced at her father then blurted out, "Pabbi, Ingibjorg wants to ask you something."

"No I don't Gudmundina. You want to ask him something," replied Ingibjorg.

"Don't be such a baby, Inga. Ask him!"

"I didn't want to ask him, you told me to," exclaimed Ingibjorg.

"What's the matter with you two?" asked their father.

"We just want to go to the pictures this afternoon and we don't have any money," Ingibjorg blurted out.

"Don't I always give you money when you ask for it?"

"This is different pabbi. The movie house is going up on their prices because the Ivanal Theatre is going to start showing a double feature, news reel and cartoons," said Gudmundina.

Digging in his pockets he asked, "How much will you girls need?"

"Well, it's not going up much," replied Gudmundina. "We've been paying ten cents for each person for the picture and five cents for a nickel bag of popcorn for each of us."

Ingibjorg moved to his side and kissed him. "Thank you, pabbi," she said taking, a one dollar bill from his hand.

"Did you ask Groa to go with you girls Ingibjorg?" asked Sigurdur.

"Yes, but she said she was too grown up to pal around with kids."

Smiling, he added, "What about Annika? She's not too grown up?"

"Of course not, but Ingibjorg and I felt she was just too young to go with us, so Ingibjorg Ottson invited Annika and mamma over to her place for lunch today." stated Gudmundina.

"Well, I can see I won't be missed today."

Streaks of the March sunshine filtered through the lifeless tree branches. Ingibjorg and Gudmundina walked briskly toward the small town where only one theatre existed. The Ivanal was very old but was kept up in excellent condition. "We're a little early," expressed Gudmundina.

"I don't think so. We'll be lucky to get a seat," said Ingibjorg.

"I think it's mostly children on Saturday matinees," said Gudmundina speeding up her gait. "Grown ups like to go at night." When they reached the Ivanal there was a small group waiting at the door. The carpeted market with a small roof sheltered the beautiful pictures of the popular movie star's coming attractions. Spellbound, Ingibjorg and Gudmundina moved slowly to each glamorous photo of the stars. "This is Greta Garbo, coming soon in Camille. Oh, I really want to see that," said Ingibjorg. "Greta Garbo is so beautiful!"

Gudmundina's eyes glanced at the photo. "I think Greta Garbo is ugly. She's so masculine and big. And her voice is like a man's. That's one picture you'll have to see without me."

"Well today we are seeing Lillian and Dorothy Gish.

At least we both like them," replied Ingibjorg.

"And who are these two mugs?" asked Gudmundina. sarcastically, advancing to another photo.

Ingibjorg bent over the picture to get a better look. "It looks like Gloria Swanson with John Barrymore," All at once the door to the theatre opened and the patrons shuffled in to choose a good seat, which to children meant a front seat by the stage.

They followed an usher down the dark aisle with a flashlight in her hand, Gudmundina called out to her. "Midway is good."

Strains of the organ began floating through the auditorium. After settling in the soft, maroon, velour seats Gudmundina glanced at Ingibjorg. "We forgot our popcorn, Inga."

"We still have time to go back to the lobby and gets some out of the machine. Come on, let's go," exclaimed Ingibjorg.

"No," said Gudmundina, "you can get mine too."

The theatre was now almost filled when the heavy, maroon colored curtain began to rise. Ingibjorg hurried back with popcorn flying out of the bags onto the aisle. "You spilled my popcorn," said Gudmundina in a whisper.

"I couldn't help it," replied Ingibjorg handing her a bag. "Oh look! The curtain is up!"

Silence enveloped the theatre. "Oh, that's Lillian Gish. Isn't she adorable?" asked Ingibjorg in abated breath.

"Shhh!" whispered Gudmundina. "Everyone is looking at us!" As time went by the picture was coming to a close. The heroine lay down on her bed, the captions read: "I am going to sleep and dream of John tonight." All at once Ingibjorg let out a bloodcurdling sigh. "Oh she's dead!" she sobbed out loud. All eyes focused on Gudmundina and Ingibjorg.

"What's a matter with you, Inga? Lillian is not dead. She is only sleeping. Didn't you read the captions?"

"They ran the words so fast I didn't get a chance to read them all."

On the way home Gudmundina put her nose up into the air and hurried ahead of Ingibjorg so as not to speak to her.

"Please don't be mad at me Gudmundina. I'm sorry I spoiled your day," said Ingibjorg catching up with her as they turned in their yard. "That's all right Inga. Actually it was rather funny upsetting all the people like that." Laughing, the two sisters joined hands and went into the house.

It was now the middle of May. School would be soon recessing for the summer. Groa was graduating from the eight grade and would be starting high school in the fall. Sigurdur had announced that the new house in Seattle was finished and that the family would be moving on the thirty first of may . . . Memorial Day.

The Blaine house had been sold and the money from the sale was much needed for the loan which was borrowed to build.

It was a beautiful sunny day. After the Maxwell was packed beyond it's capacity, Gudmundina and Groa seated themselves in the back seat of the Maxwell. "We're going to have to move over," said Groa to Gudmundina, "Here comes Ingibjorg and Annika."

"Annika will probably sit with mamma and pabbi," said Gudmundina.

Smiling, Ingibjorg with a large bag in her hand jumped into the back seat. "Isn't this fun?" asked Ingibjorg.

"Yes," replied Groa. "This is very exciting."

Noting that Porunn was not socializing Sigurdur averted his eyes from the road to Porunn's face. Are you all right, Tota," he asked.

"Yes I am fine Sigurdur. Annika has fallen asleep on my shoulder and I don't want to awaken her. I'm sure none of us slept too much last night."

Once more the sound of silence imbued the air. Sigurdur cleared his throat, then burst out in song. "My Country Tis Of Thee Sweet land of Liberty . . . Of Thee I Sing," chimed in the group." The echoing of their soft beautiful voices permeated to the sky from the open roofless Maxwell. "That was beautiful!" said Sigurdur with a tear in his voice. "I think you all would like to know we have a two hour drive to Marysville Washington where I will take my beautiful family to lunch."

"And I am getting hungry," said Annika having awakened during the sing. "Is it a larger town than Blaine, pabbi?" asked Groa.

"No, elskan it is much smaller than Blaine," replied Sigurdur, picking up speed when he noted the Marysville Inn coming into view. Parking his vehicle, Sigurdur opened the passenger side and assisted Porunn and Annika from their seats. Groa, Gudmundina and Ingibjorg deboarded the Maxwell and followed Annika and their parents into the lobby of the Inn. "Oh, this is nice," commented Ingibjorg, her eyes traveling around the large room.

After a deluxe meal they boarded the Maxwell and headed for Seattle. It was almost nightfall when they arrived to where their permanent home would be. "Is that it, pabbi?" asked Annika when Sigurdur slowed down the vehicle in front of a pretty, white ranch house then stopped.

Embracing Porunn, Sigurdur looked warmly at her, "Do you like it Tota?"

"Oh, yes, Sigurdur. It is lovely."

"Wait until you see the inside." added Sigurdur. "And I even painted the house address on the side of the porch." he added.

"I see it now," replied Porunn. "Ninety three Dayton Avenue. Well, you have always been very artistic."

"Only one thing is missing, pabbi. my concert grand piano," inturrupted Gudmundina.

"I could not move it anymore, Olof. It is getting old and needs a lot of fixing which is very costly."

"That's all right pabbi. I probably won't be playing much longer anyway."

"Your piano has found a new home in Ranveig Westman's old barn down by the creek which the Westmans don't use any more. Anyway, Olof it will always be there for you if you would ever want it."

"Oh, it is so sad!" she sighed. Proudly Sigurdur placed a new key into the lock and they walked in. A new, up-right mahogany piano stood in the parlor. "Oh, pabbi! Is this mine?"

Sigurdur pulled out the bill of sales from his pocket and handed it to Gudmundina. "I believe your name, Gudmundina Haflidason is on it."

She threw her arms around her father's neck and kissed him. "Oh thank you, pabbi! I don't know why you are so good to me."

The summer was ending and it was time for Sigurdur to enroll his children Ingibjorg, Gudmundina, and Annika at Oaklake School and Groa at Lincoln High. The ladies at the Icelandic Lutheran Church called on Porunn to invite her to join their club. She was very happy. And at this time, she also learned that Dr. Harold Palmasson, the reverend who was now the officiating minister there, was the same officiating minister who had christened Gudmundina in Canada when she was a year old. Dr. Palmasson's three sons were also men of the cloth now.

Thus ten years passed.

CHAPTER TWENTY SIX

The beautiful Icelandic sisters were now grown women. Their main interests appeared to be good times, expensive clothes and dancing. The dancing daughters spent three nights a week dancing at the Everstate Club. And now that a new dance called the Charleston came out they added another night-out to their evenings of entertainment.

Christmas was in the air. December fifteenth left nine days until Christmas Eve. Sigurdur came in from the shed with a tree stand in his hand. "Where do you want the tree, Tota?"

"Next to the piano I think," she replied.

"You don't sound too enthused," stated Sigurdur.

"Well actually I'm not. We have always had a tree for the girls. Now they don't seem to care. Last Christmas Eve we sat with the tree alone."

"It will be different now that the club changed their date for the Christmas dance. In fact they are giving it tonight."

"Yes, the girls are in their rooms getting dressed now."

Sitting down at the kitchen table with two cups in his hands he poured some coffee. He glanced at Porunn with a wry face. "I am starting to think that we've brought a lot of this dancing craze on ourselves. Or I could honestly say, you Tota are a large part of it."

"Why are you blaming me?" asked Porunn.

"Because, the first time Hanna announced she was going to a public dance I told her she could not go. That no daughter of mine would ever go to a public dance. However, I was wrong. You came in Tota and told Hanna she could go. I was humiliated as a father but I felt worse over the fact that it was no way for a young girl to start her life. I never interfered again but kept aware of dates and how late they came home. Not that I was snooping but because I cared.!" He rose and placed his arms around her." You're a wonderful mother Tota, and as you often remind me, we cannot change yesterday." He stretched his back wearily. "I think I will go to bed early tonight. But I want to finish this stand so the girls can decorate the tree tomorrow."

"I thought you had finished the stand." she replied.

"It's finished. I just need another brace in the back to make it a little stronger."

"I'm sure it can wait until tomorrow," she replied.

All at once a splash of rain was heard on the roof. "It's starting to rain Sigurdur. and it's getting dark. You mentioned you're beginning to have a hard time seeing when driving in the dark. You said something about the bright lights of the other vehicles bothering you."

"I won't take the car. I'll just walk to the little hardware store on Aurora highway. It is not far from here and they stay open until ten P.M." Sigurdur glanced up when Ingibjorg came running into the kitchen with her evening gown open in the back.

"Mamma, she called out advancing to Porunn's chair. "Will you snap up my gown in back? I can't reach it."

"Come over here, elskan."

"Thanks mamma," said Ingibjorg kissing Porunn hurriedly on the cheek.

"Ingibjorg is still that warm loving child she used to be. But somehow Ingibjorg has changed more than any of the girls. One would think she would be the last of the girls to change."

"I don't know what you mean. You're saying Ingibjorg is different since she grew up?"

"Maybe I am wording it wrong. Ingibjorg just isn't the type to be going out every night. She is never home. Either at the horse track or on a date," said Sigurdur.

"You are like most parents when their children grow up. They forget they are not dealing with children anymore. Their children are now grown people with their own desires and philosophy. Youth's longevity is short. I wanted my girls to enjoy their young years," said Porunn, with a recall of her own youth.

"You have been a wonderful mother, Tota and a wonderful wife," stated Sigurdur in deep concentration. They glanced toward the door when Gudmundina walked in dressed in a gold lame' evening gown. "Mamma, may I borrow your gold earrings tonight? Mine are all silver."

"Of course, Olof. They're on my dressing table."

There was a long pause between Sigurdur and Porunn after Gudmundina had left the room. "I am pleased to see that Olof is going to the Christmas dance. She wasn't sure she would go." stated Porunn.

"Why was that?" asked Sigurdur.

"I don't know. Olof is not a person you question."

"Well, Olof is a very independent girl. She appears cold and arrogant but I know it is all put on. Olof's hoity-toity remarks have never bothered me like it has you, Tota."

"I don't know why I couldn't see that, Sigurdur. I think I am getting to know Olof for the first time. And I now find her more sensitive than most people. Even more sensitive than Ingibjorg who cries all the time when she is hurting." stated Porunn, peering over the rim of her cup at Sigurdur.

He glanced at her curiously. "How did you happen to analyze Olof so correctly, Doctor?" asked Sigurdur grinning.

Porunn laughed. "You've been noticing Olof has been home with me when the other girls go out. It's been wonderful having her company and I have really gotten to know her. I think her demeanor of grandeur is just an escape to hide her true feelings deep beyond the surface," replied Porunn.

"It is almost dark. I think I had better get to the hardware store. I believe it has stopped raining." All at once a blatant sound of thunder in an imperative threatening tone resounded through the heavens. There was then a pause of silence. "I hope this is the end of the squall" stated Sigurdur rising from his chair. Suddenly an electrical discharge between two clouds and the earth flashed through the window. Removing his slicker and bird bill cap from the kitchen closet, he hurried into his rain attire.

"You're not going out in this rain, Sigurdur," stated Porunn firmly.

"It is only a short distance to the store. I'll be right back." He opened the rear door and disappeared down the many steps and headed for the Aurora highway.

As Porunn picked the coffee cups up from the table to wash, she observed the conversation and laughter coming from her daughters' rooms. She smiled to herself seeing them so happy. Annika dressed in a long, full-skirted, chiffon gown with a red rose pinned to the bodice, knocked at Groa's chamber door. "Are you decent?" she asked jovially turning the lock and walking in. "Groa, may I wear your black velvet cape tonight??"

"Sure it will look perfect with your white gown."

"What are you wearing, Groa?"

"I'm wearing last years gown that I wore to the New Years Eve ball last year."

"Oh, I love that on you," replied Annika. With your figure you should always wear something tight and slinky."

All at once a heavy knock was heard on the front door. "I'll get it!" Porunn called out advancing to the entrance,

Standing on the porch in the dripping rain was a tall stranger in a black slicker and large brimmed hat. "Are you Mrs. Haflidason?" he asked.

"Yes," replied Porunn in a tense shaky voice,

"I am sorry, madam. I have bad news for you. Your husband, Sigurdur Rosenkranz Haflidason was killed instantly about a half an hour ago. He was at a safety island waiting to cross the Aurora highway and a minister coming home from church hit the safety island, due to the heavy rain he could not see."

"Thank you," replied Porunn."

"You will have to go down to the morgue to night and identify the body." Resting his eyes on Porunn's vague expression for a moment, he then turned down the steps and disappeared in the squall.

"Mamma!" called out Ingibjorg. "We heard! Annika and are going down to the morgue for you." Annika and Ingibjorg slipped their rain coats over their gowns and left for the city.

Porunn requested to go back to Blaine to the Icelandic nursing home which was built for Icelandic people only. The head nurse named Rose, being an American was unable to speak Icelandic or understand, therefore the main reason for the home was lost.

So; consequently twenty years of alone and loneliness past. As Porunn lay on her bed she could hear the aides and nurses conversing and laughing in the kitchen, She knew that the patients were in bed for the night. How she would like to have a dish of Ice cream. Her mouth and throat were so dry. Then remembering that Dora Johnson an Icelandic aide there, and an old friend of Gudmundina's, told Porunn once that the staff always ate all the ice cream which family and relatives brought their loved ones for a snack. A splash of rain was heard on the window pane. She closed her eyes and asked God to have mercy once more and take her from this hell on earth. Falling asleep she awakened at short intervals. Recalling her prior thoughts before she fell asleep, Porunn decided she would have to will her life away herself. She lay quietly and her past life flashed by her. The shrill laughter of the staff in the kitchen was beginning to fade . . . Thank you God," she whispered, as her life ended.

And for only those who believe in the hereafter:

As life left Porunn's lifeless body, her soul which never dies, felt a jerk through her being. Her soul was rising to a supremacy.

The early dusk was in the late stage of evening, twilight just proceeding full dawn. Floating upward and toward the ocean a spray of mist from the sea blew cold and unfriendly leaving Porunn little hope of finding Sigurdur. "Sigurdur!" she called out desperately. "Sigurdur! I am coming home!" Then with natural impulse she acted in response to stimuli and headed for the small harbor, a shelter for ships and a arm of water shielding docks and piers to protect them from a storm.

When a pelting rain and windstorm arose she observed a small dark ship sailing into the harbor for shelter. Approaching the dock Porunn saw some dock workers loading and unloading cargo on ships. Moving closer to them she called out. "Have you seen Sigurdur Haflidason. I'm his wife, Porunn Olafsdottir.?" The workers did not seem to hear or see her. "Please help me!" she pleaded. No response. She was about to leave the harbor when she saw a man down at the edge of the water. At once her congenital instinct told her this was Sigurdur. "Sigurdur!" she repeated. "Is that you?"

"Tota! Tota! I'm down on the shore. "Oh Tota, I have waited for you so long . . . over twenty years!" Porunn floated into his open arms. They held each other without speaking in a blissful interlude. Porunn broke out in tears after not having shed a single tear since she was three years old. Souder's shoulder was wet with Porunn's tears mixed with rain. The dam that had held Porunn's tears back for so many years had finally given away.

"Let it all out, Tota. Don't hold the tears back. They are way over due."

Porunn smiled. "I have missed you so much!" she sobbed. Her eyes then rested on the small ship that had come into the harbor. "Now that the storm seems to be over, does that mean this ship will leave and push out to sea again?" She wrinkled her brows. "I don't know why Sigurdur but that ship over there looks so familiar to me."

"It should look familiar, elskan. That little ship is LARA, the ship that took us away from Iceland so many years ago." LARA is waiting to take us back to Iceland where we belong, never to part again."

Aboard the LARA the lights were bright and cheerful. Sea birds seen on the shore were singing and flapping their wings. As the ship sailed into Reykjavik harbor, Icelandic flags waved from the tall masts of the ships. "Looks like we're in Iceland all ready. It's so bright." said Porunn happily.

"Yes, Tota, we have finally reached home . . . HARBOR LIGHTS!"

Character Register

Porunn Olafsdottir's parents. (Mother) Hallbera Eriksdottir
(father) Olofur Sigurdson Freysteinsson
(their children) Sigurun age twelve
Loftur age seven
a daughter, Pordis and three
sons who died in a flood.
Porunn age three and Johanna age one.

Parents of Sigurdur Rosenkranz Haflidason were:
(father) Haflidi Helgason.
(their children) eight off-springs which Sigurdur was the youngest.

Sigurdur Rosencranz Haflidason and Porunn Olafsdottir married in 1906 in Canada. Their children Johann, died at the age of six months. Cause . . . pneumonia, born after; Johanna Rosemkranza, Groa, and Annika. Ingibjorg, and Gudmundina Olof.

Rosmunda, (Rosa) Sigudur's eldest sister remained a widow. She raised her two children, Emily and Jani with the little Indian boy giving Cheko equal unconditional love and support. Chico grew up to be a fine man and a successful builder. He moved to California where he built Rosa a fine house where she lived comfortably to the end of her life. The whereabouts of her birth children is unknown.

ABOUT THE CHARACTERS

Sigurdur Rosenkranz Haflidason: died. December 15, 1945 . . . cause of death . . . He was run over and killed by a driver.

Porunn Olafsdottir: died November 1964 cause of death . . . broken heart . . . She willed her life away alone in a Nursing Home.

Johanna Rosenkranza: died July 21, 2001 cause of death: willed her life away. She was married three times-divorced three times.

Groa: died August 16, 1958 . . . cause of death (murder) She was married once, divorced once.

Gudmundina Olof: lives in Connecticut. She is an author of seven excellent books . . . TIN Soldier . . . Devil's Tatto RED CORAL . . . HARBOR LIGHTS . . . THE KEYS . . . AMID THE RUBLE OF World War Two LOCATION GERMANY . . . BORN ON THE WRONG SIDE OF THE TRACKS, DEDICATED TO THE AMERICAN SCHOOL FOR THE DEAF. She has been married three times . . . divorced three times.

Ingibjorg died February 22, 2007 cause of death respiratory failure Married once . . . no divorce.

Annika: died October 25, 1986 cause of death respiratory dysfunction. Married once.

Johanna Olafsdotti, Porrun's baby sister, grew-up in foster homes.

She married in her twenties and gave birth to a little boy named Olafur. When the baby was two years old, and Johanna thirty, she commited suicide leaving her little boy motherless. Her husband was a very good man. I think she was as bad as her mother, Hallbera.

THE POWER
OF MOBILITY
How Your Business Can Compete and Win in the Next Technology Revolution

RUSSELL McGUIRE

John Wiley & Sons, Inc.

Library of Congress Cataloging-in-Publication Data

McGuire, Russ, 1964–
   The power of mobility : how your business can compete and win in the next technology revolution / Russ McGuire.
     p. cm.
   Includes index.
   ISBN 978-0-470-17128-8 (cloth)
   ISBN 978-0-470-22776-3 (custom edition)
1. Business enterprises—Technological innovations. 2. Business enterprises—Computer networks–Management. 3. Mobile communication systems—Management. 4. Business planning. I. Title.
   HD45.M379 2007
   658. 8'72—dc22   2007018193

Printed in the United States of America

10 9 8 7 6 5 4 3 2 1

To Donna and Kevin
Thank you for your love,
support, and patience

Contents

Foreword

Anyone who has been involved with the infrastructure business in the telecommunications industry for the past decade will tell you it's been a tumultuous time. From the Gold Rush mentality of the early Internet era, to the near total drop-off in equipment and services sales in the post-Bubble age, to the much-consolidated, more-muted, big-company-focused present day, it's been a roller coaster ride for all involved.

As with any chaotic environment, everyone is trying to make sense of everything around them. Theories are suggested and rejected. Explanations are offered and dismissed. There's lots of FUD (fear, uncertainty, doubt) going around, and yet a few tenets rise to the top as being generally accepted and reliable.

Moore's Law was one of these early suggested hypotheses that gained strength with time and therefore proofpoints. Moore's Law explained the era of plummeting costs and bursting processing capabilities in the early days of computing. It provided an ability to cull from the rapidly changing technology landscape some stability of purpose, and allow for solid planning, expectations, and in some cases, hope.

Metcalfe's Law followed. Metcalfe's Law provided a solid extension of Moore's Law into the Age of the Internet. Building on the decades of experience with other networks, from railroads to telephones, Metcalfe's Law provided a basis to value and exploit the Internet and all the businesses and concepts derived from it. Metcalfe's Law paved the way for all sorts of corollaries, from those that claimed "First To Market" advantages in riding the Metcalfe curve, to those that pursued M&A to obtain multiples on the market valuations from the resulting high subscriber numbers. "The Network Effect" was born, and the industry had its next big layer of stability to anchor its development.

Then came wireless to mix everything up again. "The Law of Mobility" is what it's been called for the past few years, posited more as a hypothesis at first, gaining steam recently as more and more industry data support the core facets of the Law, and providing yet more ability to craft sense from the chaos that accompanies the wireless onslaught. We've gone from custom military-grade communications, to $3,000 "bricks" offered to the few, to clamshell innovations like Motorola's StarTec, through to TREOs, Blackberries and the iPhone. We've gone through hundreds of "A" and "B" carriers, through flaming Iridium satellites, through cellular carrier consolidation and logo changes on trucks (bye bye, McCaw, Bell Atlantic Mobile, Cingular ...) through GSM versus CDMA versus Wi-Fi versus lots of other technology battles. We're witnessing a total and fundamental paradigm shift from staid, anchored landline phones and computers, to totally untethered, anywhere-in-the-world instant communications. There's no torch passing here, but rather a whole new flame in a new generation that is growing up on "always on" connectivity, constant network presence, and immediate satisfaction. We're seeing total abandonment of prior decades-refined habits in favor of whole new approaches to not only technology and work . . . but life itself.

Computing. Internet. Wireless. These disruptive changes have forever changed our landscape like the railroads, airlines, and telephone before them. Wireless enables Mobility, Mobility changes all around us. Those who are true strategists in their firms have no choice but to quickly make sense of all this dramatic change and plot the best path through. For many, from the landline-focused telephone companies to the historically lagging Postal Service, this is the Perfect Storm of their time—a time where fundamental industry tenets, technological capabilities and user habits all change overnight.

Russ McGuire's *Power of Mobility* hits this new age face on. He explains, with almost matter-of-fact simplicity, what's going on, where it's going, and what you need to do to 1) not be blindsided and 2) leverage the opportunity to your benefit. The *Power of Mobility* prepares you, in a step-by-step fashion, to interpret the opportunity presented by mobility into your firm's environment. He provides a literal roadmap for strategic planning and execution. Where he can't give you the answer, he leads by example.

Underlying all of this, however, is that solid, basic, stable tenet of his day, the Law of Mobility. It's the foundation for understanding the biggest single impacting trend of this age. The Law of Mobility has eclipsed from being a mere thought, even a hypothesis, or nary even a generic Law. It's Russ' Law now, appropriately so.

Moore's Law. Metcalfe's Law. McGuire's Law. A new stability is upon us.

Danny Briere

CEO

TeleChoice, Inc.

Preface: Welcome to the Mobile World

We already live in a highly mobile world that would seem foreign to a visitor of even ten years ago. Nearly 80% of Americans above the age of five own a cell phone. Our telephones, and our telephone numbers, are no longer tethered to a geographic location. We can place and receive phone calls wherever we go. In fact, nearly 10% of American homes have "cut-the-cord" and no longer have wireline telephone service.

The mobile device we carry increasingly is more than just a telephone. Device convergence is no longer just a cool concept—it's an everyday reality for corporate executives and mobile moms alike.

The most visible example of device convergence is the camera phone. According to Strategy Analytics, 257 million mobile phones with digital cameras built in were sold in 2004 ("Taking Camera Phones into Digital Still Camera Territory: Megapixels, WLAN and Printers," Strategy Analytics report summary by Neil Mawston, April 11, 2005, www.strategyanalytics.net/default.aspx?mod= ReportAbstractViewer&a0=2354). That's four times as many camera phones as stand-alone digital cameras. Our theoretical visitor from the past would wonder whatever happened to the traditional film camera. Is this dramatic shift due to camera phones having surpassed the quality of photo taken by an old Kodak Instamatic? Nowhere close. Not yet. But because we always have our mobile device with us, the camera phone's value is defined by its mobility—by the increased opportunities we have to take pictures—to capture moments otherwise lost forever.

One of my first encounters with the mobile value of camera phones was at a Major League baseball game. In the middle of an inning, all of a sudden the three young ladies sitting in front of me raised their cell phones in the air. Finally, I realized that they were taking pictures of their favorite player walking by in front of us—photos that otherwise would never have been taken.

However, an even more significant example of convergence is e-mail. Virtually all camera phones are bundled with an e-mail service specifically designed for e-mailing those captured moments to friends and family. As an extension to the mobile value of the camera phone, multimedia e-mail adds convenience value of immediately being able to share pictures and being able to skip the tedious process of tethering a digital camera to a computer to upload pictures into e-mail.

Business e-mail users see significant value in converged device-based messaging itself. Research In Motion created tremendous momentum for mobile e-mail with its breakthrough Blackberry products. As leading messaging vendors like Microsoft focus on mobility, the integration of mobile e-mail into core business systems is also becoming much simpler.

As a real-world example of the value of mobile e-mail, I'm writing this commentary while attending a conference. The only device I chose to bring to this event is my converged mobile device. During breaks in the agenda, I've been able to check and send messages, enabling me to interactively resolve a number of critical issues back at the office. Without mobile e-mail, I would have been forced to bring a laptop and would need to find a network connection and boot my computer each time I wanted to check or send messages. The net result is that I likely would have been less well connected and would not have been able to quickly resolve my team's issues during these two days.

A third area where mobility has been built into products is in basic information delivery. Combining high-speed wireless data services with the basic Web browser built into a growing share of mobile devices enables replacing a broad range of content-rich products with simple access to that content over the network. Mobile-specific Web portals provide access to specific types of data in a format that works well on the small screen. For example, I used to take my two-inch-thick Bible to church every Sunday. Now, I simply take my converged mobile device. Through the portal at m.seek-first.com I can access six different translations of the Bible plus a variety of other related resources.

Immediate access to dynamic content takes built-in mobility to the next level of value. For example, Accuweather.com/pda remembers the most recent zip code I typed in and gives me an up-to-date forecast as well as any weather advisories.

A more impressive example of mobile access to dynamic content is the emerging field of mobile television. An article in the September 22, 2005, issue of the *Wall Street Journal* began with this observation: "Alan Foster learned about Hurricane Katrina's landfall while watching news channel MSNBC—on the small color screen of his Sprint cell phone, while waiting for his wife in a shopping mall near Los Angeles." The article went on to report, "In the week that followed, he kept tuning into his cellular TV whenever he was away from a TV set. At work, colleagues gathered around his cell phone to watch live television updates on the hurricane's devastating impact." The mobility of this small-screen TV created tremendous value for Mr. Foster as he sought to keep up to date on the unfolding story ("Now, the Very Small Screen," *Wall Street Journal,* September 22, 2005, p. B1).

The integration of information about the status of the mobile device with network-hosted content provides even another level of mobile value. Since 2000, virtually all cell phones manufactured for the United States have been able to identify their location to the network. This is generally for emergency location purposes (E911) and usually involves installing a global positioning system (GPS) chip inside the device. By linking my precise current location with centralized databases, applications such as Garmin Mobile's mapping and turn-by-turn directions services are made possible.

The consumer applications just noted are simple examples of mobility's being built into everyday products including cameras, e-mail, books, weather reports, televisions, and maps to create tremendous new value. The Age of Mobility is upon us. How will it impact you and your business in the months and years to come?

What's in this Book for You

This book introduces an observation as simple as Metcalfe's Law of Network Value, but relative to mobility. I believe that this observation, this Law of Mobility, should serve as a beacon announcing the emerging Age of Mobility and indicating how new value is created in this new age.

To save you from searching ahead, the Law of Mobility, simply stated, is that the value of any product or service increases with its mobility, where the value of mobility is realized as increased availability and contextual relevance.

As the title implies, this book will help you to capture the power of mobility in your business. The core of the book is a clear and implementable framework for capturing that power: the seven steps to the power of mobility. We will introduce the seven steps, then dive into each one to explain how to implement it to capture the power of mobility in your products, services, and processes.

To further solidify these seven steps, we will introduce case studies of companies that have already successfully implemented this framework in capturing the power of mobility and redefined the rules of competition in their industries.

This book's value should be measured by how well it helps you look forward, to envision the power of mobility in your business and to implement the steps required to turn vision into reality.

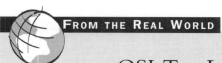

FROM THE REAL WORLD

OSI Ten-Layer Stack

Any communications technologist worth his salt will pepper his speech with oblique references to the OSI seven-layer stack (http://en.wikipedia.org/wiki/OSI_model). This very helpful model was codified by the International Organization for Standardization (OSI) in the 1970s and provides a framework for understanding how communications flow between systems across different networking technologies.

Throughout this book, I will refer to these seven layers, plus an additional three that I believe are necessary to complete the technology decision-making process, as shown in Exhibit 1.

The lowest layer (layer one or the physical layer) of the OSI stack represents the most basic physical levels of connectivity, such as how networking signals are sent across a piece of copper wire. The

EXHIBIT 1

The Pierce Ten-Layer Stack

Politics Layer
Finance Layer
Marketing Layer
Application Layer
Presentation Layer
Session Layer
Transport Layer
Network Layer
Data Link Layer
Physical Layer

FROM THE REAL WORLD (CONTINUED)

next level (layer two or data link layer) represents basic addressing and protocols for physical devices on a network. The most commonly known example of a layer 2 protocol is Ethernet. Layer three (the network layer) protocols deal with the basics of moving information across networks of physical connectivity. An example layer three protocol is Internet Protocol (IP). The transport layer (layer four) deals with network reliability. Transmission Control Protocol (TCP) is an example of a layer four protocol. And so on, up to layer seven, the application layer, which takes data transferred to and from the network and interprets that information for useful work.

Having spent 20 years in the technology industry, I am quite conversant in the seven-layer stack. However, Andrew Pierce, a friend who has spent his career helping companies actually choose and implement these technologies, taught me that it is the layers above the application layer that really matter when businesses are selecting technology solutions.

Andrew would argue for the addition of a layer eight (the marketing layer) that translates all the technical capabilities represented by layers one through seven into addressing real and perceived customer needs. If the technology doesn't solve a real problem, then it's not likely to be implemented.

Layer nine (the finance layer), he would attest, considers all of the costs of implementing the technology and balances those costs against the benefits promised by the solution. Vendor promises, heavily discounted by potential buyers, have to outweigh the cost and trouble of trying something new, or they'll never get approved.

The politics layer (layer ten), he would argue, is the most difficult to measure or predict. Who knows whom? How much clout can be brought to bear? And which parties gain and lose power through a technology decision often have the most significant impact of all in deciding whether a specific technology is deployed in a network.

Acknowledgments

Writing a book is a bigger, more complex project than I'd imagined. Without the help and support of many people, this book never could have been completed.

First let me thank my coworkers at Sprint Nextel: Mark Bonavia, Tim Donahue, Steve Funk, Walter Magiera, Bill Reed, Todd Reinglass, Charnsin Tulysathien, and Adrian Yeoh all stepped up at key times to keep the ball moving. Extra special thanks to Steve Signoff and Rebecca Sesler without whose encouragement and support this project never would have happened.

Special thanks and condolences to friends and family who have tolerated my mobility and technology babblings for years and still encouraged me to press on: Mark Volz, Andrew Pierce, Charles Mather, David Cordeiro, Howard Janzen, Mom and Dad, Mindy, Laurie, John, Bob, Ginny, Joe, Robert, Kathleen, and especially Donna and Kevin who have to put up with it every day.

Tim Burgard at John Wiley & Sons, and Susan Barry at the Barry-Swayne Literary Agency deserve special commendations for patiently educating me in all things publishing and believing in this project.

May all glory be to my God, who made all of this possible.

PART 1

The Mobility Age

CHAPTER 1

Technology Sets the Stage

The oft-repeated curse says "Those that ignore history are doomed to repeat it." I prefer the more positive twist: "If you want to know the future, understand how the past keeps repeating itself." Since this book is all about knowing the future, we will start by understanding how history continues to repeat itself. Time and time again, new technologies have been introduced and broadly adopted, resulting in dramatic impacts on society and the nature of business.

From a business perspective, a new technology can reduce a business's cost to produce a product or increase a product's value. In most cases, this improvement is relatively small but still worthwhile to the business.

Some new technologies introduce radical change to business. The reduction in cost or the increase in value may be an order of magnitude change—meaning that it is one-tenth the cost or ten times the value. These changes are so dramatic that they fundamentally change the nature of the business, the nature of the product, and the reasons why customers buy the product.

When this happens, the rules of competition change. And the new rules typically favor competitors with different strengths than the old leaders. Sometimes the old leaders can adapt and survive. Sometimes they can't.

Stories of businesses that have been crushed because they have failed to believe and have denied the changes brought by technologies in the past will likely be repeated. Now powerful companies will be crushed in the future when they disbelieve and deny the changes being wrought by emerging technologies. However, the stories of businesses that have believed in the coming changes and have turned change into value for customers, employees, and owners will also continue to be repeated.

The Gutenberg Press Unleashes Reformation and Renaissance

It is almost impossible to imagine a world without printing. In fact, arguably, all of the other technology advances we will consider would have been significantly hindered in their development if economical printing had never been developed.

And we must remember that the impact of Gutenberg's invention was purely economic. Prior to Gutenberg, there were printed documents—many made by hand (manuscripts), but printing presses were also cranking out documents by the mid-fifteenth century as well.

The innovation that Gutenberg introduced was threefold:

1. Alphabetic movable type.

2. Thicker ink that would stick to the press.

3. Perfection of the materials to be used in making the type.[1]

The result was a dramatic improvement in the cost and speed of printing. In fact, printing a book became the first assembly line process—mechanically combining replaceable parts to produce a complex end product—predating similar industrial processes by 300 years.[2] These advantages were quickly recognized by others, and lacking patent systems to protect the intellectual property (and slow its adoption), movable type printing spread rapidly.

Gutenberg began work on his first product, a beautiful Bible, in 1452. He first sold the product at the 1455 Frankfurt Book Fair, introducing his innovation to the world. Approximately 50 copies of that original Bible exist today.[3] By the early 1470s, the printing press had spread to the major trade centers in Germany; and by the early 1480s it had spread across western and central Europe.[4] Within 50 years, over 1,000 publishers had printed over a million books using Gutenberg's technology.[5]

Prior to Gutenberg's invention, there was little reason for literacy to broadly develop within society. Books were so rare and expensive that it was meaningless for the average citizen to bother learning how to read. As Walter J. Ong noted, "Many of the features we have taken for granted in thought and expression in literature, philosophy and science, and even in oral discourse among literates, are not directly native to human existence as such but have come into being because of the resources which the technology of writing makes available to human consciousness."[6]

As a simple example, Ong relates that, prior to printing, most people never knew in what calendar year they were born. With no newspapers or calendars to regularly remind them of the year, such a number would appear to have no relation to anything in "real life."

Robert Logan claims that the characteristics of Gutenberg's press enhanced and multiplied the prior impacts of the alphabet "unleashing a powerful new force that completely transformed Western civilization, leaving in its wake the Renaissance, the rise of science, the Reformation, individualism, democracy, nationalism, the systematic exploitation of technology, and the Industrial Revolution—in short, the modern world."[7]

Bacon's Law

There are two key questions we must wrestle with for each of the technologies we examine. Why was adoption so quick and why did the technology have such an impact on society and business? In most cases, we'll find that there is a simple observation, a simple truth that explains why adoption and impact were unstoppable.

In the case of the printing press, the simple observation was made in 1597 by Sir Francis Bacon in his *Religious Meditations, Of Heresies*.[8] The observation, which has become known as Bacon's Law, is that "knowledge is power."

The printing press enabled knowledge, which had been a virtual monopoly of the church and the universities, to be distributed. As Bacon observed, with the distribution of knowledge came the distribution of power. The powerless hungered for the freedom that came with the new flow of information, and, of course, those who had horded knowledge were threatened as their hold on power became challenged.

Given this true observation, once the printing press existed, nothing could hold it back and its impact on society and business was clearly dramatic.

The Steam Engine Powers the Industrial Age

The first practical steam engine was invented by Thomas Newcomen in 1712. Newcomen introduced four key innovations that made the steam engine a practical source of power:

1. Techniques for generating a vacuum.

2. The managed use of pressure.

3. Means for generating steam.

4. The piston and cylinder for capturing the mechanical power.

Newcomen built his first steam engine to operate a mine drainage pump near Dudley Castle in Staffordshire. However, it is not Thomas Newcomen who is best remembered as the inventor of the steam engine; instead, it is James Watt.

In 1764, Watt was asked to repair a Newcomen steam engine owned by the University of Glasgow. In working on it, he realized there were a number of ways in which the design could be improved. The most significant of these improvements was the use of a separate chamber for condensing the steam back to liquid at the end of each cycle. This allowed more of the energy in the main cylinder to be retained, greatly improving the overall efficiency of the engine.[9]

Watt built the first working model of his new design in May 1765, and in 1768 he applied for a patent on the invention. However, Watt did not have the capital required to build a manufacturing business around his invention, and therefore to meaningfully profit from it. He sought out investors and found them in John Roebuck and Matthew Boulton. To justify the large expense they would incur in establishing their business, the partners went to Parliament to get an extension to the normal patent to protect their intellectual property through 1800.[10]

The industrial factory predated Watt's steam engine. Water-powered factories were operational in England as early as 1721 (http://en.wikipedia.org/wiki/Industrial_revolution). But it was the steam engine that really accelerated the pace of change that became the Industrial Revolution. The first benefactor was coal mining. Pumps driven by steam engines enabled deeper and more productive coal seams to be mined, doubling British coal output between 1750 and 1800.

By 1800, cotton mills were the chief users as the steam engine provided reliable and continuous power for spinning. Up until 1750, agriculture had dominated the British economy. British agriculture was 2.5 times more productive than that of France, which itself was much more efficient than the rest of Europe. From 1750 on, three export sectors became increasingly important: coal, iron, and textiles. Cotton was insignificant as an export in 1750, but by 1810 had become 39 percent of exports by value.

In short, the steam engine radically changed the nature of business. But it also had a dramatic impact on all of society.

From 1750 to 1850 there were two dramatic shifts in the British population. The first was simple growth. Agriculture advances supported England's recovery from the Great Plague. In 1750, it is estimated that 5.8 million people lived in England.[11] By 1801, this increased to 8.3 million, and by 1851 it had nearly tripled to 16.92 million.[12]

The second shift was from country to town and to city. By 1801, about 30 percent of the mainland British lived in towns. By 1851, more than half the population lived in towns rather than in the country.[13]

London specifically reflected these shifts. In 1750, the population of London was about 700,000. By 1800, it had grown to over a million, and by 1850 it had more than doubled again to 2,362,000. London had rapidly shot past all the other cities in the world to become far and away the largest.[14]

These changes also dramatically changed the structure of society. In agricultural Britain prior to 1750, most of the farming land was owned by wealthy landowners who leased the land to tenant farmers. The farmers paid rent in the form of the goods they grew or produced. The economy was largely local, with specialized tradesmen making the nonagricultural goods needed by the community.[15]

The shift from an agricultural to an industrial economy created clear distinctions between work and home. Prior to the Industrial Revolution, most work was done in and around the home and often involved many members of the family. As work moved out of the home and into the factory, the men followed the work first, while the women stayed to care for the family and the home. However, in time, industrial productivity required even more workers, and women and then children were drawn into the workforce, creating tremendous social stress. The first child labor laws were passed in 1833 to bring the greatest dangers under control.

As referenced before, Watt's invention also sparked a new era of capitalism. The Industrial Age introduced business opportunities that required significant levels of funding. Notably, the London Stock

Exchange formally opened on March 3, 1801, reflecting this new era of capitalism.

The Second Law of Thermodynamics

As with the printing press, we must answer the questions of why the steam engine was rapidly adopted and why it had such an impact on business and society.

Bacon's Law observed the philosophical truths that answered these questions for the printing press. For the steam engine, the answer has a much more scientific foundation.

In 1865, Rudolf Clausius developed the classic statement that we know as the Second Law of Thermodynamics.[16] The statement is rather complex and is accurately quoted as "the entropy of an isolated system not at thermal equilibrium will tend to increase over time, approaching a maximum value." However, in practical terms this means that heat flows from hot places to cold places.

Big deal, right? Well, this simple truth that heat flows to where there isn't heat is what made the steam engine work and create motive power. The steam engine came onto the scene at the precise moment when mines and factories were ramping up their need for motive power. The dramatic increase in power produced by the steam engine then drove even greater productivity in industry, radically changing the shape of business and society.

The Telegraph Signals the Telecom Era

The telecommunications industry was born on March 2, 1791, in Brulon, France. On that day, brothers Claude and René Chappe demonstrated the first practical optical telegraph system. Claude Chappe wanted to call the invention the tachygraphe—meaning "fast writer"—but instead the name telegraphe—or "far writer"—stuck instead.[17]

However, it wasn't until electric telegraphy, whose invention is broadly attributed to Samuel Morse based on work he completed between 1832 and 1838, that practical telecommunications actually began to significantly impact the world. In 1843, Congress approved funds to build the first telegraph line in the United States from Washington to Baltimore, and on May 24 of that year, the famous "first message" of "What hath God wrought!" was transmitted over the line opening the American telecommunications industry.[18]

A new company, the Magnetic Telegraph Company, was formed and completed its first link, between New York and Philadelphia, in January 1846. Before this line opened, the only telegraph in the country was the original 40-mile stretch. By 1848, this had grown to approximately 2,000 miles, and by 1852 there were over 23,000 miles of telegraph lines in operation, with another 10,000 miles under construction.[19]

Writing in 1852, Laurence Turnbull noted that the growth in capacity and traffic showed "how important an agent the telegraph has become in the transmission of business communications. It is every day coming more into use, and every day adding to its power to be useful."

In 1861, the transcontinental telegraph line was completed to California. This new communications link made obsolete the Pony Express, enabling the instant communication of information that previously had taken 10 days. The Pony Express itself had dramatically improved the previous time of 20 days for a message to reach the West Coast.

International routes also began to be built. England and France were connected in 1851 and the first transatlantic cable was installed in 1858. Prior to these investments, international communications took as long as it took for ships to sail. A message from London to Bombay and back could take 10 weeks. But by the 1870s, a message from London to Bombay and back could take four minutes.[20]

The telegraph dramatically changed diplomacy, financial and commodities markets, and the news industry.

These changes in specific industries also had dramatic effects on all businesses. The telegraph effectively enabled the growth of very large businesses with centralized hierarchical command-and-control management styles. The increase in information flow also increased the pace of business decisions of all kinds and began the trend toward today's business pulse.

These changes, especially in the news industry, also dramatically changed how society looked at the world. Originally, all news was local. Local newspapers carried local news, and news only traveled to other places as the newspapers themselves were carried along. Timeliness of news was not a major focus, since it could be weeks or months before news reached distant corners of the country or world. As newspapers shifted to reporting on national and then global events, and as the news being reported increasingly was still happening (not an event already over), how people interacted with the news, and ultimately with the world, changed in the same ways as businesses. People became much more aware of places and events around them and the news of "now" really caught their attention.[21]

"Time Is Money"

Again, we must ask the question, "Why?" Why was the telegraph so rapidly adopted, and why did it have such an impact on business and society?

Writing in 1748, Ben Franklin made the truthful observation that answers our question and that should help us understand why any technology that helps us gain information and/or make a decision and/or complete a task more quickly will always be highly valued. He said, "Remember that time is money."

Businessmen using more recent information to outwit their competitors clearly learned how to use the telegraph to turn time into money. Newspapers could sell more copies of their paper with more timely news, proving that time is money.

The financial value created by telecommunications continues to this day, even as mobility enables information to reach us, and us to reach information whenever and wherever we go.

The Microprocessor Produces the Personal Computer (PC) Era

The ENIAC (Electronic Numerical Integrator and Calculator) is often credited as the first electronic computer. It was built in 1945 at the University of Pennsylvania under the direction of J. Presper Eckert and John Mauchly. The computer filled a 30-by-50-foot room, weighed 30 tons, and it took 150,000 watts of electricity to start it up. Instead of modern transistors, the ENIAC had 18,000 vacuum tubes and could store the equivalent of about 80 bytes of data.[22]

However, technically, the ENIAC was really only a big calculator. It could not store its own instructions. The first nonspecialized computer was the EDSAC (Electronic Delay Storage Automatic Calculator) built from 1947 to 1949 at Cambridge University in England under the direction of Maurice V. Wilkes. Although the machine included many concepts that we today consider standard for computers, few would confuse it with our modern products.[23]

No, the computer era, as we know it, had to wait for the invention of the transistor, followed by the integrated circuit, and finally the microprocessor.

While the Cambridge scientists were building the world's first computer, scientists at Bell Labs in Murray Hill, New Jersey, were inventing the transistor. During December 1947 and January 1948, William Shockley, Walter Brattain, and John Bardeen made the scientific breakthroughs that would be announced in June 1948 as the junction transistor. The transistor replaced the function of the energy-consuming, heat-producing, and failure-prone vacuum tubes in early computers with a tiny speck of semiconductive material.

A decade later, in 1958, Jack Kilby, working at Texas Instruments, and Robert Noyce, working separately at Fairchild Semiconductor, both figured out how to put multiple transistors and other components onto a single piece of silicon, giving birth to the Integrated Circuit and further miniaturizing the components of computers.[24]

Another decade later, Noyce was one of the founders of Intel. Through most of 1970, Intel's Ted Hoff worked to create an integrated circuit with all of the components for a complete computer on one slice of semiconductor. The first Intel "microprocessor" was delivered to Intel's customer, Busicom in February 1971,[25] and later that year Intel introduced its first microprocessor product, the 4004.

By 1977, Intel was selling microprocessors for $300 that Bob Noyce compared to the ENIAC in a *Scientific American* article: "It is twenty times faster, has a larger memory, is thousands of times more reliable, consumes the power of a lightbulb rather than that of a locomotive, occupies 1/30,000 the volume and costs 1/10,000 as much."[26]

In 1974, the 8080 became the brains behind the first personal computer product, a mail-order kit called the Altair.[27] This new class of computers inspired many new entrepreneurs, some of whom are still dominant players in the computer industry, including Steve Jobs, who founded Apple Computer in 1976, and Bill Gates, who founded Microsoft in 1975.[28]

Apple Computer was the company that really proved the concept of a mass market personal computer. Their Apple II computer, although crude by modern standards, was approachable and usable by everyday people. The company was started literally in a garage with $1,300. The real key to Apple's success was the availability of the VisiCalc spreadsheet software, which was initially available only on the Apple II. Thanks largely to VisiCalc, Apple's revenues grew from $800,000 in 1977 to $48 million in 1979.[29]

However, both the community of independent developers of software and hardware products for personal computers and the growing mass of computer users were desperate for a standard operating environment they could bet on. As businesses became increasingly interested in using personal computers to improve productivity, this need for a standard that would fit into a corporate environment became critical.

IBM stepped into this gap. In 1980, Bill Lowe, laboratory director of IBM's Entry Level Systems Unit in Boca Raton, Florida, sold IBM's senior leadership team on the vision of IBM bringing a personal computer product to market within a year. Upon gaining approval, Lowe handed the leadership of this Herculean task over to Don Estridge and a talented team, who achieved the nearly impossible. To meet the challenging timeline, the team had to work outside normal IBM operating principles, taking such innovative steps as introducing an architecture that was open to extension by non-IBM developers, using non-IBM parts and software (most notably Microsoft's operating system), and selling the product through non-IBM sales channels. Frank Cary, then IBM's chairman of the board, personally championed the personal computer effort and shielded it from IBM's otherwise smothering bureaucracy.

The resulting product, the IBM PC, was introduced on August 12, 1981 and was an immediate success. In the closing months of that year, IBM sold $43 million in PCs. By the end of 1984, the PC and related products were producing $4 billion in sales, enough to have ranked that division of IBM as number 74 in the Fortune 500 index if it had been a stand-alone company.

In time, IBM would stumble and be passed in PC leadership by more nimble startups, such as Compaq and Dell; however, the real winners were the people and businesses that adopted the PC. *Time* magazine recognized the impact of this product introduction, and for the first time in 55 years, instead of naming a "Man of the Year" or "Woman of the Year," they named the personal computer as the

"Machine of the Year." For the first few years of the 1980s, the PC market grew at 50% to 60% before leveling off to a respectable annualized growth of about 15% from 1985 on.

It is hard to imagine a world without the PC. Nearly every home in America has at least one computer, and virtually every professional uses a PC every day. So, the contrast with American business use of the personal computer less than 20 years ago is stark indeed. In 1980, fewer than 10% of small businesses in the United States were using personal computers, and within large corporations not even 3% of employees used personal computers on a regular basis.[30]

The PC and the software packages that made the computer useful were perhaps the first major example of a disruptive technology introduced from the home into the workplace. Before the PC, most technologies were first proven to be valuable at work, and then folks started using them at home. But not the PC.

Clearly, the PC unleashed tremendous power within corporations. Departments were able to make better decisions faster with fewer people. They could really get their hands on the data to run and rerun different scenarios to determine a range of possible outcomes and plan accordingly. Entire departments became obsolete overnight, including the word processing and data entry departments. And spending on big computers dropped precipitously.

But tremendous danger was also introduced. Many departments running their own analysis resulted in many, seemingly conflicting views of the "truth"—too much information became an impediment to decision making rather than an accelerator. Every white-collar worker became an untrained computer operator, searching frantically for the "Any" key. Critical data was lost when un-backed-up systems failed or critical data walked out the door on floppy disks as employees left to join the competitor. PC spending at first was out of control and literally uncontrollable since it was scattered across virtually every departmental cost center. Companies' centralized management information systems (MIS) departments were ill-prepared to deal with the tidal wave of support requests involving technologies they'd never been trained in.

"Moore's Law"

Why did the PC have such a sudden impact on business and society? The answer really comes down to the fundamental implications of Moore's Law.

The April 1965 edition of *Electronics* magazine included an article by Gordon Moore. At that time, Moore was at Fairchild Semiconductor, but later he would be one of the cofounders of Intel. Within the article were the basic points that later would be codified as Moore's Law—the observation that every year or so chip density (roughly equivalent to processing power) doubles while the price shrinks by half. Although the microprocessor wouldn't be invented until the next decade, Moore's Law became most meaningful in terms of the cost and availability of computing power.[31]

In 1965, there were very few computers and they could be used only to perform very valuable tasks. However, the continuous doubling of power and halving of costs meant that, by the early 1980s, it was economically viable for companies to move computing power out of the carefully managed data center and onto the desktops of average white-collar workers. The trend hasn't stopped, so today computing power exceeding that found in multimillion-dollar computers in the 1960s can now be included in cheap toys and everyday items.

The financial benefit of using this available power drove the rapid adoption of the PC by businesses and the embedding of computing power throughout society.

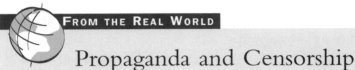

FROM THE REAL WORLD

Propaganda and Censorship

Throughout history, communications technologies have been powerfully used to bring about dramatic change in society.

As noted in this chapter, the Protestant Reformation is an excellent case in point—using the new power of the press to redraw the political boundaries across Europe, to reduce the power of the Church in society, and to encourage literacy and education. In today's terminology, we would probably call the reformers' use of rapid distribution of printed arguments "propaganda."

As can be expected, the Church in Rome (what today we call the Roman Catholic Church) was not pleased with the reformers' success in using the printing press as a tool to weaken their power. In fact, early in the history of the press, the Church attempted to gain control of the new technology, limiting the number of presses created and establishing editorial control over what would be produced. In 1487, Pope Innocent VIII commanded that all books had to be reviewed and approved by Church authorities before they could be printed.[32] Obviously, the rapid spread of printing and the relative ease with which new presses could be built, foiled those attempts at what we would today call "censorship."

Such uses and concerns over the power of communications technology did not begin with, nor have they ended with, the printing press. Going all the way back to the invention of writing, as great a thinker as Plato was philosophically opposed to the use of writing

FROM THE REAL WORLD (CONTINUED)

technology. Ong notes "one weakness in Plato's position was that, to make his objections effective, he put them into writing, just as one weakness in anti-print positions is that their proponents, to make their objections more effective, put the objections into print."[33]

Controlling the impact of writing eventually proved relatively effective due to the inefficiency of reproducing manuscripts. In fact, the Roman Catholic Church successfully censored books for centuries leading up to the Protestant Reformation, so the Church's expectation that it could continue was not baseless.

The real problem that the Church faced with the printing press was that the danger of the technology was recognized, and there were ineffective attempts made to manage that danger, but the power of the press was not recognized. Perhaps, if the Roman Church had been as aggressive as the reformers in capturing the power of the press, its ability to win the hearts and minds of European Christians would not have been so badly compromised.

Since the printing press, virtually every communications technology has been similarly used for propaganda purposes and has attempted to be censored. As I write this, the current debate centers on what some call "The Great Firewall of China." The government of the People's Republic of China recognizes both the power and the danger of today's equivalent of the printing press—the Internet. The government actively uses the Net to promote its positions while actively shutting down the use of the Internet—using technology and persecution—for promotion of opposing views.

Clearly, propaganda and censorship are powerful examples of the interaction of layer ten in the technology stack (politics) with all of the other attributes of new technologies. Politics and power can trump all of the financial, user benefit, and scientific arguments that can ever be made concerning the adoption of any technology.

Notes

1. Kreis, Steven. 2000. "The Printing Press," The History Guide: Lectures on Modern European Intellectual History. www.historyguide.org/intellect/press.html. Copyright © 2000 by Steven Kreis.

2. Ong, Walter J. 1982. *Orality & Literacy.* London and New York: Routledge, Copyright © 1982 by Walter J. Ong.

3. See note 1.

4. McNeil, Ian (ed.). 1990, 1996. *An Encyclopedia of the History of Technology.* London: Routledge.

5. Nesse, Randolph. 2000. "Printing," in John Brockman (ed.), *The Greatest Inventions of the Past 2,000 Years: Today's Leading Thinkers Choose the Creations that Shaped Our World.* New York: Simon & Schuster.

6. See note 2.

7. Logan, Robert K. 1986. *The Alphabet Effect: The Impact of the Phonetic Alphabet on the Development of Western Civilization.* New York: William Morrow.

8. www.quotationspage.com/quote/2060.htm.

9. See note 4.

10. "The Invention of the Steam Engine: The Life of James Watt." http://inventors.about.com/library/inventors/blwatts.htm. Extracts from John Lord, "Capital and Steam Power 1750–1800."

11. Langford, Paul. 1999. "The Eighteenth Century," in Kenneth O. Morgan (ed.), *The Oxford History of Britain.* Oxford: Oxford University Press.

12. Harvie, Christopher. 1999. "Revolution and the Rule of Law," in Kenneth O. Morgan (ed.), *The Oxford History of Britain*. Oxford: Oxford University Press.

13. Matthew, H. C. G. 1999. "The Liberal Age," in Kenneth O. Morgan (ed.), *The Oxford History of Britain*. Oxford: Oxford University Press.

14. Hitchcock, Tim, and Robert Shoemaker. 2003. "Gender in the Proceedings." Old Bailey Proceedings Online, www.oldbaileyonline.org (June 17).

15. Hooker, Richard. 1996. "World Civilizations." Copyright © 1996 by Richard Hooker. Washington State University, http://www.wsu.edu:8080/~dee/ENLIGHT/INDUSTRY.HTM.

16. http://en.wikipedia.org/wiki/History_of_thermodynamics#Entropy_and_the_second_law.

17. Standage, Tom. 1998. *The Victorian Internet*. New York: Walker Publishing Company, Inc.

18. Evans, Harold, Gail Buckland, and David Lefer. 2006. *They Made America: From the Steam Engine to the Search Engine*. Boston: Back Bay Books.

19. See note 17.

20. Ibid.

21. Ibid.

22. Gates, Bill. 1995. *The Road Ahead*. New York: Penguin Books.

23. Ifrah, Georges. 2001. *The Universal History of Computing*. New York: John Wiley & Sons.

24. See note 18.

25. Zygmont, Jeffrey. 2003. Microchip: An Idea, Its Genesis, and the Revolution It Created. Cambridge Mass.: Perseus Publishing.

26. See note 22.

27. See note 25.

28. Chposky, James, and Ted Leonsis. 1988. *Blue Magic: The People, Power and Politics Behind the IBM Personal Computer.* New York: Facts on File Publications.

29. Ibid.

30. Ibid.

31. See note 25.

32. "Teaching Gutenberg," www.hrc.utexas.edu/exhibitions/education/modules/gutenberg/. Copyright © by the Harry Ransom Humanities Research Center, The University of Texas at Austin.

33. See note 2.

CHAPTER 2

Redefining Communications

This is a scary chapter. If you are old enough to remember what I am about to describe, you will probably nod your head as you read it and wonder at how much the world has changed. If you are too young to remember, you probably won't believe a word of it. But it's all true.

Redefining Business Communications

In one of my first jobs, to get to my desk, I had to walk past this open window in an interior wall. Sitting behind the window was a very friendly and helpful coworker. On a sign next to the window were the words "Word Processing."

After walking past this window and arriving at my desk, I would scan my desk for messages, quickly flip through the inbox tray, and flip on my VT220 text terminal with amber letters on a black background.

This was not that long ago. I'm describing the mid–1980s.

When I think of business communications in that pre-PC era, there are three artifacts that come to mind. The overhead projector, the pink message pad, and the routing slip.

Real-time communications meant one of two things: a face-to-face meeting or a telephone call. A "multi-media presentation" in a meeting meant transparency sheets displayed on a pull-down screen using an overhead projector. The transparencies were mostly black words and were probably typed up from handwritten notes by the word processing department.

Telephone calls were definitely constrained by time and place. My telephone number was tied to the telephone sitting on my desk, but also rang at my secretary's desk. If you called me, you hoped I would answer. If I didn't answer, you hoped my secretary would answer. If she answered, she would take down your message on a pink "While You Were Out" message pad. You hoped that what you said and what she wrote were reasonably close to each other.

At some point, my secretary would carry the stack of messages into my office and put them on my desk where I was sure to see them the next time I returned to my office, whether that be in five minutes or in two weeks. If you called after 5 P.M. and I wasn't at my desk, no one would answer and there was no way to leave a message.

Non-real-time communications meant sending something by the U.S. Postal Service. When your letter arrived at my company, the mail room would sort it for delivery to my desk. My secretary might save me a little work by opening your letter for me and placing it face up in my inbox so I (or anyone else wandering in my office) could easily grasp the content of your message.

If others in my company needed to see the information you sent me, I would staple a little slip of paper to the top of your letter with the names of the people who needed to see it. I would then put the letter in my outbox, and it would spend the next several weeks making its way from outbox to inbox of each of the people on the list.

And, yes, your letter was probably typed for you by someone in the word processing department. That person's initials would appear at the bottom of the letter to ensure they received "credit" for any mistakes that might have snuck in as they tried to interpret your handwriting.

The scenario I have described is not fiction. Isn't it amazing how far we've come in just over two decades?

So, what happened? The two main things that have already happened are the PC and the Internet, and what's happening now is mobility.

Moore's Law pointed to computing power being built into everything. Falling processing costs and falling storage costs led to a major shift from analog to digital.

The real-time meeting migrated to conference calls, video-conferences, and with the Internet to Web casts. Transparencies were replaced by PowerPoint. Voice mail became broadly adopted. Word processing departments were replaced by word processing software like Microsoft Word. Letters were delivered by fax and then by e-mail. Routing slips were replaced by the "Forward" button in e-mail.

Metcalfe's Law pointed toward a single network that would connect everyone—the Internet. Point-to-point communications broadened to multipoint communications. Connection-oriented technologies that required establishing a dedicated circuit were replaced by connectionless technologies that enabled different packets to be dynamically routed and multicast across the network.

Intranets replaced employee newsletters. Web sites replaced marketing brochures. Instant messaging (IM) replaced a walk down the hall. And Web logs (blogs) replaced heated debates in smoke-filled conference rooms.

The Law of Mobility points toward a shift from communications constrained by place and time to communications that are aligned with context and capability.

Already we see that the Internet, IM, Web logs, and e-mail have had mobility built in so that they are available to me all the time, wherever I go. Soon, these capabilities will be enhanced by new applications that respond to my context—where I am, what else I'm doing, who I'm with, and what resources I have at my command.

I cannot describe exactly what business communications will look like ten years from now, but I am confident that it will make today's IM and blogging seem as prehistoric as a word processing department.

Redefining Consumer Communications

It's not just at work that we've experienced revolutionary change in how we communicate.

In the mid-1980s, virtually all telephones were connected to the wall by a cord and many of them still had a dial instead of a keypad. Answering machines were an expensive luxury that few could afford, and even those models used cassette tapes that would rewind and fast forward to play the greeting then advance to a blank spot for the message.

Even if Caller ID had existed, telephones did not have a digital display to tell you who was calling, nor did they have built-in telephone directories, logs of calls from which you could redial, or a flash button for picking up another call, even if call waiting had been offered.

Writing Mom literally meant hand-writing a letter, and the flag on the side of that metal container outside your house was the only indication that "you've got mail." A message board was made with cork. A Tupperware party was the closest thing to a chat room.

Televisions didn't have computer chips, so remote controls were rare and primitive. Cable TV was a new phenomenon that hadn't yet made it to all of the suburbs. Satellites were what the Russians used to spy on us, not a great way to get television service.

As with business communications, the PC era signaled the shift from analog to digital and the Internet era signaled the shift from connection-oriented point-to-point to connectionless multipoint communications.

Mobility is already being built into much of how people communicate, so that, for example, a football fanatic who is an NFL Mobile subscriber can use her mobile device to watch football games, draft her fantasy football team, trash talk her competitors in online message boards, and send an instant message to her buddies to celebrate a touchdown—wherever she happens to be, whatever she happens to be doing.

Where historically, our location has largely defined how we communicate, as we move deeper into the Mobility Age, the richer concept of context is becoming the dynamic regulator of our communications. The meaning of this and its implications for our lives and our businesses deserve full exploration.

FROM THE REAL WORLD

Business in
the Pre-PC World

To get a sense of what the world looked like before the PC, Internet, and Mobility eras, consider these quotes taken from a speech by Paul H. Henson, Chairman of United Telecommunications, Inc. (the company that later would become Sprint Nextel) given November, 1979.

- "You all know, and probably utilize, the time-honored practice of dictation with a secretary typing the letter after it has been drafted a couple of times and you have done some editing."

- "You may not realize that only 28% of all business calls are completed to the intended person on the first attempt. . . . We could solve that problem by sending hard copy, instantly, to the desk of somebody you want to communicate with—after you've tried your call, of course. If you don't find your party in or available to talk, hit another button and have the hard copy transmitted. We're working on it!"

- "One wonders why in the world American business has tolerated this level of productivity in the white collar sector. . . . I suspect it's probably because some of those of us who call ourselves managers never thought it appropriate for us to learn how to use a typewriter or a cathode ray tube so that we could correct correspondence, speech drafts, and other hard copy material instead of asking secretaries or assistants to do so."

- "What will emerge is the so-called 'office of the future.' . . . It is going to revolutionize the way we do business, the way we communicate with our branch offices and our other business associates. We will be using a typewriter keyboard or reading information displayed on a cathode ray tube instead of dictating and typing those letters and mailing them out in neat little envelopes, wondering if they ever will be delivered!"

FROM THE REAL WORLD (CONTINUED)

The revolution that Chairman Henson predicted is exactly what has happened over the past thirty years. Today, we can't imagine dictation or typewriters or even cathode ray tubes in our offices. We can't imagine "sending hardcopy" at a touch of a button as a futuristic concept that is hard to describe. We can't imagine a world without voice mail (a capability also enabled by computer technology). And yet, it was reality not too long ago.

CHAPTER 3

The Law of Mobility Signals Transformation

The Internet Connects the World

From the earliest days, the government, and especially the Defense Department was the biggest customer of the emerging computer industry. Much of this spending was done in university research labs.

In 1951, the Massachusetts Institute of Technology (MIT) founded Lincoln Labs, focused on air defense. The projects undertaken at Lincoln required collecting data from many sources, resulting in Lincoln becoming a hotbed for innovations in computer networking.

In the second half of 1957, the Soviet Union test-fired the first intercontinental ballistic missile and launched the Sputnik I artificial satellite, initiating the arms race and the space race. In January 1958, President Eisenhower established the Advanced Research Projects Agency (ARPA) to address these threats.

J. C. R. Licklider, a Lincoln veteran, became the first director of the Information Processing Techniques Office (IPTO) within ARPA. Early in 1963, Licklider proposed networking together the computers in research labs being funded by ARPA to make these expensive resources more available and productive. In 1966, Bob Taylor replaced Licklider as head of the IPTO and recruited Larry Roberts from Lincoln Labs to turn this concept into reality.

The network, dubbed ARPAnet by Roberts, ended up building upon advances in computer networking made by Roberts at MIT, Donald Davies and Roger Scantlebury of Britain's National Physical Laboratory, Paul Baran of the Rand Corporation, and Len Kleinrock of the University of California–Los Angeles (UCLA). These new technologies became known as packet switching. ARPA tried to get AT&T, the telecom industry leader, to participate in building ARPAnet. Bob Taylor recalls, "When I asked AT&T to participate in the ARPAnet, they assured me that packet switching wouldn't work."[1]

So the research community had to build it themselves. Boston firm, Bolt, Baraneck & Newman (BBN) was selected to build the critical piece of equipment, the Interface Message Processor (IMP) to link the computers together. The first IMP was installed at UCLA over the Labor Day weekend in 1969. The second was installed on October 1 at Stanford. The first message was sent between them and the ARPAnet, which would become the Internet, was born.

Initial growth came slowly. Four nodes were online by the end of 1969. By 1974 the network had only grown to 64 nodes, and by 1981 there were still only 213 nodes. In the 1980s, the network was roughly doubling every year, and the numbers finally started to reach significant proportions. By 1989, there were 150,000 nodes on the network. Between 1986 and 1989, the National Science Foundation slowly took over administration of the network, acknowledging the expansion of the value of the Internet beyond purely military purposes. Growth began to explode. By April 1993, there were nearly 1.5 million nodes on the Internet.

Applications also came slowly at first. Originally, the network was primarily used to log in to remote computers. In 1972, Ray Tomlinson of BBN sent the first e-mail across the ARPAnet. In 1989, Tim Berners-Lee of Switzerland's CERN started writing a program he called the World Wide Web. CERN published the program in 1991. In 1992, Congress passed a law allowing the use of the Internet for commercial purposes, unleashing an unprecedented wave of entrepreneurship.

The Internet burst into the consciousness of the general public in 1995. Most dramatically, Netscape's unbelievably rich initial public offering (IPO) of stock on August 9 captured everyone's attention and launched a thousand start-ups. However, other companies that would have a much more permanent impact on the Internet, the economy, and how we individually interact with the world were already on their way and celebrated significant milestones during the year. In March, Yahoo was incorporated, graduating from a hobby to a business.[2] Amazon's online store opened in July.[3] The first auction on eBay was launched on Labor Day.[4] So, in a short six months, three of the companies that have come to define the Internet experience came into being.

Over the coming years, the incredible power of networked computing to deliver to us dynamic content, enable us to buy and sell in new ways, and connect us more directly to our extended communities fundamentally changed how we live, how we interact with the world, and how we run our businesses.

"Metcalfe's Law"

Why did the Internet have such a broad and deep impact on the world? I believe Robert Metcalfe explains it perfectly in what has become known as Metcalfe's Law.

Bob Metcalfe is best known in technology circles as the inventor of Ethernet. As an early participant in the building and use of the Internet, Bob recognized the need for high-speed intermachine connections that responded well as traffic increased. From this recognition came the Ethernet protocol, and later Bob built a successful company, 3Com, around this expertise.

Bob didn't see growing traffic as a curse, but rather a blessing. Bob observed that the value of any network increases exponentially with the number of participants in the network, and this simple, but true observation has borne his name ever since.

What happened in 1995 is that the Internet reached a tipping point in the number of users. The value of the network outweighed the cost of connecting, so more people and businesses joined, further increasing the value. By the end of 1995, you couldn't afford to *not* be connected to the Internet, especially if you were a business.

Today, the Internet is fully integrated into our lives, our business processes, most services offered to customers, and a growing number of products.

Wireless Technologies Unleash the Power of Mobility

The wireless age can be traced back to 1888 when German physicist Heinrich Hertz demonstrated the transmission of an electrical signal through the air to a "receiver" on the other side of the room. Hertz built upon brushes with wireless signals made by Thomas Edison and James Clerk Maxwell, but wasn't able to carry these wireless signals forward into any practical applications.[5]

That task fell to a young Italian entrepreneur named Guglielmo Marconi. By 1897, Marconi had received the first ever patent for this new "radio" technology and was busy forming a company to commercialize the technology and its applications. On December 12, 1901, Marconi and his team managed to send a radio signal all the way across the Atlantic Ocean.[6]

By 1907, Marconi wireless telegraph rooms were installed on all the major transatlantic ocean liners. At first, these systems were intended as profitable ventures, with well-to-do passengers paying premium prices to send "Marconigrams" to their friends and business partners on both continents and to stay connected with the news and dealings during their journey.[7] However, with the sinking of the *Titanic* in April 1912, a new value of mobility was discovered. As the ship was going down, its Marconi operator stayed at his post frantically tapping out an SOS message with the ship's coordinates. The *Carpathia* heard the message and sailed 50 miles to save 700 passengers that otherwise would undoubtedly have perished.[8] Unfortunately, the *California*, a ship that was much closer and could have saved many more, failed to receive the signal because their Marconi operator had turned in for the night.[9] From that night on, the threefold value of wireless was clear: business, pleasure, and safety.

Wireless communications continued to develop slowly through most of the twentieth century. In 1921, the Detroit Police Department began using radio dispatching, but the system was transmit only. In 1933, the Bayonne, New Jersey, police department deployed the first two-way push-to-talk mobile radio system, filling each squad car's trunk with electronic equipment and requiring the officer to keep the car constantly running so the battery wouldn't be completely run down by the inefficient radio system.

During World War II, Motorola introduced the Handie-Talkie and the Walkie-Talkie, a backpack filled with glowing vacuum tubes and radio equipment to enable, for the first time, wireless battlefield communications.

In 1946, the Bell System began offering commercial wireless telephone service for the first time, starting in St. Louis and extending to 25 cities. The service used push-to-talk technology that an operator could then manually patch through to complete a telephone call. These systems used one set of channels to cover an entire city and surrounding area, significantly limiting the number of customers. Even as late as 1981, only 24 wireless phone users could be on the line at the same time in New York City and systems limitations kept the total number of customers down to 700. Obviously, something needed to change.[10]

That change involved both a new system architecture and new spectrum licensed from the government through the Federal Communications Commission (FCC). The new architecture was called "cellular" because it broke a city up into a number of "cells," each with its own radios, allowing channels to be reused many times over and greatly increasing the number of customers and calls that could be supported.

In 1981, the FCC announced it would offer two blocks of spectrum for this new cellular technology. The first would go to the local telephone company, most often the Bell System, but sometimes GTE or United Telephone or Centel or one of dozens of other small local telephone companies. The second was opened to new nonwireline companies. Starting in June 1982 with the 30 largest cities and working through December 1989 when the final rural licenses were issued, the FCC gave out a total of 1,468 cellular licenses covering every inch of the country.

A lot of wheeling and dealing happened over those seven and a half years largely shaping the initial cellular industry in the United States. The first surprising deal involved the Bell System. The breakup of the System was happening concurrent with the issuing of licenses. Since AT&T had performed a study that suggested the total market for cellular would only be 900,000 total U.S. subscribers by 2000, the company ceded its right to participate in the spectrum giveaway to the newly formed Regional Bell Operating Companies (RBOCs). The biggest wheeler-and-dealer among the nonwireline companies was Craig McCaw. McCaw started the 1980s as the owner of a small cable TV business in the state of Washington. By the time the cellular industry was fully formed, McCaw Cellular was the only truly nationwide wireless carrier.

The first wireless phones in no way resembled the convenient, attractive devices we carry today. At first, wireless phones were almost universally installed in cars. Later came "bag phones," which could be carried about but certainly couldn't fit in a purse or pocket. But that didn't stop folks from falling in love with mobility. By the end of 1985, there were 340,000 customers in 85 markets. Within two years, that number had more than tripled and the industry had generated more than a billion dollars in revenue. By the end of the decade, 5.3 million cell phones had been sold and annual revenues were at $3 billion. AT&T's study had missed the mark—badly.[11]

In 1994, AT&T finally got into the cellular game, buying McCaw for $12.6 billion and assuming nearly $5 billion in the company's debt. But the mid-1990s were also a period of technology advances that would further refine the industry. The first was leveraging Moore's Law to introduce digital technology into cellular systems, making them much more efficient and able to multiply the number of concurrent calls. The second was the emergence of a start-up called Fleet Call (later renamed Nextel) that used a new technology from Motorola to offer wireless telephone service using a previously inefficiently run block of spectrum called Specialized Mobile Radio (SMR). Due to its origins and regulations, the Fleet Call/Nextel service included a high performance push-to-talk capability that became wildly successful. The final new technology was called Personal Communications Systems (PCS) which would enable new data services. In July 1993, the FCC announced a new set of spectrum auctions to allow up to six new competitors to enter each market using PCS technology.[12]

One of the new nationwide carriers to emerge from the PCS license auctions was Sprint PCS. Today, in 2007, the U.S. mobile industry has consolidated down to four major nationwide players. The largest, AT&T (formerly Cingular), has been formed out of AT&T

Wireless (which started as McCaw Cellular) and three of the original RBOCs (BellSouth, Southwestern Bell, Ameritech) plus parts of a fourth RBOC (Pacific Telesis). The second largest is Verizon Wireless formed out of two of the original RBOCs (Bell Atlantic and NYNEX) plus GTE plus the most significant wireless parts of Pacific Telesis. The third largest is Sprint Nextel formed through the combination of those two mid-1990s entrants. The fourth is the U.S. arm of Germany's T-Mobile, largely formed through a rollup of PCS auction winners. So, roughly half the industry traces its roots back to the original license gifts to the big Bell wireline companies, while the other half has been formed out of scrappy upstarts that burst onto the scene in the mid-1990s.

One thing is clear—mobility has been a huge hit. According to the Cellular Telecommunications Industry Association (CTIA), in mid-2006 there were 219.4 million U.S. wireless subscribers, spending more than $10 billion per month for mobility.[13] And these customers have clearly begun to integrate their mobile devices into how they live, work, and play.

The global impact is even more dramatic. According to the International Telecommunications Union (ITU), it took 21 years for mobile technology to reach the first billion users worldwide. In comparison, it took 125 years for wireline telecom to reach that same billion. The second billion mobile users signed up in just three years. Wireline has yet to reach its second billion.[14] Philip Redman of research firm Gartner, Inc. estimates that nearly half of the world's population will be mobile users by 2010. Considering that up until now, less than 10% of the world's population has ever made a telephone call, the impact of mobility on how the world lives and communicates is huge.[15]

''The Law of Mobility''

Why has mobility so rapidly been adopted and begun to impact the world? In the fall of 2005, I made an observation as simple and intuitive as Moore's Law or Metcalfe's Law. Simply stated, the Law of Mobility observes that the value of any product or service increases with its mobility.[16]

This value of mobility is realized in two ways. First, and most obviously, making a product more mobile means that it's available for use more often. A product that is always with you and always fully functional (perhaps relying on a wireless connection) will be available for your use and translate into value much more often than a product that is usually left at home or at the office.

The classic example of this form of mobility value is the camera phone. Typically, a camera phone will not take as good pictures as a stand-alone digital camera. However, a camera phone is always with you since it's built into a product (your mobile phone) that most people take with them everywhere they go. Therefore, your camera phone is available to capture moments that otherwise would have been lost. Better yet, the camera phone also serves as a virtual photo printer since you can instantly use your phone's data connection to share the moment with any friends or family around the world.

The second way in which the value of mobility is realized is through increased contextual relevance. Mobility is the first class of technology that by definition regularly changes the conditions (e.g., location, environment) under which it is used. Since mobility is a highly personal technology, the situation (e.g., availability, with other people) of the person using it is also constantly changing. Products and services that have been mobilized have access to information about the conditions and the personal situation in which you are using them, and can use this information to be more useful and valuable given your immediate needs. The next chapter deals with this in much more detail, but consider the example of Internet search to get a sense of the value of contextual relevance.

Internet search engines, such as Google or Yahoo, do a great job of searching all the content on the Internet and ranking that information in a manner that best represents the needs of all people in all places at all times. Such tools are very valuable. All of the major search engines have created versions of their services that work well on mobile Web browsers, such as those found on cell phones. Because your cell phone is always with you, these mobile–Web-friendly versions have increased the value of each search engine by making the service available to you all the time, wherever you go.

But some search engines have gone a step further. They take into account the location from which the mobile searcher is doing their search. If they are searching for Chinese restaurants and they happen to be sitting at the corner of 119th and Antioch in Overland Park, Kansas, then a search engine that takes this context into account and brings to the top of the page the four or five Chinese restaurants within two miles of that intersection will be providing a much more relevant result and one that is dramatically higher value than one that uses the generic "all people, all places, all times" ranking algorithm. This is the value of mobility from contextual relevance.

As the cost of adding mobility (availability and context) into products continues to fall dramatically, the Law of Mobility would suggest the value of products and services would increase if mobility were built in. This potential transformation of the previously ordinary to the mobility-blessed will likely reshape our lives dramatically.

Those companies that figure out how to lead by building mobility into their products and services will redefine the rules of competition in their industries, increasing the odds they can win.

FROM THE REAL WORLD

The Beginnings of Mobility

In December 2006, the Sprint Nextel intranet featured a story recalling the launch of both Sprint PCS and Nextel networks ten years earlier. Here's the text from that story:

This holiday season, wireless consumers can download songs and videos to their phones or buy a loved one a device to keep them connected with voice and data faster than you can say "yippee-yi-yay."

But during a December just 10 years past, our employees were launching an entire industry from the ground up, one that fundamentally changed the way we communicate.

This week marks the 10-year anniversary of the launch of Sprint PCS wireless service in Fresno, Calif. Earlier that same year, Nextel refined its iDEN technology and prepared to expand to markets nationwide.

In those days, the wireless frontier was wide open and yet to be settled by nationwide carriers and hundreds of millions of customers. Employees who were there tell tales of a wild ride.

SPRINT PCS TAKES SHAPE

"I remember showing up my first day and asking the chief operating officer 'What do you want me to do?'" recalls **John Garcia**, president–Cable Joint Venture, who was then vice president–Marketing.

FROM THE REAL WORLD (CONTINUED)

"He said, 'We need help with everything.' We had to hire people who could do many things in many areas. We were true entrepreneurs."

In the early '90s, Sprint formed a task force to explore wireless possibilities, and in 1994 partnered with cable companies TCI, Cox, and Comcast to pursue a wireless venture. When the Federal Communications Commission (FCC) opened auctions for wireless licenses in 1995, Sprint Spectrum—soon renamed Sprint PCS—snatched up enough spectrum for an impressive national footprint covering 190 million potential customers.

Naysayers said it couldn't be done: Launching a multi-billion-dollar start-up that would build a nationwide network from scratch, use unfamiliar Code Division Multiple Access (CDMA) technology and introduce what *The Wall Street Journal* referred to as "so-called" personal communication services (PCS) to the mass market in a mere 18 months.

To make it happen, Sprint began a frenzied hiring process of full-timers and contractors to staff the start-up and build the network. Leading technology vendors like Lucent and Nortel stepped up, supplying manpower, equipment, and even capital to help fulfill our vision. From a blank network slate at the outset of '96, the company put 1,300 cell sites and 45 switching centers in place by year-end.

ACQUISITIONS SPUR NEXTEL GROWTH

What began as a dispatch start-up Fleet Call in 1987 quickly became an industry force in the early 1990s, thanks to aggressive acquisitions, mergers and the purchase of Motorola's SMR licenses in the United States. But Nextel really took shape in 1995 with a billion-dollar investment. This led to its 1996 evolution from MIRS (MOTR Integrated Radio System) technology to iDEN (Integrated Dispatch Enhanced Network), which combined enhanced digital cellular, two-way radio, and text-numeric paging in one phone.

Larry Krevor, vice president-Government Affairs in Reston, Va., planted his roots in 1989 as an outside counsel before coming in-house in 1992. He recalls the early days of "frenetic" acquisitions, intensive regulatory efforts to gain FCC approval and the build-out of the iDEN network. Nextel employed 300 when he started; growing to 20,000 by 2005.

Nextel employees adopted a "get it done" attitude from the start and most wore many hats. Krevor realized this while helping to open the Washington office: He bought furniture, networked computers, even connected the phone system.

But his big challenge was writing the filings for FCC approval. "I wrote all of them and even got in a cab and delivered them some-times," he says, noting that Government Affairs staffs about 100 people today. "We were the underdog who fought enormous odds and had great success."

What we now know as iDEN came into being during the 1996 Summer Olympics, with a Nextel national network rollout beginning in January 1997.

HALLWAYS AND ... HELLO?

A nimble staff meant decisions were made on the fly and impromptu "hallway" meetings frequent. A few pizzas could once feed the entire crew, and one conference room sufficed for All-Hands meetings. As Sprint PCS staffed up, leaders routinely dealt praise, worked in the trenches and did anything to keep employee motivation high.

"We once had an All-Hands meeting where our general counsel turned up in a Roman centurion costume to mimic our ad cam-paign," recalls **Lisa-Anne Uhrmacher**, manager-Partner Develop-ment & Product Innovation in Overland Park, Kan. "He came screaming into the room with his costume flapping, bare legs glaring, while a propane torch burned in his hand."

FROM THE REAL WORLD (CONTINUED)

Wireless was still in its infancy, so many employees learned by doing. **Leighton Tong** worked with Engineering & Operations technicians to build the Fresno switch and prepare for launch. The team spent long hours testing and optimizing the new network and were ''on pins and needles'' come launch day.

''We had the launch event with media, city dignitaries, and Sprint executives in a building that was half underground. We worried whether the signal would penetrate it,'' says Tong, RF Engineer-Lower Valley Design in Fresno. ''When that first call went through OK, we all took a collective breath and cheered, 'It worked—we're part of history!' ''

Gene Guevel, manager–SCS Customer Care Technology in Overland Park, experienced similar butterflies preparing to launch the first Customer Care Center in Fort Worth, Texas. He and other managers recruited, staffed, and trained 800 specialists for the 150,000-square-foot facility. Imagine their surprise when the first customer call came in the Monday before Thanksgiving in 1996 and the specialist flubbed, ''Hello?''

''We were expecting, 'Thank you for calling Sprint PCS. How may I help you?' After some fast scripting and training, we were soon activating customers very quickly,'' Guevel says.

FROM BAGS TO BRICKS

Back then, cellular was a rare commodity—bulky bag phones were the only option and calls could cost $1/minute. **Ray Kaufman**, accounting manager-IT in Lone Tree, Colo., remembers Nextel's original bag phone: ''It weighed about eight pounds and looked like a gym bag.'' Staffers were delighted when the smaller ''brick''—the Lingo—debuted, weighing ''about three pounds.''

Kaufman joined Nextel in 1994 to help set up its billing, collections and fraud systems in the Denver market. He remembers his first day, finding the conference room the only "furnished" office—with a folding table and chairs. The supply closet was equally sparse, offering blue graph paper and red pencils.

His most memorable near-crisis was the night before a big billing system conversion. During testing, his group realized they'd accidentally deleted files with customers' names and addresses. A dozen dedicated employees stayed until 4 A.M., reentering data to ensure a successful launch later that morning. "It was quite a fun time. You felt like you really made a difference with everything you touched," Kaufman recalls.

When new salespeople fret and complain about selling in today's competitive market, **James "JR" Roberts**, senior indirect account executive, Indirect Sales, Philadelphia, chuckles and reminds them about the challenges he faced when he joined Nextel's Philadelphia market in 1995. He had three products to sell, each of which cost about $1,100 and presented a downside:

- The Lingo ("A hand-held unit that doubled as a hammer. When worn on a belt, the antenna tickled your armpit.")

- The iM 370 PowerFone for your car ("Your car was out of service for up to two days while it was being installed.")

- A base station ("This was just the iM 370 with a power supply. 'You don't mind if we drill a hole in your roof for the antenna, do you?'")

Add to this two rate plan choices and coverage stemming from the market's five towers, which only provided about 20- to 30-mile coverage.

BLAZING TRAILS TOMORROW

Doing what it takes to simplify the business. Dedicating ourselves to customers. Innovating with technology to offer customers services they haven't yet dreamed of.

Notes

1. Segaller, Stephen. 1998. *Nerds 2.0.1: A Brief History of the Internet.* New York: TV Books, LLC. Copyright © 1998 by Oregon Public Broadcasting.

2. http://yahoo.client.shareholder.com/press/timeline.cfm.

3. http://phx.corporate-ir.net/phoenix.zhtml?c=97664&p=irol faq#6986.

4. http://investor.ebay.com/faq.cfm.

5. Newhouse, Elizabeth L. (ed.). 1988. *Inventors and Discoverers: Changing Our World*. Washington, D.C.: National Geographic Society.

6. Adler, Robert A. 2002. *Science Firsts: From the Creation of Science to the Science of Creation*. Hoboken, N.J.: John Wiley & Sons.

7. Murray, James B. Jr. 2001. *Wireless Nation: The Frenzied Launch of the Cellular Revolution in America*. Cambridge, Mass.: Perseus Publishing.

8. Ibid.

9. Masini, Giancarlo. 1976. *Marconi*. New York: Marsilio Publishers.

10. See note 7.

11. Ibid.

12. Ibid.

13. www.ctia.org/research_statistics/statistics/index.cfm/AID/10202.

14. www.itu.int/osg/spu/publications/digitalife/lifestylesdigital.html.

15. www.physorg.com/printnews.php?newsid=12090.

16. www.businessreform.com/article.php?articleID=11543.

CHAPTER 4

What Power?

This book is all about the power of mobility. Before we can get too far in capturing this power, we need to understand how the realities of mobility translate into power or value for your business.

For historical perspective, let's recall how the personal computer (PC) and the Internet created value. The PC provided local computing power and storage, enabling the user to rapidly adapt computer-based work to her changing needs. This was most evident with the introduction of VisiCalc, the first PC-based spreadsheet software. Using VisiCalc on a PC enabled the user to run and rerun multiple different scenarios quickly and efficiently without needing to schedule computer time. The PC price point enabled companies to buy PCs for a growing portion of their employee base to capture this power, making employees more productive and leading to quicker and better decisions.

The Internet provided network connections that crossed organizational boundaries. This enabled information to more easily flow, especially from trusted content providers. It enabled computer-based transactions to occur between companies and their customers (both business and consumer). And it enabled improved communications, facilitating stronger relationships and accelerated decisions. These value enablers are often referred to as the three Cs: content, commerce, and community.

When we talk about mobility, we see two additional Cs coming into play in creating power or value: context and convergence.

By definition, mobility means things move. The context in which products are used or services are offered changes in a mobilized world, much more so than in a premobility environment. By adapting to these contextual changes, mobilized products and services have the opportunity to be more relevant to the user, creating tremendous new power or value.

Convergence is a concept that describes things that used to be distinct and separate coming together to be one. In mobility, this is most often realized through device convergence, specifically with more and more products being built into the cell phone. This form of convergence creates value because that product (e.g., a camera) that used to be separate is now with you all the time, and because it is now always available, it is more valuable to you. However, there are other forms of convergence, including network convergence, which creates value through cost savings; application convergence, which creates value through integration that increases relevance and efficiency; and lifestyle convergence, which creates value through increased productivity.

Context Matters

Who are you? Where am I? What am I doing? Who am I with? What time is it? How powerful is my connection? Is my device's battery getting low? How busy is my schedule later today? How urgent is the topic?

All of these questions can influence how I want to communicate with you right now. Ever since AT&T patented Caller ID in 1986, we've been able to mentally evaluate many of the above questions as we see a call coming in. We can choose to take the call now or let it roll to voice mail.

However, even taking the personal evaluation approach is costly— our phone rings or vibrates consuming precious battery life, our mind is distracted from its current task to perform the complex evaluations in deciding what to do, and if we are meeting with someone else, that conversation is momentarily disrupted, sometimes changing the tone and effectiveness of the whole meeting.

What if our phone, or better yet, something inside the network, could take into account all of the contextual information and decide for us what to do with each call? How would that capability increase our productivity and effectiveness for the day?

One of the reasons that mobility's being built into every product and every process is now creating tremendous power is that all of the above contextual signals are being integrated into voice and data communications. Different applications can use different aspects of this context to appropriately take action. The voice call example is one that leverages all of the context signals, but others create even more value.

Who are you? How urgent is the topic?

As early as 1993, a telephone service called Wildfire introduced the concept of network intelligence to screen your calls. The Wildfire service provides a virtual assistant who identifies who is calling and either connects them through to you or takes a message. The action taken depends on how busy you have told the assistant you are, whether you're on another call, and whether the caller says it's urgent. Wildfire can even "whisper in your ear" while you're on another call to tell you about the incoming call and let you make the decision.

What time is it? What am I doing? How busy is my schedule later today?

Although Wildfire is still a pretty unique service, technology advances have enabled contextual communications to advance beyond what was possible in 1993. In 2003, a new company, IOTUM Corporation began offering a new service that "brings relevance to communications."

The IOTUM service takes into consideration time of day, what's on your calendar for now, what and who is on your calendar for later in the day, and your previous calling habits to determine how to handle a call.

The IOTUM solution uses a three-tier process to handle calls. First, the "contextualizer" uses standard protocols to reach into applications to check your calendar, your presence, and your connectivity. Second, the "rules analyzer" combines that context with what it knows about the caller and your past behavior to determine what to do with the call. Finally, the "services interface" completes the call, either to voice mail or to the telephone number that is right for you right now.

Who are you? Where am I?

Microsoft has taken integration with desktop applications even a step further with Microsoft Office Communicator. Communicator fully integrates with data in Microsoft Outlook, including address books and calendars, to fully identify someone, to know all the ways to connect them, and to determine everyone's availability involved in a "call."

Communicator also integrates with office telephone systems to make and receive calls, to establish conference calls, and to link incoming calls with the directory and presence information about them. Communicator can also direct calls to your mobile phone or other contact information stored in Outlook.

Where am I?

Moving beyond real-time voice communications, much attention lately has been focused on location-based services (LBSs). Since virtually all cell phones can now identify their location, that information can be put to productive use for business and personal applications.

On the consumer side, a high-profile application is child tracking, wherein parents can track where their child's cell phone currently is and where it's been. When Disney launched its mobile phone service, this type of functionality was central to what made a wireless service family friendly.

But there are other fascinating uses of location information emerging. Bones in Motion offers BiM Active, a program that uses LBS data from Sprint cell phones to record their fitness activities in real time, tracking distance, speed, location, elevation, and calories burned in outdoor activities. Kamida has introduced a service called Socialight, which allows people to leave "sticky shadows" as they move around. A sticky shadow might be a note or a photo that can be shared via cell phone with other people when they come to the same location. Users leaving sticky shadows can decide who else can see what they virtually leave behind.

Business applications may seem boring by comparison, but they are creating real business value. An example of the LBS capabilities being built for business applications is the Mobile Resource Manager product from Agilis Systems. This product includes five core modules: SmartLocate, SmartDispatch, SmartRoute, SmartCall, and Smart-Connect.

SmartLocate tracks the real-time location of an employee (based on the location of his or her cell phone). One application for SmartLocate is an automated clock-in/clock-out system based on when the employee arrives at and leaves a job site. Another is locating the employee who is closest to a customer in need. A third application is geofencing, wherein the employer is notified if any of his or her employees leave a predefined territory.

SmartRoute, SmartDispatch, and SmartCall all help improve efficiency of field personnel and improve communications with customers. These modules first generate work schedules for the day based on the employee's skills and inventory, and based on estimated drive times between locations. Throughout the day the schedule is adjusted based on actual progress, traffic delays, and the changing needs of the business (e.g., urgent customer calls). The customer is also kept updated on timing and status through SmartCall and can request rescheduling later in the day or on a different day, automatically adjusting the employee's schedule.

SmartConnect uses location information as part of an overall paperwork automation process to accelerate and simplify activities like time and expense reporting, work order updates, and inventory management. Using the context available, the employee has to input less information, and the business has more up-to-date, complete, and reliable information.

Of course, many more companies have introduced a wide variety of consumer and business location–based solutions, but these few examples clearly demonstrate how context is driving value as mobility gets built into every product and every process.

Converging Power

Convergence has been a buzzword in technology industries for at least 20 years. As PCs rapidly proliferated across businesses, many expected the PC and the telephone to converge into a single device. That clearly did not happen as a result of the PC revolution. On my desk, I still have two devices—a PC and a telephone.

Device Convergence

However, when I leave my desk, I carry with me a converged device that is both a PC and a telephone. My mobile device runs a Microsoft operating system and has within it a more powerful processor and more data storage than early PC pioneers could have imagined. My mobile device is also a highly functional telephone with features like Caller ID, call log, and built-in address book that similarly could not have been imagined in telephones 20 years ago.

But of course, device convergence has moved way past just combining a computer with a telephone. Each week at the law-of-mobility.com blog, I list the most recent announcements of convergence of products with the mobile phone. Every week, the list gets longer. For example, here's the listing from the most recent week's worth of announcements as I write this:

- Cell phone as (relatively) cheap gas finder
- Cell phone as traffic avoidance navigator
- Cell phone as parking spot finder
- Cell phone as sports radio
- Cell phone as TV remote control
- Cell phone as contraband
- Cell phone as newspaper
- Cell phone as steamy romance novel
- Cell phone as matchmaker
- Cell phone as diet aid
- Cell phone as watch
- Cell phone as blogging tool
- Cell phone as global Voice-over Internet Protocol (VoIP) phone
- Cell phone as international VoIP phone
- Cell phone as music player

Clearly, some of the items listed are more "feature" than "product," but the industry that is forming around mobility (some combination of media, content, communications, and electronics) clearly senses the value of device convergence as the most obvious application of the Law of Mobility—increasing product value by building mobility into the product.

But convergence is even more than just device convergence. At Sprint, we speak of four dimensions of convergence:

- Device convergence
- Network convergence
- Application convergence
- Lifestyle convergence

Network Convergence

Network convergence is all about making irrelevant the historical differences between distinct legacy networks.

Historically, at least in the United States, ever since the break-up of the original Bell System, there have been separate networks for local and long-distance telephone calls. These networks were interconnected, but operated separately with separate offers from different companies for local and long-distance services. Industry deregulation and consolidation have made those distinctions meaningless as providers combine local and long-distance into one all-distance service. Some of these companies own all the local and long-distance assets and some don't, but it's all irrelevant to the end customer.

Consumers and businesses have also historically recognized clear distinctions between wireline and wireless networks. Typically, they had wireline voice services from one provider and wireless voice services from a second provider, with very different feature sets, pricing structures, and value propositions. They also typically had wireline data services but did not have meaningful choices for wireless data. Today, all of that is changing. Consumers, and increasingly businesses, perceive that their mobile phone provides everything they need to replace their wireline phone. New high-speed wireless data offers are providing all of the speed and capability of most wireline data services, but with the increased value of mobility built in. The distinctions between wireless and wireline are becoming irrelevant, allowing customers to simplify down to one or the other.

Application Convergence

Another historical distinction has been between voice, data, and video networks. Typically, businesses and consumers had different wires carrying these different types of traffic, often with services provided by different carriers. Technology advances driven by the Internet era have enabled voice, data, and video services to all be carried by Internet Protocol (IP) networks, and the top service providers have focused on offering bundled solutions making the distinctions irrelevant to their customers.

Lifestyle Convergence

Finally, all of these advances enable the distinctions between different parts of our lives to be blurred, hopefully for the better—recapturing the ten-minute halftime during my son's soccer game to check my work e-mail and respond to an urgent request, using the five minutes waiting for everyone to join a midday conference call to research Mother's Day gifts, sending my sister a scenic picture from my camera phone taken from the conference room window while on a business trip. All of these represent lifestyle convergence. As one executive put it, "I used to have home and work. Now I just have life."

These four dimensions of convergence are significant proof points that mobility is happening and that it is creating real and measurable value.

 FROM THE REAL WORLD

A Cautionary Tale

In 1994, I was head of new product development for a telecom carrier. During that year, our company entered into an agreement to merge with another in our industry. In December 1994, my team reviewed our current projects with the soon-to-be chief executive officer (CEO) of the combined company. About half of our developments centered on the Internet. My future top boss ordered us to shut them all down. His words still echo in my mind: "The Internet's a toy. Businesses will never pay for it."

I recount this story not to paint this man as a fool. In fact, within a few years he would become the most powerful player in the industry, defining the course his peers would try to follow.

No, I tell this story as a cautionary tale. It was perfectly credible for a powerful technology executive to believe in December 1994, that the Internet would never be adopted for real business use. However, within 12 months, this view would be proven completely incredible.

FROM THE REAL WORLD (CONTINUED)

A decade later, I fear many business leaders risk making the same mistake in their assessment of the impact of mobility on business. Many see today's mobile applications and perceive that mobility may change how consumers are informed and entertained, but fail to see how the power of mobility can transform how their business operates.

Even worse, many will fail to prepare for the danger of mobility. By doing so, they will expose their businesses to tremendous risk. Businesses will fail and fortunes will be destroyed because smart people fail to pay attention to the leading indicators that are signaling the most significant change in how businesses operate in over a decade.

By 1994, the core technologies underlying the Internet were a quarter of a century old. Sure, improvements had crept up the venerable OSI stack (see Exhibit 4.1) from the move to fiber optics in the bottom physical layer to the introduction of the Mosaic Web browser in the top application layer. Those improvements mattered, but what really drove the explosive, chain-reaction impact of the Internet was beyond the OSI's seven layers. And it shouldn't have been a surprise to anyone.

Years earlier, Robert Metcalfe, whose layer 2 innovations in inventing Ethernet have had a tremendous impact on corporate networks, observed a reality in financial, not technical terms. Bob's observation, forever captured as Metcalfe's Law of Network Value, was that as more people used networks, their value increased exponentially.

The "so what" of Metcalfe's Law relative to 1994 was that the number of Internet users had been roughly doubling every year, but was still small enough to be below most companies' radar screens. Metcalfe's Law predicted that there was a tangible threshold of users at which point the value of the Internet would exceed the cost and trouble of connecting to it. That threshold was reached in the first half of 1995, resulting in new users flocking to the Net, further increasing the value, sparking the chain reaction that led to virtually every business wanting to be connected within a matter of months.

By failing to recognize the power that would be unleashed, as predicted by Metcalfe's Law, in the form of the value of dynamic content, electronic commerce, and virtual communities, that telecom CEO failed in 1994 to value the opportunity that was before him.

As we now look forward to how mobility will unleash new power through contextual relevance and convergence, are we properly valuing the opportunities we have before us?

EXHIBIT 4-1

OSI Reference Model

Application Layer
Presentation Layer
Session Layer
Transport Layer
Network Layer
Data Link Layer
Physical Layer

Seven Steps to the Power of Mobility

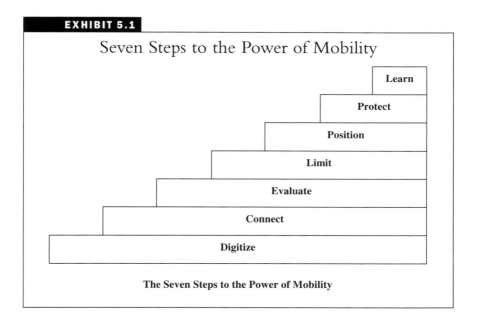

Seven Steps to the Power of Mobility

The Seven Steps to the Power of Mobility

CHAPTER 5

Introducing the Seven Steps

The Mobility Age represents an opportunity for businesses large and small to capture the power of mobility in order to create competitive differentiation and to take market share.

Large corporations and entrepreneurial start-ups alike should examine every aspect of their product or service for ways to increase value by taking things that have always been assumed to be fixed and making them mobile. Similarly, every internal process should be examined to identify ways that mobility can be introduced to increase productivity and efficiency, improving business performance.

Making a Product Mobile

In 1979, Sony introduced mobility into the world of consumer electronics.[1] The Walkman combined a small, battery-powered cassette tape player with lightweight headphones to create a personal music device that you could take with you wherever you went. Before the Walkman, people could listen to music in their homes or in their cars. Portable "boomboxes" had begun to be produced, but were intrusive, being too large and heavy for many activities and forcing the owners' listening preferences on everyone in the immediate vicinity.

The mid-1970s had been hard on Sony, as competitors like RCA, Zenith, Toshiba, and JVC adopted and improved upon technologies Sony had invented. The company lost share in critical markets and overall revenue growth slowed from 166% for the first four years of the decade to 35% for the next four.[2]

The Walkman ushered in the 1980s as a period of unprecedented growth for Sony. The company's sales and operating revenues grew from 643 billion yen in 1979 to nearly 3 trillion yen in 1989.[3] The Walkman also played a pivotal role in establishing Sony as a global brand standing for innovation and entertainment.

However, this success was not guaranteed when the product was envisioned by Sony's founder and honorary chairman, Masaru Ibuku. To keep dimensions small and the price relatively affordable, the Walkman lacked a record function. Critics claimed that no one would buy a tape machine that couldn't record. Industry experts could not yet envision that the value of mobility would outweigh any feature limitations in the product.

The Walkman truly revolutionized the electronics industry. To properly introduce the impact of the innovation, Sony held a launch event for journalists where the message was completely communicated via Walkman. The guests were ushered onto a tour bus where each was given one of the new products. The tape inside introduced the Walkman. The bus took the journalists to a nearby park where active people used the product while riding a bike and roller-skating—all choreographed to the taped explanation of the power of mobility unleashed by this radical new invention.[4]

In the first month of availability, only 3,000 of the initial production run of 30,000 units sold, seemingly validating the predictions of the skeptics. However, in the next month, the entire first batch sold out. Mobile music had become a phenomenon across Japan. Sony and its retail partners struggled to keep up with demand. Soon, fans around the world were begging Sony to take the product global.[5]

By 1986, the Walkman had become so ubiquitous and synonymous with mobile music that the word "Walkman" was added to the *Oxford English Dictionary*. More than 50 million units of the product family shipped in the first ten years, with that number doubling again by 1992.[6]

Not only was the Walkman a huge commercial success that helped put Sony on the map as a consumer electronics and entertainment powerhouse, but it also radically transformed how people listen to music.

What Sony did was take a product that, by assumption, was fixed and made it mobile. This transformation created tremendous new value for the customer. Music could now be enjoyed anywhere, anytime. Instead of being limited to the waking times spent at home or in the car, customers were listening while traveling, while playing and exercising, while commuting on public transport, and in previously musically deprived parts of their homes.

That value creation translated into growth for the consumer electronics industry, and most importantly for Sony, a strong foundation for the company's development into a global powerhouse.

Adding Mobility into Products Today

Just as Sony leveraged Moore's Law by using transistors and integrated circuits to make a small affordable tape player to revolutionize the music industry, Apple has leveraged both Moore's Law and Metcalfe's Law by applying the shrinking cost and size of data storage and accelerating network connectivity to once again redefine how people interact with the music that defines their lives.

Apple's iPod has accomplished for Apple virtually the same benefits that the Walkman accomplished for Sony, reversing a multi-year slide and establishing the company as a global brand standing for innovation and entertainment. The resulting halo effect has improved performance for the company's core computer products.

For the first six months of 2006, Apple's net revenues increased 50% over the same period the year before. Computer sales increased 6%, and software sales increased 44%, but the real growth came in iPods and other music-related sales. Music player sales more than doubled, and revenues from Apple's iTunes music service and related offers increased by nearly 150%. Most tellingly, music now accounts for more than half of the company's total revenues.

Both Sony and Apple are also participating in mobilizing other product categories.

In 2003, Sony announced the introduction of the Play Station Portable (PSP). Although clearly not the first mobile video gaming system, the product extends the company's leadership in innovation and mobility. Sony sold over 6 million PSP units in the first full year of availability.[7] Across the video gaming industry, mobility is driving growth, with mobile system sales increasing 96% from 2004 to 2005.[8]

Meanwhile, Apple is pioneering building mobility into television. In October 2005, Apple introduced a video-capable iPod and a groundbreaking agreement with ABC to sell popular television shows through Apple's iTunes online store. The company has since added content from other broadcast and cable networks. By midyear 2006, iTunes featured more than 9,000 video products and had sold more than 30 million video downloads.[9]

The television industry faces threats to conventional revenue streams, largely due to the growing adoption of digital video recorders (such as TiVo) which enable instant skipping of commercials. With the video iPod, Apple has introduced a new model for watching television that is delivering the value of mobility for consumers, redefining the business model to provide customer control while ensuring revenue for the networks, and inserting the company into the transaction flow for yet another industry.

I Thought Cameras Already Were Mobile

Like music players, cameras have also gone through two rounds of redefinition around the concept of mobility. Film cameras fell prey to Moore's Law with the rapid adoption of digital cameras. Now, Metcalfe's Law has kicked in and consumers are buying four times as many camera phones as digital cameras.

Because of this shift, consumers are enjoying mobility-driven value as they use their camera phones to take everyday snapshots.

But wait—haven't cameras always been mobile?

Cameras have certainly been portable. But for most people, cameras have tended to stay in one fixed place. I keep mine (both my retired film camera and two generations of digital cameras) in a drawer in the kitchen. I always know exactly where they are, which usually isn't where I actually need them.

By converging a camera into a device (a cell phone) that people tend to have with them all the time, the camera's mobility has increased, creating tremendous value for consumers and incremental revenue for phone manufacturers and wireless carriers.

So, what does this mean for products that already seem to be mobile? Most products can be made even more valuable by increasing their mobility. If customers aren't already taking the product with them 100% of the time, then there's still more value that can be added by increasing the mobility. And no matter how much people are using a product, if there is information or content involved, leveraging computing power and networking can further add to the product value and likely shift the power in the industry.

Specific to the camera phone, making it easy for customers to take a picture and immediately send it to a friend has dramatically changed how people take and share photographs, while the buying shift from cameras to camera phones has turned companies like Nokia, Motorola, and Samsung into photography market share leaders.

Can Mobility Increase the Value of Your Product?

But what about you? Do you have a product that you think might be a candidate for mobilizing to create more value? How can you capture the power of mobility?

The next seven chapters will guide you through the process of capturing the power of mobility in your business. We have identified a seven-step process that can be applied to virtually any product, service, or process to best capture the power of mobility.

In your business, you may have already implemented some of these steps. Even so, now is a great time to revisit exactly how you have digitized or connected your business and ensure that you are truly prepared for moving forward into the Age of Mobility.

The seven steps to the power of mobility are:

1. **Digitize**. Capture the power unleashed by Moore's Law. Digitize your product and your business.

2. **Connect**. Capture the power unleashed by Metcalfe's Law and the Internet.

3. **Evaluate**. In what ways does your product create value? In what ways is that value limited due to lack of mobility? If you could build in mobility, how would that increase the value of your product?

4. **Limit**. In mobilizing your product, what are you going to leave out? What are you going to choose to *not* do?

5. **Position**. Select the target markets, customers, and applications that fit the new value creation and what you're leaving out of your product.

6. **Protect**. Manage the danger of mobility.

7. **Learn**. Watch how customers use your product and adapt to the new opportunities.

Consider Sony's Walkman and PSP, Apple's iPod and iTunes, and camera phones. Recognize how these mobilizations first captured the available power of Moore's Law and Metcalfe's Law as foundational to mobilization. Notice that the Walkman left out the record function, and early camera phones have limited picture resolution to provide reasonable performance over second-generation wireless networks. Consider how each of these companies positioned their products for the appropriate markets, and appreciate how they have expanded their vision as they have watched their customers do new things with their mobilized products—applications that the companies couldn't initially imagine.

In the coming chapters, we will help you walk through these same steps to capture the power of mobility for your products.

Making a Service Mobile

Perhaps you are in a services business. Does the Law of Mobility apply to your industry? Is there a way to capture the power of mobility in your business?

Of course there is. In the minds of your customers, their experience with your service *is* your product. Is there an opportunity to take an aspect of your service that has always been fixed and, by making it mobile, increase value for your customers?

Consider the pizza business. This favorite food of Americans originated in Naples, Italy, centuries ago. Italian immigrants brought their local specialty to American ethnic centers early in the twentieth century. But it wasn't until GIs returned from World War II with a craving for the tasty dish that pizzerias began popping up across the American landscape. These restaurants, of course, focused on the typical dining room experience.[10]

The company most clearly associated with mobilizing the pizza eating experience is Domino's Pizza. The company that would invent

74

the cardboard pizza box and the belt-driven pizza oven had a legendary start in 1960 involving $50 cash and a used VW Beetle.[11] Today, the company is the second largest pizza chain in the world, with nearly $5 billion in annual revenues, delivering over a million pizzas a day.[12]

Domino's created a delivery-only business. They focused all of their products, processes, and systems on taking the sale, delivery, and consumption of the menu items from the fixed location of the restaurant to wherever the customers were—at their homes, at work, at parties, at the park having a picnic—anywhere, anytime. And Americans have loved the new freedom, contributing to the Italian specialty's becoming a nationwide favorite.

Of course, virtually all pizzerias and pizza chains have responded, similarly offering delivery service. But Domino's has maintained nearly a 20% share of the delivery market. Is it because they make great pizza? Apparently not. Of the 11 pizza chains with at least 50 customer ratings at RateItAll.com, Domino's scored ninth.[13]

No, Domino's success comes from delivering good enough pizza at an attractive price with the added value of mobility!

The company's focus on adding mobility into the pizza experience has resulted in corporate success, but it has also helped the entire industry grow. Since 1991, the share of the pizza industry that is delivered has grown from 26% to 35%.[14]

Pizza delivery has also changed the way Americans approach mealtime. A Roper study claims that 73% of Americans have no idea what they'll feed their family for dinner even at 4:30 on an average afternoon.[15] Pizza delivery has also become a critical component for casual gatherings of friends. More pizza is eaten on Super Bowl Sunday than any other day of the year.[16]

And all because an entrepreneur saw the opportunity to mobilize a service that everyone assumed was tied to a fixed location!

Adding Mobility into Services Today

In 1987, Avis became a pioneer in leveraging mobile technology to revolutionize an industry by taking a service process that had been fixed in a company location and taking it to where the customers were. In that year, the company introduced the Roaming Rapid Return, using a handheld terminal to bring the car return and checkout process carside.[17]

Prior to this innovation, a rental car customer had to write down her mileage, unload her belongings from the car, and then walk across the rental car lot to a hut housing the company's point-of-sale terminals. There, she would wait in line for her turn to hand over paper, the information from which would then be reentered into the terminal, payment made, and finally the customer could run to catch her flight.

Virtually all competitors have had to replicate Avis's mobilized service. Today, by the time the traveler has removed her bags from the trunk of the car, a service agent has arrived at the car, used a bar code scanner to identify the car and customer, entered the mileage into a handheld point-of-sale terminal, and often has the receipt printed and ready for the customer so she can head straight to her flight.

This approach obviously leverages Moore's Law and Metcalfe's Law along with wireless networks to create tremendous value for the customer.

Others are seeking to similarly deliver this value of mobility for their service customers in additional industries.

Dry Cleaning To-Your-Door is a nationwide franchise operation that does exactly what its name implies—taking the process of dropping off and picking up your dry cleaning to where you are instead of the company's fixed locations. The company has developed the processes and systems to enable franchisees to deliver a quality service at a competitive price. The value of mobility creates the differentiation to enable the business to rapidly grow.

Can Mobility Increase the Value of Your Service?

The seven steps to the power of mobility apply equally well for service businesses:

1. **Digitize**. Capture the power unleashed by Moore's Law. Digitize your service.

2. **Connect**. Capture the power unleashed by Metcalfe's Law and the Internet.

3. **Evaluate**. In what ways does your service create value? In what ways is that value limited due to lack of mobility? If you could untether where you provide service, how would that change the value?

4. **Limit**. In mobilizing your service, how will you define limits? Will you limit the geography in which you provide the service, or will you limit the specific services that you mobilize?

5. **Position**. Select the target markets, customers, and applications that fit the new value creation and the limits you're placing on your service.

77

6. **Protect**. Manage the danger of mobility.

7. **Learn**. Watch how customers use your service and adapt to the new opportunities.

Consider Domino's, Avis, and Dry Cleaning To-Your-Door. Recognize how these mobilizations first captured the power of service data and connectivity as foundational to mobilization. Notice that Domino's limited its menu, Avis limited its mobilization to its own return lot, and that Dry Cleaning To-Your-Door carefully selects the neighborhoods into which it expands. Consider how each of these companies positioned its products for the appropriate markets, and appreciate how they have expanded their vision as they have watched their customers ask for new value from their mobilized services—opportunities that the companies couldn't initially imagine.

In the coming chapters, we will help you walk through these same steps to capture the power of mobility for your services.

Making a Process Mobile

In any business, there likely are processes that are well suited to mobilization. Taking these processes out of a fixed location may not necessarily result in increased customer perception of value but can drive increased productivity and efficiency, improving your overall business performance.

In 2004, Sprint began a program known as the Sprint Powered Workplace. In this program, as real estate leases expire at branch locations across the company, the staff within those locations are evaluated. Approximately 40% of field staff typically qualify as "work anywhere" employees. For these employees, there's little value in tying them to a fixed location and instead there is tremendous value in empowering them to do their job anywhere.

Many of these anywhere workers are customer facing. They are most productive when they are interacting with various folks within customer organizations. However, the bulk of the tools they need to do their jobs are maintained in the fixed location of the branch office.

Sprint has taken a number of steps to free these resources from the fixed office. Work-anywhere employees are equipped with laptops with broadband wireless data cards, handheld smart phones, and broadband connections at home. Through these connections, they can now securely access the systems that previously had been accessible only from their office desktop. Sprint has also established a system so that any required documentation or collateral can be printed on demand at any of the hundreds of FedEx Kinko's Office and Print Centers across the country and around the globe.

Of course, when anywhere workers want to come into the office, shared offices are available, along with all the normal resources to provide a productive office environment. In addition to improving the productivity and job satisfaction of these employees, Sprint is also on track to reduce real estate costs by $50 million annually.[18]

Could your business benefit from those kinds of savings? Are there processes in your business that could be performed more productively or efficiently if they were no longer tied to a fixed location? Would the employees involved view this as a positive change, and if not, how critical is the current staff to company success?

The seven steps to the power of mobility are also relevant for mobilizing internal processes:

1. **Digitize**. Capture the power unleashed by Moore's Law. Digitize your processes and your business.

2. **Connect**. Capture the power unleashed by Metcalfe's Law and the Internet.

3. **Evaluate**. In what ways is your process constrained due to lack of mobility? If you could build in mobility, how would that change the effectiveness of the process?

4. **Limit**. Are there aspects of the process that must be limited as you mobilize?

5. **Position**. Select the target applications that fit how you've defined the mobilized process.

6. **Protect**. Manage the danger of mobility.

7. **Learn**. Watch how your mobilized process uncovers additional opportunities for value creation.

In the coming chapters, we will help you walk through these same steps to capture the Power of Mobility for your processes.

High Reward, High Risk

Capturing the power of mobility is a high-reward opportunity. If done right, you have the opportunity to redefine the rules of competition in your industry. You will create tremendous differentiation and advantage. Your competitors will be forced to follow your lead on your terms. The expectations you set in the minds of consumers will be well aligned with what you can deliver profitably but could drive those that blindly follow your lead into financial ruin.

However, the types of changes represented in this chapter are obviously not simple nor risk free. The complexity of restructuring your business and its offers to create tremendous new value through mobility cannot be underestimated. The impact on processes, systems, organizations, and staffing are significant. You may be well served to get help from those experienced in similar transformations.

Is it worth it?

You have a choice. You can lead and set the rules. Or you can wait for a competitor to lead and define the rules to his benefit and your demise.

 FROM THE REAL WORLD

Making Moby

To best understand how to apply the seven steps, let's consider a hypothetical case study. What if we were a toy company, specializing in stuffed animals, and we wanted to consider "mobilizing" our product. How would we go about it?

Wait a minute! Aren't stuffed animals already mobile? Of course they are. Kids carry their favorite foam-filled friends almost everywhere they go. But, like the camera, which has always been "mobile," stuffed animals could benefit tremendously by becoming even closer to 100% available and by leveraging the power of computing and networking technologies.

For fun, let's consider making our first mobile product a stuffed whale. We'll call him Moby.

Step 1 is to think about digitizing Moby. For a product like a stuffed animal, much of the value comes from the physical reality. Kids want something cute and cuddly that makes them feel comfortable and safe and helps them fall asleep at night. We can't merely reduce Moby to a bunch of ones and zeros and still be in the stuffed animal business.

But we can look to add digital technology into Moby. Since the PC revolution, many toymakers have added microprocessors into stuffed animals to make them move, talk, sing, and even respond to children in realistic ways. To fully capture the power of mobility in Moby, we should consider how to leverage these technologies.

Step 2 is all about connecting Moby. Since the Internet revolution, a few toymakers have found ways to integrate connectivity into stuffed animals so that the animals interact with information on networked computers. Given our goals for Moby, we should factor these advances into our planning as well.

Step 3 is to evaluate whether we're losing value because we haven't fully mobilized our toys. Do kids take our product everywhere they go? Some do, but many don't, or they switch off between different favorites. Would our customers perceive more value if they had our toy with them all the time? From the kids' perspective, maybe not, but let's think about the parents.

Maybe we have an opportunity to focus our marketing on guilty and paranoid parents. We could build on the common concern among today's busy grown-ups that they don't spend enough time with their kids, and their fear that their kids will end up in the wrong place, either accidentally or due to evil intent.

If we could use technology to make our stuffed animal distinctively fun for the kids so they want to take Moby everywhere, then we could use technology to help parents communicate with their kids anytime, anywhere, and make sure they don't stray from safe locations.

Given these goals, let's get specific about the opportunity to digitize and connect Moby:

- Moby could have a limited-capability cell phone built in so that Mommy or Daddy could call their child through this stuffed whale. This would also provide a microphone and speaker for other purposes.

- Moby could have location-sensing capabilities built in (e.g., global positioning system) so he could sense where he is.

- A mobile stuffed animal could have wireless data capabilities built in so he could send and receive data.

- Moby could potentially have a video camera or video screen built in.

- He likely would have some level of computing power and some level of animation robotics.

With this list of capabilities we could design a product offering powerful features for parents:

- The ability (with robust security) to call Moby for an audio or video call from either an Internet-connected computer or a telephone/cell phone.

- Geofencing, so that if Moby travels outside a predefined area, the parent is immediately called and e-mailed, and location tracking is automatically enabled.

- A "nanny camera," enabling the parent (with robust security) to see what is happening through Moby's camera at any time, and even to record pictures or short video clips for future reference.

- Special greetings, which can be recorded by the parent and will randomly play when the child squeezes Moby's tail. The greetings can be recorded with audio and video using the built-in microphone and camera.

FROM THE REAL WORLD (CONTINUED)

For the child, we could offer these fun features:

- Special greetings from Mommy and Daddy.
- Songs and videos that can be played on Moby's speakers and screen. (Mommy or Daddy can purchase additional songs and videos for download to Moby and can remove those that have become too irritating.)
- Warm and friendly gestures, sounds, and messages on the video screen in response to hugs and key phrases.
- Recognition of familiar places based on location data, and Moby expressing excitement about the location (sounds, gestures, and messages like "We're home!" "We're at Grandma's house!" or "We're going to school!" on Moby's screen).

With this combination of features, I believe Moby could be a toy that kids want to take with them everywhere and that their parents will be glad they did!

Step 4 is to limit the product as appropriate for mobility. In general, stuffed animals are relatively limited. We likely will need to make Moby not too small and not too large, but otherwise Moby can probably have just about all the characteristics of your typical stuffed animal.

We've already talked about step 5. We will position Moby to specifically appeal to guilty parents. Given all the technology built in, Moby won't be cheap. We'll need to target Moby to "financially advantaged" guilty parents. Finally, to take full advantage of Moby's abilities, these rich guilty parents will need to be somewhat tech savvy. This positioning will impact our marketing campaigns and the sales channels we use, and perhaps guide us towards some key partnerships to make the product successful.

Step 6 is all about managing the danger of mobility. Moby won't be your typical stuffed animal. He will have power and connectivity needs that are relatively unique. We'll need to ensure that these challenges are easy for our customers to manage.

Speaking of customers, customer support for Moby will go well beyond our existing capabilities. The kinds of complaints customer service is likely to receive from Moby customers will also vary dramatically from those for your typical stuffed whale. Questions about battery life, wireless connectivity, broken components, sea-faring whales (or at least bathtub-faring), Web interfaces, lost passwords, and so on will stump a typical teddy expert.

Most likely, at least at launch, we should consider outsourcing much of the operational challenge to those that are experts in developing Web interfaces, running network businesses, and operating technical support hotlines.

However, the real key to ongoing success with Moby and beyond is step 7: Mobilizing a stuffed animal won't result in just a toy with a camera, screen, global positioning system, and wireless connection built in. Once kids and their parents start playing with Moby, they will uncover for us new value from mobility that we could never predict. They'll find ways to make Moby play fun games we never knew we'd enabled, and they'll ask us to add new features that we never would have imagined.

We will need to be prepared for mobility to completely redefine how kids play with stuffed animals, simply because they are now mobile. And to be prepared to translate those learnings into continued market success!

Notes

1. Sony History www.sony.net/Fun/SH/index.html.

2. "Sony Corporation," *International Directory of Company Histories*, Vol. 40. St. James Press, 2001; www.fundinguniverse.com/company-histories/Sony-Corporation-Company-History1.html.

3. Sony Historical Data, www.sony.net/SonyInfo/IR/library/historical.html.

4. See note 1.

5. Ibid.

6. Ibid.

7. "Sony Targets 6 Million Sales of PSP," www.consolewatcher.com/2005/12/sony-targets-6-million-sales-of-psp/.

8. "The NPD Group Reports Annual 2005 U.S. Video Game Industry Retail Sales," www.npd.com/dynamic/releases/press_060117.html.

9. Apple press release.

10. Pendergast, Sara. 2006. "Pizza." *BookRags*. Retrieved July 15, 2006, from the World Wide Web, www.bookrags.com/history/popculture/pizza-bbbb-03.html.

11. "Domino's Pizza," Wikipedia, http://en.wikipedia.org/wiki/Domino's_Pizza.

12. Domino's Web site, www.dominos.com.

13. www.rateitall.com/t-103-pizza-chains.aspx?age=&zipcode=&gender=&sort=0&pagesize=all.

14. Domino's Investor Presentation, May 2006, from company Web site, www.dominos.com.

15. Ibid.

16. See note 10.

17. www.avis.com/AvisWeb/JSP/global/en/aboutavis/corp_info/historical_chronology.jsp

18. Sprint Web site, www.sprintenterprisemobility.com/mobile_workplace.html.

CHAPTER 6

Digitize
Capture the Power Unleashed by Moore's Law

These days, business runs on bits. It's no longer checks in the mail, but rather electronic transactions. It's no longer cards in a Rolodex, but a customer database. It's no longer numbers in a ledger book, but a financial accounting system.

Whether we're talking about the world's largest corporation or the gas station on the corner, every aspect of business has become digital.

Or has it?

How much information that's critical to the success of your business on a day-to-day or month-to-month basis still exists as ink on paper—or worse, locked up in someone's head? Or on one person's computer that no one else ever sees?

Those islands of information represent business risk and lost opportunity.

Digital data represents tremendous opportunity because it can be relational.

A business card is associated with a person. That person might be an employee of an important customer of yours. That customer has business information, such as the locations you ship products to and how and where they want you to submit invoices so you can get paid. The information on a business card can become digital data that is related to a person, which can be digitally related to his employer, which can be digitally related to locations, which can be digitally related to shipments and invoices. This digital data could be the heart of your revenue stream.

People place orders for companies. Those orders need to be fulfilled, which impacts your inventory. The status of your inventory may impact your production schedule and may cause you to order new supplies. Your production schedule involves your employees. The information on a business card can become digital data that is related to a person, which can be digitally related to her employer, which can be digitally related to orders, which can be digitally related to inventory, which can be digitally related to suppliers and your production schedule and your workers. This digital data could be the heart of your operations.

By interrelating the digital data about your business, you can make better decisions and improve the performance of your business.

Your supplier likes to get paid, but if you're tracking the quality of what he's sending you, and how well he's meeting his commitments, you might want to hold off on paying this supplier until you have a chat.

Your supplier has employees, too. One of them manages your account. You may have his contact information, including his e-mail address, his telephone number, and his cell phone number. You may also have a folder in your e-mail box with all the e-mails he's sent you with wonderful promises. Your electronic calendar may have recorded all the meetings you've had, and it's easy enough to send a meeting request to his calendar for yet another discussion about those wonderful promises.

These little pieces of digital data are powerful because of their relationships—person to employer, to customer, to order, to invoice, to production schedule, to employee schedule, to paycheck, to supplier, to performance metrics, to invoice, to person, to e-mail address, to calendar event, to getting your business operating at it's optimal level.

So any information that is an island rather than being a related piece of data is a lost opportunity for outperforming your competitors. It's like that little rattle that you can't quite clearly hear coming from under the hood that you know is costing a millisecond of hesitation and may even become an expensive failure in the engine of your business.

So, why isn't all the information in your business-related data? Because that's not how we work.

Our salespeople take notes with black ink pens, not laptop keyboards. Our production manager remembers what his vendor promised, but hasn't entered it into any database. We all have yellow sticky pieces of paper with important telephone numbers dangling by one last molecule of adhesive from our computer monitors. And those are the things we've already recognized as information.

What about the data that we hadn't even recognized as such. Where is the best technician for this product—I mean what is his longitude and latitude, the intersection he's driving through right now? What time does UPS expect to deliver that part today? What will the temperature be tomorrow, and how will that impact our scheduled installations? What does Joe like to order at his favorite restaurant, and what's the name of his kid's soccer team?

This is important data! But most companies haven't yet learned how to capture it and use it to beat the competition. Have you?

Thinking clearly and carefully about how your business runs on digital information, bits, data, is the essential first step in capturing the power of mobility. What are the processes that define your business and what data is essential to the success of those processes? What little bits of information are overlooked today, not even captured casually, that if you could factor them into your management of those processes could separate you from the competitive pack?

What's your product? What about it constitutes information that should be managed as data? Is your whole product open to digitization (as happened in the music industry when analog recordings became digital CDs)? What would that take and how are you going to beat your competitors to the punch?

Or are there just seemingly insignificant pieces of information that can be digitized—the owner's manual, the lot number, and serial number? Are there potential outputs from your product that, by digitizing, you could create new value for your customers—maybe information about how your product is used, how often and for what, or how well it's performing its job (validating your customers' investment)? What would it cost to add that in, and how could that translate into value (pricing, loyalty, market share) for your business?

Will digitization create opportunities for you to integrate your product or service with something you've never considered for your business—expanding the market you serve into adjacent spaces? Or are your current partners, suppliers, and customers eyeing your market as a space they can integrate into through digitization?

Capturing all of this information and turning it into relational data is not something that happens overnight at zero cost. Undoubtedly, you'll need to evaluate and prioritize the opportunities. Where are the greatest opportunities to create new value, to stand apart from your competition, and to improve the performance of your business? Where are the greatest threats from important information being lost, or competitors beating you to the punch, or partners stealing your market?

Even once you've prioritized, the business case may be hard to prove. Moore's Law has driven the cost of computing down, but empowering your employees with laptops isn't cheap, and building digital capabilities into your products will increase the unit cost. Can you afford to do it? Can you afford not to?

Once you understand the unavoidable costs, consider the incremental steps you can take to maximize the return on the required investment. If employees have laptops, how can you leverage those capabilities to reduce costs in other areas (office space, filing cabinets, copiers)? How can you drive even greater productivity by equipping each laptop with additional tools (wireless data cards, productivity tools)?

If you've built processing power into your product, can you reduce costs somewhere else by using the compute power to compensate (e.g., automatic recalibration to compensate for a less precise component)? Can you add new features that allow you to charge a premium price?

All of this digitization will also have human costs that should similarly pay rich secondary dividends. Many of us aren't native to this digital age. Expect to invest in training for your employees, either those performing new digitized processes or those assembling new digitized products. But this training will create employees capable of carrying your business forward into the remaining six steps of capturing the power of mobility.

These days, business runs on bits. Does yours?

How to Digitize

Digitizing your business does not involve a magic wand. It requires a step-by-step, need-by-need analysis, implementation plan, and execution. The specific challenges you face will differ from those of your nearest business neighbor, but there are a couple of places you can turn for help.

The first place you might turn is existing literature. Entire books have been written about the opportunities and challenges associated with integrating digital technology into how businesses operate. A few you might consider are *The Social Life of Information* by John Seely Brown and Paul Duguid (Harvard Business School Press, 2002), *Information Literacy and Workplace Performance* by Tom W. Goad (Quorum Books, 2002), *The Virtual Corporation* by William H. Davidow and Michael S. Malone (HarperBusiness, 1992), *The Digital Organization* by James D. Best (John Wiley & Sons, 1997), *The Executive's Guide to Information Technology* by John Baschab and Jon Piot (John Wiley & Sons, 2007), and *Customer Data Integration* by Jill Dyche and Evan Levy (John Wiley & Sons, 2006).

The second place you might turn is to outside help from specialists. Depending on your specific needs, you might turn to a document digitization specialist like Xerox, a consulting firm like Accenture who can help marry processes to technologies, or a mobile specialist like Sprint. Or better yet, start with the specialist firms who are already supporting your business with computer and networking expertise. They likely already understand your business and are already well connected with others in other technology specialist firms.

Digitizing your business is neither painless nor impossible, but it is necessary in today's competitive environment. And it's the critical first step in capturing the power of mobility.

 FROM THE REAL WORLD

Digitizing the Newspaper Business

Pick up a newspaper and your initial reaction is that you're dealing with a relatively low-tech product that hasn't fundamentally changed for centuries.

And in many respects, you'd be absolutely right. The creative process of identifying a newsworthy event, compiling the facts into a meaningful story, and determining the prominence of that story hasn't really changed since Benjamin Franklin's day.

But in so many other ways, the newspaper industry has been transformed time and again by technology advances that both threaten to destroy the industry and create entire new platforms for growth. The most recent series of technology waves transforming the industry started in the 1970s with the introduction of computer front-end systems into the production process. Those arrived as newspapers abandoned lead type for paper or "cold-type" page production, and adopted offset presses—which contributed to innovations in design and increases in color capacity. Desktop publishing on personal computers was introduced in the 1980s. And since the mid-1990s, the basic newspaper business models have been under attack from Internet-based replacements.

Monroe Dodd, an editor for the *Kansas City Star* and editor of *Kansas City: An American Story* (Kansas City Star Books, 1999) remembers "It used to be that a reporter had to carry a lot of dimes for pay phones."

Reporters often had to go to where the news was happening, interview witnesses and experts, dig up any background information they could possibly find, and then call in their notes to the newsroom where rewrite men would compile it all into readable prose.

Monroe notes that today a reporter also can access searchable electronic archives, online databases, and the Internet for background material and can compose and send a completed article from anywhere using his or her laptop and a mobile broadband card.

That electronic copy is then integrated into the computerized pagination system that is used to create on-screen page layout. The system integrates photos and graphics, inserts of advertisements, and then greatly simplifies the process of creating the negative from which the printing plate is created.

As a simple point of comparison, think about photos that appear in the paper. Before desktop publishing, a photo would come out of the darkroom as an 8 × 10 print and would be sent to the engraving department. The engraving department would carve a negative image of the photo into a metal plate that would then be used to print the papers. Today, the digital photo image is integrated into the desktop publishing software, which automatically creates the raster image of the page that becomes the printing plate.

However, even with the dramatic gains in efficiency, the newspaper business is under assault. The Internet threatens every aspect of the industry. Because news can be much more cost-effectively distributed as electronic network bits than as ink on paper, increasing numbers of former newspaper subscribers are turning instead to online news sources. This challenges two of the primary revenue sources for newspapers: subscriptions and advertising revenue. From at least a business model perspective, over the decades, the newspaper has increasingly become a physical container for advertisements that help pay the bills. As readers have left, the value to advertisers has declined, and the resulting revenue hit has been painful.

To add insult to injury, classified ads have more recently come under attack, first in the narrow niche of job placements (from online sites like Monster.com) and now general classified ads from geographically focused consumer ad sites like Craig's List.

Do newspapers have any hope in the face of this technology-driven onslaught?

Monroe notes that "there will always be value in local news gathering. News starts with the news makers, and being there when news happens is part art, part experience, and part relationships. Technology algorithms probably won't ever be able to replace that."

Furthermore, as contextual relevance is integrated into the "newspaper" business, the value of that local perspective will undoubtedly become more prominent. Already newspapers can increase their advertising margins by targeting specific ads to specific parts of town. Locally targeted mobile ads, based on location based technologies, are already starting to appear. Who will first figure out how to leverage contextual relevance to garage sale shoppers, reordering the classified ads based on the shopper's current location?

Case Study

Rand McNally

When I think of going mobile, I most often think of getting in my car and driving somewhere. But heading to a new destination means finding it, which, for centuries has meant breaking out the map. And when I think of maps, I think of Rand McNally.

Rand McNally & Company was founded in 1856. Today, their products are sold in over 60,000 retail outlets and their products are found in 98% of the schools in America, so it's no wonder that their brand is strongly associated with the maps that you and I grew up using to find our way.[1]

But, in today's environment, in addition to using physical, paper-based maps to navigate to new locations, we have more options available. For example, we may use an electronic global positioning system (GPS)-based navigation tool, or turn to an Internet-based mapping tool, or maybe even use a navigation tool on our cell phone.

Is Rand McNally threatened by this shift?

"Absolutely not," says Alan Yefsky, vice president of business strategy and new product development for the company. "We have found that people use different types of mapping tools depending on the situation. Print maps will always be around, and we've used them as a platform to provide continuity and familiarity to consumers as we developed our Internet and mobility based products."[2]

Case Study (continued)

Rand McNally has been a leader through each of the recent technology revolutions. The company's PC-based TripMaker® and StreetFinder® software packages broke new ground, winning awards for the company and establishing market leadership in the new digital personal navigation space. In 1997, the randmcnally .com Web site captured the dynamic power of the Internet, integrating timely road construction and weather updates into the navigation space.

In 2003, Rand McNally introduced Mobile Travel Tools™, providing mapping and navigation tools in a format that could be downloaded to a Java-based mobile phone. The thick-client approach took into account the usability and screen size limitations of a handheld phone, while still providing timely linkage to the content available at randmcnally.com.

Rand McNally has also found ways to leverage the strengths of all of their product lines. StreetFinder® Wireless combines the functional strength of the company's PC-based products with the power of mobility, and also interworks in a unique way with the company's flagship road atlas product.

A traveler may be using the Rand McNally Road Atlas during a long distance trip, but may reach a midpoint in his destination where he wants to find a restaurant or hotel. By entering an express access code from the paper atlas into StreetFinder Wireless, the traveler is immediately zoomed in to the local street maps and can dynamically search for the destination.

"Since we operate across technology platforms, we've paid close attention to the strengths and challenges of each platform and how that translates into how people actually use different types of navigation products," notes Gary Lancina, Rand McNally's vice president of marketing. "For example, randmcnally.com is a great tool for planning a trip, but people are most comfortable using our print products while en route. Our Road Atlas is great for getting

CASE STUDY (CONTINUED)

from city to city and our Street Guides are great for finding your way around your hometown, but when you arrive in a new city, our GPS-based products allow you to act like a local anywhere in America."

To build on the company's strong presence in the traditional paper-based navigation space, Rand McNally has extended its grid system across all of its products, paper and electronic. This commonality enables easy transitions from Internet to paper to mobile, as Gary described above, but also provides a sense of continuity and comfort as customers adopt new technologies.

The company has also learned a lot about how different types of people use the same products differently. For example, the average consumer probably drives the same route in the same parts of town day after day, week after week, but occasionally will venture out to a new part of town for a kids' soccer tournament or cultural event. This customer will rely on Rand McNally's street-level guides to figure out which highways to take, which side of the road to exit, down to the last turn into the sports park. A local delivery driver, however, is an expert at getting from any part of town to any other, but will turn to the street guide for the last quarter mile to his destination.

This long-standing understanding of how customers rely on navigation tools has translated into Rand McNally's mobile tools—from how they are designed for different users to how they are marketed, and finally to how they are integrated with the company's core products.

One of the challenges any company will face that is moving from traditional physical products to new technology products is preparing for new customer service needs.

Rand McNally's interactions with customers have evolved from getting letters in the mail from people wondering why their 20-year-old road atlas isn't current any more to now getting live phone calls from customers trying to navigate a new city. Some customers even expected to be able to call the toll-free number on their road atlas to get free live directions to their destination. Alan notes that "as in any business, consumer expectations are very high. We needed to adapt the strategies we had developed for addressing consumer concerns with traditional 'analog' products to address new kinds of issues specific to the digital and mobile environment."

Alan also explains that Rand McNally never underestimates the customer—they are the ones who really understand what is needed. They can provide rich feedback that translates into new opportunities for differentiation and value creation.

He cites the example of local delivery dispatchers who were regularly using randmcnally.com to figure out the best route, then copying the directions into a text message to the drivers' phones. By learning from the customer, Rand McNally was able to develop and introduce a new text-to-phone feature for their Web-based service.

Bottom line: Rand McNally has clearly executed on the seven steps described in this book. They are capturing the power of mobility while building on the strong foundation of a powerful legacy halfway through its second century. This company doesn't see it as choosing between technologies, but rather as finding the best way to help people do things they couldn't do before.

"In our business, it's clear that human behavior is messy," Alan observes. "As technology evolves, winners figure out how to use the right technology to make life a little bit less messy."

RAND MCNALLY'S MOBILIZED PRODUCTS[3]

So far, Rand McNally has built mobility into three product lines: Rand McNally Mobile Navigator (MONA), StreetFinder® Wireless,

CASE STUDY (CONTINUED)

and Rand McNally Traffic. The product desriptions that follow are provided by Rand McNally.

Rand McNally Mobile Navigator (MONA)

Rand McNally MONA gives you instant, audible, accurate turn-by-turn voice directions on your GPS-enabled mobile phone.

- Avoid the cost of getting lost with voice-prompted, turn-by-turn navigation and automatic rerouting for missed turns.
- Easily and efficiently enter addresses online or on the phone.
- Locate and route to the nearest gas station, ATM, restaurant, and other points of interest.
- Save money—Rand McNally MONA works on your existing mobile phone equipment.

Rand McNally StreetFinder ® Wireless

Easy to use, impossible to live without, StreetFinder® Wireless gives you access to maps, directions, and a directory of points of interest, wherever you are, all on the convenience of your mobile phone. Ideal for getting around town, perfect for travel.

With StreetFinder® Wireless on your phone you can:

- Save time. Quickly and easily locate addresses and points of interest in your area, and get maps, directions, and location information to help you get there.
- Be flexible—plans change, don't be caught without alternatives. StreetFinder® Wireless is always as close as your mobile phone.
- Act like a local—even when traveling! Want to find the nearest ATM, bank, or restaurant to your hotel? Need a reservation? Get it done yourself.
- Pinpoint your location. If your phone has GPS capabilities, StreetFinder® Wireless automatically maps your location, and

CASE STUDY (CONTINUED)

can provide you with a listing of local restaurants, hotels, coffee shops, gas stations, and the like. Makes getting directions easy!

- Get more from your printed maps. By using Express Access Codes built into the Rand McNally Road Atlas, you can quickly and easily use StreetFinder Wireless to get local street detail and points of interest for any area in the country.

Rand McNally Traffic

Rand McNally Traffic puts you in control. It helps you plan, anticipate, and arrive worry free. Get real-time traffic updates on your mobile phone. Know about traffic on your specific route ... before it's too late.

Available every day, all day, accurate up-to-the-minute information with traffic maps by region, city, road, or neighborhood showing:

- Accidents
- Traffic congestion
- Average road speeds (in select cities)
- Toll backups
- Road or lane closures
- Public transit delays

The handy Commute Wizard function lets you save a start and end point for fast and easy access anywhere, anytime.

Notes

1. www.randmcnally.com/rmc/company/cmpProfile.jsp.

2. www.randmcnally.com/rmc/company/cmpTimeLine.jsp.

3. *Source:* Rand McNally & Company.

CHAPTER 7

Connect

Capture the Power Unleashed by Metcalfe's Law

The Internet revolutionized how business gets done, not just because it extended the value of digitization onto data networks, but because of the reach of connectivity that was involved. Unlike previous data networks, the Internet was not limited to one location, or one company, or a limited group of collaborators, but rather it was a network for the world.

Because the Internet was everyone's network and cut across traditional boundaries, the digital value that had been captured within companies could now be amplified by extending it beyond those companies. This translated into three dominant business models from the mid-1990s to today.

The first successful business model is represented by Amazon.com. In 1995, Jeff Bezos launched "the world's largest bookstore." In reality, there was virtually nothing real about Amazon's bookstore—it was almost all digitized virtual reality. Bezos combined digital data about the books that were available from publishers with an attractive digital online storefront and the capability to accept digital payments using credit cards and Amazon.com was up and running. As of the third quarter of 2006, Amazon was reporting more than $2 billion a quarter in sales. I'd say it worked.

What Amazon.com did was not radical by today's standards, but it could be done only because the piece parts had been digitized (information about books, pictures of book covers, and credit card transactions), and Amazon.com could further use digital technology to efficiently fulfill the logistics of a customer's order (feeding orders to the warehouse for picking and packing, coordinating with FedEx for shipping and tracking).

Obviously, many others have followed in Amazon's footsteps, creating successful Internet e-commerce businesses. For example, Barnes & Noble Booksellers, an obvious target of Amazon's success, has been very aggressive with eCommerce. In the third quarter of 2006, nearly 10% of Barnes & Noble's $1.1 billion in revenue came through barnesandnoble.com.

The second successful business model is represented by Yahoo .com. Yahoo created a "portal" business that helped connect people to digital content. Much of that content is from traditional sources, such as news bureaus and traditional media companies. Yahoo leverages the digitization of this content to present customers with content they're comfortable with in a more dynamic (up to the instant) and interactive (customers have more control over what they receive and how and when) fashion that makes the original product even more valuable to the customer. Yahoo's primary revenue stream, as has been true with traditional media, is advertising. However, the digital and networked nature of Internet ads provides the advertiser with a much higher confidence that the right consumers are seeing the ads and better feedback that the ads are translating into consumer action. This makes Internet ads more valuable to advertisers. Yahoo reported $1.6 billion in revenues in the third quarter of 2006.

Yahoo's success demonstrates the opportunity to take a traditional product and, by digitizing it and extending it to customers across a network, magnify the product's value.

Many have followed in Yahoo's footsteps, with Apple Computer being a high-profile example. Apple reported $485 million in sales of "other music products" in the second quarter of 2006. This primarily consists of music and video sales through the iTunes music store.

Amazon, Yahoo, and Apple have each disrupted existing industries (book retailing, publishing, and music respectively) by taking digitized product information or the products themselves and using that digitization and networking to improve the customers' experience.

The third successful business model is represented by eBay. eBay connects people in new ways across networks. Specifically, eBay primarily connects buyers and sellers to perform their transactions in new and more efficient ways. eBay makes it easy for the members of its community to digitize all aspects of their interactions, from presenting product information and pictures to talking real time about the product (using eBay's Skype technology) to processing a digital payment (using eBay's PayPal transaction processing services). For the third quarter of 2006, eBay reported $1.4 billion in revenue.

Many others have followed in eBay's footsteps, making it easier for people to connect in new and exciting ways by simplifying the uploading and sharing of digital content and finding others with similar interests. Two currently prominent examples are MySpace (acquired by News Corporation for $580 million in 2005) and YouTube (acquired by Google for $1.6 billion in 2006).

eBay, MySpace, and YouTube have no value without the participants in their communities and yet they have created tremendous value by leveraging networking and making it easy for participants to digitize and share their own products.

Now, in 2007, most of the Internet buzz is about something people reference as Web 2.0. There are many definitions of what this means, but I would call out one particular new characteristic that has set these new Internet participants apart—the ability to integrate pieces of different services together into something new. The common phrase for this is "mashups," and these services often use new technology called Web Services and protocols such as XML (extensible markup language), SOAP (simple object access protocol), and REST (representational state transfer).

What does all this mean? It means that someone can take a data feed across the network from one source with, for example, real estate listings, and data feed from another source with housing market pricing data, geocoding data from another source to translate everything into longitude and latitude coordinates, and then present it on a map using Google's mapping service. I can do this as a tool just for myself or my employees, or I can open it up as a service for the whole world to use.

So, now that you've digitized your business, how will open networks amplify the value of your digitized data?

Is your product now a virtual digital product that can be sold and delivered across the network at nearly zero production cost? Is information about your product now digitized in a way that can be delivered across the network to customers or partners to increase sales or improve customer service and loyalty? Can you leverage networks to facilitate connecting with key communities (employees, channel partners, suppliers, customers) in ways that create value for them and for you?

What information are you willing to let across the network? What will you allow employees to access? What will you allow partners to access? What will you allow authenticated customers to access? What will you allow the whole world to access?

In what ways do you want each group to be able to access that data? Something they can "see but not touch" (e.g., as an image file)? Data they can download but not manipulate (e.g., as an uneditable portable document format [PDF] file)? Data they can download and work with (e.g., as a spreadsheet file)? A data stream they can "mash up" into a Web 2.0 application?

How will you enforce the policies we just discussed? How will you secure sensitive data? How will you authenticate authorized users? How will you protect your intellectual property rights?

These are not simple questions, and the implementation of the answers is well beyond the scope of this book. But they are critical questions to answer and successfully implement.

Choosing to share too little will likely open the door for your competitors to gain an advantaged position in the marketplace. Choosing to share too much can destroy the value of your product and intellectual property. Failing to securely implement what you decide will result in failing to gain a favored position and also destroying corporate value.

How do you decide what to share, with whom, and in what fashion?

Start with the imperatives. Have your competitors taken steps that you must match to maintain parity in the marketplace? Do you have an opportunity to take their actions one step further to gain advantage without destroying value?

Next, look for opportunities to improve your business performance. Are their networked information solutions to statements from your sales channels ("I could sell more if . . . "), your customers ("I would buy more if . . . "), your production group ("We could create a higher value product at a lower cost if . . . "), or your support organization ("We would get fewer customer problem calls if . . . ")? The benefits claimed may not always be enough to justify the investment, but it is critical to listen for these opportunities.

Once you understand the opportunities and requirements, you can move toward implementation. Given the complexity of successfully and securely implementing networked computing initiatives, if you do not already have experienced staff on board, this would be a great time to engage outside help. As always, a great place to start is with the partners who already support your technology needs, who understand your business and are probably well connected with other experts. Global information technology (IT) leaders such as IBM, EDS, and Hewlett Packard are well versed in all of the applications and technologies involved in networking your business. Application specialists, such as EMC, Verisign, and Entrust may also be worth considering, depending on your opportunities and needs.

And it never hurts to read up on the opportunities and challenges in connecting your business with the world. You may consider titles such as *Digital Capital* by Don Tapscott, David Ticoll, and Alex Lowy (Harvard Business School Press, 2000), *Service Orient or Be Doomed!* by Jason Bloomberg and Ronald Schmelzer (John Wiley & Sons, 2006), *Out of the Box* by John Hagel III (Harvard Business School Press, 2002), *Information Rules* by Carl Shapiro and Hal R. Varian (Harvard Business School Press, 1998), and *Unleashing the Killer App* by Larry Downes and Chunka Mui (Harvard Business School Press, 1998).

Successfully implementing networking initiatives will enable you to maximize the value of your digitized data and will prepare you for the next step in capturing the power of mobility.

 FROM THE REAL WORLD

Digitizing and Connecting Magazines

At the beginning of 1995, when my partners and I founded Digital Frontiers, a Web consulting firm, one of the first companies we called on was PennWell Publishing. PennWell was, and is, publisher of a diverse portfolio of magazines. However, the company is best known as the publisher of the *Oil and Gas Journal*, a 105-year-old weekly publication that keeps the entire oil and gas industry in the know.

Obviously, PennWell had seen plenty of change in the publishing industry in their time, but that didn't mean they were quick to abandon their highly successful existing business models. Over time, we were able to convince them to begin to experiment, and before long they'd jumped in with both feet. We partnered to launch OGJOnline, a new Web-based online service specifically designed to appeal to the conservative nature of the oil and gas industry. As part of this launch, we converted ten years' worth of the weekly publication's back issues to online digital format to provide the kind of archival searching that had previously been virtually impossible for PennWell's subscribers.

To address the conservatism of the *Oil and Gas Journal*'s subscribers, we developed a custom solution with a locked-down Web browser and dial-up software to ensure that oil company employees weren't "exposed" to the "dangers" of the Internet. Response was very positive. The initial business model mirrored the subscription model of the print magazine. Over time, advertising revenues became increasingly prominent in PennWell's online activities. Today, PennWell operates over 60 Web sites[1] supporting their 45+ publications. PennWell has also launched PennEnergy, a Web-based market for surplus equipment for the energy industry.

Obviously, PennWell's early adoption of digital and Web technology has positioned them well to grow their business and capture emerging opportunities.

But, the fascinating aspect of PennWell's journey has been the transformation that has occurred in their business. Online publishing radically changed PennWell's editorial perspectives. For the Web, the weekly publishing timeline could be thrown out the window. When content was ready, it could run online. Online content was no longer constrained by column lengths and traditional structures, and online-only features became possible and appealing.

The experience for readers also changed. At the time, most companies had libraries that kept back issues of all important publications for easy reference by employees. As publications like the *Oil and Gas Journal* moved online, these periodical libraries became much less critical. Many readers began looking for the online version of the publication to arrive, often days before it would show

FROM THE REAL WORLD (CONTINUED)

up in physical form. And as OGJOnline grew in popularity, what had started as a one-way publication became a vibrant industry online community.

The change wasn't without risks and challenges.

Especially in the early days, it was hard to deliver an aesthetically pleasing and usable online publication that came close to matching the quality product that PennWell was accustomed to delivering. There also were real concerns about the value of the content, copyright protections, and later, as the community became more active, editorial control over everything appearing on OGJOnline.

However, I'm sure that PennWell is thankful for their early initiative in taking their publications online and creating one of the first industry portals in the world.

Case Study

MapQuest

In 1994, printing giant R. R. Donnelly & Sons formed an entrepreneurial start-up called GeoSystems Global Corporation, which in 1996 launched the MapQuest.com Web service. The rest, as they say, is history. MapQuest became the go-to source for maps and directions for the growing online population. In 1999, AOL acquired MapQuest for more than $1 billion, but that didn't stop the innovation at the company, which continued to operate as a separate division.[2] As MapQuest's online audience has gone mobile, the company has seen the opportunity to invest in building mobility into their product so that the company remains accessible, relevant, and usable wherever MapQuest's users go.

"We actually saw both offensive and defensive reasons to extend our mapping leadership into mobility," reports Alan Beiagi, the director and general manager of MapQuest Wireless. "We recognize that the user profile of mobile users is slightly different from our traditional MapQuest base, meaning that mobility provides a way to extend our reach into this market. We also recognize that if we don't take the mapping experience mobile, others will, and our brand and leadership position will be damaged, so mobilizing became a competitive imperative."

Mapping and navigation, of course are a very natural choice for mobility. Taking MapQuest's capabilities mobile has created immediate value for the company's customers. But a critical issue for MapQuest is how to translate that customer value into shareholder value.

As a traditional Internet company, MapQuest's primary revenue stream has been online advertising. The PC Web browser screen provides plenty of real estate to wrap beautiful, enticing ads around the content MapQuest's customers are seeking. However, when that experience moves to a small mobile device, screen real estate becomes scarce and users become intolerant of anything inhibiting finding their way.

In entering the space, MapQuest has initially adopted the mobile applications industry model of charging users a monthly subscription fee to use MapQuest's solutions. This approach has been fine for an initial foray, but the company recognizes that monthly fees create a barrier to the kind of broad adoption that the company has enjoyed with the free MapQuest.com service. A different approach is required long term.

Alan notes that "it's critical to understand your customer. Why are they using your product? How are they using your product? How does that create value and for whom? When you deeply understand these factors, you can tailor your product and your business model to capture the most value.''

MapQuest is developing a contextually relevant business model. Why do people use a mobile navigation tool? Because they need to find their way. And often they need to find the place where they want to go. Using MapQuest's mobile products, a user can search for a hotel for the night or a restaurant for dinner or the nearest electronics store. Knowing that the hotel/restaurant/store exists is good, finding it is better, but often we want to call ahead to make reservations or check to see if what we want is in stock. Clicking through to call translates into an immediate highly qualified lead that's valuable to the business, translating into a revenue opportunity for MapQuest.

This points to the continuing evolution of advertising. First, we had broadcast and print advertising, where value was measured simply by exposure and the most the advertiser could hope for was awareness. Next came Internet advertising where value was measured by click-throughs, where advertisers hope customers will be interested in learning more and maybe even buying. Now, with contextually relevant mobile advertising, value is measured by capturing customers when they are in the very process of the decision, delivering to advertisers highly qualified customers wanting to make a purchase.

For MapQuest, revenue opportunities are not limited to the mobile space. A guiding factor in the company's pursuit of mobile opportunities has been seamless integration between the desktop and mobile experiences. With 54 million users of MapQuest.com, the company has a great start to building a base of mobile customers. The company has worked hard to optimize each platform for its strengths. Customers can start by using MapQuest at their desktop to research and plan a trip, and then transfer the fruits of those efforts into MapQuest's mobile products for easy access to relevant information on the go.

Just as importantly, the company has looked for ways to leverage the strengths of the mobile platform to bring customers back to the MapQuest Web-based service. A great example is MapQuest Navigator, which uses the global positioning system (GPS) capabilities built into Sprint Nextel phones to provide users with turn-by-turn, voice-guided driving directions.

The fact that MapQuest Navigator is currently available only to Sprint Nextel customers points to one of the biggest challenges MapQuest has faced in building mobility into their products. Within the mobile market, there seem to be an infinite number of combinations of network capabilities, handset capabilities, and operating system capabilities. MapQuest has broken the market down into four tiers by technology capability. Almost all cell phones can send and receive text messages. About half have some form of Web browsing capability. About a third can download an application, and less than one tenth currently have GPS capabilities.

On one hand, these differences create an opportunity to segment the market and develop specific products for the different types of users who naturally gravitate toward the devices with specific capabilities. But on the other hand, this diversity creates development costs and challenges that were beyond what MapQuest expected when they headed down the mobility path.

To help manage these complexities, MapQuest turned to two companies much more experienced in working with the countless varieties of technology combinations. MapQuest turned to Zingy to launch the MapQuest Mobile downloadable application, and turned to Telmap for help building the MapQuest Navigator GPS-based, voice-guided navigation application.

Alan acknowledges that having partners that understood the varied environments has been critical to MapQuest's success. ''It's critical that we focus on our strengths and on seamless integration

CASE STUDY (CONTINUED)

with our desktop products. Zingy and Telmap helped us maintain that focus.''

Sometimes even a navigation leader needs help finding its way through a new neighborhood!

MAPQUEST'S MOBILIZED PRODUCTS

The following product descriptions are provided by MapQuest, Inc.

MapQuest offers three products that capture the power of mobility: MapQuest Navigator, MapQuest Mobile, and the company's free WAP service for Web-enabled phones.

MapQuest Navigator represents leading edge technology in mobile navigation and gives you a powerful new level of convenience that is available when you need it most.

Enjoy in-car navigation in the palm of your hand!

MapQuest Navigator turns your phone into a full GPS Navigation system.

- Hear voice-guided, turn-by-turn directions right on your phone.
- Superior navigation display with full moving maps that automatically zoom in and out at the right time.
- Use full pedestrian navigation that ignores vehicle turning and one-way driving.
- Receive guidance and automatic rerouting even when you are out of network range.
- Find over 15 million of points of interest including restaurants, hotels, and theaters from the MapQuest.com database.
- Locate addresses, intersections, or zip codes with ease.
- Customize routes by finding the fastest or shortest route, or avoid toll roads and highways.

- Easy-to-read dynamic color maps that move as you follow the turn-by-turn directions.
- Zoom in or out, and pan and point on a map.
- Save frequently visited destinations in "My Places" menu.
- Receive phone calls without interrupting navigation.
- Make phones calls while navigating on select handsets.
- Direct dial to any of MapQuest's 15 million points of interest.

MapQuest Mobile offers U.S. and Canadian coverage from the world's leading online map provider. Instantly find your way with interactive color maps, step-by-step instructions, reverse directions, and recall of recent addresses.

The newest enhancements to MapQuest Mobile include:

- MapQuest's points of interest: Find over 15 million points of interest including restaurants, hotels, and theaters from the MapQuest.com database.
- Multipoint routing: Select multipoints along your route and receive step-by-step directions.
- Find places, get maps and step-by-step directions for Canada!
- Click to call a business directly from MapQuest Mobile (availability limited to certain carriers).
- Access recent locations and multiroutes: Access your most recent places and multiroutes.
- Save locations and multiroutes to favorites: Save your places and multiroutes to your favorites folder.
- Pedestrian navigation: Get directions for walking routes.
- Choose advanced routing options: Optimize your route by choosing the shortest time or distance and/or avoid tolls.

Next time you look up MapQuest directions, don't print them. Click on the "Send to Cell" link at the top of the page.

MapQuest Mobile was created in partnership with Zingy, one of the best-known publishers of consumer applications for mobile phones.

MapQuest® Navigator turns your phone into a full in-car navigation system. It helps you find places, get maps, and receive voice-guided, turn-by-turn directions using the latest GPS technology on your mobile phone.

Decide where you want to go and MapQuest Navigator will guide you there—quickly, easily, anywhere, anytime!

MapQuest free WAP service enables users with Web-enabled mobile phone or PDAs to access a "right-sized" version of MapQuest optimized for their phones. Users simply visit wap.mapquest.com using their mobile browser to find any destination, get detailed maps, and get turn-by-turn directions. In addition, with MapQuest's "Send to Cell" service, users can search for places and create maps and directions on their home or office desktop, and send that information to their cell phones by clicking on the "Send to Cell" link conveniently found through the MapQuest.com site. Then, while on the road, they can quickly access the information on their mobile device via a simple text link, and be directed to their turn-by-turn directions and detailed maps, all "right-sized" for their cell phone's Web browser.

Notes

1. www.pennwellpetroleumgroup.com/sites/index.cfm.
2. http://company.mapquest.com/corporate/2.html.

CHAPTER 8

Evaluate
How Is the Value of Your Product or Service Limited?

Mobility creates value above and beyond digitization and networking in three forms:

1. By increasing the availability of a product or service.

2. By using the immediate context of the product or service use to improve the relevance of the product or service to the customer.

3. By reducing the cost of a product or service.

Now that you have digitized and connected to create value for your business, you must evaluate ways in which you can increase that value through the increased availability, contextual relevance, or reduced cost promised by mobility.

Increasing Availability

What percentage of the time is your product or service fully available to your customers?

For a product, availability usually means how often your product is within their reach with its full capabilities. Do they take it with them everywhere they go? Does your product work anywhere, or are there special requirements, such as needing to be plugged in, needing to be connected to a certain kind of network, or only able to be used under certain conditions?

For a service, availability usually means when and where your customers can use your service. Do they need to go to a certain location? Are there only certain times and days that the service is available? Do your customers need something (e.g., a computer or telephone) to access your service?

What could you do to increase the availability of your product or service?

What could you do so that your customers would take your product everywhere they go? What could you do to reduce or eliminate the current requirements or conditions for your product's use?

If you have fully digitized your product, would it be possible to converge your product into a mobile phone so that your customers literally will take it with them everywhere they go? If not, but your product requires networked information, is it possible to build mobile wireless networking into your product so that it's fully available all the time?

What could you do so that your customers can use your service everywhere they go? Have you digitized your service and networked it so that your customers can access it over the Internet? If so, could you optimize that Internet access to work well with the small screen and limited keyboard of a mobile phone so that they can access it anywhere, anytime they have their phone?

If your service involves direct interaction between your employees and your customers, what can you do to make your employees available no matter where or when your customers need them? Is it possible for your service to be delivered over the telephone or the Internet? If not, can your employees become mobile to go to where your customers are? Can wireless technologies enable you to establish very short term (for a few hours, a day, a weekend, a week) service locations for special events to be where you know your customers are going to be, providing them with highly valued convenience?

Evaluating any of these options requires a deep understanding of your customers' desires and frustrations. How and when and where do they really want to use your product or service? How well does your current offer match those desires? How well could adding mobility to your product or service better align with your customers' needs?

What about your product or service currently frustrates your customers? How much of that frustration is associated with availability—where, when, and under what conditions they can use your product or service? Could these limitations be overcome by adding mobility into your product or service?

How could you translate better alignment with your customers' desires or elimination of their frustrations into value for your company? Will you be able to increase the price? Will you sell more? Will your customers be more loyal? Will you be able to reduce customer care costs or reduce billing disputes and unpaid customer invoices? Can you put a dollar figure on this value creation to help justify any necessary investment?

Contextual Relevance

Is there an opportunity to improve your customer's perception and value of your product or service by making it more relevant to the context in which they are using it?

Could your product create value by performing differently based on where your customer is using it, whom they are with, what is on their calendar, what the weather is, or what time it is? Could you make your product easier to use if it automatically adapted to the situation rather than having to be either reconfigured by your customer or tolerated in a suboptimal state? Could your product perform better, providing better results if it knew the current context and performed appropriately?

Could your service create value by taking into account where your customer is, what time it is where they are, whom they are with, what the weather is or forecast to be, or when their next appointment is (and where)? Could you save your customer some trouble or some time by automatically collecting this information instead of requiring them to tell you or type it in? Could your service perform better, providing better results if your company automatically knew the current context and performed appropriately?

Can you build into your product or service technologies to provide context, such as the current location or the current time? Can you tap into existing network-based sources to determine the weather or the traffic or the status of your customer's flight? Can you integrate with other products that your customer is using to know (with your customers' permission) what their calendar looks like or with whom they have just met or are about to meet? Can you correlate information across your customers to create value by knowing that two customers are or will be together and making your product or service work better for them together?

These questions are at the heart of evaluating the opportunity to increase the value of your product or service through contextual relevance enabled by mobility.

How will your business benefit from this increased relevance? Will you be able to increase the price? Will you sell more? Will your customers be more loyal? Will you be able to reduce customer care costs or reduce billing disputes and unpaid customer invoices? Can you put a dollar figure on this value creation to help justify any necessary investment?

Reduced Costs

Is there an opportunity to increase your customers' appreciation for the value of your product or service by reducing its price?

If you can converge your product into a cell phone, does that translate into dramatic reductions in manufacturing and repair costs? If you can deliver your product as bits, can you similarly dramatically reduce all costs associated with the physical components of your product? If your product will have network connectivity built in, can you replace more expensive components with less expensive components and compensate by receiving updated accurate information over the network?

Will mobilizing your service make your employees more efficient? Will it accelerate information flow, resulting in fewer costly mistakes? Will it eliminate expensive paper processes and duplication of effort?

Will mobilization reduce data entry requirements and associated human errors?

How much of these cost reductions do you need to apply to paying for your mobility investment? How much are you willing to pass on to customers as price reductions?

What Does It Take?

There are a number of levels of complexity possible in building mobility into your product or service.

The simplest level is to provide your service employees with effective tools for taking your service mobile and turning them loose to serve your customers. You'll likely need to invest in mobile phones, laptops, wireless data cards, and the appropriate voice and data plan to keep your employees connected and productive wherever they go. Wireless carriers can help you select the best tools and plan for what your business needs.

The next level is to enable your now mobile workers with solutions to be more effective when they're in the field. Sprint is the leading provider of mobile business solutions and offers dozens of applications ranging from simple navigation and messaging to resource tracking to credit card processing to work order and dispatch management, to vertical solutions unique to your industry, but other carriers are also developing portfolios of business solutions.

The next level of complexity is to ensure that your Web-enabled capabilities will work well for your employees and customers when they are using their mobile devices. The official standards group for the World Wide Web provides a profile for designing Web sites to work well with mobile devices. This profile is available at www.w3

.org/TR/css-mobile/. Another excellent resource is the Global Authoring Practices for the Mobile Web, available at www.passani .it/gap. Finally, a collection of large wireless industry players have created a company called dotmobi to make the mobile device as useful as a PC for browsing and data applications. They offer a collection of "Switch On!" guides for developing for the mobile Web. These are available at http://pc.mtld.mobi/mobilenet/dotmobi_guides.html.

You may decide to develop applications specifically to run on mobile devices rather than simply using a Web interface. This provides a higher level of control over security and performance and may enable your product to work well even when the network isn't. Most carriers have developers' programs to support folks developing for the devices on their network. A number of valuable resources are typically available through these programs to create, test, and deploy applications for devices on the carriers' networks.

If your product is a physical product that cannot be easily converged into a mobile phone, but that you want to consider building mobility in, then you may want to pursue a variety of options.

One is to embed mobile network connectivity into your product. You'll likely want to align with one carrier per global region to simplify your development, certification testing, and support. You'll want to work closely with the business development group at each carrier.

Another, complementary approach is to build mobility-enabling technology into your product. This could include alternative sources of power, such as solar panels and fuel cells, memory for storing data being transmitted and received, global positioning system (GPS) location tracking sensors, or any of a variety of other sensors that could provide important contextual information to increase the value of your product through increased relevance. Tremendous strides are being made in making these components cost effective, energy efficient, small, and robust for embedding into products. For example, Epson recently introduced an ultrasensitive GPS module that is only 6 mm by 7 mm by 1.3 mm in size, Yamaha recently introduced a 2 mm by 2 mm three-axis geomagnetic sensor for determining directional movement in mobile devices, and Hewlett Packard has developed memory the size of a grain of rice that can store up to 4 megabytes of data and requiring no external power.

Understanding the value that can be created by mobilizing your product will help you evaluate the different options you have for doing so. As we'll see in the next step in capturing the power of mobility, often it's deciding what *not* to do that will be critical in delivering real value to your customers and creating value for your shareholders.

FROM THE REAL WORLD

The Mobility Declaration of Independence

As a creative illustration of the revolutionary power of mobility and of the forces against which mobility is in revolt, in July 2006, I introduced a Mobility Declaration of Independence on the Law-of-Mobility.com blog. I modeled this new declaration after the American Declaration of Independence of 1776. Historically, the Americans were revolting against a ruler they considered a tyrant, so it was also necessary for me to introduce the tyrant of the Big Bell Dogma against which mobility is rebelling.

BIG BELL DOGMA

Clearly, mobility provides freedom from "fixedness." As we develop our list of charges against our oppressor, they will largely or entirely be the injustice of being tied to a specific location.

But what is forcing us into this fixed state?

As much as anything, I think what we're struggling against is a mind-set that is firmly embedded in how products and processes are designed and in how businesses operate.

For fun, I'd like to call this oppressing force "Big Bell Dogma."

According to Wikipedia, "dogma" is belief or doctrine held by a religion, ideology, or any kind of organization to be authoritative and not to be disputed or doubted.

I think this well captures the mindset against which we fight. It is the belief held by product development groups and by those that define processes that "of course it can't move, it never has."

"Big Bell" is a reference to the way AT&T built the telephone network over the past century or so. As mentioned, not all oppression against mobility is related to telephony, but I think the mind-set of that old company well reflects the mind-set we're fighting against.

In *Nerds 2.0.1,* this mind-set is well reflected by this quote from Len Kleinrock, one of the key players in the establishment of the ARPAnet, which would become the Internet: "I would say, 'Please give us good data communications,' and they would reply, 'The United States is a copper mine—we have phone lines everywhere so use the telephone network.' I would counter, 'But you don't understand, it takes 25 seconds to set up a call, you charge me for a minimum three minutes, and all I want is to send a millisecond of data.' Their reply was, 'Go away, children, the revenue stream from

127

data transmission is dwarfed by that of our voice traffic.' So the children went away and created the Internet!''

Back in 1995 when I cofounded an Internet start-up, I encountered this same mentality within the businesses that we were selling to— a sense that communications would never change. Even though the original AT&T had been broken up 11 years earlier, when I asked one of our customers who his local telephone company was, his retort was ''AT&T, of course!''

These examples are specific to the Internet, but I believe this ''dogma'' extends to a bias against mobility as well. The copper and fiber networks that have been built by the telecom industry represent truly ''buried'' costs that have historically translated into tremendous wealth creation. Obviously, these assets are well suited to continue to serve a purpose in the information economy, but newer technologies provide tremendous advantages for many applications that have traditionally been served by these fixed facilities.

Although there is still a company called AT&T, I think you recognize that the ''new AT&T'' is not really the ''bad guy'' I'm referencing here.

The original AT&T was first dismantled in 1984 as the result of a Justice Department antitrust action. The company that retained the AT&T name continued to self-destruct, first splitting out its innovation arm as Lucent and its computing arm as NCR and later spinning off AT&T Wireless.

The company formerly known as Southwestern Bell was one of the ''Baby Bells'' created in 1984 out of AT&T and has been working hard to recreate much of what the original Ma Bell had been, most dramatically acquiring the remains of AT&T and taking on that moniker in the past few years.

FROM THE REAL WORLD (CONTINUED)

However, this new AT&T is a very different company that has benefited as much from the fall of the old Ma Bell as anyone has. I'm not saying that the new AT&T is immune to the defensiveness described above as "Big Bell Dogma" (are any of us?), but I ask that no one equate the two.

What we fight against is the mind-set represented by those who defend the tethering of products and processes to specific places. This mind-set is fueled by the investments that have been made that establish power in the companies, departments, and individuals that stand in the way of mobilizing our lives and our businesses. These investments are not always in hard assets, but often are investments of time and experience to establish intellectual and relational assets.

We should expect our assault on these "fixed" ways to be defended to the death.

So, at least personally for me, this "Big Bell Dogma" is a fair representation of the oppressor that is holding back the independence promised by Mobility.

THE DECLARATION

When in the course of human events it becomes necessary for people to dissolve the technological bonds which have connected them with a specific place for a specific task and to assume among the powers of the earth, the free and mobile status to which the Laws of Nature and of Nature's God entitle them, a decent respect to the opinions of mankind requires that they should declare the causes which impel them to the separation.

We hold these truths to be self-evident:

- That all men are created equal.
- That they are endowed by their Creator with certain unalienable Rights.

- That among these are Life, Liberty, and the pursuit of Happiness.
- That to secure these rights, Technologies are implemented among Men, deriving their just powers from the consent of the enabled.
- That whenever any Form of Technology becomes destructive of these ends, it is the Right of the People to alter or to replace it, and to implement new Technology, laying its foundation on such principles and organizing its powers in such form, as to them shall seem most likely to effect their Safety and Happiness.

Prudence, indeed, will dictate that Technologies long established should not be changed for light and transient causes; and accordingly all experience hath shown that mankind are more disposed to suffer, while evils are sufferable than to right themselves by abolishing the tools to which they are accustomed. But when a long train of abuses and usurpations, pursuing invariably the same Object evinces a design to reduce them under absolute Despotism, it is their right, it is their duty, to throw off such Technology, and to provide new Enablers for their future happiness.

Such has been the patient sufferance of this society; and such is now the necessity which constrains them to alter their formerly adopted Technologies. The history of the present Big Bell Dogma is a history of repeated injuries and usurpations, all having in direct object the continuation of an absolute Tyranny over all people and businesses. To prove this, let Facts be submitted to a candid world.

- Limiting products so that they can only operate in a few fixed locations ("where they have always operated").
- Forcing services to only be offered in a constrained set of fixed locations ("where they have always been offered").
- Locking processes to only work in a relatively small number of places ("where they have always been performed").

FROM THE REAL WORLD (CONTINUED)

- Forbidding (by law or policy) constituents from adopting otherwise viable and available mobile products, services, and technologies.

- Disabling or blocking technologies that otherwise would enable the power of mobility.

- Taxing or otherwise penalizing mobile products and services so as to destroy the financial value of adopting them.

- Charging mobile products, services, and technologies with pretended offenses so as to encourage fear, uncertainty, and doubt amongst those who otherwise would adopt and enjoy the power of mobility.

In every stage of these Oppressions We have proposed solutions in the most humble terms: Our repeated proposals have been answered only by repeated injury. A Dogma whose character is thus marked by every act which may define a Tyrant is unfit to define how we run our businesses, do our jobs, and live our lives.

Nor have We been wanting in warnings to our technology brethren. We have warned them from time to time of attempts by the Dogmatists to extend an unwarrantable jurisdiction over us. We have appealed to their native justice and magnanimity, and we have implored them by the ties of our common kindred to disavow these usurpations, which would inevitably interrupt our advances in productivity and connectivity. They too have been deaf to the voice of justice and of logic. We must, therefore, acquiesce in the necessity, and hold them, as we hold the rest of mankind, Enemies in War, in Peace Friends.

We, therefore, those seeking to drive mobility into all we do and are, appealing to the Supreme Judge of the world for the rectitude of our intentions, do, in the interest of serving this society and economy, solemnly publish and declare, That we are, and of Right ought to be Free and Mobile; that we are Absolved from all Allegiance to the Big Bell Dogma, and that all forced fixed connection is and ought to be totally dissolved; and that as a Free and Mobile Society, we have full Power to develop and implement mobile technologies, introduce new mobile processes, and to do all other Acts and Things which Free and Mobile businesses and individuals may of right do. And for the support of this Declaration, with a firm reliance on the protection of divine Providence, we mutually pledge to offer each other our Products, our Services, and our efficient Processes.

 Case Study

TeleNav

H. P. Jin had long envisioned that GPS technology would have a real impact on how people lived their lives and how businesses operated. Working as a consultant for McKinsey & Company and then at the McKenna Group, H. P. was able to see the seeds of this technology be planted at many companies around the globe. But the costs of implementation were too high and the challenges of broadly deploying GPS technology were too daunting for most companies to undertake.

However, H. P. recognized the opportunity for these challenges to be broadly overcome on September 15, 1999, when the Federal Communications Commission (FCC) revised its rules for wireless-enhanced 911 services. The original rules had been passed in 1996, requiring wireless carriers to be able to locate a wireless caller within 125 meters at least two thirds of the time by October 1, 2001. The 1999 rules change allowed carriers to accomplish this goal by embedding GPS technology into the wireless handset.[1]

Suddenly, it appeared that GPS technology would literally be placed in the hands of millions of consumers within a few years. H. P.

grabbed the opportunity, creating Televigation to focus on wireless telephone–based navigation products. The company would later shorten its name to TeleNav, Inc.

In 2000, the company introduced Snap-to-Map, a solution that didn't require GPS to be installed in the handset, but used the carrier's information about the user's location and the carrier's Wireless Application Protocol (WAP) services to provide turn-by-turn directions through a voice interface so the driver could keep his eyes on the road and his hands on the steering wheel. The service was trialed with two major carriers, proving the technical viability of the approach; however, the business models supported by the carriers could not support a profitable service for Televigation.

The company continued working with the major wireless carriers. One of these carriers, Nextel, offered an approach that was particularly well suited to Televigation's needs. Nextel standardized on a single Java-based platform for all of the phones they offered. Nextel was very supportive of developers and allowed Televigation to access the serial port on the phone to connect an external GPS receiver. In 2002, Televigation introduced a new product, TeleNav on Nextel phones, using a low-cost monthly subscription model. Later that year, Nextel introduced the industry's first handsets with GPS built in, enabling TeleNav to work without an external receiver so that only the cell phone was required. The product was well received by the market and was even named a *Time* magazine "Gadget of the Week."

By building the navigation function into a mobile phone, TeleNav overcame three obstacles that had limited the adoption and success of GPS-based technologies.

The first barrier was price. Stand-alone GPS units typically cost hundreds of dollars, creating a psychological barrier for consumers. Potential customers must be convinced that they will benefit from the technology before they will make an investment of that magnitude. TeleNav priced their product as a low monthly recurring fee. Today, customers can use TeleNav for about $10 per month and can cancel at any time, making it a much easier decision to try the technology.

How could TeleNav afford to disrupt the prevailing pricing model? By adding their product onto an existing customer handset, TeleNav leveraged the hardware investment that had already been made. Their competitors have to factor in the cost of all of the hardware components into their product cost and ensure that the up-front payment from the customer covers that hardware cost. TeleNav's approach also has ongoing support cost benefits. Software updates are automatically uploaded to the customers' handsets, eliminating the multistep process stand-alone units require, and maps are always up to date, reducing customer frustration and churn.

The second barrier that TeleNav's approach has overcome is availability. Customers who purchase a dedicated GPS unit typically install the unit in their car. However, if the customer isn't in that car, if they are in their other car, or riding with a friend, or once they leave their car and start walking, their big-ticket GPS system is no longer available to them. Because TeleNav's product is integrated into the customers' cell phones, the navigation feature is available wherever the phone goes, which means that it is available virtually 100% of the time.

Finally, because the TeleNav product is integrated into a phone, it has access to the network, so it overcomes the barrier of out-of-date information. The TeleNav product always benefits from the most recently available maps and has even been extended to provide up-to-date traffic, weather, and gas price information.

TeleNav has also worked with its carrier partners to integrate information on special events. For example, Sprint Nextel is the wireless partner to the NFL, so, working together, they integrated driving information for the 2007 SuperBowl into the TeleNav product.

So, what did it take for TeleNav to achieve this level of mobility success?

CASE STUDY (CONTINUED)

As a new company, TeleNav was free to play by the changing rules in the industry. They leveraged existing digital data and saw opportunity to differentiate by using the connectivity in the cell phone to provide updated information. They evaluated and understood the value they could create for their customers by integrating the power of mobility into their navigation product.

But none of that would have mattered if they had failed to execute.

According to H. P., the early partnership with Nextel was key to Televigation's success. By focusing their resources on one carrier that had the components necessary for the TeleNav product to succeed, the company was able to gain the greatest impact in the shortest time possible. As TeleNav has enjoyed success around the world, it has generally followed this same model, choosing one carrier that is well suited to the company's products in each market, focusing efforts at that one carrier, and enjoying outsized success with that carrier.

Now that TeleNav has established its success, and as other carriers have matured their platforms to support GPS-based solutions, the company has begun working with additional carriers.

"Wireless carriers are big companies that can be very slow to make decisions, but once they set a direction, they can move very fast. You need to align yourself with partners that are positioned to deliver what you need," counsels H. P. "And when they decide to move, you need to be lockstep with them, ready to move very fast."

TeleNav has moved very fast, first in lockstep with Nextel, then with Sprint Nextel, now with partners all over the world.

TELENAV'S MOBILIZED PRODUCTS

The following product descriptions are provided by TeleNav, Inc.

TeleNav offers two main product lines, TeleNav GPS Navigator and TeleNav Track.

TeleNav GPS Navigator is easy to use. As you drive, TeleNav will give you all the information you need, such as:

- The current street.
- The next turn to take.
- The next street to turn onto.
- The distance remaining before next turn.
- The number of miles left on your trip.

Along the way, turn-by-turn directions will be announced in a clear voice and displayed on your phone. For example, TeleNav will say, "Go 1.2 miles and turn right on Elm Street." As you approach the turn, you will hear, "Turn right on Elm Street."

TeleNav will even tell you whether the destination is on the left- or right-hand side of the street.

With TeleNav GPS Navigator, it is easy to find restaurants, banks, cafés, hotels, and more from over 10 million points of interest across the United States.

- Search by category, such as "Thai restaurant" and "pharmacy"
- Search by name, such as "Thai Basil" and "ABC Pharmacy"

Once you've found what you are looking for, you can use TeleNav to get turn-by-turn driving directions or call ahead to make reservations.

Best of all, updates are free and automatic, unlike expensive GPS systems that charge for updates and require manual intervention.

As you drive, TeleNav Traffic monitors the traffic situation every five minutes. When there is slowdown or incident, TeleNav Traffic proactively alerts you with a voice and onscreen prompt, "Accident 2.3 miles ahead on Main Street, one lane closed. Press '0' to avoid."

With just one click, TeleNav Traffic will intelligently reroute you to minimize travel time, taking into account the latest traffic conditions. Or you can continue on your course.

TeleNav even updates your estimated time of arrival (ETA), so you can set the proper expectations on when you will be there.

With TeleNav Track, you can manage your mobile workforce with confidence. TeleNav Track utilizes the latest technologies to make mobile workforce and asset management reliable and affordable for businesses of all sizes. Best of all, it works with your employees' mobile phones and personal digital assistants (PDAs).

You will be able to deploy mobile employees efficiently, allowing the most effective coverage of any area. You will even be able to predict arrival times and change schedules on the fly to better serve your customers.

TeleNav Track allows your mobile workforce to do their reporting from the road. No need returning to the office and filing invoices, orders, timesheets, and more. All data can be sent wirelessly.

With wireless bar code scanning, you will have an instant handle on deliveries, inventory, assets, and more. With that kind of real-time information, you will have the power to make quick, well-informed decisions.

TeleNav GPS Navigator^{TM} is incorporated into TeleNav Track and with turn-by-turn directions—onscreen and by voice—to lead them to their destinations, saving employees time and frustration.

Notes

1. www.constructionweblinks.com/Resources/Industry_Reports__Newsletters/GPS_Nov_1999/gps_nov_1999.html.

CHAPTER 9

Limit

What Are You Going To Choose Not To Do?

Mobility is a wonderful thing. Obviously, this book is based on the assumption that mobility will be built into every product, service, and process. At the end of the day, well-defined standards and fully built-out reliable wireless networks will ensure that the infrastructure underlying mobility will work everywhere and all the time.

But we are not yet at the end of the day.

Different standards have taken hold in different parts of the world. Different network providers have selected different technologies that will work with their networks. Which provider's network works best varies from city to city, and even the best network in a city will have areas where performance is challenged.

You can't afford to wait for these issues to get resolved, so you had better figure out how to work within the current limitations to ensure that mobilizing your business does not destroy your brand, drive away customers, and kill your company.

There are four factors around which you should consider limiting the mobilization of your product, service, or process. These limitations will play out a bit differently for a product than for a service or a process, but the factors are the same:

- Wireless technology
- Network provider
- Geography
- Activities

As we will see, these four factors are all interrelated, so making the right choices will involve balancing the attractiveness of decisions in each area.

Wireless Technology

In most instances, mobilizing your product, service, or process will involve using wireless technologies. There is a broad array of technologies on the market, and new technologies being developed every year. Most of the technologies you will consider are international standards, meaning that you will have multiple vendors from which to choose in mobilizing your business.

The most meaningful way to characterize different technologies is in terms of their reach.

The shortest-reach technologies actually require wireless devices to touch or nearly touch each other to communicate. One standard in this space is near field communications (NFC) technology, jointly developed by Sony and Philips.[1] This technology can be used to pass information between two NFC-enabled devices. It is currently being targeted for inclusion in mobile phones for applications like the digital wallet (credit/debit transactions), identification, and electronic keys.

If NFC technology is broadly adopted and built into most mobile phones, it may be a valid choice for mobilizing your business. Obviously, its greatest limitation is that it requires the phone to come in close contact with another device. This may work if your employees or customers need to exchange information only when they return to a fixed location. It may also work in conjunction with a mobile NFC "reader" that is connected to the rest of the world using a different wireless technology.

A closely associated technology is radio frequency identification (RFID). RFID is being broadly adopted as the new standard for tagging items for retail, replacing the bar code system that became almost universally adopted during the PC revolution as inventory tracking and transaction processing were digitized. Because of this broad adoption, the cost of RFID tags is dropping rapidly (now as low as a few pennies each), making it a viable technology for a broad range of applications.

Passive RFID tags (those without a power source) are the smallest and least expensive and can operate up to a few meters.[2] Active tags are larger and more expensive, but can have ranges even into the hundreds of meters. An application of active RFID that you have probably encountered is the electronic toll pass, which identifies cars passing through a toll plaza allowing them to automatically pay without slowing or stopping.

The greatest limitation with RFID is that it is primarily designed for identification purposes. It is not a two-way networking protocol, and the amount of data that can be transmitted is intended to be small.

RFID may be part of a mobilization strategy, but is not likely to enable true mobilization of products, services, or processes.

The next class of wireless technologies is known as personal area networks (PANs). PANs are designed to connect multiple electronic devices together, generally for use by one person and in very close proximity. Wireless PAN technologies include Bluetooth and ZigBee.

Bluetooth has been broadly adopted for consumer electronics applications such as cordless telephone headsets, printer connections, and remote control and input devices. It can work up to about 100 meters and is designed for simple setup (which limits sophisticated features such as advanced security).

ZigBee is intended to be even simpler than Bluetooth, which contributes to a lower cost (currently in the neighborhood of $1 per device).[3] ZigBee nodes automatically form mesh networks to cover a larger area than would otherwise be associated with a PAN. Typical ZigBee applications include networks for industrial sensors, home automation, and alarm monitoring.

PAN technologies can be a great tool in mobilizing products, services, and processes, but primarily in connecting together different parts of the solution. For example, Bluetooth can be used to pass data between different components, such as to connect an RFID reader to the main data collection and networking node. ZigBee and Bluetooth generally are less useful for connecting together products or employees on a broader scale.

The next class of technology is local area networking (LAN). The most prevalent wireless LAN technology today is known as WiFi. WiFi technologies provide multi-megabit transmissions over hundreds of meters. Mesh networks are also being built out of hundreds of WiFi access points to cover entire cities. WiFi is a general computer networking technology that is well suited to carrying Internet-like data traffic and is beginning to be used for performance-sensitive applications like voice calls and multiplayer gaming.

WiFi's greatest limitations come from signal coverage and quality challenges. Users can experience challenges with signal strength variations due to a variety of factors including interference, contention from other users, and propagation through walls. WiFi is a relatively mature technology with strong tools for managing the network, including security authentication and encryption.

Using a WiFi network dedicated to mobilizing a service or process and managing that network to provide the needed performance in the area where the service is provided or the process is performed can prove highly effective. However, extending that service or process beyond the controlled area becomes a challenge.

Using WiFi to integrate mobility into a product is also worth considering. Many technology-oriented consumers have implemented WiFi networks in their homes, and WiFi has also been broadly adopted by businesses. However, security concerns have caused consumers and businesses to wisely deploy standard authentication schemes that will require the product to be configured to interact with specific secure WiFi networks, adding to the complexity of the product and likely inhibiting full use of the mobilized features. Since it will be impossible for you to ensure the quality of the network where your product is used, you will need to ensure that the product performs acceptably when the network signal is poor or even nonexistent. This could significantly limit the extent to which you can claim the increased value of your product due to mobility.

The final class of wireless technologies is the wide area network (WAN). Third-generation wireless wide area networking technologies that are broadly deployed globally include high-speed packet access (HSPA) technologies and CDMA2000 (code division multiple access) technologies such as EV-DO (evolution data optimized). These technologies are used by licensed cellular telephone companies to provide data services covering entire cities, regions, or countries. Currently, these services offer speeds in the 1-Mbps range and can work even when traveling at highway speeds.

Fourth-generation wireless WAN technologies are now emerging that provide multi-megabit data rates at highway speeds. The leading international standard is WiMax, which can provide up to 40 Mbps per channel at a cost point that is dramatically lower than existing wireless WAN technologies.[4] Sprint Nextel is currently deploying a nationwide WiMax network.

Wireless WAN technologies are well suited to mobilizing products, services, and processes. As with mobile phones today, there will be pockets of coverage challenges in any wireless network, but in general, wireless WANs provide significantly greater reach providing a much higher confidence that a signal will be present where the product is being used, the service is being provided, or the process is being performed.

Third-generation wireless WAN technologies generally require advance activation by the carrier, which can add a slight barrier to product mobility adoption. Pricing plans for third-generation offers may also inhibit broad use as a mobility value-add for products (many carriers charge based on usage, and pricing plans are typically $15 per month or more). However, these challenges are much less of an issue when mobilizing a service or a process.

Sprint Nextel's fourth-generation WiMax network is specifically being designed for integration into mobilized products. Instant, automated, over-the-air activation and pricing plans better suited to mobilized products are currently being developed. Fourth-generation technologies will also support mobilized services and processes with higher performance, perhaps even at lower costs. Intel is a strong supporter of the WiMax standards and has indicated that they will push for WiMax capabilities to be embedded into all computing products, just as virtually all laptops sold today include WiFi networking.

It is not economical to build all of these wireless technologies into your product, service, or process, so one of the first decisions you'll need to make is which technologies will best meet your goals and how that will drive additional limitations for your business.

Network Provider

Based on the wireless technologies you choose to build mobility into your product, service, or process, you will need to determine whether to build and operate your own wireless network or whether to partner with a network provider.

NFC, RFID, and PANs will almost always need to be implemented to your unique specifications. Although it may be wise to outsource the building and operating of the network, your opportunity to share the cost with other companies is limited. Still, an experienced partner can bring best practices to bear in deploying your network quickly and cost effectively and likely can centralize operations into their existing network operations centers.

Selecting an outsource partner likely will be based on a variety of factors, including your previous experience or recommendations of those you trust and a bid that appears competitive relative to others you consider. However, most important will be a partner's proven expertise supporting the technologies you've selected and how you plan on using the network. As you negotiate with your partner, keep in mind that the choices you make now may limit how quickly you can expand your mobilization efforts into new areas. A provider with proven success supporting your immediate needs and a broad portfolio of additional capabilities may enable you to rapidly build on your early mobility successes.

If you have selected wireless LAN technologies, the range of network providers available to support you broadens. If you plan on primarily using WiFi technologies in the locations that you control, then the best approach may again be to find an outsource partner to build and operate the network. If you are interested in opening this WiFi network up for your customers to use, it would be wise to look for a partner with specific expertise in this area. You will need to ensure that your partner has proven experience protecting your network and all the data on it from the general public.

However, if you hope to use public WiFi networks as your customers and/or employees travel around the world, then you should look for a network provider who has roaming agreements providing connectivity in thousands of locations. T-Mobile provides WiFi connectivity to its customers in about 30,000 locations in 22 countries. Sprint customers can use their WiFi service in over 20,000 locations around the world. Boingo, a WiFi-only network provider, offers connectivity in 60,000 locations in about 75 countries.

Again, you should choose a provider not just based on your current plans, but taking into account its ability to support you as you expand your mobilization efforts to additional technologies and applications.

Wireless WAN technologies provide the most straightforward choices and the most apparent sets of limitations. Depending on the wireless WAN technology that best serves your needs, there will be a clear set of carriers supporting that technology. For example, in the United States, AT&T currently supports the HSPA 3G technology family, and T-Mobile is beginning to build their network to support the HSPA standards. Verizon supports the CDMA2000 standards, as does Sprint, while Sprint is also building out a WiMax 4G network. In part, selecting a network partner is as simple as identifying which carriers support your current and future network technology needs.

Another limiting factor in choosing a wireless WAN provider is the device technologies that they support. If you are building a product that will be integrated into the handsets offered by a wireless carrier, then you will need to consider the openness of the carrier to your development efforts. You will need to consider the technologies built into their handsets. Do they support the operating environment that best suits your needs and skills? Do their handsets include the contextual sources (e.g., GPS) and support any peripheral devices (e.g., RFID readers, environmental sensors) that are required for your solution?

If you are going to build the wireless WAN technology into your product, does the carrier actively support embedded solutions? How robust are their support services? Will you be able to test your product sufficiently on their network? Do they see partners like you as an opportunity or a threat?

If you are mobilizing a service or process, are the applications already available to support your employees using the devices they offer for their network? How mature are their processes and organizations in supporting business mobilization efforts? Do they have experience working with an organization like yours on an application like this, or will you be providing them with a "learning opportunity" that may not go well for you?

There are also very well defined geographic limitations imposed by selecting a network provider for wireless WAN services. T–Mobile is owned by Deutsche Telekom, and therefore has some connection to European services, but in general, selecting a network provider in the United States will solve only your U.S. connectivity needs. If you need connectivity in different parts of the world, you will generally need to select different partners in each region or country.

Because of this complexity, it will likely make sense to limit your initial mobilization efforts to a single country with a single network provider and consider expanding as your experience and support resources allow.

Geography

This takes us directly to geographic limitations.

If the mobilization of your product, service, or process involves working with a wireless WAN network provider, then you will naturally want to limit the geographic reach of your solution to match the footprint of your partner. In the United States, the national carriers have extended their networks through builds and partnerships to cover virtually all of the reasonably populated areas of the country. But, as noted above, their networks do not extend beyond the borders of the country.

Wireless LAN, PAN, RFID, and NFC wireless technologies create even more significant limitations on the geographic reach of your solution.

As previously discussed, PAN, RFID, and NFC solutions will require a dedicated infrastructure, so you will need to limit the mobility of your solutions based on where you are willing and able to build out that infrastructure. You may allow your employees or customers to wander beyond that geography to perform tasks, but they will need to return to reconnect and gain the full benefit of mobility.

Wireless LAN technologies promise much greater mobility, but the real-world experiences of your customers and employees may make it challenging for you to capture the value of mobility if relying on these technologies to provide significant geographic reach. In theory, WiFi hotspots are available all over the world, including public networks, networks to which you can subscribe for access, and private (business and residential) networks that your customers or employees may be able to authenticate to. However, the coverage area of this vast array of hundreds of thousands of hotspots is just a small fraction of the area covered by wireless WAN technologies, and the performance experienced by users may vary dramatically.

Since you have almost no control over this virtual cloud of WiFi coverage, either directly or through well-established network provider relationships, your ability to influence or even monitor what your customers and employees are experiencing is virtually nonexistent. The net result may be a failure to adopt the mobility solutions in which you've invested, thus eliminating your opportunity to capture the value that should accrue from mobility.

For these reasons, especially in the earliest days of your mobilization efforts, it would be best to limit the geography over which you implement your solution to a footprint over which you either have direct control or your network providers are willing to guarantee performance through service-level agreements.

Activities

The geographic limitations you have selected for the mobilization of your product, service, or process likely will lead to natural limitations in the activities that are fully mobilized using wireless technologies.

For a mobilized product, this may dictate the features that you will support in the early releases of your industry-defining offers. As you gain experience and confidence enabling you to extend the geographic reach, you may find that additional features may be supportable. For example, if your initial product release relies on WiFi networking, you may store enough data within the product for it to work reasonably well even when a live connection is not available. The synchronization of data can occur whenever a WiFi connection can be obtained. However, once your product is upgraded to include WiMax network technologies, and as WiMax network coverage gets expanded, your confidence that a connection will almost always be available will enable you to include live information and even real-time communications in your product features.

Similarly for service and process mobilization efforts, if you've chosen WiFi as your networking technology, then you will limit the mobilized activities that can occur within the footprint of the infra-structure you have built and can manage. However, if you have selected wireless WAN technologies, then you can mobilize activities that can be performed virtually anywhere there are people (cities, towns, highways).

Remember, the goal is to increase the value of your product, service, or process through mobility. That value creation comes from increased availability of the product or service and its contextual relevance. The opportunities for contextual relevance are almost limitless as location information (from GPS receivers), environmental information (from a variety of sensors), health information (from medical telemetry devices), time and date (from various time sources), and a variety of network sources of data can all be built into your product. However, the choices you make about wireless networking technologies and providers will have a direct impact on how limited (or not) the availability gains are that you are introducing.

To ensure that your mobilization efforts create value by increasing availability and contextual relevance rather than destroy value by failing to work where and when your customer or employee expects, it is critical that you appropriately limit the geographic reach and activities/functions to match the choices you have made in network technologies and provider.

And these limitations will likely lead directly to your selection of target markets, customers, and applications.

FROM THE REAL WORLD

When Less Is Best

Sometimes even wireless carriers need to narrow their focus to maximize success.

When Sprint Nextel introduced Advanced Wireless Solutions in 2006, it was already the market share leader in wireless solutions for businesses. The company had the broadest portfolio of available solutions, with dozens of products meeting the diverse needs of functional groups across several industry vertical markets.

But, in fact, all that choice wasn't making life easier for Sprint's customers. As businesses recognized building mobility into their processes and services was becoming a competitive imperative, actually figuring out what they needed and how to implement it became daunting. Sprint's Advanced Wireless Solutions were designed to dramatically simplify the decision process and accelerate the implementation of mobility for these businesses.

Paul Deering, vice president of Advanced Wireless Solutions recognized that fewer was better. "By initially focusing on just the six challenges that are best solved with mobility solutions today, and then picking a short list of partners that consistently deliver the best results, we have amplified our impact many times over."

By limiting the number of mobility solutions, Sprint has developed deep expertise in those solutions and tight relationships with the software partners. This allows Sprint to tightly integrate the applications into its core operations, thoroughly test the solution with its chosen handsets across its network, and focus all of its resources on delivering a great experience for six right solutions.

Sprint's customers directly enjoy the benefits of this focus. Not only is the selection process simplified, Sprint has used its broad experience to pick the best software and the best handsets running over its powerful networks, but the application of that solution to the customer's unique needs is well served by Sprint's deep knowledge and close partnering for this select group of solutions.

By choosing to do a few things very well, Paul's team can also deliver an exceptional implementation and ongoing support experience that is critical to Sprint customers fully capturing the power of mobility.

FROM THE REAL WORLD (CONTINUED)

"In a big company like Sprint Nextel, saying 'no' can be hard," says Paul. "But we've learned that it takes discipline and focus to deliver a solution that's going to really make a difference for our customers."

Case Study

Sport Clips

I am not a big fan of getting my hair cut.

Having a stylish "do" is not high on my list of priorities (if you have seen me, it shows).

Getting my hair cut takes time, especially since I prefer the types of salons where you don't need an appointment and the value proposition is all about a decent cut at a low price. Sitting and waiting for my turn while flipping through some entertainment magazine looking for something interesting to pass the time is downright painful.

And then, finally, I get in the chair and the stylist wants to talk to me about my day. What's the deal? And what's that smelly stuff you're putting in my hair?

Thank goodness for the Sport Clips concept. Sport Clips provides high-quality haircuts in a fun sports environment, complete with TVs at every stylist's station tuned to sports. Every Sport Clips has "guy smart" stylists who focus on providing the highest level of service to every client.

Apparently, the concept resonates with more guys than just me. Sport Clips is one of America's fastest-growing franchises, with more than 400 locations in 33 states, and that number is doubling every year. In fact, one franchisee is planning on building 30 new Sport Clips stores in Las Vegas alone.[5]

However, since guys like me don't really care about our hair, Sports Clips will grow only if my experience is positive instead of painful so I will be willing to go out of my way and pay a little bit more for that experience. Each shop's business will grow or decline based on how well they manage that positive experience, but what I tell my buddies will also impact the brand and growth of the overall franchise.

"Our job is to ensure that guys that come into a Sport Clips store will get a quality haircut and have a great experience," notes Kerin Haney, vice president of field operations for Sport Clips.

The national Sport Clips brand stands for something, and poor performance by local stores can undermine that brand and quickly destroy the growth potential of the overall business.

Sport Clips clearly understands this dynamic and manages it closely. The company has 60 field district managers and coaches who regularly visit each shop to provide coaching and to ensure that franchise standards are being met so that clients' experiences support the brand. These field managers complete a lengthy site survey during each visit. Historically, this process has been paper based, with the field personnel mailing in completed survey forms.

As the company was evaluating options for equipping the field force with updated wireless devices, the timing seemed perfect to consider setting the new standard for franchise brand management by mobilizing the entire site survey process.

"Believe it or not, word of mouth moves even faster than we're growing," observes Clete Brewer, Sport Clips president. "When our folks in the field uncover a problem, we need to move quickly to resolve it."

Case Study (continued)

Sport Clips worked with Anyware Mobile Solutions to transform their paper-based process into a paperless application running on Palm Treo smart devices connected back to Anyware over the Sprint Nextel mobile broadband network. Anyware collects and compiles the data input by the field technicians and immediately sends out alert notifications via e-mail to key Sport Clips personnel.

As field managers move through the different stations within each store, they click off results of the survey. As soon as they are done, any combination of factors that indicate a problem is flagged for that field manager and reported back to headquarters. The field personnel can immediately begin working with the local "team leader" (the franchisee) to develop an action plan to resolve the issues.

The survey results are also captured in the Anyware database and are used to produce historical trend results on key metrics that can help identify developing issues before they can become significant problems that could damage the brand. Sport Clips has also been able to use this data to identify differences between stores and to translate those differences into standard best practices that can benefit all team leaders.

In addition to the immediacy of the reporting, Sport Clips has also benefited from the improved accuracy and efficiency that comes from not having to key in data at headquarters that has been collected on paper in the field. Field personnel can also attach electronic files, and all of the information gets integrated into the company's customer relationship management (CRM) system, enabling a much richer and timelier view of each franchisee and location.

As with any championship team, excellent execution and clear communication are keys to gaining a competitive advantage. The combination of Treo smart devices, mobile e-mail, and the mobilized site survey application have Sport Clips operating at the top of their game.

"Every entrepreneur has a choice," Clete notes. "Our franchisees have bet their life on our brand. By mobilizing our field interactions, we've dramatically increased the odds of that bet paying off for our franchise partners."

But mobilization has been a big bet for Sport Clips as well. To increase their odds, the company standardized on one device on one network, and they turned to an expert who has worked extensively with those technologies. Outsourcing the collection, tabulation, and reporting functions further simplified the overall deployment and increased the likelihood of success.

Of course, Clete clearly understands this model: "The great thing about the franchise model is that our franchisees can focus on a small set of decisions. They trust us to be experts in everything else, empowering them to succeed in running their business. It's been the same way with Sprint and Anyware. We know they're the experts and that they've spent years getting the devices, network, and application model working well together. We just need to focus on making our business a success."

And from the looks of it, Clete and team are hitting the ball out of the park!

Notes

1. http://en.wikipedia.org/wiki/Near_Field_Communication.

2. http://en.wikipedia.org/wiki/Rfid.

3. http://en.wikipedia.org/wiki/Zigbee.

4. http://www.wimaxforum.org/technology.

5. www.sportclips.com/about_us/press_box/pr201.asp. "A Cut Above the Rest," February 16, 2007, Las Vegas Business Press, Staff Report.

CHAPTER 10

Position
Select Your Target Markets, Customers, and Applications

Building mobility into your product, service, or process requires investment and introduces change for your employees and customers. That change may be embraced, or it may be rejected. Because of this uncertainty, and to limit your initial investment, it's wise to carefully select a limited initial deployment to gain experience, fine tune the mobile integration, and prove the business case for maximum success with minimum pain moving forward.

For these reasons, in selecting the initial target markets, customers, and applications for your move into mobility, it is critical to think in terms of three factors:

1. Risk

2. Reward

3. Replication

Risk

The old saying is "with the greater the risk, comes the greater reward," but we all know that's not always accurate. Great rewards are rarely gained without any risk, but a wise businessman will find ways to eliminate unnecessary risk and balance the necessary risk with the available rewards.

When mobilizing a product, service, or process, risk takes three primary forms. The most obvious is the risk that things just won't work when your customers and employees expect them to. We'll call this *performance risk*. The second very scary risk is that your mobilized product, service, or process will work perfectly, but your customers and employees will reject it. We'll call this *acceptance risk*. The third kind of risk is the best kind of all—*success risk*. Success risk represents the chance that your customers and employees will so strongly embrace your mobilized product, service, or process that they will demand that it expand where it works and what it encompasses faster than you can keep up, leading to frustration for them and stress on your operations for you.

Since eliminating these risks is likely impossible, the key is to evaluate them up front, making key decisions to limit the likelihood or impact of each type of risk, and actively monitoring and managing your mobility introduction to respond well if the risks become reality.

Let's start with performance risk. Carefully evaluate the potential sources of failure that can cause your newly mobilized product, service, or process to fail. The most obvious sources of failure will be any newly introduced components.

Are you adding in new pieces of hardware? How reliable are these components? Are there conditions under which they are more likely to fail than others? Is a component susceptible to failure from interference or weather conditions or long periods of continuous use? How difficult, expensive, and time consuming is it to replace a failed component? In choosing your initial implementation, what choices can you make to limit the likelihood of failure of each new hardware component? What choices can you make to accelerate and minimize the cost of fixing any failures? What choices can you make to minimize the impact on your customers and employees if there is a failure? Can you choose specific applications for specific target customers/employees in specific geographies that will both reduce the likelihood of failure of your new hardware components and minimize the impact of any such failure?

Are there software components in your new mobilized implementation? Is it possible to allow frequent updates of the software to fix diagnosed problems with minimal impact to the users? Can you choose specific applications for specific target customers/employees in specific geographies that will reduce the impact of software failures and increase the opportunity for painless software upgrades?

Are you reliant on communications networks as you mobilize your product, service, or process? Where do those networks operate most reliably? Under what conditions are they likely to fail? How well does your product, service, or process work if the network isn't working? For how long can it continue to be valuable between successful network connections? Will network failures be more noticeable and frustrating for different types of customers or employees? What decisions can you make to minimize the risk and impact of network failures? Can you use local data storage to ensure that your product, service, or process will still be valuable even when the network isn't working? Can you limit the geographies for your product, service, or process to increase the likelihood that the network will be available and reliable? Are there applications that are better suited to use local data storage when the network is down, but that will still benefit from mobilization when the network is active? Can you select target customers or employees who will be best suited to the anticipated reliability of the network?

Acceptance risk is much less scientifically managed than performance risk. Understanding how people will perform is inherently more challenging than understanding how hardware, software, and networks will perform.

Acceptance risk is best managed by carefully selecting initial target customers or employees, communicating with them well in advance of the coming changes, providing sufficient training for them to rapidly gain the benefits of mobility, and providing effective and timely support when they do encounter uncertainty or problems.

Consider the combination of hardware, software, and networking that you're introducing as you mobilize your product, service, or process. Are there target customers or employees who are already comfortable with these technologies or who have previously demonstrated openness to advances in these directions? Are there users who have proven willing to work with you in introducing new technologies and are therefore both willing and able to adapt, even through early performance challenges?

Are there target users, applications, or geographies that are better suited to the communications, training, and support tasks required to ensure successful acceptance and adoption? Is there a subset of potential users that are located where face-to-face communications, training, and support can easily and cost effectively be provided, increasing likely success? Are there target applications that would simplify the communications, training, and support efforts? By limiting the geographic reach of the mobilized product, service, or process, can you significantly increase your ability to provide timely and effective support to quickly resolve issues and concerns and increase the likelihood of acceptance?

Success risk shouldn't be shrugged off with an offhand statement like "That will be a good problem to have." Success risk must be carefully considered from the beginning and managed just as actively as other risks to your mobility implementation.

There are two fundamental approaches to managing success risk. The first is to be prepared to scale up when success hits and demand outpaces current capabilities. The second is to select initial implementations with dimensions of expansion that reduce the scale of expansion required.

Demand for expansion can come in any of several dimensions. Current users may desire that you expand the value of mobility into an increasing range of capabilities, products, services, or processes. They may desire that the mobilization work in a broader geography. Or additional customers or employees may demand that they have access to the successfully mobilized product, service, or process. And these new users may require slightly different applications in different geographies than your original target.

What would it take for you to scale in each of these dimensions? What preparation can you take to be prepared to quickly expand each dimension? Are their choices you can make in the technologies, components, and networks used in mobilizing your product, service, or process that would make it easier to scale up? When choosing suppliers, which suppliers are best prepared to support your potential future expansion? What can you do to prepare for potential expansion in manufacturing or support? What impact will potential geographic expansion have on your technology, component, network, supplier, manufacturing, and support decisions?

Once you understand what it takes to be prepared to scale in each of these dimensions, and which you can afford to put in place advanced preparation, you're better prepared to evaluate which initial target customers or employees, geographies, and applications expose you to the greatest likelihood to expand in areas where you are least prepared to scale. Can you choose initial users who have limited additional uses into which they will ask you to expand, or who have limited geographies they will expect you to cover? Which initial users and applications can limit the appeal to additional users who you are best positioned to expand to serve?

Taking into account each form of risk—performance risk, acceptance risk, and success risk—you should be able to develop a clear picture of the portfolio of risks as they associate to the potential target customers or employees, applications, and geographies that you could initially target with your newly mobilized product, service, or process.

Reward

Identifying the best target users, applications, and geographies shouldn't just be about managing risk. You must also consider the potential reward associated with these choices.

Your reward will likely take the form of some combination of profitability, share of decisions, and loyalty. For mobilized products and services, these rewards specifically are premium pricing, market share, and customer lifetime value. If your mobilization involves a service or process, profitability may also come from reduced operating costs, and share of decisions may include your attractiveness to potential employees, and loyalty extends to employee loyalty, yielding a variety of benefits to your business.

Within the context of managing performance, acceptance, and success risks, your choices for target customers, applications, and geographies will be selected based on opportunities to maximize market share, profitability, customer loyalty, employee attractiveness, and employee loyalty.

In choosing to maximize these rewards, you likely will consider the opportunity to clearly differentiate your product or service from competitors through mobilization, leading to the opportunity for premium pricing, to take market share, and to gain customer loyalty. You likely will also consider the opportunity to reduce costs, increasing profitability. Finally, you will also consider whether your new mobilized products, services, or processes appeal to your current and prospective employees, making it easier to hire and retain the talent you need for your business to be successful.

To fully maximize the rewards of your mobilization initiatives, you will want to achieve all of these benefits on the largest scale possible, supporting the largest possible collection of customers and employees with the broadest possible array of applications, across the most expansive geographic reach.

However, that, of course, flies in the face of managing the risk. Therefore, the right choices will balance the desire to maximize the reward while minimizing the associated risks.

Replication

Both of these desires, reducing initial risk and maximizing the reward, are well served by making choices that enable rapid replication.

Can you choose an initial set of customers or employees for your mobilization efforts that are well suited as a model for a much broader base, so once the implementation is reliable and supportable, it can quickly be expanded to many others?

Can you choose an initial geography that involves a set of regulatory, market, and technology conditions that make an excellent blueprint for replicating the implementation over time to new geographies? This may mean designing for the worst geographic environment and then knowing that "if it works here, it will work anywhere." Or it may mean designing for a cutting-edge environment that is setting the standards that the rest of the world is likely to follow. Both approaches are valid, but each obviously represents different timing and different levels of capability.

Can you choose an initial set of applications that can serve as a prototype from which many additional applications can quickly be supported by making relatively minor adjustments to the initial implementation? Is there a base application on which many other applications can be layered?

Wrapping It All Together

Taking all of these factors together, the key decisions you will make in your initial mobilization efforts include choosing which users (customers or employees) to initially target, for which applications of your product, service, or process, and in which geographies.

The right answer will depend somewhat on your tolerance for risk, but will be the combination that both minimizes your risks around performance and acceptance and that positions you to rapidly replicate your success to maximize the rewards that you reap.

Mobility creates tremendous opportunity to win in your industry by increasing your market share, increasing your profitability, and attracting and retaining the best talent. But, if you stumble with your first mobilization efforts in the wrong place in front of the wrong customers and employees in a way that is devastating to how they value your company, then your mobilization efforts will destroy value rather than create it.

Choose well!

FROM THE REAL WORLD

Laying a Firm Foundation

One of my side activities is work I do with Living Stones Ministry (www.lstones.com). Living Stones provides software building blocks that churches and other ministries can use to make their Web sites more dynamic and interactive.

Unlike most of the entities featured in this book, Living Stones had neither an existing base of organizations it was serving nor an existing set of services that it was offering. As a start-up ministry, it had the freedom to choose any offers to first bring to "market" and it did not have a base to "sell" into. The ministry could choose virtually any starting point—any target "market" and any initial set of applications—and grow from there.

Although the technologies that Living Stones is working with are not specifically mobility-centric, the thought processes, and the balancing of risk, reward, and replication are very similar to what you may face as you consider mobilizing your products, services, and processes.

Living Stones' model is to provide a software building block that provides a specific dynamic and interactive capability that can immediately create incremental value for a church's existing Web site. Living Stones faced the exact same three risks described in this chapter: performance risk, acceptance risk, and success risk.

Software products seem to attract bugs. Therefore, our expectation was that the software would face performance challenges. Our hope was that we would work through the most significant problems quickly with the first few "customers." From the beginning, we structured the product so that new versions could easily be downloaded and installed without a lot of reintegration required. However, we are currently on our third model for distribution. The first made it too difficult to notify users that a new version of software was available. The second required too much up-front registration work so it became a barrier to adoption. We're hoping we finally have found a balance between the two. In establishing the overall architecture, we knew that we needed to be prepared to fix performance problems in a way that would scale rapidly if we experienced tremendous success. This isn't any easier than it sounds, but we still believe it's essential to our ability to truly make an impact.

Acceptance risk has become a multiheaded beast that we haven't yet conquered. We made a number of up-front choices specifically to ease the adoption of the Living Stones software. We chose to use technologies that would be supported on the vast majority of Web hosting platforms that churches are likely to already be using, so technology isn't an issue. We chose to create a new open-source styled license with no licensing fees, so price isn't a barrier to adoption. We put intense focus into truly creating "building blocks" that are easy to add to an existing Web site so that complexity wouldn't become a barrier to adoption. All of those decisions have been essential to reducing the acceptance risk.

However, we've found that our current offers still require some knowledge of how to edit the files on the Web server and how to access a database system. For most church administrators, this is scary stuff! The folks who have been willing to try the Living Stones software have proven to be technically competent individuals. Unfortunately, most technically competent folks aren't necessarily attracted to the simplicity and "building block" model represented by Living Stones offers. Many of them would rather struggle through trying to build the same capabilities themselves than drop in a building block we've provided. Obviously, there are plenty of churches that have technically competent Web support folks who are happy to implement what we've provided, but needing to find that "middle ground" market has been an acceptance risk that we hadn't originally anticipated.

We managed the success risk from the beginning by building the product for easy replication. As a zero-income nonprofit, we've had to ensure automation and plug-and-play success to create any meaningful value.

The reward equation is dramatically different for a nonprofit than it is for a corporation. Our reward is not measured in profitability, but we do hope that many churches and ministries will choose our solution and will continue to use and derive value from it for years to come.

The two key decisions we made early in the start-up of Living Stones were to pick two key applications we would initially deliver and to pick one church that we would work closely with as a "beta-test" customer to refine the product and our processes.

FROM THE REAL WORLD (CONTINUED)

The two applications we targeted were a Bible interface and a sermon database. Christian churches base their authority and their ministry on the Bible, so it is only natural for a church Web site to include the ability to read and search the scriptures. However, from our personal experience, we knew that it was very difficult to add this functionality to a church Web site. In short, there was almost universal pent-up demand for this capability on church Web sites.

Similarly, most churches have a desire to enable their sermon content to have an impact beyond the half hour it is heard in the church sanctuary and even beyond the life impact it has on those sitting in the pews that Sunday morning. A growing number of churches have figured out how to add sermon notes and audio files to their Web sites, but it's generally not easy and it's even harder to maintain these files over time. Therefore, we believed that these two applications would provide nearly universal appeal, enabling us to have the greatest impact as church after church replicates these applications into their Web sites. These choices have proven to be well directed.

In choosing a single church to start with as a "beta" site, we wanted one that placed high value on the capabilities of their Web site, that especially valued our two target applications, that had the right technical capabilities to make it work, and that was open to implementing something new like Living Stones. It turns out that my local church, Oak Hills Presbyterian (www.oakhillspca.com) was a perfect candidate. The original Web site design by Toby Becker and John Burke was both progressive and based on the same technologies Living Stones relied on, so adding in the Living Stones building blocks did not encounter any acceptance barriers. The two pastors, Russ Ramsey and Jon Dunning, are both young men with a strong appreciation for modern technology, so they both embraced the new Bible and sermon capabilities, but also became active supporters of Living Stones, providing exactly the kind of input and feedback necessary of a beta customer.

FROM THE REAL WORLD (CONTINUED)

In the case of Living Stones, with zero advertising budget, that first customer also became the marketing platform—using it as a visible example when approaching other churches to serve and reaching out to others through the personal network of pastors that Russ and Jon had developed.

In short, those early decisions have proven foundational to the ongoing success of Living Stones Ministry.

Case Study

Montclair State University

Have you heard of Montclair State University? Many haven't yet, but it is New Jersey's second largest university with over 16,000 students on a 246-acre campus just 14 miles from New York City.

The school, like many universities today, was facing a widening communications challenge. Today's students are more connected than any previous generation. A typical freshman shows up with a cell phone he's had for years, a Web mail address all of his friends have memorized, and instant message and text message accounts that keep his fingers flying almost nonstop throughout the day.

In other words, most students have fully embraced mobile communications and need no help from the university in getting reconnected. Although the university provides telephones in the residence halls and e-mail accounts for all students, the kids would rather use the cell phones and Web mail accounts they know and love. They rarely use the dorm phones and don't bother checking their school e-mail accounts.

CASE STUDY (CONTINUED)

So, although today's students are more connected than ever before, they are shunning the communications channels provided by the university and on which schools have relied in getting critical information out to students. Short of showing up at a student's dorm room at 7 A.M., there's no way to ensure that a student receives critical academic, community, or emergency information.

Since universities are always resource constrained, spending budget dollars and staff time to maintain a phone system that students won't use proves increasingly hard to justify.

To overcome these challenges, Montclair State University turned to Sprint Nextel and Rave Wireless to implement an innovative wireless solution that perfectly fits students' lifestyles, addresses the school's communications and budget challenges, and greatly enhances the University's ability to engage its students and improve their living and learning experience.

"Communications are at the center of any modern university," notes Dr. Susan A. Cole, president of Montclair State University. "Students are used to universities being one step behind them. With our Campus Connect mobile phone program, we're one step ahead of them and it's created an interesting cultural shift."

Typically, universities feature grand buildings built to serve generations of students. These robust structures weren't built with wireless signal penetration in mind. Therefore, campuses are plagued with coverage dead spots, often in the areas where communications could be most valuable. As students have increasingly adopted mobile phones as their primary communications tool, universities, like Montclair State, have found the need to partner with a carrier to ensure excellent coverage everywhere and to better connect faculty and staff to the students using wireless technologies. Frost & Sullivan estimates that university spending on wireless voice and data services will more than double between 2006 and 2009.[1]

Sprint Nextel has built out the wireless infrastructure on the Montclair State campus to ensure that students always have reliable coverage. Students use Sprint Nextel phones and service even as they leave campus and travel home to their families. Montclair designed the program to provide the commuter population with a virtual on-campus experience through the Campus Connect device. The Sprint Nextel solution also provides the unified messaging platform that the university needed. Depending on the urgency of the message, university officials can immediately communicate with everyone on campus via text message, e-mail, and/or voice mail.

Dr. Karen L. Pennington, vice president for student development and campus life, observes, "the quality of the student's experience is extremely important. Students who are happy and connected to an institution are integrated into the environment. After many years of research, we know that those are the students who do well academically and succeed better socially. Campuses that have students who connect, they connect not just in the short term, but they connect in the long term; they connect as alumni which helps improve alumni giving."

The biggest challenge is truly connecting. Students show up with a cellphone in their pocket. Why would they change to a phone provided by the school? Without broad student adoption, Montclair State University would never achieve its objectives. Three keys to driving adoption at Montclair State have been number portability so students can stay in touch with their friends, the excellent wireless coverage across the entire campus, and the suite of mobile applications and content provided by Sprint Nextel and Rave Wireless.

"We decided to launch the mobile phone program at Montclair State to actually create a situation for students to become much more engaged with their peers and with the faculty and have ready access to the various services we provide," recalls Dr. Edward Chapel, chief information officer, Montclair State University. "Choosing the small number of applications that have fully engaged students into the virtual and on-campus experience has been critical to student acceptance and even enthusiasm."

Students love many of the applications that are available to all customers on Sprint Nextel's network. Push-to-talk is a great fit with the campus lifestyle, and the opportunity to customize the phone with features like hip ring tones goes a long way toward making students comfortable moving to a new device. Additionally, Rave has created a suite of applications specific to the campus environment.

Dr. Chapel's team surveyed students to identify the applications of greatest interest to students. They initially launched a trial involving 200 users (students and faculty) to prove the value of the solution. And the university and its partners have been very responsive to new requests and ideas from students. The most heavily used applications to date are the BlackBoard Course Management Service and applications that provide basic community-building features such as a student directory integrated with the phone's calling, texting, and e-mailing features, user-generated content publishing, and group management.

The cell phone then moves into the classroom. Montclair State University wireless users can tap straight into the course management software that drives the university's academic programs. Instructors can also easily communicate with students and even use phones for in-class polling. A wide array of campus information, from class schedules to dining hall menus to shuttle bus schedules are all available to students through their phones.

But the two applications that have really driven broad adoption are the shuttle bus tracker and the Mobile Guardian feature. Campus shuttle buses are tracked via GPS signals. Students love the fact that they can monitor the bus location and keep studying (or developing important lifetime social skills) to the very last minute before rushing out to catch the bus.

Students and parents both love that a student can set a tracking timer for anywhere from a few minutes to a few hours through the Mobile Guardian. The system tracks their location and if they don't deactivate the tracker before the timer expires, the campus police will call them to make sure they are okay and will know their precise location if there's any problem.

"It is important for students to know that they are safe and comfortable in their environment, but I would say it is even more important for the parents," remarks Dr. Pennington. "The Mobile Guardian feature allows a student to send an alert in a passive mode to the police station that they have activated Guardian and they want to be tracked. They want people to know where they are."

Campus safety is one of the top criteria parents use in evaluating a university. Academic capabilities and social opportunities certainly also play a critical role as students choose where they want to spend four years preparing for the rest of their lives.

To ensure overall success, the program had to first gain the acceptance and adoption of students. That required intense focus on community and safety features that appeal much more strongly to students than the rest of the university community.

"This is a journey. At the outset we were very concerned with providing a network with the quality of service and capacity to support our rapidly expanding population of users. In hindsight, I wish we'd invested more time getting key faculty and support team members fully on board from the beginning of the journey," Dr. Chapel notes. "These mobile devices have the potential to be powerful tools in the learning environment. We have created a plateau from which we intend to greatly expand the use of this technology as an integral part of the campus curriculum. We have very creative professors who I'm confident will find new ways to unleash the power of mobility in preparing our students for the future."

By building mobility into all critical aspects of what they offer, Montclair State University has differentiated itself from other universities and started to redefine how higher education operates.

"It is a good feeling to know that your university is paving the way for something that I think will ultimately become part of the culture of higher education across the country," concludes Dr. Cole.

Have you heard of Montclair State University? Many haven't, but they will. The school's innovative approaches to creating a richer, safer, and more connected campus experience have contributed to their position as New Jersey's fastest growing university.

Note

1. "U.S. Education Vertical Telecom Services Markets," Frost & Sullivan, 2006.

CHAPTER 11

Protect
Manage the Danger
of Moblity

T he previous chapters describe how businesses can capture the power of mobility to create tremendous differentiation as mobility gets built into every product, service, and process. As noted there, capturing the power of mobility will be full of challenges. In some respects, these challenges can be viewed as dangers of mobility to be managed.

However, this chapter deals with more mundane dangers that all companies will face as mobility becomes integrated into how we do business. Whether or not a company chooses to capture the power of the new technology, it will need to manage the danger. Even businesses that fail to use mobility to lead their industries in creating differentiation eventually will need to adopt mobility to close the gap created by their competitors.

What Are These Dangers?

An entire book could be written on the dangers that we can already see from mobility. Unfortunately, new dangers will emerge as mobility is increasingly integrated into how we live and work, so this chapter should not be viewed as a comprehensive checklist against which you should manage your mobility risk. However, history also gives us a solid foundation for understanding the general areas of challenge that businesses will face.

In short, we should be prepared to manage three key interrelated classes of danger:

1. Data security
2. Financial exposure
3. Third-party claims

Data Security

Perhaps the greatest danger related to mobility is that mobile devices are, well, mobile. They go everywhere. And sometimes they don't come back. Mobile devices, including cell phones, smart phones, and laptop computers are attractive targets for thieves because they are, by design, easy to carry away. But these devices are also small enough that they can easily slip out of a pocket, purse, or briefcase without being noticed. And honestly, we're human and sometimes we just forget to pick them up after we've set them down.

According to a research report from Pointsec Mobile Technologies, 8,701 electronic devices were left in taxicabs in the Washington, D.C.–Baltimore area during a six-month period in 2006. Over 6,000 of these devices were mobile phones. Eighty percent were eventually reunited with their owners. Another 339 laptops were left in cabs in the Washington-Baltimore area, all of which found their way home.[1]

London travelers apparently are less diligent in tracking down their lost devices. According to another Pointsec study, around five laptops and ten mobile phones are handed in at Heathrow Airport each day, most of which were simply forgotten at security checkpoints. Only 60% of these devices are reclaimed by their owners. After three months, the devices are sold at auction. By Pointsec's math, that translates into 730 laptops and 1,460 mobile phones auctioned off each year. Imagine the wealth of sensitive competitive information being auctioned off by Heathrow each year![2]

The danger to companies from these lost and stolen devices is twofold. On one hand, many mobile devices store important company information that could damage your business or help a competitor. Mark Komisky, chief executive of Bluefire Security Technologies Inc., was quoted by the *Washington Post* describing his panic when he lost his smart phone. The device stored e-mails, details of his company's strategy, and phone numbers of executives at Bluefire's most strategic partners. Thankfully, as a security company, Bluefire had put in place the mechanisms to remotely erase the information from the device.[3]

Wired magazine reported on a BlackBerry that had been owned by a Morgan Stanley vice president of mergers and acquisitions that was sold on eBay. The buyer had full access to the address book of Morgan Stanley executives and clients, debt-restructuring strategies for specific companies, e-mails on preliminary talks for potential merger deals, financial spreadsheets, and other documents that, at the very least, could inform a competitor's understanding of how Morgan Stanley conducts its business.[4]

The second threat from these lost or stolen devices is the configuration information that the device owner uses to connect securely into corporate networks. Even if the new owner of the device can't access any sensitive information stored on the device, they may be able to access your networks and find a way to access confidential information stored elsewhere in your business.

When dealing with mobile network users, the process should follow the policies that have developed over the years for any user connecting into the network. The first step is authentication—are you who you say you are? The second step is interrogation to determine whether the connecting device represents any type of threat—are the security policy requirements met and is the device free of viruses and other malware. Based on that information, a decision can be made as to whether any issues can be remedied and what level of access will be allowed.

Another major area of threat to data security comes from criminals tapping into your networks without using a lost or stolen device. Network hacking is not a new profession, so many of the tools developed over the years to defend against attacks, detect them when they occur, and to limit the exposure from an attack are just as valuable for wireless networks. However, wireless networks also represent new forms of threat. Wireless messages passing through the air to and from your employees' devices can theoretically be intercepted, and even the data flowing across wired networks from mobile employees are at risk, for example when connecting through a public WiFi access point or when connecting through a hotel's network. Employees need to be kept informed as network hackers move beyond today's tricks, like WiFi spoofing, into new areas of deception.

Use of a mobile virtual private network (VPN), including encryption of data to the device can go a long way toward securing your sensitive information that is flying through the air.

Mobility also introduces new data security threats through the proliferation of camera phones into the workplace. In all businesses, across all technology eras, the greatest security threats have come from those we trust—employees and partners—those who walk through our doors each day and have access to sensitive information. Camera phones represent a new tool for trusted criminals to walk out the door with our secrets. Maintaining control and visibility over the mobile devices in use by employees is a good first step toward minimizing this threat.

Financial Exposure

Of course, any of the risks associated with data security threats can easily translate into financial exposure, but mobility also introduces new forms of expense into the business.

The most obvious new expenses are from mobile devices and the service plans to keep your employees connected. U.S. wireless carriers currently heavily subsidize most mobile devices in exchange for long-term commitments to use a given carrier's service, but even if you negotiate for a heavy subsidy, smart phones that are best positioned to deliver the power of mobility for your employees likely will cost several hundred dollars apiece. It's also not unusual for monthly voice and data service fees per employee to be in the $50 to $100 range or perhaps even higher for your most mobile communications–intensive workers.

You may think that you've got it easy if employees are already using their personal mobile devices to do their work. It might appear that you're getting the benefits of mobility without having to pay for them. However, I'm guessing that at least some of those employees are expensing back their mobility costs to the company. These somewhat invisible costs are even more dangerous since they are unmanaged and can't benefit from the negotiating power of your entire firm. Even worse, the devices and connections likely are also unmanaged, opening the company up to mostly invisible security risks. Carefully consider the costs and benefits of each approach before assuming that the status quo is financially attractive.

In addition to the basic mobile communications device, you likely will also consider enabling your workforce with applications that are specifically suited to increasing their productivity in their jobs. Depending on the application, purchasing and deploying these applications will likely incur up-front costs and may also have ongoing recurring charges. Undoubtedly, in deploying these applications, you will have evaluated the business case and have justified the additional expense, but these costs do represent new incremental items that likely haven't previously been in your budget.

Finally, be sure to plan for your own internal staff needs to support a newly mobilized workforce. What you have traditionally called *desktop support* and *network support* will now take on entirely new responsibilities that likely will require additional headcount and cross-training in new technologies and applications.

And keep in mind that mobile technology is advancing rapidly, so you should plan for a shorter refresh cycle than you currently enjoy with PCs and other assets. You may be able to squeeze two years of use for handsets for most of your employees, but power users may need to be upgraded every year.

To get a sense for the impact of these types of technology changes, J. Gold Associates analyzed the costs associated with switching from one mobile e-mail system to another. Their analysis concluded that the cost of switching was $845 per user, with the cost split evenly between information technology (IT) infrastructure and end-user deployment costs.[5]

Beyond your IT budget, mobilizing your workforce also introduces financial risk in the form of lost productivity. Workers who previously relied on paper-driven processes may have been less efficient, but their pens and pads worked everywhere, all the time. Unfortunately, the same cannot be said for mobile technology. Device and network failures can cause your team members to be stuck, sitting idle waiting for a replacement or the network to recover instead of being able to do their jobs.

Other threats to employee productivity include the temptation to play games or surf the mobile Internet (remember the early days of Windows as workers discovered Solitaire and when the Mosaic browser opened new worlds for employees to explore), and interruptions that come now that your employees can be reached anytime, anywhere for both business and personal needs. Obviously, this is more of a management challenge than a technology challenge, and these issues will be more of a problem for some employees than others, but don't overlook the need to actively incorporate these new challenges into your management team's supervisory and coaching activities.

Finally, mobile devices are increasingly becoming targets for malware—software intended to do damage. Mobile viruses, worms, Trojan horse programs, and spyware are beginning to show up on mobile devices. These pests invade using the same tricks that PC crackers have used in the Internet era—getting installed with "free" software, riding along with e-mail attachments, and sneaking in through infected Web pages. But mobility represents a new threat as well, with some viruses spreading through the Bluetooth connections most typically turned on for cordless headsets. All of the major vendors of PC-based antivirus software are introducing mobile products to help ward off attacks.

And these attacks can be expensive. In addition to lost productivity for the handset owner, IT resources are often consumed cleaning up the mess. Critical data may be lost. And some attacks result in a significant increase in network traffic, resulting in financial exposure for network fees.

Third-Party Claims

The final area of danger closely follows from the risks to data security and financial exposure. Mobility can open your firm to new forms of third-party claims against your company and new flavors of old third-party claims.

Following directly from the threat of data loss when a mobile device is lost or stolen is the liability that comes from your firm's failure to properly protect that data. The list of companies and government entities that have been exposed to the possibility of significant third-party claims continues to grow. Just as a sample, here's a list of events from May and June 2006:

- U.S. Department of Veterans Affairs lost a laptop containing personal information on 26.5 million veterans and active-duty soldiers.
- New York state government lost a laptop with 540,000 names.
- Ernst & Young Global Ltd. lost a laptop with 243,000 names.

- YMCA of Greater Providence, Rhode Island, lost a laptop with 68,000 names.

- ING Groep NV lost a laptop with 13,000 names.

- Equifax Inc. lost a laptop with 291 names.

In each of these cases, data was lost that could contribute to the growing problem of identity theft. Because of these potential liabilities, the costs associated with a lost device are significantly higher than just the price of a replacement. At least 35 states have passed laws placing additional burdens on companies that have a security breach that involves personal information.

Every year, the Computer Security Institute with participation from the San Francisco Federal Bureau of Investigation's Computer Intrusion Squad conducts a survey of computer security practitioners in U.S. corporations, government agencies, financial and medical institutions, and universities. The 2006 survey included 616 responses. While the percentage of respondents reporting laptop or mobile theft held relatively flat at 47%, the losses increased by more than half from $19,562 per respondent to $30,057 from 2005 to 2006.[6]

Such data security failures can also trigger regulatory violations including the Health Insurance Portability and Accountability Act (HIPAA), Gramm-Leach-Bliley, and Sarbanes-Oxley. For example, HIPAA clearly states that patient data must be protected against unauthorized disclosure with penalties for failure to adequately protect that data.

But even new forms of third-party claims are emerging, and these are coming from the very employees that are being empowered with mobile technology. The fact that mobile technology enables us to work anywhere, anytime has led to us working everywhere and all the time. This creates a variety of potential dangers.

A recent article in Britain's *The Independent* reported on three such dangers that have translated into employee lawsuits. In one, a business consultant is suing her employer for damages because she was constantly checking her BlackBerry for messages, which led to her marriage collapsing and her losing custody of her children. In a second case cited by the paper, a woman sued her employer because she was so distracted by her BlackBerry that she put cleaning fluid on her baby's diaper instead of baby oil. And in a third case, a company ended up paying substantial damages to an employee who was using her BlackBerry while driving, resulting in a crash that killed a motorcyclist.[7]

Obviously, in each of these tragic cases, the primary fault is with the employee, but as we push mobile technology onto our employees and raise our expectations of their availability, responsiveness, and performance, lawsuits such as these are sure to follow. Teaching managers to restrain their expectations is an important step, but official policies that employees may sign up to as they are empowered with mobile technology can also be an important tool in managing your firm's liability.

Policies can also play an important role in keeping employees happy in the workplace. As cell phones have become increasingly media capable, new risks and challenges have emerged. Perhaps the most openly discussed is the challenge of personally selected ringtones. According to a workplace survey by staffing company Randstad USA, 30% of employees listed cell phones ringing as one of their top workplace pet peeves.[8] Some companies have established policies requiring cell phones to be set to vibrate in the workplace to combat this contributor to worker stress.

However, the topic that may be even more dangerous to companies deals with pornography and other content that can create a hostile environment for employees. Employees every day are carrying into the workplace personal devices with multimedia capabilities that exceed what many of them go home to in their private homes every night. This opportunity to take personal content wherever they go can create new challenges for employers as we strive to maintain a healthy and productive workplace.

Taming the Dangers

Two critical steps are required to keep the potential dangers of mobility from bankrupting your company.

The first is to update your company policies to reflect the new realities of the mobility age. Employees need clear guidance on what they can and can't do to keep your business out of trouble. Policies should address the dangers represented in this chapter:

- Protecting company assets and data.

- Ensuring secure mobile access to company networks.

- Minimizing expenses related to devices, service plans, applications, and associated infrastructure.

- Effectively receiving support needed to maintain productivity.

- Minimizing personal and nonproductive use of mobile devices during work hours.

- Restricting the use of mobile devices while driving.

- Appropriately limiting expectations for work-related activities beyond normal work hours.

- Reducing ringtone-induced workplace stress.

- Controlling mobile content in the work environment.

Of course, policies are useless if no one knows about them. Ensure that every employee agrees to your mobility policies when they are issued and that every new employee agrees to them as they join the company.

The second critical step is to ensure that you have established an effective support infrastructure so that you are getting the full benefit of your investment in mobilizing your business. This includes establishing a knowledgeable support staff that is able to respond to workers who are trying to be productive anywhere, anytime. It includes putting in place the hardware and software infrastructure required to manage the security and reliability of your mobile assets. It includes a commitment to ongoing monitoring of new technology advances and the willingness to refresh your infrastructure as mobility continues to advance.

This is a big commitment. Especially in these early days of mobility, it's probably worth considering outsourcing to experts for at least part of the deployment or ongoing support.

In any case, managing all of the dangers of mobility may sound expensive, and in reality may represent significant new expenditures. These costs should be factored into your overall evaluation of the value of mobilizing your products, services, and processes. When balanced against the value created by mobility, these costs may not seem so expensive.

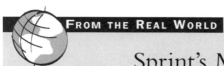

FROM THE REAL WORLD

Sprint's Mobility Management Services

The following content is provided by Sprint Nextel, Inc.

Sprint Mobility Management is an award-winning suite of managed services that allows your company to securely manage the wireless devices, data, rate plans, and user profiles throughout your enterprise. The suite is comprised of three primary sets of options: Billing Management, Device Management, and Security Management.

BILLING MANAGEMENT

A billing analytics service that provides a robust, easy-to-use Web portal to manage mobile communications. Billing Management enables businesses to:

- Control wireless spending:
  - Consolidated view of accounts and expenses.
  - Visibility of corporate wireless plan by user profile and department, including trending, usage and overage expenses.
  - Enforce and monitor expense policies.

DEVICE MANAGEMENT

Device Management offers businesses the ability to manage multi-carrier mobile devices via a self-service Web portal. Device Management enables business to:

- Manage devices from multiple carriers:
  - Manage multiple user configurations and profiles.
  - Synchronize data, files, and applications.

- ○ Deploy software updates.
- ○ View software and hardware inventory.
- ○ Backup and restore files and applications.
- ○ Push all functions Over the Air (OTA).

SECURITY MANAGEMENT

Sprint Mobile Security provides end-to-end security for laptops and handheld devices. Mobile Security enables businesses to:

- Enforce corporate compliance:
  - ○ Manage devices, data, and security policies from a single Web portal.
  - ○ Update noncompliant programs with automatic remediation.
- Secure corporate data:
  - ○ Flexible security with device "kill" or "lock."
  - ○ Enforce password policies across all devices.
  - ○ Encrypt data on mobile devices and memory cards.
  - ○ Allow users to securely connect to the corporate intranet.
- Prevent internal and external threats:
  - ○ Monitor and control network access.
  - ○ Detect and automatically protect against viruses, worms, and malicious code.

CUSTOMER CARE

At Sprint, we provide multiple levels of support allowing you to define exactly how much control you have over your mobile environment. Customer Care includes:

- Multicarrier support for multiple devices.
- Premium level of support available 24/7.
- 24-hour fulfillment for Sprint phones.

FROM THE REAL WORLD (CONTINUED)

- Self-care Web portal.
- Reporting and activity logs.

Case Study

AllState GES

AllState GES, an appliance distribution and installation company in the Phoenix area, is focused on delivering good products at a great price when the customer needs them.

That mission requires a three-way focus on quality, cost, and time management that can be hard to balance. To help make those goals become a reality, AllState turned to Xora, a mobility software company. By installing Xora's TimeTrack software on their employees' cell phones, AllState can track the location and project-specific activities of their team members.

When it comes to a quality installation, proper site preparation is critical. AllState clearly communicates to its customers the required condition of the site for a successful project. When AllState installers arrive on-site, they type into their phone the job number, clocking into the project. They also key in any conditions on the job site such as existing damage or any issues with site readiness. Using the camera built into their phone, they can also attach photos further documenting issues. These records not only are helpful in quickly resolving disputes with contractors, but in educating their customers in what is required for a successful job that lives up to AllState's quality standards.

As the AllState installers leave a job site, they clock out of the project, creating very accurate records of the time required for each

CASE STUDY (CONTINUED)

project. These records help the company to improve performance of the work force, reducing overall costs. But an even greater cost savings has been realized in the communications between the mobile workers and the AllState office. Prior to deploying the Xora software, drivers and installers would regularly call in to report their location and job status. Since automating with Xora, the number of calls to the office have been cut to less than half, saving an hour or two of telephone time each day.

"The time savings have been tremendous, but the biggest benefit to Xora is in customer service," said AllState dispatcher Jackie McCarter. "Prior to Xora we could tell customers their appliances would be delivered that day; now we can say in a two to three hour window."

That precision comes from the real-time information the office has on the mobile workers' location and job status. Jackie and her teammates can see where each installation team is at any time on a Web-based map, and can view the comments being typed by field workers through a Web-based reporting tool, enabling the company to not only deliver appliances when their customers need them, but to predict that delivery time with great precision.

Quality service, when you need it, at a competitive cost. Isn't that what all of us want from our suppliers? By mobilizing their workforce, AllState has managed to step up their performance on all three competitive dimensions. Their customers have got to love that!

Notes

1. Pointsec press release. 2006. "New Survey Reveals Thousands of Mobile Devices Left Behind in Major U.S. City Taxi Cabs,"

November 28, www.pointsec.com/news/newsreleases/release
.cfm?PressId=386.

2. Pointsec press release. 2006. "40% of Mobiles Left at Airports This
Summer Will Never Be Reclaimed," August 31, www.pointsec
.com/news/newsreleases/release.cfm?PressId=313.

3. "Lost a Blackberry? Data Could Open a Security Breach."
Washington Post, July 25, 2005, p. A01.

4. Zetter, Kim. 2003. "BlackBerry Reveals Bank's Secrets." *Wired
News,* August 25, www.wired.com/news/business/1,600520
.html.

5. J. Gold Associates press release. 2006. "J. Gold Associates Releases
Report on the High Cost of Change in Wireless E-mail," January
13, www.jgoldassociates.com.

6. CSI/FBI Computer Crime and Security Survey, 2006.

7. Goodchild, Sophie, and Martin Hodgson. 2006. "CrackBerry
Addicts: Why the Workers Who Can't Switch Off Are Suing
Their Employers," *The Independent,* October 1, http://news
.independent.co.uk/world/science_technology/article1777821.ece.

8. Randstad USA press release. 2006. "Loud Talkers among Biggest
Workplace Pet Peeves, According to Randstad Survey," March 14,
http://us.randstad.com/webapp/internet/servlet/News?id=53.

CHAPTER 12

Learn from Your Customers

I f you've taken the steps described so far in this book, you're on a great path toward capturing the power of mobility, and you're already creating new value for your customers and translating that power into value for your employees and owners. That's great!

But, almost definitely, you still haven't captured the full power of mobility for your customers. In reality, you simply can't know how your customers and employees are going to change their behaviors once you take the first steps into mobility.

But that's not a bad thing.

It's critical to take the first steps. But it's at least as critical that you do not stop there, but rather that you learn from your customers how to make your mobilized product, service, or process even more powerful!

Sounds easy enough.

But, unfortunately, listening to customers is a skill that does not come naturally to most of us. Really listening and really learning from your customers will require intense focus and likely will require significant changes in your business.

Can you remember the last time you made a specific change in your business because of a specific comment from a specific customer? Sure, most of us do customer surveys and we use those generalized results to guide decisions we make about products and pricing and perhaps how we interact with our customers. But, as we'll discuss, survey percentages do not really teach us the innovative ways that our customers are taking our products to the next level.

Can you remember the last time you made a specific recommendation to a company you do business with and actually saw the resulting change? I can't. In fact, most of us rarely bother providing constructive input because we come to accept the fact that it never does any good.

Can we break that cycle?

It's hard on both sides, but I would argue that it is well worth it. It's hard for us to change our companies to be good at listening to customers and acting on their recommendations. And it's hard to get our customers to actually start giving us input with the confidence that it will make a difference.

So, how can you make the change?

I suggest that learning from your customers requires that you achieve three imperatives and that you pursue those imperatives through three progressive levels of learning from your customers.

The Three Imperatives

The three imperatives are:

1. Make it easy.

2. Make it count.

3. Pay it back.

Make It Easy

If we want to learn from our customers, we need to be willing to go to them. We need to respect what they can teach us and eliminate all barriers to their fully sharing with us what we need to learn. In the different levels of learning, this will take on different meanings, as we will see through the rest of this chapter.

Make It Count

The reason most of us never provide input to companies is that we doubt it will really make a difference. If we truly want to learn from our customers, and if we want to change the attitude of those customers toward helping us learn, then we need to do something meaningful with what they tell us. We need to make their input count. If they recommend changes to our product or service, we need to seriously consider those changes. It's as simple as that.

Pay It Back

Customer insights are valuable. We need to reward our customers for sharing them with us. Again, this takes different shapes for the different levels of learning, but we need to "pay" for the value they are creating—perhaps in the form of acknowledging their input or perhaps in more tangible forms, such as discounts and free add-ons.

The Levels of Learning

The three levels of learning are:

1. Listen
2. Engage
3. Employ

Listen

How easy do you make it for customers to give you unsolicited input on how your product or service could be improved? Do you force them to conform to your way of interacting, or will you "come to their house" and accept their feedback on their terms?

If they are most comfortable doing business through the Internet, how easy is it to provide feedback through your Web site? If there's a friendly form, is it easy to find? Is it easy for them to find an e-mail address that clearly communicates that at that address you welcome product or service ideas and feedback?

How easy is it to find a phone number where customers can call you? When they call, how frustrating is their experience? Is one of their first options the opportunity to provide you with product or service input? Is there an option to actually talk to a knowledgeable person about your products or services? Do you limit the hours when calls are accepted to hours that may be inconvenient for your customer?

Your answers to these questions may indicate that you are loudly telling your customers that you have no interest in learning from them. You do not want to hear what they have to say. Or your answers may indicate that you are listening with open ears and an open mind.

Even if you have made it easy for your customers to tell you what they think, do you make their input count? Who sees or hears what your customers tell you? Do you ever make changes based on input from your customers?

In a recent Harvard Business School *Working Knowledge* article, HBS professor Frances X. Frei identified Intuit, the financial software company, as an example of a company that makes their customers' input count. At Intuit, the customer service department resides within product development and the people fielding customer service calls take the input they receive directly to the software engineers developing the next generation of Intuit software. Intuit pays higher wages for their customer service staff to attract a different type of individual and to recognize that they are expected to do more than just open trouble tickets. The end result is higher product satisfaction and fewer but more valuable calls from customers.[1]

As another example, Mark Federman of the University of Toronto, in a speech to the Conference Board of Canada, cited a drug store chain that provided immediate responsiveness to the feedback from customers. "For instance, one of the callers to one store noted that the aspirin was on too high a shelf for her—she was short, and her arthritis prevented her from reaching up. The very next day, the aspirin was relocated to a lower shelf. That's value."[2]

It does you no good to pretend to listen to your customers but then do nothing with what they tell you, or simply bury their input into a generalized statistical result that gets broadly shared every few months.

Your product or service will not reach its full potential and your customer's cynicism will increase.

So, how do you pay customers for simply telling you what they want? For starters, truly listen. Unfortunately, in today's marketplace, so few companies are willing to listen that for customers that really care and are willing to share, finding a company willing to listen and take customers seriously is reward enough. But then, follow-through on what they say and keep them informed of progress. At the end of the day, your final update to the customer may say, "Thank you for your input. Your ideas will undoubtedly shape our future offers as we continue in our mission to deliver the best products and services in the industry. However, we have completed evaluation of your specific product idea and we are unable to justify the investment in this particular capability at this time. Please continue to share your challenges and your dreams with us. We value your partnership and your business."

Even though that message may indicate a disappointing specific outcome, more importantly it communicates that you truly value your customer's input and that you took their input seriously. Unfortunately, there are few companies that will similarly interact with their customers.

Engage

But listening is just the first step. Actively engaging with customers in an ongoing dialog creates an even richer environment for you to learn from them.

Sprint Nextel recently launched a Web site called Buzz About Wireless (www.buzzaboutwireless.com) intended to provide a comfortable place for customers to share their experiences, good and bad, and engage with other customers and with the company. The site provides forums where folks can talk about what they love and hate about Sprint's products and services, where they can ask questions and expect a more useful and meaningful answer than official documentation, and where they can express their desires for how they wish the company and its products to develop.

Tristan Kime, the Sprint customer experience and community manager who managed the launch of the site, acknowledges that it can be risky offering to engage with customers in a new way. "If we aren't responsive in the way that folks in online forums expect, then we can do more damage than good."

This difference was amplified in the first few days after the site launched. A customer asked in the public forums a question about the company's network plans in his state. A well-meaning Sprint employee responded with the standard company answer. Immediately, other community participants slammed the company for providing a "boilerplate" response and not truly engaging the customer's need.

Tristan and his team immediately corrected the mistake and reminded everyone helping out that engaging with customers in this way is more than just business as usual.

"We're hearing lots of good ideas from customers. One of the challenges is that evaluating the merits of each idea within our business takes time, so we have to manage customers' expectations and keep the dialog and information flowing," Tristan notes.

The Sprint team found that launching the site wasn't that hard or expensive, compared to the value of the input, feedback, and engagement. To make the launch as quick and successful as possible, the team evaluated a variety of outsource partners, selecting Lithium Technologies as the one that best fit Sprint's specific needs. The whole launch process from initial concept through live customers took less than three months.

Few companies can manage to establish a rich and engaging relationship with all of their customers. Netflix is one of those companies. When you talk to folks at Netflix, the first thing you notice is that they don't use the term *customers;* instead, they say *members.* It's easy to brush this off as corporate-speak pushed down from marketing, but the more you understand their business, the more overly formal even the term *members* seems. The conversation turns to the nature of the relationship between customer and Netflix as being more of a trusted friendship.

According to the company, more than 90% of Netflix members would recommend the company to friends,[3] and according to research firm Foresee Results, Netflix has the highest online customer satisfaction of any company in the world.[4]

How has the company established this kind of trusted relationship with customers? Although Netflix is in the business of renting DVDs, the core of the business is the company's customer software. That software keeps track of the movies and TV shows each customer has rented and the DVDs the customer has queued up to rent next. When a customer returns a movie, they are sent an e-mail reminding them to rate the movie they just watched. Most importantly, Netflix makes it simple to rate movies within the flow of a member's normal interactions, and the payback is immediate, with instantly improved recommendations. Netflix has collected more than 1.6 billion individual ratings in their database. This simple exchange allows each member to be presented with a custom view into Netflix, connecting members to the movies they will love.

The result is threefold. First, customers get all the benefits of an incredibly broad portfolio of titles (more than 70,000 and growing) without the pain of needing to wade through thousands of uninteresting titles to find the one they might enjoy. Second, the value to the customer increases with every rental and every review (the more movies I review, the better targeted are the recommendations to me). Third, the customer sees value in providing input to Netflix. In short, Netflix has nailed the "Make it easy," "Make it count," and "Pay it back" imperatives I mentioned earlier.

But the company does not stop at customer ratings and great recommendations. Netflix overinvests in customer research. While the methodologies are not significantly different from the surveys, focus groups, and experiential research that other firms perform, the existing trusted dialog with the customer and the company's customer database seem to enable Netflix to get feedback faster and with greater richness than most companies.

An example of how the company has used that feedback is the Previews feature through the Netflix Web site. Customers said they would love to easily watch the kind of preview trailers that typically precede a movie in the theater. Netflix was able to leverage its software to dramatically improve on that process. Now, when a member opens the preview feature, they see a continuous stream of preview trailers that are specifically selected and sequenced based on what the customer will love, and it is simple to order a movie directly from the Previews section.[5]

Unfortunately, not all companies have the luxury of the software and database capabilities on which Netflix has built its business. How can the rest of us hope to engage in a meaningful dialog with our customers?

A recent article by Jennifer Alsever at BNET.com provides some valuable direction. In the article, titled "How to Get Your Customers to Solve Problems for You," Jennifer recommends four key steps to "harness the intelligence of customers that love your business":

1. Decide if you really care what customers think.
   o Engage in a true dialog with your customers, or don't bother at all.

2. Learn who loves you (and who hates you).
   o Identify customers who will provide the most useful insight.

3. Make engaged customers feel special.
   o Reward passionate consumers with insider perks and benefits.

4. Bring customers inside the tent.
   o Give participants clear goals and integrate their ideas into your decision making.

As Jennifer notes, one of the critical steps is to find the right customers to engage with. She recommends looking for the customers that contact you the most often—whether with positive or negative interactions. She also recommends looking for the most active participants in online forums that discuss your firm's products or services. These are the folks that have demonstrated that they care and that they want to be heard. When you reach out to them, they will engage and they will value the dialog—if you make it count and are willing to make changes based on their input.[6]

So, now that you've opened a dialog with customers so you can learn from them how to improve your product, what do you ask?

BDC Consulting, a service of the Business Development Bank of Canada (BDC), recommends a discussion flow that asks three key questions:

1. What are the top three problems your product or service should solve?

2. What are three things they dislike about your product or service?

3. What are the top three things they would add to your product or service?[7]

These questions are likely to lead to a rich discussion that will help you better understand the strengths of your product and the opportunities to create new value for your customers.

Employ

The final level of learning from your customers is to actually put them to work!

My favorite example of a company that does this well is the Lego Group. The company offers free Lego Digital Designer software that makes it easy for customers to design their own custom building sets. Those designs are then uploaded to legofactory.com, where they can be ordered. The custom sets then arrive in the mail in a box with a picture of the customer's unique design on the front. Customers can even make their designs available for others to purchase.

The Lego Group doesn't just passively observe this customer activity. The company has taken several sets designed by customers and fully productized them—giving them traditional Lego packaging (with the addition of the designers' photos) and making them available in Lego stores, catalogs, and the company's main online store. The designers even get paid royalties![8]

However, even the designs that don't turn into official products inform Lego's ongoing product development. Those that visit legofactory. com are the most passionate customers, and the time they invest in designing a new creation represents what they really wish Lego was selling!

But Lego doesn't stop there. When the company was beginning work on a new version of its Mindstorms robotic building set, they identified a handful of the most passionate and talented Mindstorms customers from around the world. This "Mindstorms User Panel" (MUP) actively worked with the company over 11 months leading up to the formal introduction of the Mindstorms NXT. The MUP members were invited to Lego headquarters in Denmark and played a critical role in helping the company introduce a product that was a hit right out of the gate. What did it cost Lego? Well, they paid their MUP "employees" in Legos and with the honor of making their input count.[9]

However far you are willing to go, your customers are ready to go with you. Take the time to learn from them, and together you can capture more power from mobility than you ever could have imagined on your own!

FROM THE REAL WORLD

Sipping Their
Own Champagne

TechSmith (www.techsmith.com) is the world's leading provider of screen capture and recording software. The company's flagship product, SnagIt, is recognized worldwide as the premier tool for capturing an image of the computer screen for use in documents, presentations, and for training purposes. The company has extended that leadership into a number of related areas

Two of TechSmith's products particularly relevant to learning from your customers are UserVue and Morae.

UserVue™ is a Web-based service that allows a product manager to remotely connect to, interact with, observe and record users as they navigate an application or Web site. UserVue shares the participant's screen, providing a truly accurate view of the user experience. Up to ten people can view a live session and collaborate over chat, without disturbing the participant. As soon as a session ends, the product manager can create a Windows Media Video (WMV) file of the recording to view and share. You can analyze, edit, and share UserVue recordings in Morae Manager.[10]

Morae is a complete, all-digital application for user experience research. It enables organizations to observe and record how customers really interact with a Web site or application. By showing a product manager not just *what* actions the user took, but also *why* and *how,* Morae gives them a complete and accurate understanding of user needs. Morae has three components—Recorder, Remote Viewer, and Manager. These three components work together to record, log, observe, analyze, and share the user experience.[11]

Morae Recorder captures the total user experience by recording screen video, user audio and video, and a chronicle of system events, all automatically synchronized. It also sends the screen video, camera video, and audio to observers using Remote Viewer. Anyone logged into a Remote Viewer can observe the recording session and set markers, with text notes, to flag important moments. This marker information can be searched for and viewed later using Morae Manager. Within Morae Manager, you can import recordings and quickly analyze the data and calculate metrics. The integrated editing functionality makes it easy to assemble the important moments into a highlight video to share.[12]

FROM THE REAL WORLD (CONTINUED)

What better way to learn from your customers than to actually watch how they use your product—the challenges they encounter, the rabbit trails they pursue, and the frustration they display on their faces and express under their breath.

Obviously, TechSmith believes in the value of learning from customers! And, of course, the company uses its own products to watch how people use TechSmith products and the TechSmith Web site to accomplish specific tasks. For example, in preparing for the 8.0 release of SnagIt, the company brought in a variety of users and used Morae to observe the usability challenges with the current release of the product.

The resulting SnagIt 8 benefited tremendously from what customers were able to teach the company, making the product approachable to a new, much broader set of customers. "With SnagIt 8, we are knocking down barriers and bringing screen capture to new audiences," said Tony Dunckel, product manager at TechSmith. "We've brought the most popular features to the forefront so new users can realize immediate benefits while still having the option to customize SnagIt for maximum effectiveness. The learning curve has essentially been eliminated. New users can be up and running within minutes after installing SnagIt 8, and we've enhanced SnagIt's editing capabilities, including PDF output, so users don't have to use additional and expensive software to embellish their captures."[13]

But TechSmith doesn't stop there. Formal usability testing and watching your customers use your products are great ways to learn how to improve, but the company also creates opportunities for customers to talk and listens carefully to what they have to say.

Betsy Weber, chief evangelist for TechSmith, estimates that she attends 30 trade shows a year. Even though her title implies that her job is to talk, Betsy acknowledges that it's much more valuable to listen.

From the Real World (continued)

At a trade show, it's not unusual for customer to show up and share their perspectives on what they like and don't like about TechSmith products. Betsy is not shy about grabbing a Webcam and having the customer speak through it, creating an internal video document, complete with nonverbal nuances, that then gets shared with the product development teams back in Michigan.

Betsy has also led creation of a number of customer advisory boards, organized by product line and by industry vertical focus. TechSmith has established online group discussion areas where these customers can talk to each other and share their questions and perspectives about TechSmith products. Throughout the development process, the company will introduce these customers to ideas and demos being considered for future releases and collect feedback on initial reactions, what the board members like, and what they don't like.

"It's critical that we recruit a very diverse set of members for our boards. We make sure that we have people who love our products and folks who may be our biggest critics," Betsy notes. "We also look for diversity, from newbies to power users, to make sure that we're neither turning our back on our base nor missing out on opportunities to reach new customers."

So, how does Betsy find these advisory board members? She looks for them everywhere she goes, and she has help. She asks people that approach her at industry events who have passion for TechSmith products (positive or negative) if they'd like to help make TechSmith products better. She e-mails folks who are passionate in blogs and technical forums. The company's technical support team knows that Betsy wants to hear about the folks who are trying to use their products in new and unusual ways.

And recruit them she does. All she has to offer is the opportunity to be heard and the chance to really make a difference in improving

Case Study

Portable On Demand Storage

Portable On Demand Storage (PODS®) is revolutionizing the moving and storage industry through the power of mobility!

Storage has always been fixed. You go to a storage location and you put your stuff into the storage container or building. When you want your stuff again, you go back to where you stored it and you get it out.

That sounds simple enough—and we have been willing to put up with that model forever because we could not imagine any other approach. The founders of PODS were able to see well beyond the assumption that storage is always fixed.

In 1998, by taking something that had always been fixed and making it mobile, the company created tremendous new value for people needing to store or move their stuff:

- Saving customers time and money.
- Making both on-site and dry storage more convenient and accessible for the customer.
- Eliminating many of the complexities and stress associated with moving and storage.
- Putting customers in control of how they moved and stored their belongings, with as much or as little help packing as they wanted.
- Making moving and storage safer and more secure.
- Creating a totally different relationship between the customer and his or her moving/storage company—one based on superior service and trust.[14]

Today, PODS offers service to over 200 million people in more than 20,000 cities in 53 states, provinces, and territories throughout the United States, Canada, and Australia. In 2006, the company rolled out its 100,000th PODS brand storage container and served its 500,000th customer reservation.[15]

This phenomenal growth has come from taking a service that has always been assumed to be fixed and making it mobile.

PODS introduced the concept of portable storage containers that are delivered to the customer. With PODS, the customer packs the storage container at his leisure and doesn't have to worry about finding a friend with a pickup truck or making lots of trips back and forth to the storage location. When the container is fully loaded, PODS comes and picks it up again, taking it to the PODS warehouse. When the customer is ready to unpack, at the original or their new location, PODS delivers the container, and once again the customer has complete control over unloading at his convenience and with minimal effort.[16]

Of course, there's a reason that storage has always been non-mobile.

Case Study (continued)

For one thing, storage buildings are designed to withstand the weather. Part of PODS's innovation has been to create a portable container that is as weather resistant as a fixed-location storage building. PODS containers come in two sizes: 8 feet by 8 feet by 12 feet and 8 feet by 8 feet by 16 feet. They are made with steel frame construction, a marine-grade wood interior, and aluminum skin exterior. They are designed to withstand winds up to 110 miles per hour.[17]

For another thing, once I pile my boxes of eight-track cartridges on top of my old dorm room sofa and lay my ten-speed bike on top of all of that, I'm not sure jerking that big box around is such a wise idea. Packing a PODS container may require a bit more care and wisdom than throwing stuff into a fixed storage building, but to minimize the challenges, PODS invented the Podzilla lift and transport system—a hydraulic system that picks up the storage container and keeps it as steady as possible during transportation to and from the warehouse.[18]

Finally, when I take my stuff to a storage building, I know exactly where it is. When the PODS truck drives off with all my stuff, how do I know where it's going?

"By definition, we are a business on the move," notes Peter S. Warhurst, president and CEO of PODS. "Keeping track of the containers holding our customers' precious belongings and our drivers could only be met with an innovative wireless solution."

PODS has implemented a solution that increases customer peace of mind. The company's 700 drivers and 200 warehouse staff use a mobile device from Motorola, wireless services and Advanced Wireless Solutions from Sprint Nextel, and software custom designed by PODS to keep a constant eye on each customer's container throughout the entire process. The solution incorporates bar code scanning, customer signature capture, and global positioning system (GPS) technologies to tie together containers to customers to precise location information. At any point in time, the company knows exactly where every container is. Since, most of the time, those containers are either at the customer's location or in the PODS limited-access warehouse, customers can feel more comfortable that their precious belongings are safe and secure than in traditional storage facilities.[19]

"We know our business and have developed the systems that create our sustainable business advantage," observes Tammy Carr, VP of corporate training and development for PODS and executive lead of the project. "But we wanted a partner who knows wireless and knew how to combine the right communications technologies to deliver a solution that meets our business needs. Sprint brought that value to our partnership."

PODS is also leveraging these technologies to be as responsive as possible to customer requests. When a customer requests their container out of the warehouse, the company can instantly locate the container and, as quickly as possible, load it onto a truck. On every trip to customer locations, drivers are guided by GPS-enabled voice navigation to ensure the most efficient route and to eliminate wasted time searching for an address. Drivers are also provided with precise customer information to ensure authorized transfer of the containers to each customer.[20]

"Our technology platform ensures that deliveries and pickups are on time," said Peter. "This provides control and visibility into the customer experience from start to finish: from quoting and booking to final delivery, resulting in a worry-free experience for the customer."

PODS introduced the wireless solution to nearly 1,000 personnel in over 150 company-owned and franchise locations. This user population had very diverse levels of technology skills, technical support staff, and buy-in to the program.

CASE STUDY (CONTINUED)

"Training was essential to meet the needs of teaching a typically computer illiterate delivery driver team on the use of the handheld device," Tammy recalls. "We met that need by using a variety of technology-based training tools such as simulation training, webinars, and our online University of PODS Virtual Classroom. Location management teams were supported by a 'T-minus-21-day' Countdown to Success Calendar of Events and CD based 'Managers Toolkit.' The Corporate Training team prepared warehouse and delivery teams before the handhelds arrived to ensure success and an expedient launch."

The wireless solution has resulted in measurable improvements in efficiency and has been well received by most employees and locations.

"We are a company not unfamiliar with using technology as a solution to improvement," concludes Tammy. "Obviously, we believe in the power of mobility and we look forward to continued improvement in our process efficiencies and asset management while pushing the wireless technology envelope wide open!"

Notes

1. Lagace, Martha. 2004. "Your Customers: Use Them or Lose Them," Harvard Business School *Working Knowledge,* July 19, http://hbswk.hbs.edu/item/4267.html.

2. "Listening to the Voice of the Customer," presented by Mark Federman, Chief Strategist, McLuhan Management Studies, McLuhan Program in Culture and Technology, Univeristy of Toronto, Luncheon Keynote, Conference Board of Canada, Customer Relationship Management Conference,

November 28, 2001. Copyright © 2001 by Mark Federman. www.utoronto. ca/mcluhan/VoiceoftheCustomer.pdf.

3. Netflix press release. 2006. "Netflix Opens Customer Service Division in Oregon and Hires Stephanie Sanford as Director," July 25, www.netflix.com/MediaCenter?id=5364.

4. Gupta, Shankar. 2006. "ForeSee: Amazon, Netflix Tops In Consumer Satisfaction," *Online Media Daily,* December 27, http://publications.mediapost.com/index.cfm?fuseaction= Articles.san&s=53040&Nid=26108&p=248134'.

5. Netflix press release. 2006. "Netflix Launches 'Previews' Feature for Instant Viewing of Movie Trailers," August 31, www .netflix.com/MediaCenter?id=5360.

6. Alsever, Jennifer. "How to Get Your Customers to Solve Problems for You, www.bnet.com/2403-13241_23-52960.html.

7. "BDC Perspective: Use Your Customers to Develop Winning Products," www.bdc.ca/en/my_project/Projects/articles/ marketing_ bdc_perspective.htm.

8. Lego press release. 2005 "Lego Group Launches Infinitely Customisable Lego Factory," November 27, http://factory.lego.com/ news/Europe%20news%20item.aspx.

9. Koerner, Brendan I. 2006. "Geeks in Toyland," *Wired News,* January 4, www.wired.com/news/culture/0,69946-0.html.

10. Mostly quoted from http://techsmith.com/uservue.asp.

11. Mostly quoted from http://techsmith.com/morae.asp.

12. Mostly quoted from http://techsmith.com/morae/features.asp.

13. TechSmith press release. 2006. "TechSmith Launches SnagIt 8; Debuts Interactive Screenshots," January 26, http://techsmith .com/company/press/pr060126.asp.

14. www.pods.com/subpages/about_pods.asp.

15. PODS press release. 2006. "PODS® Inc. Announces over 500,000 Customer Reservations and 100,000 Containers in Service—Expands National Service Market," May 17, www.pods.com/press.asp? rls_id=8.

16. www.pods.com/subpages/PODS_Innovations_Page.asp? navid=&id=8.

17. Ibid.

18. Ibid.

19. Sprint press release. 2007. "Sprint Extends Advanced Wireless Solutions to PODS to Enhance Its Delivery Capability" (draft), February.

20. Ibid.

CHAPTER 13

Conclusion: Go Capture the Power!

We started way back in Chapter 1 by recognizing that new technologies can result in dramatic impacts on society and the nature of business. We noted that a new technology can reduce the cost for a business to produce its product or it can increase the value of that product in the market. We observed that sometimes these changes are small, only incrementally improving the business, but sometimes these changes introduce radical change to business—an order of magnitude improvement—fundamentally changing the nature of the business, the nature of the product, and the reasons why customers buy the product.

By now, I hope that you have gained a vision for how mobility will impact your business. You've evaluated ways that, by building mobility into your product or service, you can increase the value of your offer to your customers. Do you think this is an incremental increase, or an order of magnitude improvement? It is important to consider how much of an impact your mobilized offer will have in the marketplace. It is also important to consider how quickly your competitors will follow you down the mobility route.

You've undoubtedly also considered ways that, by building mobility into your internal processes, you can reduce your costs or increase your revenues, resulting in increased profitability. Again, you must consider how significant an impact mobilization will have on your processes and your profitability.

Me-Too-Plus or New Category?

As you gain understanding of the magnitude of the improvement in your offer, you likely will need to consider how to position your new offer in the marketplace. In technology marketing, one of the key questions is whether your new offer represents a new category, or whether it just represents an incremental improvement to an existing category.

What's all this talk about categories?

Well, the concept of a product (or service) category is that it is a label that helps the target customer associate attributes to your product. For simplicity's sake, let's consider pizza as a familiar product category.

Everyone knows what pizza is, so when a company comes out with a new kind of pizza, customers understand the value of pizza and all they need to do is determine whether they find the incremental improvement to pizza to be appealing enough to try. For example, when Pizza Hut introduced a stuffed crust pizza, folks immediately understood the value of the offer as a pizza offer, and only had to evaluate the incremental change of the stuffed crust.

Pizza Hut didn't need to focus marketing dollars on educating their customers on a new product category. Instead, they could leverage the deep understanding their customers had of pizza and focus all of their attention on convincing customers they'd rather have a pizza that happens to have a stuffed crust.

Oklahoma-based Mazzio's Pizza tends to push the envelope, regularly introducing innovative new offers that dramatically alter the traditional pizza offer. One of their most recent innovations is the Quesapizza®, which combines aspects of a pizza with a quesadilla. Mazzio's has registered the name of their new creation as a trademark so that competitors can't quickly duplicate their offer. However, the company also has to work harder to educate customers on what a quesapizza is and why they might like it more than traditional pizzas offered by competitors.

In the technology marketing vernacular, quesapizza is a new product category and Mazzio's is a category maker. Stuffed crust pizza is a "me-too-plus" offer—it too is pizza but it has something that sets it apart.

What's the right answer for you? Now that you have mobilized your offer, should you position it as a new category or as a me-too-plus offer?

The right answer depends on a number of factors.

At its most basic level, the decision should be based on what best serves you and your customers. Will your customers best be able to decide whether or not to buy your new offer by starting from an understanding of an existing category and simply understand how you have improved it? Or will forcing your offer into an existing category misserve your customers because they will associate characteristics to your product (from that category) that are inappropriate and inaccurate, leading them to make a wrong decision? Neither you nor your customer are well served when they buy your offer with wrong expectations, or when they fail to buy your offer because they do not understand what is true and valuable about your offer.[1]

However, category-making decisions are never that simple. There are three fundamental factors that can impact your decision.

Perhaps the most critical factor is your current market position. If you are the market leader in an existing category, then you likely will be best served continuing in your existing category. For a new category to be successful, it has to be positioned against the existing category, proving to the customer how the "old way" has been devalued by new innovations. In other words, launching a new category devalues the category in which you are already the leader, undoing years of previous investments. In many cases, market leaders will be tempted to position their innovation as me-too-plus, even though it truly is a new category.

Challengers face the opposite temptation, seeing every innovation as a new category, even when customers will be better served by understanding the innovation as an incremental improvement to an existing category.

The second factor is defensibility. Market challengers who try to create a new category without considering how difficult it will be for the market leaders to convince customers that they can add the new capabilities to their existing offers are setting themselves up for a nasty fall.

TeleChoice, a strategic consultancy that has helped several companies create new categories in telecom and networking, cites the need for defensibility at an architectural level. If the current market leader can duplicate enough of the new advantage without having to change their technical or operational architecture, then challengers who attempt to make a category around this innovation are at particularly high risk.[2]

Danny Briere, CEO of TeleChoice, recalls Ipsilon as an example of a company that unadvisedly attempted to make a new category at the beginning of the Internet era. Ipsilon introduced a concept known as IP switching as a distinct category with order of magnitude performance improvement over the IP router category dominated by Cisco Systems.

"Ipsilon was the hottest game in town, for exactly six months," remembers Danny. "Then Cisco announced tag switching as a way to accomplish the same gains within the existing routing category. At that point, the game was up for Ipsilon."

For a new category to succeed, the category maker must have confidence that existing market leaders cannot or will not follow for several years given their technical and business constraints.

Within two years, Ipsilon was put out of its misery, acquired by Nokia for a fraction of its previous estimated value.

The third factor is budget. Convincing customers to take a risk on a new category is hard and expensive.

The decision to go with a new category offer is more involved for customers than simply comparing among the best alternatives in an existing category. Customers must understand what is wrong with the existing category and what is essential about the new category. They must become convinced that the dimension of improvement represented by the new category is important to them.

The decision to go with a new category is also dramatically higher risk for customers. For starters, new categories are unproven, and if they are well positioned, they involve an entirely new architecture for solving a problem that has been solved differently for years. Layer on the fact that categories are most often created by unproven market competitors, and the risk is amplified. Given that, by definition, a new category starts with only one provider, a customer betting on a new category cannot switch providers if there are problems with their first supplier.

To overcome these barriers, the category maker has to invest substantially in evangelism—preaching the good news of the new category and trying to win converts. This requires marketing and publicity expenditures well above what is required in introducing a new product in an existing category.

Is it worth it? If done well, category making can dramatically launch a company into the upper echelons of their industry. An example that Briere cites is TiVo.

TiVo defined a new way to watch television by introducing the digital video recorder (DVR) category. DVRs were positioned against VCRs, but offered order of magnitude improvements in usability and storage capacity. VCR manufacturers couldn't match TiVo's benefits with their existing architecture. TiVo became a huge success, rapidly establishing brand recognition, market share, and customer loyalty rarely matched by start-up companies.

However, the same results can be achieved by successfully marketing your new value in an existing category. Briere contrasts the success of Juniper Networks with the failure of Ipsilon. In the same year that Ipsilon failed to make a new category against Cisco Systems in IP switching, Juniper successfully launched products in the core routing category that Cisco had created and dominated. Juniper's innovations delivered meaningful incremental improvements along the performance dimensions that Cisco had defined for the category.

Within four years, Juniper had taken 30% market share away from Cisco. The two companies owned the market, accounting for 98% of all sales.[3] If you choose not to create a new category, then the challenges are different, but no less daunting. Standing out in a mature market where the rules of competition have been defined by powerful incumbents is never easy. Even in an existing category, customers must be convinced that the new value created through mobility is meaningful to them. This too requires investments in marketing and publicity.

Deliver the Value, Capture the Power

Whether or not you choose to position your mobilized product or service as a new category, communicating the benefits of mobility will be essential to translating the value you're creating for customers into power for your company in the competitive market.

All the work you have done up to this point should flow naturally into a launch plan. You have evaluated the ways in which mobility creates new value for customers. You have identified the best target customers and applications. You have put in place appropriate safeguards and you are ready to learn as your customers find new ways to derive value from mobility.

As you take your mobilized offer public, you may consider new ways to maximize your impact in the market. Should you develop a new vocabulary to create immediate traction around the value unleashed through mobility? Can you handpick some optimal customers who are willing to serve as case studies to clearly communicate how mobilization is creating tremendous new value? Can you participate in some high-profile events that will attract media and customer attention and that are particularly well suited to a mobilized offer? Can you convince a leading industry association or publication to add the value of mobility to the criteria they use in evaluating products and services for awards they issue each year, or perhaps to create a whole new award category?

At the end of the day, you need to execute flawlessly to truly deliver the power of mobility to your customers, but you must also create a market awareness of the value of mobility to make your investment pay off.

When the dust settles, and the rest of your industry wakes up to the fact that a technology revolution has once again redefined the rules of competition, will you be the one who has first grabbed hold of mobility and set the new rules? Having completed this book, I believe you will!

FROM THE REAL WORLD

The Equilibrium of the Marketplace

In the preface to this book, I introduced the concept of a ten-layer stack that drives technology decisions, at least within communications networks. I presented the argument that the seven layers codified by technology standards as the OSI seven-layer model really only matter within the context of three additional layers: marketing, finance, and politics.

Whether any given technology truly matters to customers, ultimately gets adopted, and therefore has the opportunity to impact business and society rests in which of these three layers or forces has the greatest impact on decisions being made in the marketplace. I refer to this as the *equilibrium of the marketplace*.

The status quo has tremendous power in society and in business. Newton's first law—that a body at rest tends to stay at rest—is true in much more than just the science of physics. This truth is captured in many wise sayings, including "Let sleeping dogs lie" and "If it ain't broke, don't fix it." All of this truth and wisdom represents inertia that impedes the adoption and success of new technologies.

Marketing comes into play by communicating the value of the new technology in addressing the "latent desires" of the target market. People want things to be different, but they assume that their desires cannot be met, so they do not even bother asking. And realistically, their desires *can't* be met, until a technological breakthrough enables it. The role of marketing is to make people aware that the previous barriers have been broken and to awaken within them the desire for this capability.

This is a powerful force. Unchecked, even the smallest, simplest desire that could be met by new technology would overcome the marketplace inertia and would be immediately adopted. But neither society nor business is a frictionless world. There are largely unseen forces that impede this adoption and that must be overwhelmed if the technology is to disrupt the equilibrium and move the market.

The most powerful of these forces is politics. Continuing our Newtonian analogy, politics acts very much like friction. The force is virtually unnoticed until there's an attempt to move, and the force appears stronger as the force attempting to move the market increases.

FROM THE REAL WORLD (CONTINUED)

The reality behind this is that those in control have much power and are generally happy with the status quo. Their power lies in the fact that they often have the most money, the most influence, and the most control over what people hear. They can out-shout, out-influence, and out-buy any attempt by challengers to disrupt the equilibrium of the marketplace.

As you can imagine, a new technology has to unleash powerful desires to overcome the incredible force of politics.

The third force, finance, is often the swing vote. Often, early in the life of a new technology, finance votes against adoption. But as the technology matures, finance can shift its vote, creating enough additional force for the desires unleashed by marketing to overcome the friction of politics and to upset the equilibrium in the marketplace.

Finance has three basic variables that come into play. The first is capital. How much does it cost to adopt the new technology? The second is operational expense. How does adopting the new technology change how much we will spend in the future—does it increase or decrease our need to spend? The third is revenue. Does the new technology enable me to make more money? These three variables are dispassionate, unlike the desires often unleashed by marketing and the power wielded by politics, but they can play the deciding factor in the minds of either consumer or business customers.

Early in the life of a new technology, the capital costs may be high and the operational expenses may be increased by the use of the technology. Potential new income from adoption of the new technology may be unproven. However, fine-tuning of the technology and the ability to share up-front costs over an increasing base of customers can reduce the capital and operating expenses, shifting the balance in favor of adoption, even as growth opportunities become clearer.

FROM THE REAL WORLD (CONTINUED)

In the end, these forces all play against each other, as shown in Exhibit 13.1. Either the status quo survives and the new technology disappears into oblivion or the desires of the marketplace and the economic advantages of the new technology overcome the political resistance of the ruling parties and the new technology emerges to disrupt society and business.

EXHIBIT 13.1

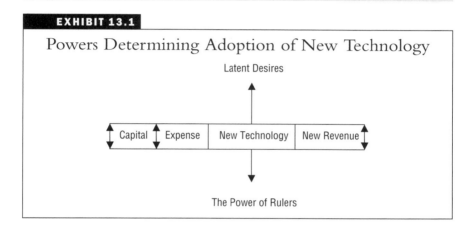

Powers Determining Adoption of New Technology

Notes

1. TeleChoice. 2002. "Category Making in a Down Market," white paper, March 19.
2. Ibid.
3. Moritz, Scott. 2000. "Juniper Snatching Router Market Share From Cisco," November 22, www.thestreet.com/tech/network ing/1184179.html.

Index